Social Mobility and Modernization

The *Journal of Interdisciplinary History* **Readers**

Health and Disease in Human History
Edited by Robert I. Rotberg

Social Mobility and Modernization
Edited by Robert I. Rotberg

Social Mobility and Modernization: A *Journal of Interdisciplinary History* Reader

Edited by Robert I. Rotberg

The MIT Press
Cambridge, Massachusetts
London, England

David Herlihy, "Three Patterns of Social Mobility in Medieval History" *JIH* II, 4 (Spring 1973); Theodore Evergates, "The Aristocracy of Champagne in the Mid-Thirteenth Century: A Quantitative Description" *JIH* V, 1 (Summer 1974); Gregory Clark, "The Political Foundations of Modern Economic Growth: England, 1540–1800" *JIH* XXVI, 4 (Spring 1996); E. A. Wrigley, "The Process of Modernization and the Industrial Revolution in England" *JIH* III, 2 (Autumn 1972); Franklin F. Mendels, "Social Mobility and Phases of Industrialization" *JIH* VII, 2 (Autumn 1996); Joel Mokyr, "Industrialization and Poverty in Ireland and the Netherlands" *JIH* X, 3 (Winter 1980); Louise A. Tilly, "The Food Riot as a Form of Political Conflict in France" *JIH* II, 1 (Summer 1971); John Bohstedt and Dale E. Williams, "The Diffusion of Riots: The Patterns of 1766, 1795, and 1801 in Devonshire" *JIH* XIX, 1 (Summer 1988); Gloria L. Main, "Inequality in Early America: The Evidence from Probate Records of Massachusetts and Maryland" *JIH* VII, 4 (Spring 1977); Raymond A. Jonas, "Peasants, Population, and Industry in France" *JIH* XXII, 2 (Autumn 1991); Michael B. Katz, "Social Class in North American Urban History" *JIH* XI, 4 (Spring 1981); Claudia Goldin, "The Changing Economic Role of Women: A Quantitative Approach" *JIH* XIII, 4 (Spring 1983); Gale Stokes, "Cognition and the Function of Nationalism" *JIH* IV, 4 (Spring 1974)

Selection and Introduction copyright © 2000 by the Massachusetts Institute of Technology and The Journal of Interdisciplinary History, Inc.

Library of Congress Cataloging-in-Publication Data

Social mobility and modernization : a Journal of interdisciplinary history reader / edited by Robert I. Rotberg.
   p.   cm.—(The journal of interdisciplinary history readers)
  Includes bibliographical references.
  ISBN 0-262-18208-4 (hc : alk. paper)—ISBN 0-262-68123-4 (pb : alk. paper)
  1. Social mobility—History. 2. Social classes—History. 3. Industrialization. 1. Rotberg, Robert I. II. Journal of interdisciplinary history. III. Series.

HT612 .S63 2000
305.5′13′09—dc21

00-033254

Contents

Contributors

Robert I. Rotberg is Co-Editor of the *Journal of Interdisciplinary History,* President of the World Peace Foundation, Director of Harvard University's Program on Intrastate Conflict, Adj. Professor at the Kennedy School of Government, and former professor of history and political science at MIT. He is the author or editor of three dozen books on Africa, Asia, and the Caribbean. His most recent book is *Creating Peace in Sri Lanka: Civil War and Reconciliation* (1999).

John Bohstedt is Associate Professor of History at the University of Tennessee, Knoxville, and wrote *Riots and Community Politics in England and Wales, 1790–1810* (1973).

Gregory Clark is Professor of Economics, University of California, Davis.

Theodore Evergates is Professor of History, Western Maryland College, and the author of *Aristocratic Women in Medieval France* (1999), and *Feudal Society in Medieval France: Documents from the County of Champagne* (1993).

Claudia Goldin is Professor of Economics at Harvard University and an Associate Editor of the *Journal of Interdisciplinary History.* She is the author of *Human Capital and Social Capital: The Rise of Secondary Schooling in America, 1910–1940* (1998), and *The Origins of Technology-Skill Complementarity* (1996).

David Herlihy, now deceased, was Professor of History at Harvard University and an Associate Editor of *the Journal of Interdisciplinary History.* He wrote *Pisa in the Early Renaissance: A Study of Urban Growth* (1958), *Medieval and Renaissance Pistoia: The Social History of an Italian Town* (1967), and *The Black Death and the Transformation of the West* (1997); and (with Christiane Klapisch-Zuber) *Tuscans and their Families: A Study of the Florentine Catasto of 1427* (1985).

Raymond A. Jonas is Professor of History, University of Washington. He wrote *Industry and Politics in Rural France: Peasants of the Isère, 1870–1914* (1994).

Michael B. Katz is Professor of History, University of Pennsylvania, and the author of *In the Shadow of the Poorhouse: A Social History of Welfare in America* (1986) and *Improving Poor People: The Welfare State, the "Underclass," and Urban Schools as History* (1995).

Gloria L. Main is Associate Professor of History at the University of Colorado, Boulder, and the author of *Tobacco Colony: Life in Early Maryland, 1650–1720* (1982).

Franklin F. Mendels, now deceased, taught at the University of Maryland, Baltimore County. He wrote *Industrialization and Population Pressure in Eighteenth Century Flanders* (1977).

Joel Mokyr is Professor of Economics and History at Northwestern University and the author of *Industrialization in the Low Countries, 1795–1850* (1976), and *The British Industrial Revolution: An Economic Perspective* (1993).

Gale Stokes is Professor of History at Rice University and the author of *From Stalinism to Pluralism: A Documentary History of Eastern Europe since 1945* (1996), and *Legitimacy through Liberalism: Vladmir Jovanovic and the Transformation of Serbian Politics* (1975).

Louise A. Tilly is Professor of History and Sociology, the New School for Social Research, and the author of *Politics and Class in Milan, 1881–1901* (1992), and *Women, Politics, and Change* (1990).

Dale E. Williams is a lawyer and the author of articles on riots in England.

E. A. Wrigley is Professor of Economic History and Master of Corpus Christi College, University of Cambridge, an Associate Editor of the *Journal of Interdisciplinary History,* and the author (with Roger Schofield) of *The Population History of England, 1541–1871: A Reconstruction* (1989).

Robert I. Rotberg

Gaining Their World: Modernization and Its Impact on Mobile and Aggrieved Peoples How the West modernized, and what modernization meant to human society, is the central theme of this volume. Within that frame are several distinct sub-themes of direct relevance to a study of society and social history: the process of industrialization in Europe and elsewhere, including precursors and antecedents; social mobility, class structures, and class differences, and the impact of modernization on those aspects of human interaction; social unrest and the stresses of modernization and industrialization; economic and social equality and inequality and their markers; the role of women in modernization; and the origins of nationalism.

Each of the chapters in this volume fits into one or more (and sometimes several) of the sub-themes. For the most part, all of the chapters seek clarity on exactly how the West accomplished and endured modernization. Chronologically, these chapters examine similar issues from medieval times through the twentieth century, with abundant overlap but not always total agreement. The eighteenth and nineteenth centuries are the main focus, as is Western Europe and America.

The chapters in this volume are drawn from the pages of the *Journal of Interdisciplinary History,* which published its first quarterly number in 1970. They are representative of the very best articles on modernization, industrialization, social mobility and unrest, nationalism, and methodology that have appeared in the *JIH* since its inception. They are also representative of three decades of American and European scholarship on the same and analogous subjects. The criteria of their inclusion were their intrinsic and lasting scholarly importance, their subject matter, and their interdisciplinary significance.

David Herlihy's "Three Patterns of Social Mobility in Medieval History" opens this volume with a major revision of existing notions about the closed and stable nature of medieval society. The received picture of medieval society, with its official discouragement of social mobility, was, Herlihy explained, distorted. Moreover, it was based on a reading of texts, not attention to life as it was lived. Medieval Europe was much more plastic—a work in progress—than had earlier been believed.

Drawing on hitherto underused manorial surveys and the subsequently renowned Tuscan Catasto of 1427, Herlihy delineated distinct forms of social mobility in medieval society that responded and reacted to early medieval economic stagnation, growing per capita productivity from the eleventh to the fourteenth century, and increasing urbanization. Overall, medieval society was living close to the margins of its available resources, and the access to those resources was hardly equitable, heavily favoring the top of the social pyramid. As a general pattern, medieval mobility showed a downward trend even, or more particularly, for the descendants of the higher classes. But this result also meant that as a few privileged families descended, room at the top was created for newcomers.

The new patterns of social mobility reflected the age of medieval expansion from 1000. During the early centuries of the second modern millennium, when Europe was colonized from within and trade was well on the rise, towns became centers of exchange and of manufacture, labor became more specialized, and new economic and social wealth was created. The feudal nobility and the urban patriciate became prominent, the latter growing out of the experiences of the proto-bourgeois property owners of the pre-urban countryside. The entrepreneurial spirit of medieval times emerged from the ranks of these petty landlords, and became a driving force.

The urbanization of Europe simultaneously encouraged class differentiation, with the welfare of the poor declining over time, as compared to that of the rich. Likewise, because the possibility of slipping backward in terms of class was progressively greater for elites as the cities swelled, pressures to compete and to be entrepreneurial grew among generations of young adults of the upper echelon. This period also witnessed an influx of artisans and other workers to fill the new need for specialized skills in the urban areas. Pressures on the rich and opportunities offered to the talented poor combined to give medieval society a creative vitality—a portrait unlike that displayed in the older historiography.

The emerging aristocracy is one of the mobile classes in Herlihy's catalog. Theodore Evergates' chapter deepens and particularizes Herlihy's paradigm. He focuses on one sector of France—Champagne—and on one century—the thirteenth. He measures fief incomes, one of the components of Herlihy's examination of social mobility, to explain the survival of aristocratic families. Evergates based his measurements on administrative records for Champagne, similar in purpose to the Catasto. The *Roles des Fiefs* listed fief holders, annual incomes, military obligations, and possessions. Evergates subjected this census, collected by a roving inquiry team (even with a pilot run), to a level of statistical analysis that was then rare in medieval studies.

This analysis immediately revealed the slippage in status for descendants of the knights about which Herlihy had written. Evergates' research showed that knights could become non-knights in a succeeding generation, and that women were assuming more responsibilities in the thirteenth century than they had in the twelfth. His data also divulge disparities in income for knights as a class and for knights relative to others classes. Some fief holders gained income from multiple fiefs, others from single fiefs only. An inferior category called rear-fief holder was characterized by smaller, single fiefs, and lesser incomes.

Evergates concludes that the fief system in Champagne was more horizontal than vertical, and that the knights were divided into a four-fold class division: the wealthy descendants of the great baronial families of the twelfth century, who were closely tied to their count; an intermediate group with multiple fiefs; the offspring of "simple" knight families, whose fiefs were few and modest; and, finally, those who held rear-fiefs only. All were aristocrats, but only the first two groups, with their distinctive residences and abilities to tax trade, possessed superior standing in medieval society. Moreover, the mobility was as striking in Champagne as it was in Tuscany.

The chapter by Gregory Clark takes this volume from a discussion of the precursors to modernization and economic growth directly to a discussion of the changes in law, politics, economics, and society that permitted the rise of capitalism and of more rapid entrepreneurial activity, culminating in the Industrial Revolution. Clark takes distinct issue with the many scholars who call the establishment of property rights for citizens a sufficient condition for economic growth, and he links property rights to the prior creation of representative democracy. For Clark, the Glorious Revolution of 1688 in England was not so much of a watershed as hitherto supposed.

Using new information about the return on capital and land prices before and after 1688, Clark shows that secure property rights existed in England as early as 1600, if not before. In his words, "Nothing special happened in 1688" (65). Thus, even if secure and stable property rights are a necessary condition for economic growth, they are not a sufficient one. Nor was the move to representative democracy necessary to secure property rights since, for most people, those rights had existed since 1540.

Autocratic regimes drive up the return on capital, reduce its supply, and, consequently, reduce material output and stifle innovation. Likewise, contests for political power can make property rights insecure and private acquisition precarious. When the state confiscates personal wealth, the ensuing adverse political climate deters investment in capital, or new techniques, unless the rate of return on capital rises commensurate with enhanced risk. Autocratic rulers, in other words, cannot provide the kind of certainty that keeps returns stable. In pre-1688 England, the danger of expropriation was rife.

Before 1688, taxes were raised inefficiently and inconsistently, in a climate of politically influenced corruption. Rival armies vied for control, looting and damaging property in open warfare throughout the seventeenth-century. The century-long conflict between the monarchy and parliament came to an ostensible end with the restoration of kingship in 1660, but uncertainty prevailed as further civil rebellion ensued. But the success of the Glorious Revolution was not immediately obvious until the Land Tax of 1692 and the establishment of the Bank of England provided a new sense of predictability for investors and landowners.

Clark used data from wills and land sales recorded by the Charity Commission to investigate the operation of the private capital market in England and Wales from 1540 to 1837. These data suggest that the capital market was integrated geographically across location and by type of asset throughout the three centuries. The private rates of return across time, however, seemed to ignore political events. Neither uncertainty nor stability appear to have influenced rates of return. Instead, the rates of return trends are smooth and show longer cycles. "None of the political and military convulsions of the seventeenth century seems to have had quantitatively significant effect on private capital markets" (329). Whereas the South Sea Bubble of 1720 caused an abrupt and measurable fall in rates of return, the Glorious Revolution and its associated events caused only a very slight decline. Clark asserts that political events from 1540 to 1770 in England and Wales (unlike in

Holland) did not influence the private capital market. Nor did they influence land prices.

The evidence presented and tested by Clark indicates that in England and Wales prior to the Industrial Revolution, political stability was not crucial to economic development. Nor was security of property, as measured by rates of return on capital. The foundations of the Industrial Revolution were not necessarily in place in the seventeenth century (as opposed to the sixteenth or eighteenth centuries). The Glorious Revolution, according to Clark, hardly ushered in a stable regime of taxes and property rights. To misunderstand is to write Whig history. If James III had succeeded James II, England's economic success may have been just as great.

In the next chapter of this collection, E. Anthony Wrigley argues that the connection between modernization and industrialization, at least in England, was contingent rather than necessary. He defines industrialization as more than the expansion of total output, and more than major changes in material technology and the tapping of new sources of energy. Real incomes per capita must also rise. Associated with the onset of industrialization in England were a migration of people from the countryside to the new cities, and a significant alteration in the structure of aggregate demand.

Industrialization was possible only as a result of a concatenation of societal shifts that are together known as modernization. But defining modernization is more difficult than defining industrialization. Wrigley's prescription includes a cultural shift to more rational individual economic behavior—the maximizing of economic returns at various societal levels. Self-interest on all fronts goes hand in hand with modernization.

Modernization also implies social, geographical, and occupational mobility, as Herlihy's research stressed. Mobility increases as achievement (merit) replaces ascription as a determinant of status, kin ties and extended families decrease in importance, and individual roles in society become more specialized and differentiated. Literacy and numeracy levels rise.

Likewise, vigorous states play larger roles in enhancing self-interest and rationality and in maintaining order and enforcing contractual obligations. Bureaucracies grow in size and in importance; the new mandarinate is chosen less by ascription than by examination. Rational action, after all, flourishes within an energetic administrative framework. With it, however, comes a tension in the traditional relationships between individuals, between individuals and the state, and between old ways and new imperatives (not only of self-interest). Hostility between authority and individual autonomy often arises, and violence can result.

Wrigley takes issue with the then received wisdom about the stages of modernization that supposedly culminated in England's industrialization. He argues that a society could modernize without necessarily industrializing. It was more happy coincidence than "ineluctable necessity" that the steam engine and the coke-fed blast furnace were invented where and when they were. Those innovations occurred thanks to the peculiarity of conditions in England—a relative scarcity of raw materials and favorable local factor endowments.

England had coal and little wood. Yet, since the mines that produced coal were prone to flooding, techniques had to be developed to solve England's pre-industrial problems. Likewise, iron production in England was hindered at first by impurities in the coal. When that problem, too, was solved, limitations to production vanished. In the case of cotton goods, the introduction of improved manufacturing techniques occurred at a different stage. All of these changes, however peculiar to England, rescued England from the stress that would otherwise have followed a period of unusual population increases.

Wrigley, explicitly learning from both Adam Smith and Karl Marx, suggests that the Industrial Revolution was not inevitable; its events were surprising and its course uncertain. That England was modernizing in no way guaranteed the success of industrialization nor the institutionalization of specific patterns.

Inevitably or not, many regions of Europe experienced unprecedented manufacturing growth well before the era of true industrialization. Franklin Mendels calls this phase proto-industrialization, a period characterized by craft specialization, especially in towns and cities. But inhabitants of both the rural areas and the towns contributed to manufacture, the assembling and finishing usually being performed in the urban centers. There was upward social mobility from the countryside to the towns, and within the towns, especially as townspeople became more specialized and the proto-industrial towns grew. Artisans with "some spirit of enterprise" could, Mendels suggests, become merchant-manufacturers with comparative ease in the eighteenth century and the early part of the nineteenth century. At the same time, much of the country-side experienced downward social mobility. Cottage and farm workers were to become more and more dependent on wages and the labor market, which implied lower status.

Although changes in mobility and social status did not necessarily prepare Western Europe for industrialization proper—the introduction of the factory system—the household could remain the focus of economic growth only for so long. The rewards of specialization severed townsmen from the countryside and ended the era when households could both farm and manufacture. The workplace separated from the home, and full-time wage laboring became the norm.

The social consequences of these developments are much debated. Mechanization meant loss of status and earnings, but as less-skilled artisans were displaced, others—formerly landless la-borers—enhanced their social standing. So did the most skilled of the artisanal class, some of whom became managers and entre-preneurs. "It was an age of unprecedented opportunities for those already endowed with skills, capital, or entrepreneurship" (141).

With the rise of heavy industry in the second half of the nine-teenth century, white-collar talents became a new source of status. Heavy industry needed clerks and accountants as well as engineers. Laborers remained in demand, but the handicraft industries that had depended on specific skills and techniques were superseded by mass-manufacturing processes, which required smaller suppliers of components. As the cities expanded to harbor these economic de-velopments, banks and shops, and bankers and shopkeepers, came to the fore. Formal education became important for entry as well as advancement, and increasingly became a determinant of income and status. Indeed, although patronage (ascription) remained rele-vant for many years—more so in some European countries than in others—educational attainment ultimately overcame patronage as the main accelerator of mobility.

Mendels portrays patterns of social mobility in industrializa-tion that were diverse across nations and complex within them. Groups and individuals descended as much as they ascended. The classes churned and mixed, especially from the end of the nineteenth century, and though barriers to upward mobility existed, they were neither high nor impermeable. Industrialization had its discontents, as Marx noted, but it permitted greater mobility and opportunity than did earlier eras.

Joel Mokyr puts some of these arguments to the empirical test in his chapter on industrialization and poverty in a very poor Ireland and a very rich Netherlands during the first half of the nineteenth century. The social structures of these two countries were vastly different and their histories of innovation and wealth creation widely divergent. In one, land ownership was narrowly concentrated; in the other, it was broad and variegated. Yet, neither experienced deep industrialization before mid-century, and both were seriously affected by the great famine of 1845 to 1850. Moreover, their economic performances in the early nineteenth century were comparatively stagnant, even though at different levels.

Mokyr measures poverty in an innovative way: Poverty is higher when a random individual is more likely to fall below subsistence level. Poverty can thus be measured by the severity and frequency of subsistence crises; as those crises diminish, so poverty is alleviated as a general phenomenon. Excess national mortality helps to locate subsistence crises. So do traditional measures like incomes per capita.

Nineteenth-century Europe experienced fewer and fewer subsistence crises, especially after 1816/17. Yet, the 1845 to 1850 episode contained years with unusually high death rates, notably in Austria and France, and catastrophic mortality levels in the Netherlands and Ireland. Between 1846 and 1851, about one-eighth of the entire Irish population perished from hunger caused primarily by the potato blight. The potatoes of the Netherlands also suffered blight, leading to severe famine, excess mortality, and averted births. (Cholera was also a factor during the first years of the crisis.) By comparison, Belgium and Scotland, which both produced potatoes for subsistence, experienced far fewer excess deaths from famine.

Mokyr shows that Ireland and the Netherlands suffered more during the crisis of the late 1840s because, compared to Belgium and Scotland, they were less industrialized and thus more dependent on harvest successes. They industrialized late and remained poverty prone longer not because they lacked iron and coal (in addition to having low labor costs, Ireland had peat and water power; the Netherlands had peat and wind power), but because of economic rigidities. The Netherlands cushioned economic misfortunes by means of a highly advanced system of poor relief. Ireland's poor relief was rudimentary, but its colonial condition and patterns of land ownership encouraged massive out-migration, even before the famine of 1845 to 1850. Indeed, since Ireland's main export was labor, not manufactured goods, it proved difficult to accumulate capital in Ireland.

Self-sufficient economies were more vulnerable to disaster than commercialized ones. The Netherlands and Ireland, for different reasons, remained self-sufficient and agriculturally dominant longer than their neighbors, and suffered. Yet, after 1850 Ireland remained the poorest part of Europe, and the Netherlands recovered from the subsistence crisis and prospered. The latter was able to accumulate capital and join its industrialized neighbors. Ireland, denuded of labor and without capital, took much longer to attain rapid growth.

As Europe modernized, relations among communities and classes altered, sometimes dramatically. For that considerable number who felt deprived or disregarded, the search for personal satisfaction, or the removal of discontent, found little relief. At times, grievance became protest, and protest became riotous. The chapters by Louise Tilly and John Bohstedt and Dale Williams discuss why and how inhabitants of the French and English countryside and towns rioted, and to what ends. Tilly establishes the long-term secular trends that motivated rioters. Bohstedt and Williams focus primarily on the diffusion of the impulse to riot. Tilly covers two centuries. Bohstedt and Williams confine their study to the late eighteenth century in one county, but both chapters examine local self-interest in an age of inexorable economic transformation.

Tilly's study of the food riot as a form of conflict in France differentiates rural and urban types of riot—in the cities to ease shortages, in the countryside to prevent (as in Devon) grain from being exported to the towns. But both types were responses to perceived hunger and perceived injustice. The riots cited by Tilly were triggered by short-term price shifts. As Clark suggested, the long-term secular trend of prices for grain and bread from 1693 to 1854 bears no relation to the resort to rioting over food. Indeed, the most severe subsistence crises in France concluded a century before the final food riots; peasant life in France was palpably better, with reduced hunger and misery, during the last phase of food riots, which persisted into the mid-nineteenth century.

According to Tilly, food riots became increasingly important as a method of political expression because France was centralizing, particularly in economic policymaking, and because a national market had superseded local ones. Paris became a price maker by the end of the seventeenth century on the back of Bourbon fiscal demands and more efficient/onerous collection of taxes. In response, grain was sold and transported more widely across the country than before. Rioting was an attempt to exert countervailing control over the new forces that peasants and townspeople regarded as oppressive and/or irrational.

In part, the consumer food riot reflected, and was intended to influence, the two-century-long debate within France between those who advocated regulated trade and price fixing and those who espoused free trade. Even though Tilly's converging price series demonstrate the development of a national market in the eighteenth century, the tension between paternalism and competition, and between fair prices and just prices, was considerable. Was the just price for grain or bread the market price? Was the fair market local or national?

The Crown traditionally intervened to regulate prices and prevent grain exports in response to demand (and price). It even established grain reserves and added to market supplies in times of shortage. But storing grain successfully, even in the capital, was often difficult, subject to political and military requisitions as well as the need to provide subsidized prices for the poor. Most of all, it became increasingly difficult to repeal the law of supply and demand, particularly since state control inhibited the growth of industry. Articulate theorists also claimed that competition would prevent the immiseration of the poor.

The populace reacted to the enlargement of the market and to the perceived removal of state protection by rioting. In almost every case cited by Tilly, local people took matters into their own hands. They forced bakers to lower bread prices; they seized grain to prevent it from being exported. They did what they thought was better for them, often in response to the state or the locality's failure to do so. Counterintuitively, more violence occurred where the harvests were normal or ample (to prevent redistribution); where there were real shortages, fewer riots took place. Ultimately, the acceptance of a modernized and centralized France, the creation of more efficient national markets, and the rise of an industrial economy moderated the recourse to local food riots as a primary form of political participation.

Bohstedt and Williams write about the spread of riots in England during early industrial times. They apply diffusion theory to the phenomenon, especially to the social structure and organization that permits discontent to escalate to riot.

As in Tilly's France, harvest failure provided the context for a contagion of riot in late eighteenth- and early nineteenth-century England. But the deeper reason for rioting in Devon, a southwestern county, was the shift of its woolen-cloth manufacturing to Yorkshire in the north. As employment and wages fell, and the status deprivation of master weavers was exacerbated, harvest failure led to steep rises in the cost of bread grains amid general economic misery. Most southwestern English rioters in the eighteenth century were on the edge of starvation. To their minds, they "might as well be hung [for rioting] as starved" (219).

Nevertheless, as in France, rioting never took place where prices were highest and, in some cases, riots began with a lowering of grain prices. The poorest people never rioted; most rioters were from a class above, albeit still poor. Indeed, in some instances, the most prosperous of the English working classes were in the vanguard of the riots.

Nor were English riots part of a contagion; they did not radiate from a central or precipitating event. If the inhabitants of one town rioted, its neighbors did not necessarily follow suit. Instead, it is the density of social intercourse that explains microregional differences in the incidence of rioting. The phenomenon was most prevalent in those sections of Devon where the woolen weaving trade had declined, and where there were few cattle and a great reliance on grains. Since market towns were the focus of information, riots tended to galvanize around them. After all, prices were set there, and food was kept there. From the market towns the message of rioting might spread along trade, transportation, and communications axes to susceptible towns, but not necessarily to adjacent rural settlements. Social networks also diffused knowledge of, and the motive to, riot. Moreover, towns that had seen riots in the eighteenth century were almost certain to experience riots in the nineteenth. There was, Bohstedt and Williams say, a tradition of rioting.

Riots were stimulated by the export of grains and other goods from the market towns of the county to other parts of England, and to France. As Tilly also explains, rioters aimed to prevent the outflow of scarce grains and other foodstuff from places of shortage. Rioters in Devon also reacted adversely against the conversion of tillage to pasture. Plymouth, with its dockyard, and Bristol and London, drained its food supplies. Locals felt disempowered, unable to compete for their own sources of food.

Bohstedt and Williams conclude that riots happened only where strong supportive community networks existed. In places without such supportive networks, discontent never flamed into riot. Prudent charity also helped to quench the fire.

Neither of the two preceding chapters attempts to estimate the levels of economic equality in pre-industrial or early industrial France or England. It is never clear whether the rioters were more or less advantaged than the average citizen. Crossing the Atlantic, Gloria L. Main carefully mines probate inventories and tax records to discover relative levels of wealth in the colonies and their early successor states over time. Not surprisingly, the early American South exhibited greater and progressive degrees of inequality than the North—even the urban North. In Maryland, representative of the Upper South, probate inventories show an increase in the proportion of the richest 10 percent throughout the eighteenth century. This accumulation of wealth in the hands of a new elite resulted from mercantile and financial activities, not the plantation cultivation of tobacco. Nonetheless, the wealthiest 10 percent owned one-half to two-thirds of all agricultural land during the century. Slavery was growing at the same time in Maryland, but Main contends that wealth permitted slavery, not vice versa.

During this period in Massachusetts and Connecticut, however, wealth distribution remained stable. Living standards rose without exacerbating inequality. Equilibrium was maintained, in part, by the diversity of regional occupational opportunities and the growth and openness of trade (especially overseas).

But this New England egalitarianism was reduced during the nineteenth century. By 1830, Massachusetts had seen striking rises in inequality. Urbanization and industrialization, where it displaced agriculture, were the driving forces. Cities grew markedly after 1830, but only after 1847 did the great influx of foreign immigrants begin. Nevertheless, Main's examination of the probate records suggests that technological change was not the prime reason for increased inequality. The availability of credit helps explain the changes, and the locations, of inequality. Overall, she finds that the rich grew proportionally richer, especially in the cities, but that the poor did not become poorer or more propertyless.

As France—like the United States—industrialized during the nineteenth century, so did cottage manufacturing give way to urban mechanization and the aggregation of scale that took place in factories. Peasants moved off the land and into the cities. This dislocation was profound; in the early years, it resulted in the popular reactions that Tilly describes. But the adverse reaction was not just to mechanization as such, but also to the control and regimentation that arrived with industrialized manufacturing. Domestic weaving could persist only in good times. In poorer times, factory owners looked to the investment in their machines, and produced only in the factories. This generalization was true even in the Isère region, where cities were few, water power ample, and labor plentiful, if dispersed. The new factories remained small and scattered.

This pattern of mechanized silk weaving in the Isère meant that farmers, for a while, were able both to labor in the small factories and to commute daily from their agricultural holdings. But factory owners later built dormitories to house their workers during the week. Gradually, a French peasant society was converted into a rural proletariat. Raymond Jonas' chapter suggests that these smaller textile mills created "a vigorous hybrid social tissue, richer and more vascular . . . than that traditionally associated with insular . . . peasant society" (298). His "binary economy" put a limit on rural depopulation. Elsewhere in France there was a more thoroughgoing rural exodus. In the Isère, however, rural numbers remained stable until about 1900, after which there was a major out-migration, when the silk industry lost its comparative advantage.

The silk industry, like other new manufacturing processes in France, encouraged the demand for new support services—new shops and bakeries, new builders, new transporters, and new schools. The multiplier effect of small, scattered mills in a series of towns and villages was more dramatic than would have been the impact of one large factory in one large city. Just as twentieth-century rapid per capita economic growth depends on technological change and the proliferation of small enterprise, the Isère flourished so long as there were export markets for silk produced in small, cost-efficient locales.

In its later years, starting in the 1860s, the silk industry prospered by increased mechanization. That development meant that women were more desirable workers than men; by 1865, two-thirds of all mill hands were women. They lived in dormitories from Monday through Saturday while their men stayed home and tilled the barely fruitful local soils. Family relations and domestic routines so changed that even before the 1870s, when German and Swiss competition reduced the comparative advantage of French mechanized silk weaving, industrialization had caused severe disturbances in traditional society. Worse was to come. The collapse of silk weaving precipitated a great exodus from rural land—not just to the regional towns this time, but to the larger cities and to distant Paris. Rural industry had prepared peasants to become urban workers.

Running through the chapters in this book, including Jonas', is the notion that class is a meaningful category of analysis—that social mobility from earliest times reported movements into and out of classes, and that human populations across time and geographical place could be divided roughly along class lines. Michael B. Katz's chapter asserts that for North American history, social class remains an appropriate organizing category and a useful, operational concept more robust than orderings by occupational stratification, wealth, or income.

To Katz, class refers to the social relationships that derive from the ways in which material life is reproduced. Class designates positions within social relations of production, and between individual actors and groups of actors. Classes are groups of people who share a common association with a mode of production and a sense of identity. Class divisions are predominantly sharp.

In eighteenth- and early nineteenth-century America, Katz sees class exemplified by the competition between capitalist entrepreneurs and independent yeomen farmers and independent artisans. Capitalism made labor power into a commodity; artisans and yeomen resisted the trend. Later, in the mid-nineteenth century, cities were the home of three classes: a business class, a working class, and an artisanal class. Artisans eventually became wage workers and merged with the working class.

Katz sampled nineteenth-century occupations in Buffalo and in Hamilton, Ontario, to determine the relationship of individuals to their modes of production, and thus their classes. Occupational titles were an imperfect indicator. Using a variety of statistical sieves, Katz sought to discover whether either city was bifurcated into two or more classes by deciding whether the distinction between classes was greater than the differences within them. He found that in both Hamilton and Buffalo, economic rank was more attributable to class than to occupation, or that individual variation apparently stemming from occupation was in fact the product of class. Nor was it influenced by the life cycle, with younger men moving out of one class and into another as they aged. Adult skilled wage workers became masters only in small number, compared to sons of masters and manufacturers. An intermediate group of mobile masters sometimes suffered downward mobility, falling into the working class.

Katz rejects the notion that a middle class belongs in his otherwise binomial schema. On theoretical grounds, because class expresses a relationship to production, there is no opening for a middle class. Regardless, whether or not the mobile masters (and others) considered themselves a middle class needs further clarification. How should the employees of businesses be classified? Given their wage levels and their clerical duties, it might seem wrong not to include them as workers. Yet, in the nineteenth century, clerical employment was the route to commercial endeavor. Furthermore, clerks were salaried, not the recipients of wages.

Class membership was reflected by attitudes to property and home ownership, and to length of schooling. Fertility patterns were also class related. Class was a central fact of life within nineteenth-century urban America, especially before the 1880s.

Katz's chapter does not deal with the changing economic role of women in the American economy. That is the subject of Claudia Goldin's essay. Using labor-force participation rates, she focuses her attention particularly on the expansion of the market role of married white women in the United States during the twentieth century. Earlier, the employment of white single women had grown steadily as industrial manufacturing and the demand for assembly workers and clerical staff in northern cities, and then in the South and the West, became more pronounced.

Goldin's examination shows that in every cohort of white married women born since 1855, participation in the labor force increased within marriage until about age fifty-five. Each successive decade brought an expanded participation of married women, attracted partly by increases in women's earning capabilities. The work experiences of many married women began when they were single. Young married women experienced larger increases in participation than older women through the 1930s, but from 1940 to 1960 participation rates for women over thirty-five rose dramatically. These data do not only represent a movement of women out of agricultural and into urban employment, but also their persistence after marriage.

The cohort of women who experienced the largest increase in labor-force participation, especially in the 1950s, was the one that benefited from the rapid rises in years of schooling from 1915 to 1928, when high school educational opportunity experienced a massive growth in the United States. This change also reflected the shift of young, single white women out of the home and home employment and into school, before joining the clerical labor pool. Median years of education increased much less rapidly for women born between 1910 and 1940.

By using a pooled time series and cross-section model, Goldin attributes the rise in married white women's participation in the labor force to wage rates for women but not for their husband's, or family's, income levels. Schooling attainment and fertility rates were also significant in determining participation. One-third of the total change in cohort participation rates was caused by increases in the earning abilities of women. Another third was caused by educational attainments and fertility experiences. Other posited variables exerted insignificant effects.

The intervention of World War II, despite conventional wisdom, made little difference to women's participation rates. Indeed, Goldin finds structural stability throughout the twentieth century in the rates at which women became more and more fully a part of the American workforce.

As modernization begat industrialization, so, in a loose sense, did industrialization make nationalism possible. Gale Stokes, after reviewing the historiography of nationalism at the beginning of the final chapter of this book, notes the disdain among historians of nationalism for psychological and behaviorist explanations. His own hypothesis is that the development of interdependent economic systems led to the creation of a cognitive state well suited to the appeals of nationalism. This development enabled nationalism to become a powerful mobilizing and legitimizing ideology.

Stokes follows Jean Piaget in suggesting that the transition from cognitive realism to operationalism (terms derived from Piaget's psychological stages) was essential in human society before nationalism could become a dominant societal preoccupation. Following Karl Mannheim, Stokes describes the culmination of the modernizing impulse—large numbers of people leaving a life of local isolation, traditionalism, and political apathy toward a deeper involvement in a wider, more vibrant society—as the movement from realism to operationalism.

The new life created opportunities for new kinds of interpersonal contacts and broadened organizational structures and, hence, for a vast new pool of capable individuals. Interdependence led to the achievement of operationalism, first for the few and then for the many. Political figures sought to mobilize these new masses; nationalism appealed to the modern person because it offered community together with autonomy and the capacity to behave in a self-directed manner.

The nation-state provided the most satisfactory opportunity to forge a community compatible with autonomy because of the unique importance of language as a basis of national consciousness. Only when those who share community and language also share a recognized political unit can the need for autonomy by operational persons be satisfied. Appeals by socialism to the community of class failed to oust those for whom the appeal of linguistic community, and nationalism, was paramount. Throughout the modern era, nationalism continued effectively to mobilize political support because the integrity of the nation gave operational persons a field for the exercise of autonomy.

The chapters of this volume bear witness to the continuity of tension, between the modernizing impulse and its ensuing social discontent from medieval times to the present. The scale of human endeavor has increased over time; so have the many methods of incorporating and opposing that aggregation. Change has bred discontent, but it has also created opportunities for new orders and classes. Examining the ultimate fate of French fief holders and French silk weavers, or the suffering of Irish, as opposed to continental, potato growers, creates an appreciation of how modernization both harmed and enhanced individuals and groups, and how shifting the prism of concern alters the final judgment of gain and loss for societies, groups, and individuals.

Although this is not a collection of normative essays, collectively they can be read as reflecting normative concerns for the fate of the poor, the dislocated, the dispossessed, and the many others who individually were reduced in income, status, or opportunity while their more favored, more able, or more adaptable colleagues successfully embraced the nettle of modernization and industrialization. Ultimately, this volume is about the causes and results of that evolving struggle across eight vigorous and creative centuries.

David Herlihy

Three Patterns of Social Mobility
in Medieval History

Medieval rulers and philosophers repeatedly affirmed that the divine will had established social inequality, and that the good Christian should be content with his station in life. "Let everyone," Charlemagne instructed his subjects in the early 800s, "serve God faithfully in that order in which he is placed."[1] In an oft-quoted poem written about the year 1000, Adalbero, Bishop of Laon, described the Christian community, which appeared to be one, as divided into those who prayed, those who fought, and those who labored; all functional groups had to fulfill their lawful duties, to assure for the people peace, justice, and salvation.[2] "The dispensation of divine providence," Pope Gregory VII declared in 1079, "ordered that there should be distinct grades and orders."[3] He went on to state that the community could not exist without a diversity of social ranks, and without the subordination of the lesser orders to the greater. In 1302 Pope Boniface VIII reiterated: "According to the law of the universe, all things are not reduced to order equally and immediately; but the lowest through the intermediate and the intermediate through the superior."[4] The members of each order should not aspire to the prerogatives and honors allotted to those in other social positions. Nor should Christians seek to surpass their peers in wealth or dignity. "He who has enough to satisfy his wants," the scholastic philosopher Henry of Langenstein concluded in the fourteenth century, "and nevertheless ceaselessly labors to acquire riches, either in order to obtain a higher social position or that subsequently he may have

David Herlihy is Professor of History at Harvard University and in 1972–73 a Fellow of the Center for Advanced Study in the Behavioral Sciences. He is the author of *Pisa in the Early Renaissance: A Study of Urban Growth* (New Haven, 1958) and *Medieval and Renaissance Pistoia: The Social History of an Italian Town* (New Haven, 1967). An earlier version of this paper was presented to the Conference on International Comparisons of Social Mobility in Past Societies, sponsored by the Mathematical Social Science Board and the Institute for Advanced Study, Princeton, New Jersey, in June, 1972.

1 "Unusquisque in eo ordine Deo serviat fideliter in quo ille est." Missi cuiusdam admonitio, a. 801–812. *Capitularia regum francorum*, A. Boretius (ed.), (Hanover: 1883), I, 240.
2 Carmen ad Rotbertum regem, in *Patrologia Latina*, J. P. Migne (ed.), (Paris, 1853), CXLI, 782. "Triplex ergo Dei domus est quae creditur una: / Nunc orant, alii pugnant aliique laborant."
3 E. Emerton (trans.) *The Correspondence of Pope Gregory VII* (New York, 1932), 142.
4 From the bull *Unam Sanctam*, dated November 18, 1302. For the complete text, see Coleman J. Barry, (ed.), *Readings in Church History* (Westminister, Md., 1960), I, 465–467.

enough to live without labor, or that his sons may become men of wealth and importance—all such are incited by a damnable avarice, sensuality, or pride." [5]

These and similar statements convinced historians of an older generation—Sombart, Max Weber, Tawney, and many others—that medieval society was based upon a system of closed and stable estates, in which social mobility was officially discouraged and rarely in fact achieved.[6] This familiar thesis has, however, two weaknesses, which recent research has made blatantly apparent. It was founded upon a distorted interpretation of social values and policies of the Middle Ages. Although medieval moral counselors were suspicious of personal ambition, which they equated with avarice or pride, they never advocated a social system based on hereditary, impenetrable castes. On the contrary, one of the most powerful religious movements of medieval history—the reform of the Church in the eleventh century—aimed at outlawing clerical marriage and abolishing clerical dynasties. The success of the reform assured that one of the most important elite groups in society, the clergy, would be open to new men. The clergy had to be recruited anew with every generation, and this made the Church the most visible avenue of social advance in the medieval world. Although most great prelates continued to be drawn from the prominent lay families, still, low-born men of talent could occasionally attain the highest levels in the ecclesiastical hierarchy. Pope Gregory VII, who gave his name to the eleventh-century reform; Pope Urban II, who summoned the first crusade; Abbot Suger of Saint-Denys, chief adviser to two French kings; Thomas Becket, the ill-fated archbishop of Canterbury; and many other famous clerics were of relatively humble (or at least obscure) social origins.

Moreover, Sombart and others erroneously believed that the ideals expressed and the exhortations found in theological and moral treatises accurately depicted life as it was lived in the Middle Ages. Current research has focused sharply upon the realities, as well as the aspirations, of medieval society, and our picture of social mobility is

---

5 Cited in R. H. Tawney, *Religion and the Rise of Capitalism* (New York, 1963), 38.
6 According to Werner Sombart, in the precapitalistic economy, which allegedly persisted in Italy until the fifteenth century and elsewhere in Europe until the sixteenth, peasants, artisans, and merchants worked only as much as was necessary to maintain themselves in their stations in life, and did "nothing more." Cf. *Der moderne Kapitalismus* (Leipzig, 1916, 2nd ed.), 188–198. For an evaluation of the work of all of these historians in the light of recent research on the medieval economy, see J. Gilchrist, *The Church and Economic Activity in the Middle Ages* (New York, 1969).

now much transformed. Historians today recognize that both the feudal nobility and the urban "patriciate" (as the great city families are now usually called) were largely formed in the tenth, eleventh, and twelfth centuries.[7] The very appearance of these aristocratic classes is irrefutable evidence of social mobility. And new men continued to penetrate the ranks of both privileged orders during the subsequent Middle Ages.

The reality and importance of social mobility in the Middle Ages are today unquestioned. Its further investigation promises to illuminate the origins, functions, and character of the rural and urban aristocracies. The conclusions of this inquiry should also have considerable theoretical interest. Medieval Europe was very much a world in formation. Its history offers a precious opportunity to identify and observe the forces which, over a lengthy span of years, on the most fundamental levels, shaped and reshaped society.

In this paper, we shall describe three specific patterns or models of social mobility, which are observable at various epochs and in various parts of medieval Europe. We do not claim that these models offer an exhaustive description of this type of social movement; they are, however, comparatively well illuminated in this period of sparse sources. The models are distinguished primarily by varying economic conditions which affected their functioning. The three sets of conditions were: (1) the economic stagnation, which gripped the medieval world until about the year 1000; (2) the expansion and the rising per-capita productivity which marked the medieval economy between approximately the years 1000 and 1300; (3) the social and economic conditions specifically associated with the medieval towns, which become most visible in the late Middle Ages (c. 1300–1500).

---

7 For an excellent discussion of social mobility in medieval society, with a bibliography of recent research, see David Nicholas, "Medieval Patterns of Social Mobility," forthcoming. Among the many useful studies which could be cited, see especially L. Genicot, "La noblesse dans la société médiévale. A propos des dernières études relatives aux terres d'Empire," *Le Moyen Age*, LXXI (1965), 539–560; *idem*, "The Nobility in Medieval Francia: Continuity, Break or Evolution?" *Lordship and Community in Medieval Europe. Selected Readings*, Fredric L. Cheyette (ed.) (New York, 1968), 128–136; Georges Duby, "Une enquête à poursuivre: la noblesse dans la France médiévale," *Revue historique*, CCXXVI (1961), 1–22; K. Bosl, "Ueber soziale Mobilität in der mittelalterlichen 'Gesellschaft.' Dienst, Freiheit, Freizügigkeit als Motive sozialen Aufstiegs," *Vierteljahrschrift für Sozial- und Wirtschaftsgeschichte*, XLVII (1960), 306–332; *idem*, *Die Gesellschaft in der Geschichte des Mittelalters* (Göttingen, 1966). For a discussion of recent views concerning the origins of the town patriciate, see B. Hibbert, "The Origins of the Medieval Town Patriciate," *Past and Present*, III (1953), 15–27.

Before examining medieval social mobility against the background of these differing sets of economic conditions, we must first consider one force or factor which will have fundamental importance in each of the three patterns we shall explore. Medieval society was divided into many social estates, orders, strata, or groups, which performed specific functions for the community. Considerations of security, welfare, or salvation made many of those functions essential. In order to provide a constant level of services, the community had to maintain a roughly stable or proportionate allocation of its members among its various functional groups. It had to preserve this proportionate distribution over time and across generations. Otherwise, the ability of one group or another to perform essential services would be compromised, and this the community, whether for economic or cultural reasons, could not tolerate. Paradoxically, therefore, the very ideal of a society divided into stable orders, which performed fixed duties, could result in considerable social movement. The implementation or the defense of the ideal could well require that members from one order be encouraged or forced to transfer to another, for the purpose of preserving a traditional and necessary numerical balance.

A shift of members would clearly be indicated whenever one functional group was not replacing itself by natural means at an appropriate rate in comparison with the others. The recruitment of the Christian clergy once again offers a salient example of differential rates of replacement engendering social movement and mobility. As the clergy did not replenish its members through natural reproduction, so the community, demanding the services of a clergy, had to recruit individuals, from differing social backgrounds, to enter upon an ecclesiastical career. The need to muster a new clergy every generation made the Church, as we have already noted, the most open avenue to social preferment in medieval society. But differing rates of natural reproduction and replacement could also generate movement among the other social strata and orders as well. We thus confront this question: did all social and functional groups in medieval society maintain their numbers over time through natural reproduction at comparable rates?

Whenever the sources allow us insight, the conclusion they consistently indicate, for nearly every documented period of the Middle Ages, is this: success in rearing children, in bringing up heirs and successors, was closely related to welfare. Those blessed with the goods of this earth were also blessed (or burdened) with children. In a

Biblical passage which medieval writers were fond of quoting, "where there are great riches, there are also many to eat them" (*Eccl.* 5:10). In contrast, the deprived, the heavily burdened, the poor left comparatively few heirs to follow in the traces of their miserable lives. This principle, that welfare affected replacement, is so central to our argument that we must illustrate some of the data from which it derives.

The earliest surviving sources which allow us to observe how medieval communities perpetuated their numbers over time date from the late eighth and ninth centuries. They are surveys of serf or peasant families subject to the authority of a particular manor. Although limited to the peasant population, the surveys sometimes record the number of adults and children in the households, and they frequently give indications of status and welfare. They therefore allow us to identify who in the population were supporting the larger numbers of children, and to compare this distribution with indices of welfare, such as the status and size of the tenure, the dues imposed, or the number of animals owned.

One survey from the monastery of Farfa in central Italy, redacted between 789 and 822, describes nearly 300 peasant households and identifies the kinds and (although not consistently) the number of farm animals owned.[8] Table 1 is a cross tabulation of household wealth, as indicated by animals present, with average size and average number of minors recorded. Because of defective reporting, the kinds, rather than the numbers of animals, are used as the index of wealth, on the assump-

Table 1 Animals Owned and Household Size at Farfa, c. 800

KINDS OF ANIMALS	HOUSEHOLDS	MEMBERS	AVERAGE	MINORS	AVERAGE
0	170	745	4.38	397	2.34
1	43	193	4.49	105	2.44
2	37	184	4.97	109	2.95
3	35	204	5.83	127	3.63
4	9	55	6.11	35	3.89
5	1	11	11.00	9	9.00

Source: I. Giorgi and U. Balzani (eds.), *Il regesto di Farfa compilato da Gregorio di Catino* (Rome, 1892), V, 254–263.

8 The kinds of animals are *boves* (oxen and cows), *vitelli* (calves), horses, donkeys, and pigs.

tion that the more prosperous farms would also own a greater variety of animals. "Minors" include all persons in the household who are younger, in terms of generations, than the household head; children, nephews, their possible spouses, and grandchildren are all counted as minors.

Both the average size of households and the average number of minors present show an unmistakable correlation with the kinds of animals owned, and indirectly with the prosperity of the peasant family. This survey illuminates, of course, only part of the total spectrum of Carolingian society; but even among the peasants, the influence of welfare upon reproduction, and eventually upon replacement, seems apparent.

The largest and in many respects the most detailed of all the Carolingian manorial surveys is the "polyptych" of Irminon, who was abbot of the monastery of Saint-Germain-des-Prés near (and now part of) Paris in the first quarter of the ninth century.[9] It describes the estates and the dependent farms, called manses, subject to the monastery's authority in the vicinity of Paris. The manse, as the basic tenurial unit, was classified into three types: free (ingenuilis), "lidile" (lidilis), and servile (servilis). Presumably these categories recalled the personal juridical status of the peasants who had first held the manses—free cultivators (coloni), slaves (servi), or half-free lidi. This last group is of uncertain derivation, but may possibly have been recruited from barbarian captives. In any case, at the time the survey was redacted, the status of the manse had no fixed correspondence with the personal status of the peasants settled upon it. The free tenures were usually the largest and the least burdened with charges; the servile tenures were the smallest and the most heavily taxed; and the "lidile" tenures occupied an intermediate position. Roughly, then, families settled upon a free manse were better off than those which held a servile tenure. The polyptych also identifies children (usually called infantes) in the peasant households, and once again permits us to identify who were the most successful rearers of children in these peasant communities.

It should be noted that servants or household helpers are not mentioned in these surveys. If they were present, their numbers were

9   On the nature of the source and the character of the families resident upon the estates of Saint-Germain, see most recently the studies by Emily R. Coleman, "A Note on Medieval Peasant Demography," *Historical Methods Newsletter*, V (1972), 53–58; *idem*, "Medieval Marriage Characteristics," *Journal of Interdisciplinary History*, II (1971), 205–219.

doubtlessly small. Moreover, hired helpers in these agricultural communities would more likely be able-bodied adults rather than *infantes* (the word itself implies dependency). Servants, hired helpers, and similar groups, if they were present at all, could not have much affected the distribution of children.

Table 2 Tenures, Children, and Adults at Saint-Germain-des-Prés

	TENURES			
	FREE	"LIDILE"	SERVILE	TOTAL
Number	1430	25	191	1646
Persons:				
Children	4615	133	568	5316
Percent	86.8	2.5	10.7	100.0
Adults	4028	124	558	4710
Percent	85.6	2.6	11.8	100.0
Ratio:				
Child/Adult	1.14	1.07	1.02	1.13

Source: Auguste Longnon (ed.), *Polyptyque de l'abbaye de Saint-Germain-des-Prés* (Paris, 1886–95), I, 237–238. The calculations were made by B. Guérard.

Among the serfs of Saint-Germain-des-Prés, children were not distributed in the same proportions as adults among the three types of tenures. There were relatively more children on the favored free manses, and fewer upon the heavily taxed servile holdings. Although the differences may appear slight, still, if the population remained fixed on the holdings and if all children survived equally well, then the proportion of those living upon the servile manses would be reduced by approximately 10 per cent with each generation. Ultimately, most peasants would look back to ancestors who at one time had been settled upon the free, rather than the servile tenures.

These surveys usually included only peasant families, but it is worth noting that four of the households at Farfa were headed by a *scario*, who was an official or steward responsible for the administration of the monastic estates. The *scario* thus occupied a high social position. The four households were among the largest surveyed. Their average size was 9.5 persons (as opposed to 4.7 for the entire population) and the average number of minors or dependents counted in them was 7.5

(the comparable figure for all households was 2.7). Although the four households constitute a minuscule part of the survey, these important families were substantially larger than those of the ordinary peasants: much wealth, many to consume it.

Our last example takes us far from the Carolingian countryside to a vastly different if still medieval world: the Florentine dominions in the year 1427, which then included nearly the entire province of Tuscany. A survey of that year, called the Catasto, has preserved a unique insight into a population of 260,000 persons, resident in 60,000 households. The survey meticulously records possessions as well as people, and permits a precise differentiation between rich and poor. This was a much more complex society than the small peasant communities previously considered, and it included a large proportion of urban residents. About a quarter of the population was living in cities of more than 3,500 inhabitants—a very high figure by medieval standards. Because there may be a tendency for the wealth of households to decline as their heads pass beyond the prime of life, we shall consider the population by three age categories: minors, aged 0–17; young adults, aged 18–47; and older adults, aged 48–99.[10] In the Catasto, servants were not counted in the households of their masters but were considered to form households in their own right and name. The children in the survey are thus the natural or legal dependents of the person named as household head.

Again, the distribution of minors and dependents in the Tuscan households is not the same as the distribution of young adults across these various wealth categories. In particular, the two richest categories of households, with 34.3 per cent of the young adults, contained 36.5 per cent of the children. On the assumption that the children survived equally well and that no subsequent adjustments were made in the distribution of the population across the wealth categories, then the two richest categories would grow by more than 6 per cent in relative size over each generation. Where, in Florentine society, there was much

10 The word "minor" here designates all persons, married or unmarried, who appear in the Catasto with a stated age of 17 years or less. In reporting ages, the population tended to favor years exactly divisible by 10 and 5, and this "age heaping" is particularly pronounced among the poor and the rural segments of the population. In order to diminish possible distortions arising from this tendency, the intervals are broken at age 17 and 47, rather than the favored ages 15 and 45. This avoids placing a favored age at the margins of the intervals. On the character of the Catasto and the reliability of the data it contains, see Christiane Klapisch, "Fiscalité et démographie en Toscane (1427–1430)," *Annales-Economies-Sociétés-Civilisations*, XXIV (1969), 1313–1337.

Table 3 Welfare and Age Distributions in Tuscany, 1427

	ASSESSMENT (FLORINS)				
	0	1–100	101–400	OVER 400	TOTAL
Ages:					
0–17					
Persons	10901	57200	24053	15139	107293
Percent	10.2	53.3	22.4	14.1	100.0
18–47					
Persons	9635	50595	19938	11402	91570
Percent	10.5	55.2	21.8	12.5	100.0
48–99					
Persons	6366	35761	12972	5540	60639
Percent	10.5	59.0	21.4	9.1	100.0
Total	26902	143556	56963	32081	259502
Ratio:					
Minor/Young					
Adult	1.13	1.13	1.21	1.33	1.17

Only persons with stated ages are included. Assessment is the total value of taxable assets before allowable deductions and is expressed in gold florins.

wealth, so there would be many to consume it. Interestingly, the absolutely destitute at Florence, with no taxable assets, replaced themselves as well as those with some but little property. A large number of apparently destitute families were sharecroppers (*mezzadri*) who lived on well-stocked farms owned by urban landlords; presumably they benefited from the use of capital invested by the city. Taxable wealth may not be a flawless index of welfare, but it still provides a sufficiently accurate measurement.

In spite of the great differences in location and character of the communities we have considered, consistently in the medieval world those families and social strata which commanded the larger part of available resources were also rearing the greater number of children. Doubtless other factors influenced rates of reproduction and replacement. There are indications that the poor segments of society were more sensitive than the rich to long-term economic swings. Bad times delayed marriages among the poor and discouraged procreation; the resources commanded by the wealthy gave them partial immunity from such pressures. Bad times therefore heightened the contrasts between poor and rich in average household size, children supported, and eventual replacement. Such contrasts seem to have diminished in prosperous years without, however, disappearing.[11] Residence was another factor affecting replacement, particularly residence in towns; this we shall consider when we examine our third pattern of social mobility. The forces affecting reproduction and replacement were thus complex and shifting. It remains true, however, that whenever our sources permit us to judge, welfare was exerting an important influence upon the ability of medieval social groups to preserve their numbers across generations.

The consistency with which this principle operated is remarkable (we have not cited all possible examples), but not perhaps the principle itself. Medieval society was living close to the margins of what its available resources could produce; access to those resources was not distributed evenly among all members. Those favored with resources could therefore afford to support more children, heirs, and successors than the economically deprived. If all segments of society reared as many children as they could reasonably support, then the contrasts in replacement rates, which we have observed, would inevitably appear.

The correlation of welfare and replacement had profound repercussions for the pattern of social mobility in medieval society. If the argument so far presented has validity, then the conclusion is obvious: the dominant direction of social mobility in medieval society had to be *downward*. The more rapid expansion of the higher social strata tended to create a top-heavy social pyramid. Stability had to be sought by forcing a continuous downward settlement of family lines from higher to lower social levels. No society can function with all chiefs and no warriors, with all stewards and no serfs, with all lords and no laborers. The children of the privileged thus faced an uncertain social future, and, barring extraordinary efforts, many of them would have to accept a lower status than their parents had enjoyed.

Support for this conclusion—that the dominant direction of social mobility in medieval society was downward—can be found in many literary texts. References to impoverished nobles and other *déclassé* persons are in truth far more numerous in medieval sources

---

11   At Verona, for example, in 1425, when the economic depression of the late Middle Ages continued to affect the city, the correlation between taxable wealth and the number of children aged 0–15 in the city households is 0.434. But in 1502, during an economic upswing, the coefficient drops to a weak 0.199. Wealth, in other words, no longer was exerting so strong an influence over the number of children households were supporting under prosperous times as it had during the previous economic slump. For the data upon which these figures are based and further discussion concerning them, see my "The Population of Verona in the First Century of Venetian Rule," forthcoming.

than allusions to self-made men. The Carolingian capitularies frequently mention free but impoverished persons. Many abandoned their freedom and became serfs; still others "because of need become beggars, thieves or criminals." This awareness of the instability of status probably contributed to the notorious medieval sense of the fleeting character of worldly honors. "I myself have often observed," Lotario Segni (later Pope Innocent III) lugubriously observed in the 1190s, "how much and how many important men are in want. Wealth does not make a man rich, but puts him in need."[12] Medieval literature has preserved many somber reflections on the great families of the past, now much diminished:

> It will not seem or strange for thee or hard
> To hear how families degenerate,
> Since even cities have their term of life.[13]

There is, however, a paradox. The dominant downward drift of family lines could also favor a small but significant upward movement. This downward drift tended to obscure juridical distinctions among persons, as, for example, those separating the free from the unfree. It therefore blocked the formation of impenetrable status barriers between the orders. The decline of some important families also opened room at the top, which persons from humbler origins could hope to fill. Above all, the tendency for privileged families to lose status created a fluid situation, which allowed some social movement in all directions.

We are now prepared to consider our three patterns of social mobility in medieval society.

THE AGE OF STAGNATION   The European economy seems to have achieved little real growth over the five centuries that constitute the early Middle Ages (c. 500–1000). The population remained small, but it was not evenly distributed across the countryside. Rather, it was

---

12 Cf. Boretius (ed.), Capitularia missorum specialia, a. 802, *Capitularia*, I, 100, "De oppressionibus liberorum hominum pauperum, qui in exercitu ire debent et a iudicibus sunt oppressi." *Ibid.*, 125, ". . . propter indigentiam mendici latrones seu malefactores efficiantur." "Quot et quanti magnates indigeant, ipsemet frequenter experior. Opes itaque non faciunt hominem divitem, sed egenum." De contemptu mundi, in *Patrologia Latina* (Paris, 1855), CCXVII, 720.
13 "Udir come le schiatte si disfanno, / non ti parrà nuova cosa nè forte / poscia che le cittadi termine hanno." Dante Alighieri, *Paradiso*, XVI, vv. 76–78. The translation is from Courtney Langdon (trans.) *The Divine Comedy of Dante Alighieri* (Cambridge, Mass., 1921), III, 16.

concentrated into "population islands."[14] The cultivators mounted little concerted effort to push back the wilderness which hemmed them. Constraints of various sorts—insecurity, fear of the wilds, strong manorial discipline, kinship ties, lack of capital—kept the peasants huddled together in packed communities, in which signs of over-population and land crowding frequently appear. The imbalance between such factors of production as land and labor imposed poverty on the people and frequently subjected them to famine and starvation.

As the surveys of Farfa and Saint-Germain-des-Prés show, these impoverished communities were far from stable in their social structures. Rather, the surveys record some extraordinary social shifts. It is instructive to observe, for example, the relationship between the personal status of the cultivators and the tenurial status of the lands they worked on the estates of Saint-Germain-des-Prés. Table 4 displays this relationship.

Table 4. Status of Tenures and Status of Persons on the Estates of Saint-Germain-des-Prés

| | TENURES | | | |
	FREE	"LIDILE"	SERVILE	TOTAL
Number	1430	25	191	1646
Tenant Families:				
Liberi	8			8
Coloni	1957	29	94	2080
Lidi	29	5	11	45
Servi	43		77	120
Mixed	160	25	101	286
Unknown	199	8	42	249

Source: Longnon (ed.), *Polyptyque*, I, 237–238.

The term *liberus* in Carolingian records usually refers to a free man not bound to the soil, but subject to heavy obligations of military service. The word therefore often designates nobleman, in the sense of one who fights but does not work. The eight families of *liberi* in the survey clearly had lost status, since they appear as tenants upon

14 Cf. Georges Duby (trans. Cynthia Postan), *Rural Economy and Country Life in the Medieval West* (Columbia, 1968), 14; R. Fossier, *Histoire sociale de l'Occident médiéval* (Paris, 1970), 85–112, where the author discusses the "force des contraintes internes" which kept the population huddled into packed communities.

holdings primarily responsible for agricultural rents. The *coloni* were technically free cultivators, but bound to the land which they worked. A deterioration in the status of many *coloni* is also apparent. More *coloni*, according to Table 4, were working inferior "lidile" tenures than *lidi*, and, more remarkably, more *coloni* were holding heavily burdened servile tenures than *servi*. The status of tenures, presumably established when the manses were first settled, was relatively stable, but the status of persons, altered with each generation, was not. At the time the survey was taken, if we exclude the "mixed" category, the proportion of free (*coloni*) families—92.6 per cent—surpassed the proportion of free tenures—86.8 per cent. If we also exclude from consideration the eight families of *liberi*, which were too few to have much of a demographic impact, the conclusion is apparent: as the generations passed, the members of the community were being assimilated under the most favored social status. Families in the favored social categories had more sons than were needed to take their fathers' places, and these sons were forced to replace the missing children of slaves, on servile tenures.

But there is also evidence of upward mobility. Some 29 *lidi* and 43 *servi* enjoyed the possession of a free manse. Moreover, in marriages between persons of unequal juridical status, it was more common for men to marry women of a higher, rather than a lower, social station.[15] They did this probably to assure a higher status for their children, who assumed the status of their mothers. Still, they had to have some resources in order to win brides from more exalted social levels. We do not know how exactly the resources were gained that made possible this limited but visible upward social movement. Chance probably played a role. A *servus* might inherit several tenures. Since the replacement rates for the servile population were generally low, the concentration of inheritances in the hands of few heirs was statistically not unlikely, and such property could serve as a platform for an upward thrust in society.

From other sources it is apparent that a principal avenue to vertical social mobility was service—to the manorial lord or to other great men in the neighborhood. With large manor houses to administer, there was need for supervisors and stewards, and the personal contact with powerful persons could provide numerous advantages. One phenomenon evident in early medieval sources is the transformation of

15 For a study of this phenomenon, see Coleman, "Marriage Characteristics."

titles, the tendency for names, which first appear as designations of slaves or servants, to evolve into terms referring to high personages in the aristocracy. "Knight," for example, derives from a word originally meaning "boy" or "servant" (modern German, *Knecht*). "Vassal" or *vassus* similarly comes from a Celtic word for "boy," "slave," or "servant." "Baron" may derive from a term meaning "rustic lout." "Marshal" originally referred to a servant in charge of horses, and "constable" to one who cared for the stables. The Anglo-Saxon *thegn* was in its earliest appearances equivalent to the Latin *puer*, in the sense of "boy" or "servant." Another word adopted in the language of feudalism to signify "vassal" was *homo* or "man" (cf. "homage"). It too had disreputable beginnings, as its earliest comparable meaning seems to have been "slave." This vertical upward drift in social terminology is quite striking, even if the stages of the evolution cannot be dated with precision. The process seems to reflect the experience of many servants, who through valued services to powerful men rose from low to high social levels and added dignity to the names they bore. In the early Middle Ages, as subsequently, service was one important way to social preferment.

The pattern of social mobility in early medieval society thus indicates a circulatory movement through the body social. The tendency of family lines in elevated social positions to lose status was partially balanced by the penetration of lucky or talented persons of humble birth into the higher social levels. Both movements worked to obliterate the traditional juridical distinctions separating one status from another. The erosion of the ranks of the unfree is particularly notable, as it may be considered to represent the last phase in the disappearance of ancient slavery in the West. Still, under conditions of a stagnant economy, it may be doubted that the lot of the lowest social classes was much improved.

THE AGE OF EXPANSION   From about the year 1000, the European population began to pour out of the settlement islands which had hitherto contained its numbers. Within Europe, a vigorous attack was launched upon the forests and wastes that still dominated much of the landscape. Still other colonizers pushed beyond the frontiers of the former Carolingian empire, to eastern lands beyond the Elbe River and down the Danube valley, to the south into the heart of the Iberian peninsula, and into southern Italy and the western islands of the Mediterranean Sea. The crusades to the east are only the most famous, but probably not the most significant example, of the advancing frontiers of Europe in the central Middle Ages.

Although no figures can be given, there can be little doubt that this movement resulted in real economic growth, in the sense of rising per-capita productivity. The newly settled areas were marked by a better balance between the factors of land and labor, and their opening relieved population pressure and factor imbalances in the older centers of settlement. The development of regions with different "factor endowments" and resources gave a powerful stimulus to the growth of trade and markets. The influence of the market in turn promoted a greater division of labor and more specialization in productive efforts. Even without dramatic changes in technology, the cultivators of the twelfth century could work more efficiently than their predecessors of the Carolingian epoch.

The growth of trade further stimulated a rebirth of urban life, and the towns became centers of exchange and of various manufacturing processes, especially involving textiles. Again, gains in productivity came from the advancing specialization of labor, and urban markets facilitated the flow of both goods and capital. In sum, the economy of the central Middle Ages was changing considerably; it placed at the disposal of society a greater social wealth, which could be divided among its various institutions and members.

Social change accompanied economic change. In particular, two new groups came into prominence: the feudal nobility and the urban patriciate. Most historians today maintain that neither group was directly connected with the older aristocracies of barbarian or Carolingian Europe.[16] At least there is no evidence of continuity in the aristocratic classes across this period of profound social transformations. The appearance of both nobility and patriciate thus offers an exceptional chance to study how this vertical social mobility was achieved against the background of a growing economy.

We shall first consider the feudal nobility, and we shall begin our analysis by relating a "success story" which seems to illustrate a pattern

16 See the now classical discussion by Marc Bloch, (trans. L. A. Manyon), *Feudal Society*, (Chicago, 1961), 283–285. "The most striking feature of the history of the dominant families in the first feudal age [i.e. those families established by 1100 or 1150] is the shortness of their pedigrees . . . To speak of nobility is to speak of pedigrees; in the case in point, pedigrees did not matter because there was no nobility." Only a few of the greatest families, according to Bloch, can trace their lineages as far back as the ninth century. For most families the traces disappear in the tenth and eleventh centuries. This problem has been much discussed; see n. 7.

widely repeated in the growing Europe of the tenth, eleventh, and twelfth centuries. One of the principal feudal families of northern Italy was the house of Canossa, which at the height of its wealth in the eleventh century controlled a vast assemblage of lands in Tuscany, Emilia, the Romagna, and elsewhere. The most famous member of the family was Matilda of Tuscany, who supported Pope Gregory VII during the bitter Investiture Controversy with the German emperor Henry IV. Her castle of Canossa, near Modena, was the scene of Henry's penance and submission in the snow, in January, 1077.

The pedigree of Matilda's house is, however, notably short. The earliest known ancestor of the family, and indeed the founder of its fortunes, was a man called Adalberto-Atto, who first appears in a charter of 958. Recently, an Italian scholar has intensively studied the career of Adalberto-Atto in order to determine how he carried his household and his lineage to such social heights.[17] Adalberto-Atto had no known connection with the older Lombard or Frankish aristocracies, but from his earliest appearances in the sources he was already a property owner with some resources. He seems, in other words, to have sprung from the rural "middle class" of small landlords. The secret of his spectacular success was the contribution he made to the resettlement of the lands of the lower Po valley, between the river and the Apennines. Settlement in the region had been traditionally concentrated on the higher, drier lands forming the approaches to the Apennines. The low lands close to the banks of the Po River were poorly drained and largely deserted, but they were potentially fertile. One great need of new settlers was protection, and protection was best afforded by the construction of castles. Adalberto-Atto seems to have achieved his success primarily as a builder of castles. At times he built his fortresses while the surrounding lands were still dominated by woods and marshes. But they attracted settlers into their environs and became centers of new communities. The farms laid out on the reclaimed lands were larger and more productive than the crowded holdings in old-settled areas; the colonizers improved their own economic position, and were simultaneously able to pay Adalberto-Atto for the protection afforded them. "New lands for a new lord," is how Fumagalli summarizes this process of resettlement and social advance for Adalberto-Atto and his house. By 962, this new lord had several vassals, who were rising in society along with their chief. When the German king,

17 Vito Fumagalli, *Le origini di una grande dinastia feudale Adalberto-Atto di Canossa* (Tübingen, 1971).

later emperor, Otto I arrived in Italy, he showered favors on this already powerful man in order to win his support. In the years after 962, Adalberto-Atto became count of Reggio, Modena, and Mantua. He thus arrived at the pinnacle of the new, feudal aristocracy of northern Italy.

Careers comparable to that of Adalberto-Atto can be noted widely across Europe during the central Middle Ages. There is a still better-known example in the accomplishments of the Hauteville brothers, sons of a petty knight in Normandy named Tancred. Facing impoverishment at home, three sons of Tancred emigrated to southern Italy in the 1030s, where they distinguished themselves first as hired mercenaries, then as castle builders, and then as rulers. Two younger brothers soon followed. One of them, Robert Guiscard, took the title of count (later duke) of Apulia, and his brother Roger eventually became count of Sicily. Roger's son, Roger II, claimed to be and was recognized as king of Sicily. The descendants of a petty Norman knight thus established one of the most powerful feudal dynasties in Europe.[18]

Still another example of a comparable rise is given by the career of Rodrigo Diaz of Vivar, called the Cid, the great Spanish hero of the Middle Ages. The Cid came from a class of minor landowners called *infanzones*. Through his exploits as a frontier fighter and governor, he was to attain wealth, power, and renown. "Today the kings of Spain," the later *Poema de Mío Cid* states with justification, "are among his kinsmen."

Both along frontiers and in old-settled areas, those warriors and castle builders who could provide protection were well rewarded in this age of expansion. It has been estimated that the number of fortresses constructed in this epoch in France alone came close to 10,000.[19] These sellers of protection undoubtedly formed a chief component in the new feudal nobility.

It is important to note that Adalberto-Atto, the Hauteville brothers, the Cid, and others, derived not from the highest levels of the older society, and certainly not from among the destitute. They came

18 Cf. the classic account offered by C. H. Haskins, *The Normans in European History* (Boston, 1915), Ch. 7.

19 For the Cid's historical career and his place in literature and legend, see the excellent study by Stephen Clissold, *In Search of the Cid* (London, 1965). For a list of medieval castles by *département*, see Camille Enlart, *Manuel d'archéologie française depuis les temps mérovingiens jusqu' à la Renaissance* (Paris, 1916) II, 623–753. See also Jacques Levron, *Le château fort et la vie au Moyen Age* (Paris, 1963), 30.

from the hard-pressed middle ranges of society—those petty land-owners who, in spite of some resources, were most sensitive to the threat of a deteriorating social position. Literary sources contain frequent allusions to the pressures operating upon these men. In summoning the first crusade at Clermont in 1095, Pope Urban II is reported to have told the knights:

> ... the land which you inhabit, shut in on all sides by the sea and surrounded by mountain peaks, is too narrow for your large population; nor does it abound in wealth; and it furnishes scarcely food enough for its cultivators. Hence it is that you murder and devour one another.[20]

Peter Damian, an Italian leader of the reform movement of the eleventh century, complained about how his contemporaries, pressed by need, entered the service and assiduously cultivated the favor of rich men; others sought "to increase their moneys in ambitious business"; still others hired themselves out as mercenary soldiers. According to Damian, these energetic and ambitious men were claiming: "We cannot obey the commandments of God, because we do not have enough earthly property for our needs."[21]

Leadership in the new enterprises of the medieval world seems primarily to have come from those social levels which had to struggle to repair their perpetually sinking fortunes, but which controlled some property to help support their efforts. A large share of the resources controlled by these social groups was likely to be turned to entre-preneurial purposes. Aided by a buoyant economy, this entrepreneurial drive and willingness to commit resources carried many men of low and middling origins to high social positions.

The origins of the second aristocracy of medieval society—the urban patriciate—show many similarities to the patterns which marked the formation of the feudal nobility. The Belgian historian

---

20 According to the account of Robert the Monk. See August C. Krey, *The First Crusade. Accounts of Eye-Witnesses and Participants* (Princeton, 1921), 31.

21 *Patrologia Latina* (Paris, 1853), CXLIV, col. 524. "Ubi sunt illi qui dicunt: Nos Dei praecepta servare non possumus, quia terrenam substantiam ad usos necessarios non habemus ... Egestatis quippe angustatus inopia, non ad obsequendum cujuslibet domum potentis intravit, non adulari divitibus, ut mos est pauperum, studuit, non ambitiosa negotatione augere pecunias anhelavit, non periculosae militiae quae sine peccato bajulari non potest stipendium concupivit, sed muliebri contentus officio simplicem victum manu et arte quaerebat ..." Peter is comparing the simple life of St. Severus of Ravenna with the exaggerated efforts of the men of his own times to find sustenance.

Henri Pirenne advanced the famous thesis that the great urban families were recruited primarily from the "proletariat" of feudal society, from those "foot-loose adventurers" who owned no property and had no vested interest in preserving things as they were.[22] Only the destitute, argued Pirenne, had reason to cultivate an entrepreneurial spirit. Pirenne had a gift for clear and appealing exposition, but today, after more than two generations of research, little remains of his thesis. Intensive investigation of the origins of the great urban families, both in Flanders and in Italy, identifies them as small property owners even before their immigration to the city.[23] Moreover, the contention that families with property were therefore devoid of incentive ignores the problem of younger sons or too many sons, which is everywhere visible on the medieval social scene. The heir with some property, but not enough to live after the manner of his parents, is most likely to engage in *ambitiosa negotatio*, in Damian's phrase.

In sum, the model we propose as a generalized description of social mobility in this age of expansion is this: the upper levels of society continued to replace their numbers more successfully than the lower, and this created a continuing downward pressure upon family lines. That pressure was particularly intense within those ranks of society with some, but limited resources. The sons of petty landlords, warriors, or knights either had to contemplate an imminent loss of status or seek to repair their fortunes through effort and daring. From the ranks of such small landlords, the great entrepreneurs of the age—Adalberto-Atto, the Hauteville brothers, the Cid, and many urban patricians—were primarily recruited. An entrepreneur requires, after all, both incentive and some initial resources. The processes we have explored explain why men from the low but still propertied ranges of society would have both incentives and ambitions, and the means to pursue them.

CITY AND COUNTRYSIDE   The economic expansion from approximately the year 1000 brought to Europe a rebirth of urban life, particularly notable in such regions as northern Italy or Flanders. The

22 The thesis is developed in his *Medieval Cities* (Princeton, 1925).
23 See especially J. Lestocquoy, *Les villes de Flandre et d'Italie sous le gouvernement des patriciens (XIe–XVe siècles)* (Paris, 1952). The problem is discussed by Lucien Febvre, "Fils de riches ou nouveaux riches?" *Annales-Economies-Sociétés-Civilisations* I (1946), 139–153. For Florence, the work which reversed the older assumption that the urban population was recruited mainly from escaped serfs and the destitute was J. Plesner, *L'émigration de la campagne à la ville libre de Florence au XIIIe siècle* (Copenhagen, 1934).

economic crisis of the closing Middle Ages (fourteenth and fifteenth centuries) does not seem to have influenced the proportion of the population living in towns. In Tuscany, for example, about a quarter of the population continued to live in cities during the last two hundred years of the Middle-Ages.

How did the presence of a large urban sector affect patterns of replacement and mobility in medieval society? The rich data from the Florentine Catasto of 1427 can give us partial but suggestive answers. Table 5 shows the distribution of minors, young adults, and older adults according to residence in the city of Florence, in the small cities (Pisa, Pistoia, Arezzo, Prato, and Volterra), and the surrounding rural areas.

Table 5 Residence and Age Distributions in Tuscany, 1427

	RESIDENCE			
	FLORENCE	SMALL CITIES	COUNTRYSIDE	TOTAL
Ages:				
0–17				
Persons	15671	9930	81692	107293
Percent	14.6	9.3	76.1	100.0
18–47				
Persons	13230	8793	69547	91570
Percent	14.5	9.6	75.9	100.0
48–99				
Persons	7083	6543	47013	60639
Percent	11.7	10.8	77.5	100.0
Totals	35984	25266	198252	259502
Percent	13.9	9.7	76.4	100.0
Ratio:				
Minor/Young Adult	1.18	1.13	1.17	1.17

Only persons with stated age are included.

The most remarkable result which emerges from Table 5 is the success with which the population of the city of Florence was maintaining its members. There is apparent no replacement deficit, in the sense of a smaller portion of minor children in comparison with that of adults, in the Florentine urban population, and only a minuscule deficit can be observed in the small cities. To be sure, the countryside included many stricken areas, such as the high mountains, and the global replacement ratios cannot be considered representative of the prosperous rural areas. Still, cities have a long-standing reputation for being, in comparison with rural areas, poor producers of children; this is not apparent in the Florentine domains in 1427.

However, to gain a better grasp of the patterns of replacement present in Tuscan society, we must take a closer look at our data. Did welfare, for example, have a different impact upon replacement in the cities than in the rural areas? Table 6 illustrates the distribution of minors, young adults, and older adults, according to four wealth categories, exclusively for the households of the city of Florence.

Table 6 Welfare and Age Distributions at Florence, 1427

	ASSESSMENT (FLORINS)				
	0	1–100	101–400	OVER 400	TOTAL
Ages:					
0–17					
Persons	1713	2564	2969	8425	15671
Percent	10.9	16.4	19.0	53.7	100.0
18–47					
Persons	1635	2566	2770	6259	13230
Percent	12.3	19.4	20.9	47.3	99.9
48–99					
Persons	1095	1581	1788	2619	7083
Percent	15.5	22.3	25.3	36.8	99.9
Total	4443	6711	7527	17303	35984
Ratio:					
Minor/Young					
Adult	1.05	1.00	1.07	1.34	1.18

Only persons with stated age are included.

If the results of Table 6, for the city of Florence, are compared with those for the entire population of the Florentine dominions (Table 3), then it becomes evident that the poorer households of the urban population were conspicuously less successful than poorer families generally in rearing children. With "minor–young adult" ratios of 1.07 and less for the three lowest categories of assessed wealth (Table 6), those segments of the urban population were clearly not maintaining their numbers through natural increase. The apparent success of the city in rearing children was exclusively the success of its richer families, those with more than 400 florins of assessed wealth.

The influence of residence upon replacement seems, therefore, to have been strongest among, and indeed limited to, the poor and the lower middle classes. Table 7 cross-tabulates residence and age distributions for Florence, the small cities, and the countryside, but only for those persons found in households assessed at 400 or fewer florins.

Table 7 Residence and Age Distributions in Tuscany, 1427 (Households Assessed at 400 or Fewer Florins)

| | RESIDENCE | | | |
	FLORENCE	SMALL CITIES	COUNTRYSIDE	TOTAL
Ages:				
0–17				
Persons	7246	7416	77492	92154
Percent	7.9	8.0	84.1	100.0
18–47				
Persons	6971	6785	66412	80168
Percent	8.7	8.5	82.8	100.0
48–99				
Persons	4474	5469	45156	55099
Percent	8.1	9.9	82.0	100.0
Total	18691	19670	189060	227421
Percent	8.2	8.7	83.1	100.0
Ratio:				
Minor/Young Adult	1.04	1.09	1.17	1.14

Only persons with stated ages are included.

Table 7, which incidentally surveys about 87 per cent of the inhabitants of the Florentine dominions, confirms that urban residence interfered with reproduction and replacement, but only at the lower levels of the social scale. (The assessment level between 300 and 400 florins would, however, include many artisans and shopkeepers in the city, who would have to be described as "middle class" in their social position.) The patrician families, in spite of their urban residence, continued to support large numbers of children in their households.[24]

24 The median age of the population resident in households with more than 400 florins of assessment was 18, and for those with 400 or fewer florins it was 26. The rich households, in other words, were prolific in the numbers of children they were supporting. As servants were not registered in the Catasto, the children were all the products of the natural reproduction of the rich families.

On the assumption that the size of the population and its residential distribution were constant over time, then about 10 per cent of the middle and lower classes of the urban population would have to be recruited by means other than natural reproduction and replacement. The replacement deficit of these groups could be overcome either by encouraging immigration from the more prolific countryside, or by absorbing persons from the higher and more prolific urban social strata. The patrician families were, however, likely to resist this second alternative.

Two principal conclusions flow from our data. The threat of losing status, which particularly pressed the lower but still propertied classes in the countryside, reached into much higher social levels in the city. The urban patriciate had to find careers for its plentiful children, or watch them sink to lower social positions. Many, but clearly not all, of the patrician sons and daughters could enter upon ecclesiastical careers or join religious orders. Many more had to make their way in a highly competitive world. Contemporaries were quite aware of the pressures working upon the patrician families. A historian of Florence, Goro Dati, who appears in the Catasto, offered this striking account of the behavior of the Florentines in the face of demographic pressures:

> ... the city of Florence is placed by nature in a rugged and sterile location which cannot give a livelihood to the inhabitants, in spite of all their efforts. However, they have multiplied greatly because of the temperate air, which is very generative in that locale. For that reason, for some time back it has been necessary for the Florentines, because they have multiplied in number, to seek their livelihood through enterprises. Therefore, they have departed from their territory to search through other lands, provinces and countries, where one or another has seen an opportunity to profit for a time, to make a fortune, and to return to Florence ... For some time now it has seemed that they were born for this, so large is the number (in accordance with what the generative air produces) of those who go through the world in their youth and make profit and acquire experience, daring (*virtu*), good manners and treasure. All of them together constitute a community of so large a number of valiant and wealthy men which has no equal in the world.[25]

25 L. Pratesi (ed.), *L'istoria di Firenze dal 1380 al 1405* (Norcia, 1904), Bk. IX. For the character and date of Dati's chronicle, see the recent comment by Hans Baron, *From Petrarch to Leonardo Bruni. Studies in Humanistic and Political Literature* (Chicago, 1968), 138–150. Baron believes that the work was written in 1409.

Goro Dati was clearly not describing the humbler inhabitants of Florence, few of whom wandered great distances through the world, few of whom made fortunes. He described the life style of the patricians. Still, in his estimation that demographic pressures demanded that the sons even of the privileged assume and maintain an entrepreneurial stance, he now confirms what data from the Catasto also reveal.

The second conclusion from our data is that the replacement deficit from the middle and low classes of urban society engendered a recruitment of new men, partially from other cities, but pre-eminently from the villages and small towns of the countryside. Numerous men of talent responded to the call, and they especially filled the ranks of artisans, notaries, and government servants—careers where skill counted more than capital. Many great literary figures of Renaissance Florence came from rural or small-town origins—Boccaccio, Coluccio Salutati, Leonardo Bruni, Poggio Bracciolini, Marsilio Ficino, Angelo Poliziano, and others. Many artists were of similar derivation—Giotto, Masaccio, Leonardo da Vinci, Desiderio da Settignano, and more. Few of these gifted immigrants penetrated in the fourteenth and fifteenth centuries into the ranks of the patriciate. One ominous result of this mass recruitment of talented men was that it introduced them into society at levels—the middle urban classes—where their own reproduction was hampered. Ultimately, massive immigration may have been destructive of talented lines and wasteful of human capital. But in the short run, these gifted newcomers were given an opportunity to display their skills, and Florentine culture was immeasurably richer for it.

These, then, are the principal conclusions which our considerations of social mobility in the Middle Ages suggest. Because of differences in rates of replacement across the social spectrum, families in favored positions produced more heirs and successors than those on the less advantaged levels of society. The dominant trend of social mobility in this traditional society was therefore consistently downward. Still, markedly different results could follow, which pre-eminently reflected the economic conditions of the period. In the stagnant epoch of the early Middle Ages, the privileged tended to lose position, while some few lucky or talented persons gained it. The overall result was a shuffling of status; in consequence, juridical differences, notably between slave and free, were progressively obliterated. The economic takeoff from the year 1000 enabled those facing a threat of losing status to assume the function of entrepreneurs. They had powerful incentives, and enough property, to be both willing and able to gamble upon their talents. Conditions of urban life heightened pressures on the privileged, requiring them under penalty of loss of status to keep their sons in an entrepreneurial stance. Also, in increasing the difficulties of reproduction for the city poor, urban conditions forced a continuous recruitment of new men from the countryside, to which the talented and the motivated were especially prone to respond. The pressures upon the rich, the opportunities offered to the talented poor, combined to lend to the late medieval and Renaissance town its creative vitality. In sum, medieval society, rural and urban, presents dynamic patterns of social movement, which historians are only today coming to appreciate and study.

Theodore Evergates

The Aristocracy of Champagne in the Mid-Thirteenth Century:

A Quantitative Description

Quantification is one of several techniques employed by historians in the past two decades to give increasing precision to our understanding of French feudal society, but its major results have been limited as yet to rough measurements of the survival of the aristocracy and the relative levels of fief incomes.[1] Comparisons of the total numbers of aristocratic families in several periods in the Mâconnais, Namur, and Flanders have demonstrated the essential continuity of the aristocracy as a social group in the eleventh to thirteenth centuries.[2] In the thirteenth century, however, aristocratic families appear to have been unstable: in Forez one third of the thirteenth-century families disappeared by the next century because an average lineage lasted only three to six generations, while in Picardy only one quarter of the aristocratic families in 1190 survived to 1290.[3] An analysis of thirteenth-century fief incomes has been possible in

Theodore Evergates is Assistant Professor of History at Western Maryland College.

This project was made possible by an initial allocation of computer time by The Johns Hopkins University Department of History and by a grant from the Johnson Fund of the American Philosophical Society which helped to defray additional computer and computer-related expenses. The author is grateful to Solis James, Director of The Johns Hopkins University Computing Center, for his encouragement and guidance in the development of the project. For their comments on earlier drafts of this paper, the author thanks Robert Forster and Arthur Lyons; the latter also contributed by playing devil's advocate in discussions on the methodological problems of extracting and interpreting the data.

1 The contributions of prosopography and sociolinguistics to the analytical study of feudal society will be reviewed in another paper. Excluded here, of course, are strictly economic measurements, such as prices. Demographic studies for the tenth through the thirteenth centuries probably cannot be realized, but the model for any such undertaking would be Edouard Baratier, *La démographie provençale du XIIIe au XVIe siècle* (Paris, 1961). The Carolingian polyptiques have only recently been subjected to quantitative analysis; see Emily R. Coleman, "Medieval Marriage Characteristics: A Neglected Factor in the History of Medieval Serfdom," *The Journal of Interdisciplinary History*, II (1971), 205–217.

2 Georges Duby, *La société aux XIe et XIIe siècles dans la région mâconnaise* (Paris, 1953); Léopold Genicot, *L'économie rurale namuroise au bas moyen âge (1199–1429)*, II: *Les hommes. La noblesse* (Louvain, 1960); Ernest Warlop, *De Vlaamse adel voor 1300* (Handzame, 1968), 3v.

3 Edouard Perroy, "Social Mobility among the French *Noblesse* in the Later Middle Ages," *Past & Present*, XXI (1962), 25–38; Robert Fossier, *La terre et les hommes en Picardie jusqu'à la fin du XIIIe siècle* (Paris, 1968), 2v.

Forez, where all extant charters have been catalogued: Ordinary knights had much lower annual revenues (25 pounds) than the castellans (100–500 pounds), who in turn had much less than the few great lords (1,000–2,000 pounds) and the count of Forez (12,000 pounds).[4] Such seemingly modest attempts at quantification in medieval social history are, in fact, substantial contributions to the systematic analysis of "feudal society," which is too often depicted in legalistic or impressionistic terms.

Unfortunately, the above determinations were based on charter evidence, for which quantitative operations are at best difficult and often questionable. Most charters are ecclesiastical records of property transactions, usually acquisitions, of particular houses, and as a type of source they present discrete, fragmentary situations. The extant acts and their copies in cartularies most frequently mention the constant benefactors of the Church, the wealthy and powerful families whose representativeness of the fief-holding group has not been established, and do not necessarily mention all members of the secular aristocracy; therefore, they do not constitute a series in the statistical sense. In Forez, for example, 215 aristocratic lineages can be isolated at one time or another in the thirteenth century, but because of lacunae in charter references, the genealogies are not continuous; and it can only be estimated that about 150 families existed at any given period. Furthermore, it is quite possible that there were other aristocratic families which do not appear in any of the extant charters. Since it is impossible to obtain a "fix" on the entire group at a specific date solely from charter references, it would be unsound procedure to generalize about an aristocracy from these sources alone. There are also the crucial problems of charter terminology and conceptual models: What criteria should be used to identify a medieval aristocracy? Neither the titles of knights (*milites*) and castellan lords (*domini*), nor similar terms of qualification (e.g., "noble") were assigned either consistently or uniformly by local ecclesiastical scribes. Even more critical, the connotation of various titles and terms changed, as in the case of both *dominus* and *miles* from 1150 to 1250. In any analysis of a medieval aristocracy it is important to make explicit whether knights are to be counted in the aristocracy of the twelfth century, according to the traditional Guilhiermoz-Bloch-Duby model, or not until the thirteenth century, as the more recent Belgian thesis

---

4 Perroy, "Social Mobility"; Count of Neufbourg, "Puissance relative du comte et des seigneurs en Forez au XIIIᵉ siècle," *Le Moyen Age*, LXI (1955), 405–432.

holds.[5] In sum, there are serious methodological and conceptual problems entailed in the quantification of charter information; although some difficulties are due to the inherent nature of charters and are insoluble, others can and must be consciously controlled before quantification will yield significant results from charter evidence.[6]

Another type of source—one which remains relatively unexplored—is particularly susceptible to quantitative analysis and offers considerable possibilities for medieval social history: the administrative record was developed as a basic tool by the nascent bureaucracies of the great territorial states which emerged in the twelfth century. Large-scale surveys of fiefs or of domainal rights and revenues were reporting systems of standardized information on entire spectra of persons, conditions, or rights in lay principalities; they were further organized according to geographical or political areas defined by contemporaries. Early examples of such records are the Norman *Enquête* and the Champagne *Feoda Campanie*, both of c. 1172 and both essentially lists of barons and

[5] The standard interpretation of aristocratic development in medieval France is Paul Guilhiermoz, *Essai sur les origines de la noblesse en France au moyen âge* (Paris, 1902), esp. chs. 3–4, and Marc Bloch trans. L. A. Manyon, *Feudal Society*, [Paris, 1939–1940] (Chicago, 1961), 282–344. According to this thesis, members of the aristocracy assumed knighthood in the eleventh century; their status was assured by birth alone and guaranteed by new legal sanctions in the thirteenth century, when they gave up their military functions. Duby, *La société mâconnaise*, furnished the first local documentation of the thesis and argued that the closed, cohesive, and privileged aristocracy of castellan lords and knights in the eleventh century was the result of a common *genre de vie*, based on military service. The attribution of aristocratic status to the knights in the eleventh century has been increasingly resisted, by the Belgians in particular, since the appearance of Genicot's study in 1960. The alternate model sees the Carolingian aristocratic families not only surviving as lineages, but also preserving their social exclusiveness into the thirteenth century. The knights were distinctly inferior, essentially armed retainers, until the late twelfth or early thirteenth century, depending on the region, when they gradually acquired status comparable to that of the castellan lords. Thus, an aristocracy of lords and knights with uniform social and legal standing did not exist until the thirteenth century, two hundred years later than the French model would have. The separation of aristocratic and knight lineages is clearly shown in Warlop's study (see note 2 above), and most recent monographs confirm the Belgian interpretation. The best general statement of the new formulation is Léopold Genicot, "La noblesse au moyen âge dans l'ancienne 'Francie.' Continuité, rupture ou évolution?" *Comparative Studies in Society and History*, V (1962), 52–59.

[6] Fossier's *Picardie* illustrates both the strengths and weaknesses of full-scale quantitative analyses based on charters alone. An example of a controlled approach is George Beech, "Personal Titles and Social Classes in Medieval France (Poitou), Ninth to Twelfth Centuries" (read at the American Historical Association meeting, 1971). The Belgians have undertaken to subject all texts on the aristocracy before 1000 to computer analysis; see Léopold Genicot, "Naissance, fonction et richesse dans l'ordonnance de la société médiévale. Le cas de la Noblesse du Nord-Ouest du Continent," in Roland Mousnier (ed.), *Problèmes de stratification sociale* (Paris, 1968), 83n.

knights with their military obligations, and the Flemish *Gros Brief* of 1187, an account of revenues from the count's domain.[7] In the thirteenth century, administration became more complex and its documents more ambitious; the inquests of Alphonse of Poitiers and Charles of Anjou reflect the growing importance of good "paper work" in the normal functioning of territorial states.[8] Less well known but equally impressive as a model of administrative competence and as an incomparable source for the study of a medieval aristocracy are the *Rôles des fiefs* of Champagne, drawn up under Count Thibaut IV le Chansonnier in 1249–52.[9]

The *Rôles* furnish an extraordinary amount of information: the names and titles of all fief holders of the count; the annual incomes, military obligations, and components of their fiefs; and the names, titles, and possessions of their rear-fief holders. The information was collected by two traveling *enquêteurs*, a knight and a canon, with whom Count Thibaut asked his "barons, castellans, knights, and other fief holders" to cooperate by giving the appropriate information on their fiefs and rear-fiefs.[10] A test-run was conducted in 1249 for Provins and four neighboring castellanies, and by 1252 the *enquêteurs* had canvassed all thirty-seven Champagne castellanies. Registers for twenty-three (62 percent) of the thirty-seven castellanies survive as the fullest and most systematic collection of data on an entire medieval aristocracy. Since the data constitute a closed series in the statistical sense—the inventory theoretically covered all fief holders of the count—the *Rôles* can be analyzed quantitatively without the methodological problems involved in the quantification of charter information. The following results of a computer analysis are basically descriptive; they are the prerequisite of more complex correlations for a larger study of the Champagne aristocracy in which quantitative data will be integrated with specific family histories.

7 Preliminary analyses are in Jacques Boussard, "L'enquête de 1172 sur les services de chevalier en Normandie," *Recueil de travaux offert à M. Clovis Brunel* (Paris, 1955), I, 193–208; A. Verhulst and M. Gysseling, *Le Compte Général de 1187, connu sous le nom de "Gros Brief," et les institutions financières du comté de Flandre au XIIe siècle* (Brussels, 1962).
8 Edouard Baratier, *Enquêtes sur les droits et revenus de Charles Ier d'Anjou en Provence (1252 et 1278)* (Paris, 1969).
9 The text is in Auguste Longnon (ed.), *Rôles des fiefs du comté de Champagne sous le règne de Thibaut le Chansonnier, 1249–1252* (Paris, 1877). A discussion of the manuscripts and dating is in *idem, Documents relatifs au comté de Champagne et de Brie (1172–1361)*, I: *Les fiefs* (Paris, 1901), xxiii–xxviii.
10 Letter of 1250 addressed to his "baronibus, castellanis, militibus, et aliis feudatis," Joseph de Laborde (ed.), *Layettes du Trésor des Chartes* (Paris, 1875), III, 122–123.

In the refinement of the raw data of the *Rôles*, two types of entries —duplications and multiple fief listings—must be controlled. Ordinarily, fief holders appeared before the *enquêteurs* to report their holdings on oath; absentees were represented by their wives, agents, close friends, or even by letter, as in the case of the *dame* of Trainel, who in spite of illness penned a long report in the vernacular. A separate register was allotted to each castellany, so emendations could be made at the end of each set of entries for changes which occurred while the inquest was still in progress. For example, if a man died after reporting his holdings, his widow and son might then be listed at the end of the register for the same possessions by reason of dowry and inheritance. For the purpose of this analysis, the later entries are considered duplications, and only the original holder and his possessions are counted. In like manner, a person who is listed in two or more castellany registers is here assigned to the one in which he had his "main" holding, defined as the fief with the highest income or the greatest amount of castle guard; his less important fiefs are then counted as his second, third fief, etc. Thus, each person and each fief is counted once only.[11] The *Rôles* contain 1,358 entries for the twenty-three castellanies, but the elimination of duplicate and multiple listings (− 13 percent) reduces to 1,182 the total number of persons who held directly from the count. Of the 1,182, 977 (82.7 percent) were men and 205 (17.3 percent) were women. Although some women were temporary holders, as guardians for their sons or as respondents for their husbands who were away in the East, many held in their own right for inheritances and dowries, and one fourth were identified as widows. The presence of women making up about one fifth of all fief holders in 1252 contrasts with their absence from the 1172 inventory of fief holders (*Feoda Campanie*).

In the twelfth century, the knights and castellan-lords of Champagne, as in most of France and Belgium, constituted distinct social, economic, and lineage groups.[12] But in the last decades of the century, ecclesiastical scribes increasingly gave the *dominus* title, hitherto reserved for lords, to knights who had neither genealogical connections with

11 In order to obtain a static situation, I have ignored the fact that a few registers were actually composed in 1249 rather than in 1252. In the few cases in which a "main" holding cannot be ascertained by income or castle guard, the entry in which the scribe provided the most precise description of the person (e.g. status) or fief (e.g. components) is taken here to indicate the "main" fief.

12 See note 5 above and the works cited in notes 2–4. See also George T. Beech, *A Rural Society in Medieval France: The Gâtine of Poitou in the Eleventh and Twelfth Centuries* (Baltimore, 1964).

nor the concomitant military and economic attributes of the castellan families. By the early thirteenth century, *miles* and *dominus* were employed indiscriminately in the charters for the descendants of both castellans and knights, and the count's scribes adopted the convention in the *Rôles* of 1252. At the same time a new social distinction emerged: It became common for the sons of knights and, to a lesser extent, of lords to retain the non-knighted status (*armiger, escuier*) for many of their adult years before acquiring knight status, and by the mid-thirteenth century many remained non-knighted for their entire lives. A parallel, although less pronounced, development occurred among women: Some retained the *domicella* title even after marriage, when earlier they would have become *dominae*. According to the *Rôles*, the breakdown of fief holders by status in 1252 was 42.2 percent *domini/milites*,[13] 14.0 percent non-knighted *armigeri*, 12.6 percent *dominae*, 2.1 percent *domicellae*, 5.1 percent others (viscounts, townsmen, clerics, and lesser administrative officials), and 24.0 percent without any title indicated. Some of the nontitled can be located in the charters, mostly as *domini/milites*, as might be expected, since the latter were most often involved in charter transactions in the first place. Pierre of Floregny, for example, who held a 30-pound fief lacked a title in the *Rôles*, yet he was qualified as a knight both in an earlier administrative survey and in a charter of 1263.[14] In this and other specific cases which can be checked there is no evidence that the countal scribes systematically omitted status, and the purely quantitative analyses so far have failed to reveal distinctive characteristics of the nontitled group.[15] Therefore, the omission of status is tentatively taken as a random factor which has no influence on the relative distributions of the other specifically mentioned status groups. Thus, the closest approximation of status distribution for the entire population of fief holders is the one for known status

13 The *dominus* category here includes 411 *domini*, 64 *milites*, 19 persons with both titles, and 5 counts and dukes. In the charters of the first half of the thirteenth century, *dominus* was synonymous with *miles*, but the *Rôles* are the first countal record to employ the new convention. The fact that Thibaut's letter (note 10 above) referred to *milites*, whereas the *Rôles* recorded mostly *domini*, demonstrates the equivalence. Several specific cases in the *Rôles* also confirm it: Hugh of Montfey, for example, was entitled *dominus* as a direct fief holder (Ervy, no. 337) but *miles* as a rear-fief holder (Bray, no. 122). The reason for double *dominus/miles* titles is not evident.

14 *Feoda* IV (*milites* of the countess, no. 3941), c. 1222–43, in Longnon, *Documents*, I; charter of 1263 in Charles Lalore (ed.), *Collection des principaux cartulaires du diocese de Troyes* (Paris-Troyes, 1875–1890), III (Paraclet), no. 268.

15 The only significant quantitative trait of the nontitled group is its rather low median fief value; otherwise, it shows the same general characteristics as the other groups; see notes 20, 21.

Fig. 1   Fief Holders

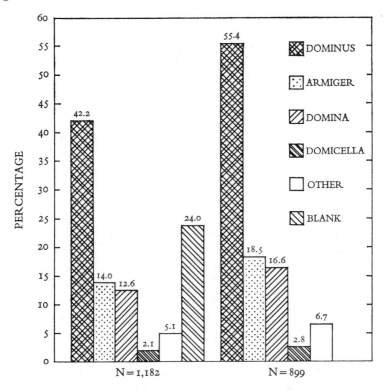

alone (899 persons) which is: 55.4 percent *domini*, 18.5 percent *armigeri*, 16.6 percent *dominae*, 2.8 percent *domicellae*, and 6.7 percent others (Fig. 1). This mid-thirteenth-century breakdown represents a substantial change from the composition of fief holders in the twelfth century as revealed both in charters and in the *Feoda Campanie* of 1172, which identified almost all fief holders as knights and only a few percent as *domini*. Many descendants of the twelfth-century knight families were entitled *domini* in 1252, but others, although they remained direct fief holders of the count, had slipped into the non-knighted, *armiger* status. Thus, the first half of the thirteenth century witnessed a profound change in the social organization of the Champagne fief holders: As the simple lord-knight dichotomy of the twelfth century was erased by a fusion of the two groups for tenurial purposes, two new groups, women and the non-knighted, emerged to constitute together one third of all fief holders.

The *Rôles* were primarily an account of fiefs, and the scribes organized all information by individual fief. Of the 1,182 fief holders, 956 (80.9 percent) held a single fief, 184 (15.5 percent) held two fiefs, and 42 (3.6 percent) held three or more. In spite of some clear examples of fief holders who held additional fiefs from great lay or ecclesiastical lords, it appears that in most cases the fiefs held from the count furnished the entire, or at least the major, family incomes. For example, in cases where fief holders alienated their fiefs to ecclesiastical houses and then both they and their properties disappeared from the Champagne registers and the charters, it is evident that the alienations were of unique family fiefs.[16] The fief holders who also held fiefs from other Champagne barons were accountable in the *Rôles* as rear-fief holders, but only 14.9 percent of the direct holders had such rear-fiefs.[17] Moreover, persons who can be shown by charter evidence to have held fiefs from lay and ecclesiastical lords outside the count's fief system generally had neither a fief nor a rear-fief from the count. In short, both the Champagne registers and the histories of individual families which can be traced confirm that, except for an occasional alod which could be disposed of at will, most persons who held from the count held only from him and usually a single fief.

Most fiefs in the *Rôles* were valued in *libratae terre* (*l.t.*), according to their estimated annual yield from all sources of revenue, including domain produce, rents, taxes, justice, and banal monopolies.[18] A simple entry is: "*Dominus* Pierre of Rizaucourt holds at Villeneuve men, a mill, lands, fields, justice, about 50 *libratae terre*."[19] Fief incomes can be measured by several methods, most obviously by individual fief or by

16 For example, Gautier II of Ruvigny, whose father had been assigned a countal fief c. 1190 (*Feoda* I, Troyes, no. 1912, in Longnon, *Documents*, I), alienated that entire fief ("omnia bona sua tam mobilia quam immobilia") to Montier-la-Celle in 1223 (Lalore, *Collection*, V, nos. 85, 153). He was dead by 1245 (*ibid.*, no. 80) when his wife entered the abbey as a convert. Neither his fief nor any of his descendants appeared in the *Rôles*, in any later countal survey, or in a charter; the countal fief and its holder had effectively disappeared.

17 See note 25.

18 The *librata terre* was a unit of value employed throughout the county, as it was throughout England (F. M. Stenton, *The First Century of English Feudalism, 1066–1166* [London, 1961], 165n), and did not refer to a specific coinage, such as pounds Provins or Troyes. When the count assigned a revenue in *libratae terre*, the amount was collected in the local currency, so the actual purchasing power of the *librata terre* varied slightly from one locality to another. One of the earliest references to this type of valuation is c. 1200 (*Feoda* II, Rosnay, no. 2164, in Longnon, *Documents*, I): A fief was listed as *quindecim libratas terre*. Another expression for the same form of valuation is in the *Rôles*, Bar-sur-Aube, no. 10: "que omnia valent circiter sexaginta annuatim."

19 *Rôles*, Bar-sur-Seine, no. 76.

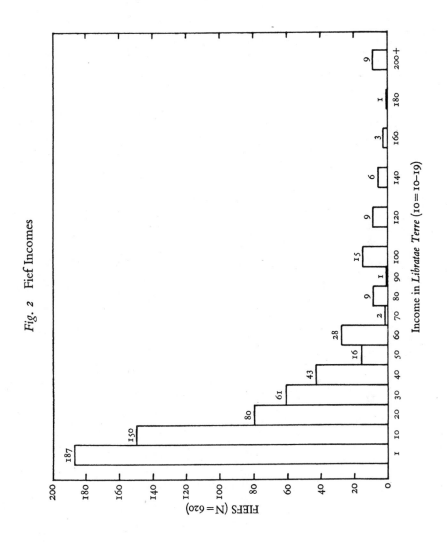

Fig. 2 Fief Incomes

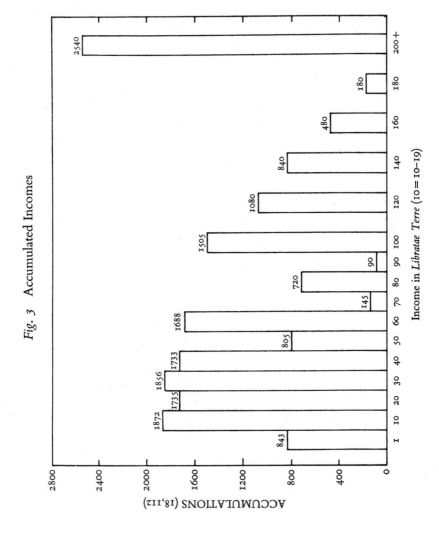

Fig. 3 Accumulated Incomes

total personal income, neither of which is satisfactory here.[20] However, since 80.9 percent of the fief holders had only one fief, and since the values of the second and third fiefs were, in fact, distributed in the same manner as those of the sole or first fiefs, the most efficient method of linking fief value with the status of the fief holder is to tabulate the values of the sole fief (for the 80.9 percent) together with the values of the first fief of multiple holdings (for the 19.1 percent). In this way 620 (52.5 percent) of the 1,182 persons have their sole or first fief valued in *libratae terre* (Figs. 2, 3). The average income was 29.2 *l.t.*, but the median of just under 20 *l.t.* indicates a preponderance of lower-valued fiefs. The status of the holder does indeed account for some discrepancy in fief values: The average fief of a *dominus* (35.7 *l.t.*) was almost twice as valuable as that of an *armiger* (21.7 *l.t.*). Compared to all other groups, the *domini* had proportionately fewer fiefs in the 1–19 *l.t.* range and an increasingly larger share of fiefs over 20 *l.t.* Clearly, they and, to a lesser extent, the *dominae* had the more valuable fiefs *vis-à-vis* the *armigeri* and nontitled. But in each case the discrepancy between average fiefs is far greater than that between median fiefs: For example, the difference between an average *dominus* and *armiger* fief (14 *l.t.*) is twice that between their respective median fiefs of 25 *l.t.* and 18 *l.t.* (7 *l.t.*). That is, the significant disparity was not so much between status groups as between the minority of fief holders, of whatever status, who held very valuable fiefs and the overwhelming majority of persons who had comparatively modest or even low-valued fiefs.[21] Since there is no satisfactory index

20 Although it is possible to link status with total personal income, in many cases total incomes are deceptive because second fiefs were enjoyed only a few years before being transferred out of the family as dowries. Tabulation by individual fief alone does not permit the crucial linkage of fiefs with the status of their holders. Furthermore, a lower percentage of *all* fiefs than of *sole/first* fiefs were valued in *libratae terre*, so the latter group contains a larger and hence more reliable sample of valued fiefs. In fact, the distribution of values for all individual fiefs is almost identical to that for sole/first fiefs; thus, the latter can be taken as an accurate reflection of the former but with the additional linkage of personal status and fief characteristics. The percentage of valued fiefs in each status group is similar to the total percentage of fiefs held by that group: the *domini* had 42.2 percent of all sole/first fiefs and 40.9 percent of all valued sole/first fiefs; the *armigeri* had 14.0 percent and 16.4 percent respectively, the *dominae* 12.6 percent and 12.4 percent, and the non-titled 23.9 percent and 24.2 percent. Thus, the valuation of fiefs was not itself a function of status.

21 For example, although the median fief value of the nontitled (12 *l.t.*) was half the median of the *domini* (25 *l.t.*) and two thirds the median of the *armigeri* (18 *l.t.*), the nontitled nevertheless possessed a number of very valuable fiefs. Furthermore, the fact that some of the nontitled can be located with titles in the charters means that the non-attribution of status in the *Rôles* did not of itself deliberately define a particular group. Status alone was not the key function of income.

Fig. 4 Fiefs and Accumulated Incomes

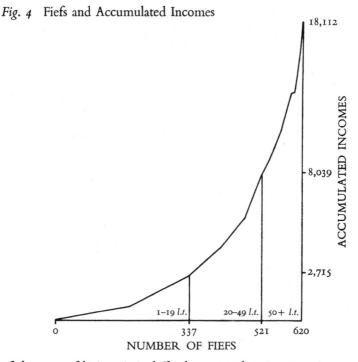

of the cost of living, it is difficult to translate incomes into equivalent levels or styles of living, but the relative difference in income distribution can be derived by tabulating the fiefs against their accumulated incomes (Fig. 4). Of valued fiefs, 54.4 percent (337) provided 1–19 *l.t.* annually, but their accumulated incomes constituted only 15.0 percent (2,715 *l.t.*) of the total accumulated incomes. In contrast, the great fiefs which extended from 50 *l.t.* were only 15.9 percent (99) of the fiefs but absorbed more than half (55.5 percent) of the total accumulated incomes. An intermediate level ranging from 20 *l.t.* to just under 50 *l.t.* was an open-ended layer between the many smaller fiefs concentrated below 20 *l.t.* and the few valuable fiefs. The three income levels corresponded in great part to family origins: Descendants of the twelfth-century castellan families were in the over-50 *l.t.* level, descendants of knight families rarely went over 30 *l.t.*, and members of both groups mixed at the intermediate level. Although several baronial fortunes may well have approached the 1,000 *l.t.* mark (the count of Brienne, for example, whose possessions were not valued), none came close to the count of Champagne who had about 27,000 pounds.[22] The ranges and

22 For the estimated income of the great princes, see John F. Benton, "The Revenue of Louis VII," *Speculum*, XLII (1967), 84–91.

concentrations of these 620 fiefs are the most accurate obtainable for an entire fief-holding group, and they suggest that, as with the several hundred families in Forez, there was a deep divide between ordinary fief holders who composed the bulk of the aristocracy and the relatively few great families who controlled a disproportionate share of economic resources. The differences were also reflected in the composition of their respective fiefs. Only one tenth of all fiefs had rights of *péage, tonlieu,* or market. Rights of justice were present on only 16.7 percent of the fiefs and were clearly associated with fief values: Found least often on fiefs worth less than 10 *l.t.* and increasingly on the more valuable holdings, they were universal on fiefs of 50 *l.t.* or more.[23]

The last important aspect of the Champagne fiefs to be systematically inventoried was military obligation. Of all fiefs, both valued and nonvalued, only 31.1 percent incurred an annual castle guard obligation; 22.0 percent explicitly did not owe guard (*non debet gardam*); and 40.0 percent had no mention of guard in their entries and probably did not owe any because the scribes apparently queried each person on that point and even entered responses of uncertainty ("he doesn't know about guard") for 6.9 percent of the fiefs (Fig. 5). Of the 367 (31.1 percent) fiefs which did owe some regular military service, one fourth owed five to six weeks and about one sixth each owed unspecified terms, up to four weeks, seven to eight weeks, or nine to twelve weeks. No single term of duty seems to have been standard, and there is no correlation between either the obligation of guard or the length of service and the value of the fief. But there was great fluctuation from one castellany to another in both the ratio of fiefs owing service and in the length of service: Castellanies bordering Burgundy and the Empire had significantly higher ratios of castle guard (up to 60 percent for Chaumont) than areas bordering the royal domain (only 23 percent for Provins). It would seem that local military situations rather than fief values dictated the terms of guard. Of course, there was an exception with castles, which were found on the most valuable fiefs, and fortified

23 Additional correlations between the various income levels and the components of the respective fiefs will be required for a more precise interpretation of fief incomes. A full analysis is impossible here, but the findings for justice are reported because of its particular importance. The 16.7 percent may be slightly low in reality because the most valuable estates were not described in their numerous components, but certainly the actual percentage would not be over 20 percent. Unlike the status of fief holders, components of fiefs were strictly accountable to the count and were reported on oath; it seems unlikely that rights of justice and of taxation on trade and transportation would not have been reported, except on the largest estates for which any enumeration would have been superfluous.

Fig. 5 Castle Guard

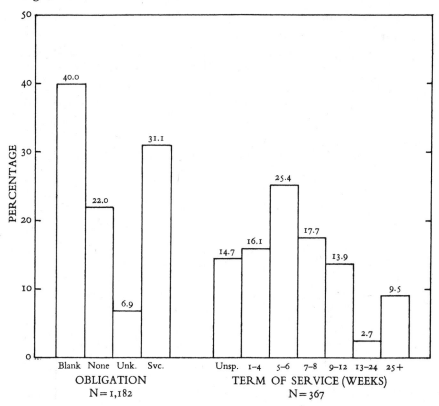

houses (*domus fortes*), which were clustered on the intermediate fiefs of 30–50 *l.t.* The holders of both types of structures were exempt from duty in the count's castles unless their fortifications had been constructed on fiefs which had previously owed guard, in which case they were still obligated. But significant fortifications were found on a minority (15.1 percent) of all fiefs: There were 48 (4.0 percent) castles and 131 (11.1 percent) fortified houses.[24]

At the end of each *Rôles* entry came the names and possessions of rear-fief holders, generally in much less detail than for the direct holders. Of the 1,519 rear-fief holders, 1,215 (80.0 percent) were men and 304 (20.0 percent) women—about the same ratio as for the direct holders. Their distribution by status, however, is more difficult to determine because a

24 As mentioned in the previous note, the great estates were usually not inventoried by components. The actual number of castles may have been higher, especially for families with several, but the overall percentage cannot have been significantly higher.

Fig. 6 Rear-Fief Holders

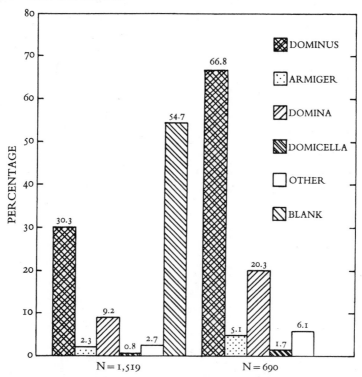

high percentage (54.7 percent) were not so identified in the *Rôles*, and seldom do rear-fief holders appear in charters. Although the omission of status may be more significant in identifying a particular social group among the rear than the direct holders, a final evaluation of the rear-fief holders who lacked titles in the *Rôles* is not yet possible. The breakdown by known status (45.3 percent or 690 persons) is: 66.8 percent *domini*, 5.1 percent *armigeri*, 20.3 percent *dominae*, 1.7 percent *domicellae*, and 6.1 percent others (Fig. 6). Compared to the direct holders, the rear holders had proportionately more *domini* (66.8 percent vs. 55.4 percent) and fewer *armigeri* (5.1 percent vs. 18.5 percent), but the other status groups had similar ratios.

Most rear-fief holders (85.0 percent), like most direct holders (80.9 percent), had a single holding from the count, and of the 1,519 sole or first rear-fiefs, 759 (43.4 percent) were valued in *libratae terre*. The average and median rear-fiefs were both 14 *l.t.*, compared to the direct fief average of 29 *l.t.* and median of 18 *l.t.* Again, the *domini* had the more valuable holdings. But there is an additional factor here because 177

Fig. 7 Rear-Fief Holders per Fief Holder

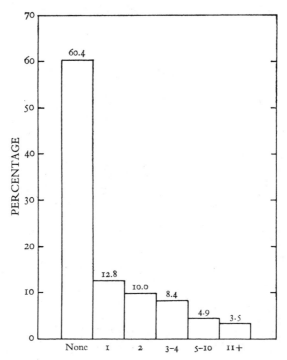

(14.9 percent) of the direct holders also had rear-fiefs: Of the valued rear-fiefs they held 79 (10.4 percent), which absorbed 20.4 percent of the accumulated rear-fief incomes; without these, the average rear-fief value drops from 14 *l.t.* to 12.4 *l.t.*[25] That is, the 14.9 percent of the direct fief holders who also held rear-fiefs generally held the more valuable rear-fiefs. Valued or not, only a handful of all rear holdings contained large units of land or rights of justice, taxes, or banal revenues; most rear-fiefs consisted of fragmentary revenues, often only grains or other minor rents. Both the values and composition of rear-fiefs put them on a decidedly inferior level in comparison to direct fiefs.

The system of fiefs and rear-fiefs was neither uniformly hierarchical nor symmetrical, for 60.4 percent of 1,182 direct fief holders had no rear-fief holders at all, and of the remaining 39.6 percent who

25 177 (14.9 percent) fief holders were also rear-fief holders. Of their rear-fiefs, 79 (44.6 percent) were valued, compared to the 43.4 percent of all rear-fiefs which were valued; that is, each group is similarly represented. As with direct fiefs, only the sole or first rear-fiefs are counted here in order to permit the linkage of status and rear-fief value (see note 20); since 85 percent of the rear-fief holders had a single holding, the operation has the same validity.

Fig. 8 The Fief and Rear-Fief System

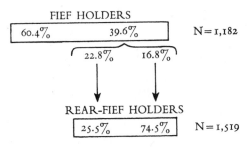

did, about half (22.8 percent) had only one or two rear holders (Fig. 7). In effect, 199 (16.8 percent) direct fief holders accounted for 1,132 (74.5 percent) rear-fief holders (Fig. 8). The Champagne fief system seems more horizontal than vertical, with only a few direct holders controlling most rear holders, and it reflects the two origins of the count's authority over fief holders. Descendants of simple knight families in the twelfth century who received their fiefs directly from the count usually did not have any rear-fief holders, or if they did, it was because of family transfers (e.g., dowry, escheat); those with numerous rear-fief holders derived from the great baronial families of the twelfth century, and when they had been effectively subordinated by the count, their own fief holders who did not become liegemen of the count became his rear-fief holders.

The distillation of registers for 62 percent of the county provides a reasonable measure of the basic quantitative attributes of the Champagne aristocracy as a whole. There were, of course, variations by castellany, often ranging up to 10 percent, but such discrepancies only reflect local geographical and historical peculiarities, and the fact that none of the figures except those for castle guard contain erratic variations proves that the county-wide figures are accurate in representing a level of generalization above that of individual castellany. Perhaps the single most striking impression is of the great range and variety of conditions encompassed by the mid-thirteenth-century aristocracy. Yet, in spite of the diversity, the overall system of fiefs and rear-fiefs mirrored four distinct layers within the aristocracy: 1) the rear-fief holders had the fewest resources, derived mostly from scattered and fragmentary revenues (12 *l.t.* median); 2) the small fief holders had more concentrated properties and greater revenues (about 20 *l.t.*), an increase in degree but not in kind over the rear holders; 3) the intermediate group of fief holders (30–50 *l.t.*) often held more than one fief, usually with rights of justice and taxation on trade, and at least one fortified house, as well as several rear-fief holders; 4) the great families (over 50 *l.t.*) retained their hereditary castles, extensive estates with all concomitant rights, and usually a sizable contingent (10 to 40) of rear-fief holders. All four groups by virtue of their status and tenure composed the aristocracy, but only the latter two groups, a distinct minority of all fief and rear-fief holders, possessed the attributes of superior standing— distinctive residences (castle, fortified house), rights of justice and taxes on trade, and sizable followings of rear-fief holders.

By canvassing the entire range of fief holders, not merely those best represented in charters, the *Rôles* reveal the predominance of rear-fief and smaller fief holders in the thirteenth-century aristocracy. Of course, the structure of feudal society cannot be expressed in quantitative terms alone, for the reality of lineage in medieval society was a central aspect of social life and accounted for much of what was the aristocracy. Nevertheless, the analysis of a cross-section of an entire group in 1249–52 provides an important corrective to the charter evidence, which can seldom be controlled by independent and quantifiable data and from which feudal society has usually been cast in the image of its most prestigious members. According to the *Rôles*, a composite, typical fief holder might have been a *dominus* with a single fief worth less than 20 *l.t.* annually and with no rear-fief holders; he did not perform castle guard, had no rights of justice or taxation, and did not possess a residence which clearly distinguished him from other rural inhabitants. Indeed, the economic and physical proximity of many fief and especially rear-fief holders to other rural inhabitants was compelling reason for the insistence on the absolute separation of the fief and peasant tenure systems in the thirteenth century. For it was fief tenure which guaranteed the poorer knights and non-knighted *armigeri* their social and judicial privileges.[26]

26 The Champagne *Coutumier* of c. 1290 contains several judgments of the Jours of Troyes (1270–1290) and statements of general principles which stress the separation of the fief and peasant tenure systems; see P. Portejoie (ed.), *L'ancien coutumier de Champagne* (*XIIIe siècle*) (Poitiers, 1956), 150–152, 155–158, 180–181. Perroy, "Social Mobility," reaches the same conclusion about the low incomes of ordinary fief holders in Forez and is able to furnish several interesting examples of relative life styles.

Gregory Clark

The Political Foundations of Modern Economic Growth: England, 1540–1800

In a recent article, North and Weingast argue that the political history of England in the period before the Industrial Revolution illustrates two important propositions: the first, that the establishment of secure and stable property rights for private citizens is a necessary and sufficient condition for economic growth, and the second, that the establishment of such rights depended on the creation of a representative democracy. Thus, they believe that there was an intimate connection between the Glorious Revolution of 1688 and the Industrial Revolution of 1760 and thereafter.[1]

Many scholars cite England during the seventeenth and eighteenth centuries as an example of how stable democratic politics causes economic growth. The Glorious Revolution replaced a corrupt, autocratic monarchy, which financed itself by a variety of extortionary means, with a political system in which Parliament, admittedly drawn from a limited franchise, controlled the monarch. This political system was remarkably stable. There were no coups, and few attempted coups, after 1689, but an unbroken line of governments elected by a popular franchise. When James II was deposed, the throne passed first to William of Orange and James' daughter Mary, and then to Mary's sister Anne. When Anne died childless in 1714 (despite giving birth to eighteen children),

Gregory Clark is Associate Professor of Economics, University of California, Davis. He is the author of "Factory Discipline," *Journal of Economic History*, LIV (1994), 128–163; coauthor, with Michael Huberman and Peter Lindert, of "A British Food Puzzle," *Economic History Review*, LXVIII (1995), 215–237.

The data used in this article was made possible by NSF grant SES-91-22191"i" and a scholarship from the IRIS (Institutional Reform and the Informal Sector) program at the University of Maryland. The author thanks Peter Lindert, Larry Neal, and the participants of the ALL-UC Economic History Conference at the University of California, Los Angeles, in 1993 for helpful comments and suggestions. Eddy Van Cauwenberghe kindly supplied data about the silver content of pond groten from 1550 to 1750.

1 Douglass C. North and Barry Weingast, "Constitutions and Commitment: The Evolution of Institutions Governing Public Choice in Seventeenth Century England," *Journal of Economic History*, XLIX (1989) 803–832.

James II's son was laying claim to the throne from exile in France. Yet, Parliament was able to install in his place an obscure German princeling who never learned to speak English well, without any serious threat to its control.

The years between the Glorious Revolution and the Industrial Revolution saw widespread change in the British economy: The transport system was radically improved; a large scale conversion to a purely private agriculture was accelerated; new institutions of finance and commerce were put in place; and the government's debt was regarded as the safest asset in the economy. Hence, many have been tempted to argue that the Glorious Revolution created the preconditions for the Industrial Revolution. As Olson notes,

> With a carefully constrained monarchy, an independent judiciary, and a Bill of Rights, people in England in due course came to have a relatively high degree of confidence that any contracts they entered into would be enforced and that private property rights, even for critics of the government, were relatively secure. Individual rights to property and contract enforcement were probably more secure in Britain after 1689 than anywhere else, and it was in Britain, not very long after the Glorious Revolution, that the Industrial Revolution began.[2]

Cameron agrees with North and Weingast on the importance of the Glorious Revolution, though his reasoning focuses more on the stability of public credit.

> The so-called Revolution of 1688–9 constitutes a major turning point not only in political and constitutional history, but in economic history as well. . . . [T]he ease, cheapness, and stability of credit for public finance reacted favorably on private capital markets, making funds available for investment in agriculture, commerce, and industry.[3]

This article argues, to the contrary, that 1688 did not represent a significant change in regime for private actors in the English economy. It employs data about the return on capital and about

2 Mancur Olson, "Dictatorship, Democracy, and Development," *American Political Science Review*, LXXXVII (1993), 574.
3 Rondo Cameron, *A Concise Economic History of the World* (Oxford, 1989), 155.

land prices to show that secure private property rights existed in England at least as early as 1600, and probably much earlier. As far as most private investors were concerned, nothing special happened in 1688, or, for that matter, in any period between 1600 and 1688; yet, for most of this long period before 1688, there was little economic growth. Secure and stable property rights may be a necessary condition for economic growth, but the history of England shows that they are not a sufficient one. Moreover, the information from capital markets implies that the move to a representative democracy was not necessary for the establishment of secure private property rights. For most people, such rights existed under the plethora of political arrangements that occurred in England between 1540 and 1688, including the autocracy of Charles II and the dictatorship of Oliver Cromwell.

POLITICS AND ECONOMIC GROWTH   North and Weingast argue that to produce economic growth, political systems need to be both stable and nonautocratic. A key assumption that this article shares with North and Weingast is that adverse political regimes reduce material output principally by driving up the return on capital, and hence reducing its supply. This state of affairs affects both the immediate output and the rate of economic growth, since the advance of production technique depends on the investment of resources. Innovation does not just happen; it occurs because producers spend time looking for new techniques.

Consider, for example, political instability. As factions vie for control of the state, property rights are uncertain, especially if the successful factions seek to reward their members and punish their opponents. It is estimated, for example, that nearly one-fifth of all land was confiscated from the king's followers after the Civil War in England, and that approximately the same amount of land was seized from the supporters of Parliament after the Restoration. When political struggles involve the use of force, property may be destroyed in the fighting and economic activity disrupted. Insecure regimes may suppress economic activity if the groups who benefit from it include those hostile to the regime. Driven by the short-term needs of survival, the insecure regime may plunder capital owners or innovators periodically, depriving the economy of investment or innovation and keeping it impoverished. Thus, in the 1630s, Charles I fined those enclosing common lands largely as a revenue expediency, even though enclosure increased the rental value of lands. The contest for political power can make all property insecure and all private attempts at accumulation fruitless; it supports the enrichment of individuals only through the capacity of the state to confiscate it from others. This political climate tends to deter investment in capital or in new techniques unless the return on capital rises sufficiently to compensate for the enhanced risk.[4]

The expected effect of political instability on returns on capital is evident in a number of cases. At the end of the English Civil War in 1650, for example, the victorious Parliament sold most of the deposed king's estates. In 1650, the perpetuities owned by the crown sold for an average implied rate of return of 11.2 percent, at a time when private perpetuities yielded a return of about 5.5 percent. Land confiscated from royalists, church, and crown sold for an implied return of 9.5 percent; the return on private lands was just above 5 percent. The huge premium in returns available to investors in the confiscated property reflected the political uncertainty that attached to these property rights; and, indeed, the purchasers lost those assets upon the Restoration in 1660.[5]

According to North and Weingast, even the stable regimes before 1688 created conditions of uncertainty that drove up private returns. Such autocratic rulers as James I and Charles II could not offer their subjects the security to invest without fear of expropriation. The argument of North and Weingast, however, depends crucially on autocrats being purely self-interested and having limited time horizons. If autocrats have dynastic ambitions,

---

4 Christopher Clay, *Economic Expansion and Social Change: England, 1500–1700* (Cambridge, 1984), I, 80.

5 For crown perpetuities (fee-farm rents), see Sidney J. Madge, *The Domesday of Crown Lands* (London, 1938), 237. See figures 4 and 5 herein for private perpetuities and land. H. J. (John) Habakkuk, "Public Finance and the Sale of Confiscated Property during the Interregnum," *Economic History Review*, XV (1962), 70–88, discusses the sale of land by Parliament. Land was sold mostly in exchange for government debt, but, since this debt had a market price, the implied return can be calculated. A more modern example of the effect of uncertainty on returns from capital is the Mexican Revolution of 1910–1917, which left industrial capital largely undamaged by the fighting but created great uncertainty about which property rights would prevail in the end. Investment nearly ceased, and share values plummeted. See Stephen Haber, *Industry and Underdevelopment: The Industrialization of Mexico, 1890–1940* (Standford, 1989), 122–149.

Fig. 1   Interest Rates on New Issues of Government Debt, 1540–1800

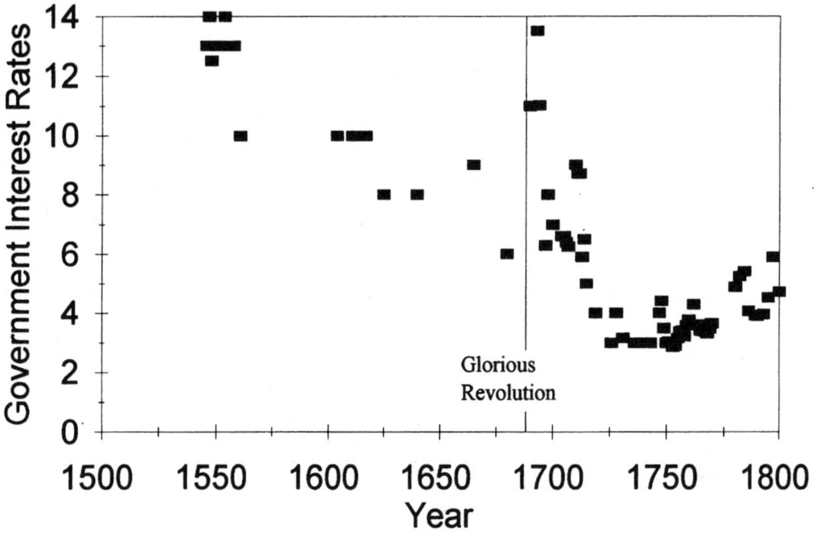

NOTE   The loans before 1688 often had an element of coercion in them, so the actual rates would be higher.

SOURCES   Robert Ashton, *The Crown and the Money Market, 1603–1640* (Oxford, 1960), 118–119, 123, 127; Peter G. M. Dickson, *The Financial Revolution in England* (London, 1967), 48–49, 60–63; Sidney Homer and Richard Sylla, *A History of Interest Rates* (New Brunswick, 1991), 113, 126.

then they can credibly commit to moderate expropriation without stifling investment.[6]

Whatever the source of the alleged political pathology, if it is to have pervasive effects in the economy, it should appear as a widespread increase in the rate of return on capital. North and Weingast themselves point to the sharp decline in the rate of return on government borrowing in the decades after 1689 as a sign that the government operated differently after the Glorious Revolution. Rates of return of 10 percent gave way to rates as low as 3 percent by the mideighteenth century. Figure 1 shows the rate of return on a variety of government loans between 1540 and 1800.

North and Weingast interpret the dramatic decline in government interest rates in the 1690s and in the 1710s as showing

6   North and Weingast, "Constitutions and Commitment."

that, in the new stable regime, private capital markets with low interest rates flourished, and private incentives to invest improved, fueling growth: "Thus were the institutional foundations of modern capital markets laid in England." North and Weingast note that, unfortunately, data about capital markets for the period before the Glorious Revolution are "almost non-existent."[7]

THE POLITICAL BACKGROUND   Between 1540 and 1770, England experienced numerous periods of political turmoil, internal warfare, and important changes of political regime. In the late sixteenth century, the impending death of the childless Elizabeth I created great political uncertainty. By 1578 when Elizabeth reached the age of forty-five, it was clear that she would die childless and that the Tudor dynasty would come to an end. The end of her reign saw five serious contenders for the throne, none of whom the aging Elizabeth seems to have shown any favor. Although James VI of Scotland was the successor by the laws of primogenitor, he was king of the traditional enemy of England, Elizabeth had executed his mother in 1586, and Henry VIII, through parliamentary act and his own will, had barred the house of Stuart from the succession. Lady Arbella Stuart was descended from the same line as James, but had the advantage of being English. Under the terms of Henry VIII's will, the crown should have passed to the House of Suffolk and to the descendants of Catherine Grey. But her marriage as well as that of her mother to the Duke of Suffolk was of doubtful validity. The last major claimant was Philip II of Spain and, barring him, his daughter the Infanta. The claims of the Infanta were pushed by the Catholic minority. Elizabeth herself increased the confusion by having an act passed imposing severe penalties on anyone making claim to the royal succession without Parliament's affirmation but then preventing Parliament from making a selection.[8]

The implication is that rates of return on capital should have risen for two reasons in Elizabeth's waning years: The uncertainty of the succession presaged a bloody power struggle after her death, but it also meant that Elizabeth could not credibly commit to any

7 Ibid., 825, 826.
8 Joel Hurstfield, Freedom, Corruption and Government in Elizabethan England (London, 1973), 104–134, gives the details of the succession debate. Peter Wentworth—an MP who spoke in the House of Commons about the succession and published a pamphlet—was sent to the Tower in 1593 and died there four years later (107).

long term contract with her subjects, if monarchs indeed behave like predators in North and Weingast fashion. Elizabeth could have expropriated property in the declining years of her reign at little cost to herself.

After the death of Elizabeth I in 1603, the Crown passed peaceably to the Scottish House of Stuart. But the Stuart kings did not enjoy a happy relationship with the English Parliament. The interminable power struggle between Crown and Parliament between 1603 and 1688 was fueled after 1660 by the Catholic sympathies of the monarchy and the Protestantism of the people. Unlike in many other European countries where the monarch had control of taxation, in England this power belonged to Parliament. The monarch had the revenue of the royal estates at his or her disposal, but even Elizabeth I had to deplete these estates by sales to meet war and other expenses because of Parliament's reluctance to levy taxes. As a result, the monarchy was always short of funds and had to resort to various illegal and semilegal exactions and confiscations to raise revenue.[9]

The Crown had some success with these measures in the early seventeenth century. It deliberately allowed obsolete regulations introduced in the midsixteenth century that limited economic activity to remain in force, and then encouraged professional informers to inform against transgressors, who were fined. So systematic was this revenue-collecting device that, in some cases, private individuals were given the monopoly of the right to inform and the power to treat with transgressors for payment of fines. The Crown similarly sold monopoly privileges for new and for existing products, and resorted to forced loans and to the revival of feudal privileges in its scramble for money. Even when Parliament consented to levy taxes, the assessment of wealth was often wildly unrealistic and heavily influenced by political connections. Thus, the tax burden on the richest was light, some magnates being omitted from the tax lists altogether. The middle income groups, being less influential, bore more than a proportionate burden.[10]

---

9 See Robert Ashton, *The English Civil War: Conservatism and Revolution, 1603–1649* (London, 1978); Christopher Hill, *The Century of Revolution, 1603–1714* (Edinburgh, 1961); James Rees Jones, *Country and Court: England, 1658–1714* (Cambridge, Mass., 1978).

10 Clay, *Economic Expansion and Social Change: England, 1500–1700* (Cambridge, 1984), II, 256–257. In 1616, James I also began to raise revenue by selling peerages.

In the early seventeenth century, taxation was slight and collection inefficient, unpredictable, and subject to political influence and corruption. A measure of the corruption in the governing classes is evident in the admission by Francis Bacon—the famous philosopher and the chief justice of the land—to his accusers in 1621 that he had taken substantial "gifts" from those on whose cases he was ruling (he denied any venal intent).[11]

The conflict between king and Parliament resulted in open warfare in the years 1639–1640, 1642–1646, 1648, and 1651, when rival Royalist and Parliamentary armies vied for control of the country. One author describes these years as "one of the most damaging periods in the history of England." Armies marched across the countryside destroying crops and requisitioning food. Property damage resulted from sieges, raids, and the strengthening of fortifications in such towns as Birmingham, Colchester, Gloucester, Worcester, and York.[12]

From 1649 to 1660, the country fell under vacillating Puritan control that gradually dissolved internally. The property of the king and his supporters formed a major source of revenue in the years 1649–1653. Meanwhile, Parliament debated all kinds of radical proposals that would have affected property rights—proposals for further sales of Royalist lands, and for the abolition of tithe rights. As the control of the Puritans unraveled, the army had to quarter itself on the population, and open plunder seemed but a short step distant.

The restoration of the monarchy in the person of Charles II in 1660 led to further uncertainty. Some, but not all, confiscated property was restored to its original owners, and the conflict between Crown and Parliament was seemingly resolved. But soon the old strains were appearing. Charles had Catholic sympathies in a Protestant country where religion was an important political issue. In 1670, Charles entered into a secret treaty with France, wherein the French committed to subsidizing him and, in return, he agreed to collaborate with the French in a war on Holland and to declare himself a Catholic at a suitable moment. As the 1670s

---

11 See "Political Corruption in Modern England: The Historian's Problem," in Hurstfield, *Freedom, Corruption, and Government*, 145–147.
12 Anthony Baker, *A Battlefield Atlas of the English Civil War* (London, 1986), 8; Stephen Porter, "Property Destruction in the English Civil Wars," *History Today*, XXXVI (1986), 36–41.

proceeded, it became clear that Charles would be succeeded by his openly Catholic brother, James, the Duke of York. In 1679 after a rebellion by Protestant dissenters in Scotland, Parliament passed a bill excluding James from the succession. Disaffected Royal advisors planned a coup in 1682, and, in 1683, a plot to murder Charles II and James was uncovered.

When James II became king in 1685, there was an unsuccessful Protestant rebellion in the west, led by Charles' illegitimate son, the Duke of Monmouth. Nevertheless, the policies of James, particularly his introduction of Catholic officers into the army and his raising of an Irish army of dubious loyalty to the English Parliament, resulted in widespread fear and disaffection. When James II had a son and heir in 1688, William of Orange—a claimant to the throne in his own right and the husband of James' daughter Mary from a previous marriage—invaded from Holland in collusion with English allies. James found little support and fled, and, in 1689, the Parliament announced his abdication, installing William and Mary as monarchs. Under the new constitutional order—the foundation of the modern British state—Parliament gained more control over the actions of the monarchy. In 1700, it so discouraged William that he left for Holland and threatened to abdicate.

The success of the Glorious Revolution was not immediately obvious, for its outcome depended on the power struggle that engaged Europe in the late seventeenth century. William had claimed the English throne, in part, because the Dutch needed to preserve England as an ally against French hegemony. From 1688 to 1695, William's new regime waged war against France on the continent, and against the partisans of James in Ireland and Scotland, who were supported by the French. Only in 1697, when William and Louis XIV made a peace treaty that recognized William as king of England did the new political settlement appear secure.[13]

Though most historians give little importance to it after 1695, the Jacobite cause did not die immediately; it was the popular rallying point for various disaffected groups until the 1740s. In

13 See Daniel Szechi, *The Jacobites: Britain and Europe, 1688–1788* (Manchester, 1994), 41–58; Jones, *Country and Court*, 256–278.

1715 and in 1745/6 Jacobite rebels in Scotland penetrated as far south as Derby, causing a brief panic in London.

The new political regime ushered in a host of political and administrative changes, among them the Land Tax of 1692, which provided a large new source of funds for the government, from a relatively predictable exaction on property owners. Since reassessments were rare, it entailed no disincentive to investments in land improvement. In 1694, the Bank of England was formed as the principal lender to the government, ushering in a series of financial developments now called "The Financial Revolution."

THE DATA   The existing information about the English private capital market before 1725 is limited, particularly before 1650. A few studies treat the rate of return on land—mainly in the south—but information for the period before 1688 has been largely impressionistic.[14]

This article uses information from 2,882 transactions or wills recorded in the Charity Commission reports, as well as supplementary information, mainly about land sales from the depositions of the directors of the South Sea Company in 1721, to examine the operation of the private capital market from 1540 to 1837. Also employed are 1,824 observations on land sales between 1600 and 1749 from the Charity Commission reports to examine the movement of land prices. The Charity Commission examined the asset holdings of charities in most parishes in England and Wales during the course of its investigation, which lasted from 1818 to 1837. The commissioners often gave details on the purchases and sales of such assets as land, tithes, houses, rent charges, mortgages, and private bonds that they could glean from the documents retained by the charity to ensure that no land had been lost to the charity over time, and that rent charges bought earlier were all still being paid. The Charity Commission reports generally gave the location of the asset purchased or sold, permitting a determi-

---

14   Clay, "The Price of Freehold Land in the Later Seventeenth and Eighteenth Centuries," *Economic History Review,* XXVII (1974), 173–189, calculates the rate of return on farmland in the south of England and the midlands for 1650–1659, 1670–1689, and 1700–1813 from 248 transactions or offers for sale. Habakkuk, "The Long-Term Rate of Interest and the Price of Land in the Seventeenth Century," *Economic History Review,* V (1952), 26–45, gives an impressionistic survey of the market for land in the sixteenth and seventeenth centuries.

nation of how representative the data are. Since the commissioners wanted to ascertain whether the charities were being used for the purposes specified in the donors' wills, they also frequently detailed what donors expected as rates of return on their charitable assets. For example, a donor might have bequeathed £100 to buy land or a rent charge at a yield of at least £5 per year to purchase bread for the poor.[15]

The various types of capital instrument are to be distinguished according to their ramifications. Land and houses were real assets, the current returns of which would approximate to their real rate of return so long as real land and house rents were not changing rapidly. There were no usury restrictions on returns on land. Rent charges were nominal assets with an infinite term the real return of which depended on the rate of price inflation; these were not affected by usury restrictions either. Bonds and mortgages were also nominal assets, but the return on them was limited by usury restrictions. Bonds were short term assets that could be terminated by either side of the contract at will.

How representative are the Charity Commission observations of capital market conditions for the country as a whole? The observations from these sources are well distributed geographi-

---

15 Between the years 1819 and 1840, the Charity Commission published 32 reports containing 27,000 pages in the House of Commons papers. A typical reference to the return on capital is "By indenture, bearing date 22nd March 1772, . . . John Sampson, in consideration of £20, granted to the parties of the second part and their heirs an annuity of £1 issuing out of the said John Sampson's one-fourth part of the messuages, lands, and tenements, called Colehouse, situate in the parish of Broadwood Kelly" (Great Britain, Parliamentary Papers, *Reports of the Charity Commissioners, Vol. 11,* XIV [1824], 24).

The data assembled herein represents a set of transactions in the land and rent charge markets—typically with the charity as a buyer—as well as a set of dated wills recording the amount of each bequest and the return that each bequestor expected the charity to achieve from investment in land or as a rent charge. A rent charge was a fixed perpetual nominal obligation secured by a house or a piece of land. It could be redeemed only if the owner of the rent charge agreed to accept a capital sum for it.

Rent charges, sometimes referred to as "fee farm rents," existed from at least the twelfth century and were still being created in the eighteenth century. Eventually, the main transactions involving them were sales to third parties, or to the owners of the land. When tithes were commuted after 1839, they were often replaced by "tithe rent charges," which were fixed money payments from the land to the tithe holder in perpetuity. The legal properties of the rent charge went largely unchanged between the middle ages and the twentieth century. See William Douglas Edwards, *A Compendium of the Law of Property in Land and Conveyancing* (London, 1904; 4th ed.); Geoffrey Chevalier Cheshire, *The Modern Law of Real Property* (London, 1962; 9th ed.); Frederick Pollock and Frederick W. Maitland, *The History of English Law before the Time of Edward I* (Cambridge, 1895).

Fig. 2 The Distribution of Observations Geographically, Prior to 1770

cally, as Figure 2 shows. The local clusters around London, Bristol, south Lancashire, and the West Midlands correspond with areas of dense population before 1837. The land purchase data similarly cover most of England and Wales.

As is illustrated in Table 1, breaking down the Charity Commission data into various types by location, the data pertain to both urban and rural capital markets. London and the four other large towns of preindustrial England—Bristol, Exeter, Norwich, and York—are all well represented in the data set in terms of returns from land and rent charges. London alone is responsible for 13.5 percent of the observations on returns from both land and rent charges, but this figure is close to the city's share of the population in England and Wales in 1700. There is almost no land actually purchased in London, but many dated wills record legacies from Londoners to buy land, stipulating a rate of return to be achieved. The Charity Commission data seem to be representative of the urban/rural split of the population as well.

The distribution of observations for each type of asset is not uniform across time. For the early period, the most numerous

Table 1   Distribution of Return Observations

	TOTAL	URBAN (LONDON, BRISTOL, EXETER, NORWICH, YORK)	
	N	*N*	%
All Returns			
Land	690	115	16.7
Houses	117	58	49.6
Rent charges	753	131	17.4
Bonds and mortgages	287	56	19.5
Actual Returns			
Land	309	6	1.9
Houses	51	20	39.2
Rent charges	606	88	14.5
Bonds and mortgages	193	37	19.2
Expected Returns			
Land	381	109	28.6
Houses	66	37	56.1
Rent charges	147	43	29.3
Bonds and mortgages	94	19	20.2

observations are the actual and expected returns on land holding and rent charges and in the later period, private bonds and mortgage lending.

The changing frequency of observations for different types of lending over time reflects the development of the capital market and the survival of certain types of records. Rent charges, for example, were steadily superseded by government perpetuities after 1727, since the latter were as secure as rent charges and much more liquid. Thus, many of the observations in the later period are rates of return at which rent charges were bought out by the owners of property charged with them. However, since these deals could have been done only with the consent of both parties, they still should have represented a market interest rate. Records of bond and mortgage lending in the early years tended not to survive because such lending had a higher default rate than investments in land or rent charges, meaning that the money would be lost over time, and also because when the loans were paid, there was no reason to keep the records on them. The distribution of the observations in different time periods is shown in Table 2.

The data also suggest that, from an early period, the capital market was reasonably integrated both by location and by type of

Table 2 Composition of Rate of Return Observations, 1540–1770

TYPE	PRE-1642	1642–1688	1689–1770	TOTAL
Real Assets				
Land	203	159	328	690
Tithes	6	3	3	12
Houses	40	14	62	117
Nominal Assets				
Rent charges	218	248	287	753
Mortgages	0	6	40	46
Bonds	32	45	164	241
Total	499	475	884	1858

NOTES   The number of observations from The Parliamentary Papers, *Reports of the Charity Commissioners, Vols. 1–32* (1819–1840) is 1,699; for the years 1715 to 1721, from The Parliamentary Papers, *The Particulars and Inventories of the Estates of the Late Sub-Governor, Deputy-Governor, and Directors of the South-Sea Company* (1721), reprinted in Sheila Lambert (ed.), *House of Commons Sessional Papers of the Eighteenth Century, Vols. 4–6* (Wilmington, Del., 1975), 159 observations.

asset. The period before 1700 shows evidence of a slight increase in returns as distance from London increases for both rent charges and land, but the remotest parts of England and Wales still returned less than 0.5 percent more on capital than the London market. The decline in returns in London between 1630 and 1730 is echoed in all the other parts of the country. Land and rent charges were almost equally secure, though only returns on land were secure against inflation. Since, on average, rates of inflation were less than 1 percent per year between 1550 and 1837, the average difference between these two assets should have been a slightly lower return for land, which was indeed the case. In all decades but one, land yielded less than rent charges, but the overall difference was merely 0.5 percent. Thus, at least these two different capital assets seem to have been traded in an integrated market.[16]

A more important issue is how representative of the private capital market these returns from charity would be. Could charities have been careless purchasers and poor managers of assets with returns lower than those in the general marketplace? Two pieces of evidence prove otherwise:

16   For more details, see Clark, "The Land Market in Pre-Industrial Society: England and Wales 1540–1837," working paper 76 (Agricultural History Center, University of California, Davis, 1995).

Fig. 3 Return on Farmland, 1540–1837

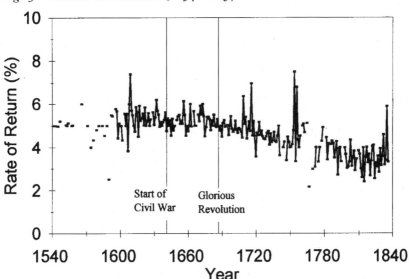

(1) Comparison of the returns expected on land and rent charges, as expressed in wills, with the actual returns charities achieved when they purchased land or rent charges shows that, for both land and rent charges, the actual returns are insignificantly different from the expected returns, both quantitatively and statistically.

(2) Comparison of the returns that charities achieved on land purchases with the returns achieved by private purchasers of land in the eighteenth and early nineteenth centuries, as reported by Clay, and Norton, Trist, and Gilbert, shows that these are close when the series overlap.[17]

Even if charities, on average, achieved marginally lower returns on capital invested in land or rent charges than private purchasers, detecting the effects of changes in political regime on rates of return would be a problem, as long as this difference in returns was stable over time. There is no reason to expect that

17 Clay, "The Price of Freehold Land"; Norton, Trist, and Gilbert (law firm), "A Century of Land Values: England and Wales," in Eleanora Carus-Wilson (ed.), *Essays in Economic History, III,* (London, 1962), 128–131. The comparison is done explicitly in Clark, "The Land Market in Pre-Industrial Society."

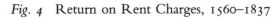

Fig. 4 Return on Rent Charges, 1560–1837

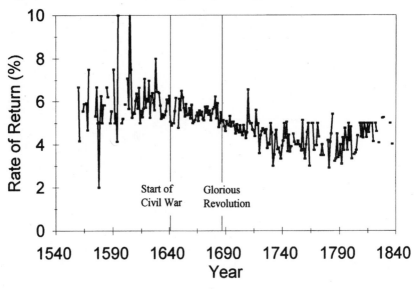

charities would perform any better or worse than private purchasers in 1550 than in 1750.

POLITICAL REGIMES AND THE RATE OF RETURN   Did any of the supposedly important political events of the sixteenth and seventeenth century affect rates of return in the private capital market? Figures 3 and 4 show the annual average rates of return on farmland and rent charges from 1540 to 1770. The private rates of return change slowly with time, indicating no dramatic upward movement in any of the periods of political uncertainty: neither the last years of Elizabeth's reign (1578–1603); the period of turmoil before and during the Civil War (1639–1648); the interregnum (1649–1659); the final years of the Stuart dynasty (1670–1688); nor the difficult years of the new regime (1689–1696). Instead, the trends in returns on both land and rent charges are longer and smoother. Both seem to have increased slowly and slightly from the 1550s to the 1620s, before beginning a long gradual decline that continued for more than 100 years.

A formal test of three series—real property (land, houses, and tithes), rent charges, and bonds and mortgages—demonstrates

Table 3 Definition of Variables in Regression Equations

VARIABLE	DEFINITION
T	Year
DX	Dummy equal to 1 when the return is expected (as in a will)
DH	Dummy equal to 1 when the asset is a house
DT	Dummy equal to 1 when the asset is a tithe right
DBUB	Dummy equal to 1 in 1720 (South Sea Bubble)
DOLD	Dummy equal to 1 in 1578–1602 (years of Elizabeth's reign with clear absence of successor)
DCIV	Dummy equal to 1 in 1639–1648 (Civil War)
DINT	Dummy equal to 1 in 1649–1659 (interregnum)
DSTU	Dummy equal to 1 in 1670–1688 (last years of the Stuarts)
DNEWREV	Dummy equal to 1 in 1689–1696 (early Glorious Revolution)
DREV	Dummy equal to 1 in 1697–1770 (Glorious Revolution established)

whether the periods of political turmoil had any effect on rates of return in private capital markets. Did rates of return on any of these three classes of asset rise during periods of political instability? For real assets, the estimated coefficients of the regression equation are

$$RET = \alpha + \beta_1 T + \beta_2 T^2 + \gamma_1 DX + \gamma_2 DH + \gamma_3 DT + \delta_1 DBUB + \delta_2 DOLD + \delta_3 DCIV + \delta_4 DINT + \delta_5 DSTU + \delta_6 DNEWREV + \delta_7 DREV + \varepsilon, \qquad (1)$$

the variables of which are defined in Table 3. The regression formally tests for any break from long term trends in interest rates during periods of turmoil or regime changes. If political uncertainty mattered, then the estimated values of δ_2, δ_3, δ_4, and δ_5 should be large positives, reflecting the periods of turmoil, and either δ_6 or δ_7 should be a large negative, depending upon perceptions of when a new regime was established. Included also is an estimate of a similar regression for rent charges, as well as a further estimate of the same equation for both types of returns with only two regime dummies—the Civil War and the years after 1696, when the new regime was established.

Table 4 Rates of Return and Political Changes, 1540–1770

PERIOD	LAND, HOUSES, AND TITHES		RENT CHARGES	
1720 (Bubble)	−1.18**	−1.19**	−0.95	−0.96
	(0.13)	(0.13)	(.56)	(0.56)
1578–1602	−0.47*	–	−0.33	–
(Elizabeth's reign without	(0.19)		(0.21)	
clear successor)				
1639–1648	−0.26	−0.16	−0.04	−0.01
(Civil War)	(0.15)	(0.14)	(0.19)	(0.18)
1649–1659	−0.13	–	0.00	–
(Interregnum)	(0.18)		(0.16)	
1670–1688	−0.23	–	0.05	–
(Last years of Stuarts)	(0.15)		(0.15)	
1689–1696	−0.27	–	−0.35	–
(Early Glorious Revolution)	(0.22)		(0.21)	
1697–1770	−0.09	0.12	−0.25	−0.18
(Late Glorious Revolution)	(0.20)	(0.14)	(0.21)	(0.15)
R^2	0.27	0.26	0.29	0.28
N	819	819	753	753

* The estimate is significantly different from 0 at the 5% level.
** The estimate is significantly different from 0 at the 1% level.
NOTE   The numbers in parentheses are standard errors.

Table 4 shows the estimated values of the coefficients for each of the seven crucial periods. None of the political and military convulsions of the seventeenth century seems to have had any quantitatively significant effect on private capital markets in the predicted direction. The estimated movement of interest rates are mostly by fractions of a percent and mostly in the wrong direction. Yet the precision of the estimates is high enough that, in most of the episodes, a 0.5 percent movement up or down in interest rates would be detected as a significant deviation by the regression estimate. The only episode before 1770 that seemed to make any difference to rates of return was the South Sea Bubble, when, for six months in 1720 the prices of South Sea stock rose to extraordinary heights in a speculative mania. Rates of return on both real assets and rent charges fell by about 1 percent in the year of the Bubble. The Glorious Revolution, counted either as an event of 1689 or of 1697, once the new regime achieved a measure of security, is associated with, at best, a 0.14 percent estimated decline of returns on land from the late Stuart period, and a decline of 0.40 percent for rent charges.

Redoing the estimates and keeping just two indicators of political instability—the dummy for the Civil War period and the dummy for the confirmation of the new regime in 1697—finds very small effects—an estimated rise of 0.12 percent on returns on land and a decline of only 0.18 percent in returns on rent charges. Political events in the period 1540 to 1770 do not seem to have mattered in the private capital market.

The experience in southern Netherlands during the same period is in direct contrast to that of England and Wales. De Wever reports the rate of return implied by land purchases in the town of Zele, Flanders, between 1550 and 1795. The countryside near Zele was subject to several long periods of destructive military activity and of uncertainty from 1550 to 1750. The struggle for Dutch independence took place mainly in Flanders during the years 1581–1592. Both Dendermonde to the northeast and Ghent to the west were recaptured from the rebels in 1584 after fierce fighting. After 1585, most of Flanders was in Spanish hands, but the Dutch continued to raid the countryside until 1607. There was also warfare in Flanders from 1672 to 1697, during the wars of the Dutch and the Habsburgs against Louis XIV and later during the War of the Spanish Succession. In 1706, the French besieged Dendermonde and, in 1707, captured Ghent, only to lose it to the Allies again in 1709. As Figure 5 shows, the three major military convulsions—particularly the War of Independence in 1581–1607—drove up the rate of return on land sharply in Zele.[18]

18 For the land sales, see F. de Wever, "Rents and Selling Prices of Land at Zele, Sixteenth to Eighteenth Century," in Herman van der Wee and Eddy Van Cauwenberghe (eds.), *The Agricultural Development of the Low Countries as Revealed by the Tithe and Rent Statistics, 1250–1800* (Leuven, 1978). For details about the conflicts in this period, see Geoffrey Parker, *The Dutch Revolt* (Ithaca, 1977); van der Wee, *The Growth of the Antwerp Market and the European Economy* (The Hague, 1963); E. Theon, "Warfare and the Countryside: Social and Economic Aspects of the Military Destruction in Flanders during the Late Middle Ages and the Early Modern Period," *The Low Countries History Yearbook*, XIII (1980), 25–39; John Childs, *The Nine Years' War and the British Army 1688–1697: The Operations in the Low Countries* (Manchester, 1991). Van der Wee notes that, in Flanders, "the situation until 1580 was generally speaking not so bad" (247), but "looting by freebooters, and not less by Spanish troops, did not cease in 1587" (269).

Fig. 5 Return on Land Holding, Zele, 1550–1750

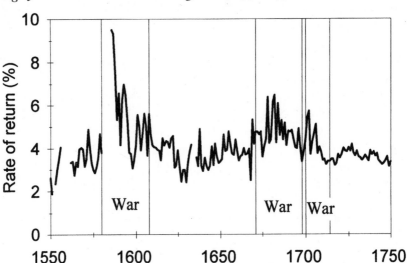

The rate of return from land holding at Zele was estimated from the regression

$$RET = \alpha + \beta_1 T + \beta_2 T_2 + \gamma DWAR_1 \\ + \delta DWAR_2 + \phi DWAR_3, \quad (2)$$

where $DWAR_1$ is 1 for the years 1581–1607, and 0 otherwise, $DWAR_2$ is 1 for 1672–1797 and 0 otherwise, and $DWAR_3$ is 1 for 1701–1713 and 0 otherwise. All the periods of warfare were associated with much higher rates of return. The estimated increase in the rate of return for the years of the Spanish reconquest of Flanders is 1.6 percent, on a base rate of 3.4 percent. This warfare seems to have driven up the rate of return to capital either by destruction of the capital stock, making capital scarcer, or by increasing the risks attached to investments in land. The second long period of warfare from 1672 to 1697 produced an increase of 0.9 percent from a base rate of 4 percent. The third period produced the smallest effect—an increase in rates of return of about 0.5 percent again on a base of 4 percent. In all three episodes, the effects of warfare were much greater than those from the civil strife or changes in regime that occurred in England during the same period.

Testing for a significant change in English rates of return in the years 1689, or 1697—when the new regime finally seemed secure from overt internal and external opposition—could be regarded as unfair. After all, it might have taken twenty or thirty years to convince the populace that the country actually had a new political regime. The decline in government interest rates portrayed in Figure 1 took nearly twenty-five years after 1689, and interest rates initially seemed to have increased between 1689 and 1695. Testing for a break in the series only after 1697 may not have given the new regime a fair chance. What transpired after 1689 could have been an acceleration of a decline in rates of return that figures 4 and 5 show to have been occurring before 1689, rather than a sudden break in the series. The estimated expression for this new test, done for returns on land, rent charges, and mortgages and bonds combined, is

$$RET = \alpha + \beta T + \gamma REVT + \delta DBUB + \varepsilon, \qquad (3)$$

for the years 1660 (the Restoration of the Stuart monarchy) to 1729, where T is the year, $REVT$ is 0 from 1660 till 1696 and thereafter equals the year T, and $DBUB$ is a dummy variable equal to 1 in the year of the South Sea Bubble. The coefficient on $REVT$ measures how the trend in rates of return changed after 1697 as a result of the Glorious Revolution.[19]

In all cases, the coefficient on T, the time trend, is negative, showing that returns on all assets were falling before 1697. But neither in the case of real assets, rent charges, nor bonds and mortgages was the estimated coefficient γ significantly different from 0 either statistically or quantitatively, indicating no acceleration in decline of returns after 1697. The Glorious Revolution leaves no trace on rates of return in the English economy between 1660 and 1730. As shown in Table 5, rates of return were falling in the years 1660 to 1696, and they continued to fall at the same rate once the new regime was established. The same results obtain

19 Estimation of the bond and mortgage returns, as in equation (1), was not possible because the usury limit requires a Tobit estimation; the usury limits, however, changed several times between 1550 and 1770.

Table 5   Rates of Return and the Glorious Revolution

	LAND, HOUSES, AND TITHES (1660–1730)	RENT CHARGES (1660–1730)	BONDS AND MORTGAGES (1660–1714)
T	−0.0096*	−0.0128**	−0.0122
	(0.0044)	(0.0034)	(0.0083)
REVT	0.0002	−0.0001	−0.0002
	(0.0001)	(0.0001)	(0.0002)
DBUB	−1.11**	−0.97*	−
	(0.15)	(0.47)	
R^2	0.30	0.18	−
N	521	413	86

* The estimate is significantly different from 0 at the 5% level.
** The estimate is significantly different from 0 at the 1% level.
NOTES   The numbers in parentheses are standard errors. The bond and mortgage equation was estimated using the Tobit procedure, because of usury limits, and only for the years 1660–1714, since the usury limit changed in 1715.

if we use 1689 as the break point between the old and new regimes.

   Another way to measure the effect of politics on capital markets is to look at asset values—in particular, the value of land. Both England and Zele allow many more observations on land prices than on returns to land. Asset values should rise sharply in stable periods and decline in unstable periods. This effect is even more pronounced than the effect for returns on land in Zele. Figure 6 shows the average annual price of arable land in Zele between 1550 and 1749, measured in terms of bushels of wheat to control for the effects of movements in the price of output. Although there are modest long-run movements in land values, it is clear from Figure 6 that, in the war periods, land prices fell sharply. In certain years during the war of independence, real land prices fell to less than 6 percent of their value at the outset of the war. In the later war, land prices fell by more than 50 percent at their minimum. The average fall in prices during the first period was 84 percent, in the second, 30 percent, and in the third, 11 percent.[20]

20   Both land rents and land values fell in the war periods, but the former more than the latter. The price of wheat is from Wilhelm Abel (trans. Olive Ordish), *Agricultural Fluctuations in Europe from the Thirteenth to the Twentieth Centuries* (London, 1980), 432–433, which gives

Fig. 6 Real Farmland Prices, Zele, 1550–1750

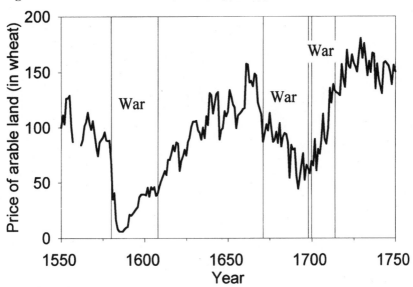

The Charity Commission data reports 1,824 land prices for the years 1600 to 1749, throughout England and Wales. Did land prices fall in periods of political instability, and did they rise after the Glorious Revolution? Because movement in the price of agricultural output will be associated with movement in land prices, as in Zele, all prices have been deflated according to Bowden's index of the price of output, which was constructed here as a ten-year moving average to avoid spurious variation caused by harvest failures and successes. Individual plot prices varied considerably. Information on land use, the enclosure status of land, the location of the land, and the numbers of buildings on the land are included to control for this variation. Figure 7 shows the average annual price of land in England and Wales from 1600 to 1749, controlling for these factors, constructed as a centered three-year moving average. The corrections were derived by regressing land prices on the variables, and then adjusting the price

the average wheat price in Bruges, Dixmude, Nieuport, Anvers, and Brussels, converted from silver to nominal values using information on the silver content of the pond groten, supplied by Van Cauwenberghe.

Fig. 7 Real Farmland Prices, England and Wales, 1600–1750

NOTE   The individual land prices were corrected for the parcel size, the use of the land, buildings upon the land, the location of the land, and the fraction of the land that was enclosed. The figure shows a centered three year moving average of land prices.

SOURCES   Great Britain; Parliamentary Papers, *Reports of the Charity Commissioners, Vols. 1–32* (1819–1840). Nominal values deflated by agricultural output prices are from Peter Bowden, "Statistical Appendix," in Joan Thirsk (ed.), *The Agrarian History of England and Wales* (Cambridge, 1985), IV, 849–850; V, 847–849.

for each plot to remove the price variation caused by differences in land characteristics.[21]

As evident in Figure 7, the two major events of the period— the Civil War of 1639 to 1648 and the Glorious Revolution of 1688—had no obvious effect on land prices. The contrast with Zele is more marked for land prices than for rates of return. Political events had little effect on land prices in England from 1600 to 1749. Even if charities were not the most astute purchasers of land, there is no reason to suppose that their purchasing abilities improved or worsened as a result of changes in political regimes in this period.

21 Peter Bowden, "Statistical Appendix," in Joan Thirsk (ed.), *The Agrarian History of England and Wales* (Cambridge, 1985), IV, 849–850; V, 847–849.

A more formal test for the effect of political events on land prices is the regression equation predicting the logarithm of land prices per acre in terms of land characteristics, a time trend, and political changes. That is,

$$LOG(RENT) = \alpha + \beta_1 T + \beta_2 T^2 + \sum_{i=1}^{n} \gamma_i CHAR_i$$

$$+ \delta_1 DCIV + \delta_7 DREV + \varepsilon, \qquad (4)$$

where $CHAR_i$ is a set of land characteristics, such as plot size, $DCIV$ is a dummy variable for the Civil War period (1639–48), and $DREV$ is a dummy for the Glorious Revolution (the years after 1688 or 1696). The logarithmic form for rent is chosen so that land characteristics and other independent variables have a proportionate effect on land values. Controlling for the long time trends in land values, the estimated effect of the Civil War is an increase of 0.1 percent in land values. The effect of the Glorious Revolution, as dated at 1697, is a 9.7 percent decline in land values, with an estimated coefficient significantly less than 0 at the 5 percent level. The decline in land values is stronger if 1689 is taken as the break point.

Did the Glorious Revolution represent just a turning point in the trend of land prices? That is, did land prices gradually rise after 1689 or 1697? The data from the period 1660 to 1730 reveal that real land values were rising before the Glorious Revolution and that the rate of increase of land values was the same after the Glorious Revolution. There was a growth of land prices from 0.6 percent to 0.8 percent per year that predated the Glorious Revolution (taking either 1689 or 1697 as its date) and that continued after the Revolution at almost exactly the same rate. Neither way of treating the problem indicates that the Glorious Revolution had an effect on land prices.

IMPLICATIONS   The evidence suggests that England in the period prior to the Industrial Revolution cannot be cited as an example of the importance of political stability to economic development, contrary to institutionalists such as North, who seeks institutional explanations of growth and development. The key issue concerning the growth that began with the Industrial Revolution is the investment of energy and resources in the development of production technology. North and his followers account for the rapid rate of technical progress in eighteenth-century Britain by an enhanced incentive to invest in new technology, created by an enhanced security of property rights. One measure of such security of property is the rate of return on capital. Institutionalists were stretching a point when forging the link between the institutional changes of 1688 and the Industrial Revolution beginning in 1760.

England, as far back as the reign of Henry VIII, seems to have enjoyed secure capital markets. The private economy in England after 1540 was largely insulated from political events—even from the strife of the Civil War. To read the Glorious Revolution as ushering in a stable regime of taxes and property rights that laid the foundation for the Industrial Revolution is to write Whig history of the most egregious sort.

Rates of return on capital fell in the 100 years prior to the Industrial Revolution, but in such a way as to show no connection with political events. Within the pre-1688 regime, rates of return on capital rose slowly to a peak in 1625 and then declined again. Within the post-1688 regime, rates of return on capital again moved, but with no indication that the change in regime was a causal factor.

Similarly, land values show little or no response to the political convulsions of the era. Farmland values are estimated to have fallen as a result of the Glorious Revolution. Given the sampling errors in the data, we can conclude that there is only a one in twenty chance that land values actually rose by as much as 6 percent as a result of the Glorious Revolution. There is no evidence from returns on capital that, had James II remained on the throne and been succeeded by his son James III, the economic history of England in the eighteenth century would have been any different.

Stable property rights may have been a necessary condition for the Industrial Revolution, but, since they had existed in England and Wales for more than 200 years prior to the Industrial Revolution, they were certainly not a sufficient condition. An adequate explanation for the Industrial Revolution requires factors other than the emergence of stable private property rights.

E. A. Wrigley

The Process of Modernization and the
Industrial Revolution in England

Modernization and industrialization are terms widely used in descriptions of the changes which have occurred in Western societies over the last two or three centuries. Whether they represent concepts able to sustain adequately the explanatory and descriptive loads borne by them is disputable. Yet they enjoy very wide currency and form the most convenient point of departure for a general discussion of the Industrial Revolution in England.

In this essay I shall describe a view of the relationship between modernization and industrialization which seems to me to be both widespread and unfortunate when applied to the Industrial Revolution in England. In particular, I shall argue that the connection between the two is contingent rather than necessary. I shall begin by offering brief definitions of modernization and industrialization as a preliminary to a discussion of the way in which the assumptions which underlie the use of the terms have clouded our appreciation of the Industrial Revolution. The definitions will serve to introduce both a discussion of the views of percipient contemporaries, especially Adam Smith and Karl Marx, and an examination of some features of the Industrial Revolution itself. I have tried to present the definitions in the form in which they are most widely held—what might be called highest common factor definitions. This means a loss of rigor, but it conforms to the requirements of the essay. At times, it will be evident that the definitions of modernization and industrialization offered are used as stalking horses as much as chargers, underlining the point that they are at once convenient and yet inadequate.

E. A. Wrigley is a Fellow of Peterhouse, Cambridge, England, and a Member of the Cambridge Group for the History of Population and Social Structure. He is the author of *Industrial Growth and Population Change* (Cambridge, 1961), and *Population and History* (London, 1969), and editor of *An Introduction to English Historical Demography* (London, 1966) and *Nineteenth Century Society* (Cambridge, 1972).

This essay was written during a year spent at the Institute for Advanced Study in Princeton. The author's work for that period was supported by a grant from the Carnegie Corporation and the Russell Sage Foundation. He wishes to make grateful acknowledgment of their generosity. The author also benefited greatly from the discussion of an early draft of this essay at an Institute seminar. He is especially grateful to Carl Kaysen, Theodore Rabb, and Fred Weinstein for their helpful comments on that draft, and to Michael Anderson, Bob Coats, Geoffrey Hawthorne, Alan Macfarlane, and Quentin Skinner for their excellent advice on a later draft.

The views of contemporaries are of great value in this regard. Smith and Marx stood closer to the Industrial Revolution than we do today. I shall argue that they identified the salient characteristics of their times in a manner from which we can still learn much—that we have been partially blinded by our knowledge of subsequent events, and so see some things less clearly than they. Finally, I shall point to some parallels and differences between English history and that of her neighbors, France and Holland, in order to throw into relief those features of English experience which set it apart from the continent and have a peculiar relevance to the question of the relationship between modernization and industrialization.

Economists and sociologists have perhaps had the most to do with attempts to define the concepts connoted by the words modernization and industrialization, but the terms are also much used by historians, political scientists, social anthropologists, geographers, and others. It is not surprising, therefore, that the two words have been put to so many different uses. Often they are simply convenient umbrellas to shelter a miscellany of less ambitious ideas.

Of the two terms, industrialization is the narrower in scope and presents fewer difficulties of definition. This is because industrialization has come to be used as a synonym for sustained economic growth. It is said to occur in a given country when real incomes per head begin to rise steadily and without apparent limit, and is always associated with major and continuing changes in material technology, including the tapping of new sources of energy. The prospect of rising real incomes per head has caused industrialization to be widely and ardently pursued. To free men from the dread of periodic cold, privation, famine, and disease, and from the hardship of long bouts of heavy labor in the fields or at the loom by creating the means to meet men's main wants and many of their fancies implies a vast change from the preindustrial past. It has placed the golden age in the future and the lure has proved universal and irresistible.

Expansion of total output alone is not a sufficient criterion of industrialization since, if population is rising more rapidly than output, it is compatible with declining real incomes per head. Nor can mere abundance of capital and land (which might give rise for a time to growing real incomes per head) produce a growth in the economy which can be described as industrialization if material technology remains unchanged. A country which retains a large, even a predominant, agricultural sector may be described as industrialized if real incomes rise and technology changes. New Zealand is an example of this possibility, although the proportion of the labor force engaged in agriculture has now fallen to a modest level. The popularity of Rostow's analogy between the behavior of an economy during industrialization and the takeoff of an airplane speaks to the same point. The crucial change is identified as a rise in the proportion of net national product invested (say from 5 to 10 per cent), but it is implicit in the selection of this criterion that population growth rates and capital-output ratios shall be such that real incomes rise, and rapid technological change is also assumed to take place.[1]

Associated with industrialization are a number of economic and social changes which follow directly from its defining characteristics. For example, as real incomes rise, the structure of aggregate demand will change, since the income elasticities of demand for the various goods available differ considerably. Again, and partly for the same reason there will be a major, sustained shift of population from the countryside into the city. These, and many other related changes, are generally understood to accompany industrialization, but whereas there is room for argument about the length and makeup of any list of the concomitants of industrialization, there is near unanimity upon the central identifying characteristic: the rise in real income per head.[2]

There is also general agreement that industrialization is possible only as part of a wider set of changes in a society which have come to be

1 "The process of take-off may be defined as an increase in the volume and productivity of investment in a society, such that a sustained increase in *per capita* real income results." Walt W. Rostow, *The Process of Economic Growth* (Oxford, 1953), 103–104.

2 For example, Kindleberger's discussion of what he calls economic development, in which he is at pains to be authoritative without provoking controversy, runs along these lines. "Economic growth is generally thought of as unidimensional and is measured by increases in income. Economic development involves as well structural and functional changes. In the absence of effective measures of the latter, however, states of development are estimated by levels of income, and rates of development by the growth of income." Charles P. Kindleberger, *Economic Development* (New York, 1965; 2nd ed.), 15. As Bruton remarks, "Per capita income is chosen as the main measure of growth for two simple reasons: One, almost all writers direct attention to this variable; two, despite some obvious weaknesses in its use there does not seem to be a practical alternative." Henry J. Bruton, "Contemporary Theorizing on Economic Growth," in Bert F. Hoselitz, et al., *Theories of Economic Growth* (Glencoe, 1960), 241. See also W. Arthur Lewis, *The Theory of Economic Growth* (London, 1955), 201–303.

known collectively as modernization. Indeed, in discussions of the developing world today, industrialization and modernization are often used interchangeably,[3] or the former is treated as one aspect of the latter. Much the same point can be made in a different way by noting that almost everyone regards modernization as a necessary condition of industrialization, and that many writers implicitly treat it as also a sufficient condition.

If these assumptions cause difficulty in the study of the Industrial Revolution in England, it is not because historians have been unwary enough to transfer to past time ideas developed by economists and sociologists with only the present in mind. Adam Smith, Marx, and Max Weber, prominent among the host of those who have helped to fashion the concepts now known as industrialization and modernization, had the history of Western Europe chiefly in mind when they wrote. The discussion of change in Asia and Africa today is more often conducted in categories devised for the European past than *vice versa*. Yet, ironically, it may be that the understanding of European history has suffered the more.

It is less easy to define modernization in a way that is likely to command a wide acceptance than is the case with industrialization. There is no equivalent to the measurement of real income per head that can serve as a touchstone for the extent and rate of advance of modernization. It is usually regarded as a congeries of changes which are found together and are related to each other, but the length, composition, and ranking of the list of associated changes vary. The nature of the relationship between the changes is also much disputed. A cynic might say that modernization has come to be a term of convenience used by those who are aware of the profound difference between traditional and modern society, and need a word which can convey their appreciation of its importance, but which does not commit them to any one interpretation of the causes or the course of change.

3 · The two terms are often used almost as synonyms. Hoselitz, for example, in his "Main Concepts in the Analysis of the Social Implications of Technical Change" (11–31), writes: "The use of pattern variables has had the advantage of putting some of the strategic mechanisms of social change associated with industrialization and technical progress into sharper focus. Universalistic norms need not generally replace particularistic ones. However, the transitions from allocating economic roles according to a system of ascription to assigning them on a basis of achievement, and the replacement of functionally diffuse by functionally specific norms for the definition of economic tasks, appear to have occurred in all cases of successful modernization." Bert F. Hoselitz and Wilbert E. Moore (eds.), *Industrialization and Society* (Paris, 1963), 18–19.

In what follows, I shall do little to allay the suspicions of such a cynic. My description of modernization contains no new features. It is eclectic and is intended simply to summarize views that have often been expressed about the changes underlying the transformation of Western European society between the sixteenth and nineteenth centuries. To proceed in this way cloaks issues of the greatest importance since it tends to imply that all concepts of modernization are equivalent, that the apparent differences between Adam Smith, Marx, Ferdinand Tönnies, Weber, Sigmund Freud, Talcott Parsons, and others are more terminological than substantial. In a different context, this would be tendentious if not absurd. In this essay, however, my purpose is simply to provide a backcloth for a discussion of the relationship between modernization and the Industrial Revolution in England, and this must be my excuse for glossing over matters which would otherwise require fuller treatment.

That modernization and greater economic efficiency are closely linked is universally accepted, and the connection is usually made explicit. For this reason, the concept of rationality which underpins much of the discussion of the modernization of Western European society has acquired a limited, almost technical, meaning. Given the values which obtain in a traditional society, for example, it may be perfectly "rational" to retain in a family group, living on a small peasant holding, adult male kin who produce less than they consume. To expel them would do violence to the social system, and cause damage not offset in the eyes of members of the family by any gain in income per head for those who remained on the holding.[4] Such behavior, however, would be counted irrational in the context of modernization because marginal labor productivity in agriculture is held down as long as attitudes like this persist. Rational behavior has come to be defined as that which maximizes economic returns either to the individual, to the nuclear family, or to the state (the interests of the three do not, of course, necessarily coincide, and this has been and still is a source of difficulty with the concept). In comparison with traditional societies, the utilities to be maximized are concentrated in a narrower band and are pursued with a new urgency.[5]

4 It is sometimes argued, following Ferdinand Tönnies, that the essential difference between modern and traditional attitudes lies less in the degree of rationality involved in decisions of this type than in the degree of consciousness on the part of the individual of the moral bases of his actions. Perhaps we overstate the uniformity of traditional societies in this respect. See the brief description of Tiwi life (below) in this connection.
5 This changing emphasis is well illustrated in the chapter by Joseph J. Spengler, "Mercantilist and Physiocratic Growth Theory," in Hoselitz, *Theories of Economic Growth*,

In order to achieve this end, there must be a common measure of value, a means by which all goods and services can be related to a common yardstick, and a calculus by which alternative courses of economic action can be compared. Money provides a common measure of value and will solve the first problem if most goods and services are bought for money rather than bartered. The operation of the market in such an economy will enable goods and services to be valued on an interval scale, and so solve the second problem. And monetary accounting, if sufficiently developed, makes it feasible to estimate the costs and returns of every possible course of economic action; to balance a given present utility against some greater future utility; and to compare the potential returns from a capital sum which may be invested in several different ways, thus meeting the third requirement.

Arbitrary action and any circumstance which makes prediction difficult are held to be antipathetic to rational behavior. The greater the accuracy with which the outcome of alternative courses of action can be foreseen, the greater the scope for rational choice and the incentive to employ rational accounting. Hence the stress first upon the importance of replacing customary arrangements by legally enforceable and specific contractual obligations, and second, upon the attractiveness of a sophisticated governmental bureaucracy to nascent capitalism striving to reduce the range of the incalculable. A government which is unable or unwilling to enforce the law and maintain public order, or which levies large exactions arbitrarily and without due notice, will inhibit rational calculation and is incompatible with modernization.

If rationality is defined along these lines and is regarded as central to the modernization process, it is possible to examine each aspect of social structure and function and, in many cases, define pairs of polar opposites, one of which is regarded as congruent with modernization and likely to further it, while the other is inimical to it and apt to prevent its development. Mention of three such pairs will suggest what is at issue. They are widely held both to be particularly important and also to be closely interlocked. Needless to say, no society has ever been either perfectly "rational" or "irrational" in regard to them. They represent

---

3–64, esp. in the appendix to the main chapter. It is, of course, the total social context which determines what is "rational" in each society. There are no absolute touchstones: Hence such charming ironies as the effect of a rise in the price of beaver fur upon the supply of pelts in French Canada. Since the Indians who caught the beaver wanted little from the French—a gun, a blanket, or a knife—they were able to satisfy their wants by trapping fewer animals when prices were high, a rational if inconvenient response.

limiting possibilities and each pair defines a spectrum on which, in principle, each society may be placed.

The first pair concerns the way in which men are recruited to discharge roles within a society. The rational method of selection is to consider only the fitness of the candidate to carry out the tasks associated with the role regardless of his parentage, kin, status, age, nationality, religion, race, or sex. At the other extreme, recruitment to a particular role is confined to a restricted group within the whole population, which in the limiting case might contain only one member. The group may be defined by kinship, status, race, or in any other way which has gained the sanction of social consent. Open, competitive examination for a governmental administrative post is an example of the first type of recruitment, while entry into a craft with preference given to sons of present members is an instance of the second. The opposite ends of the spectrum are sometimes termed achievement and ascription. The former both favors modernization and helps to define it, while the latter is the dominant form of recruitment in traditional societies.

Rationality bears not only on methods of recruitment to social and economic roles, but also on the definition of the roles themselves. The criteria for recruitment can be more exactly specified, and, at the same time, greater economic efficiency achieved if roles are strongly differentiated. A jack-of-all-trades is master of none. Division of labor tends both to increase productivity and to help ensure that the men appointed to each job are well qualified to discharge it efficiently. This is one aspect of the second spectrum, that which runs between functional specificity and functional diffuseness. In traditional societies, a man may be called upon to perform a number of different roles because of his position in society. Actions and attitudes toward him will be conditioned by the consciousness of this fact. If he is a merchant, for example, men's behavior toward him may be affected not simply by the type and price of the wares he has to offer, but by the status of merchants in the society generally, by his kinship ties, by his religion, and so on. Similarly, his attitude to his customers may be influenced by considerations other than their financial means. And what is true of merchants, is true *a fortiori* of peasants or craftsmen. In economic relations, these influences are compounded by the fact that in traditional societies, the play of the market is limited and transport costs are high. Specialization of economic function cannot, therefore, be carried very far either on the peasant holding, where a substantial measure of self-sufficiency in food and simple consumer goods may be necessary, or in the craft workshop, where the size of the market and the personal predilections of customers prevent long production runs of standard products, and hence division of labor.

It is a short step from these first two polar pairs to the third, which deals with the criteria for membership of a group. At one extreme, this may be particularistic; at the other, universalistic. The latter is typified by the view that all men should be equal before the law and that the law should be the same for all men. It is at odds with this universalistic principle, for example, that a priest in holy orders should be able *qua* priest to invoke immunity from the civil courts, or that because a man is born a serf he should suffer disabilities before the law. Again, the long struggle by local communities in France to retain control of the grain supply within their areas, setting its price and limiting its export as seemed best in their interest, was particularistic in spirit. The central government moved toward the view that trade in grain should be free, with the market being the sole arbiter of price and the movement of grain no longer inhibited by local regulation.[6] In this it was exemplifying the universalistic principle that all franchises, liberties, and privileges which distinguished particular groups, areas, or communities were to be deplored. Formal equality is mandatory.

Consideration of the several linked aspects of social and economic behavior which change during modernization has, in turn, produced paired terms intended to connote the changes as a whole: feudal-capitalist, traditional–modern, and *Gemeinschaft-Gesellschaft*. When the elements of change are analyzed, and especially when their causes are discussed, major differences of interpretation appear, but the definition of modernization may be extended a little by referring to some further points which are common ground to most views of modernization.

Self-interest is the twin pillar to rationality in supporting the concept of modernization. Self-interest is held to be the guiding principle of action in a modernized society to a degree which would appear both aberrant and abhorrent in traditional communities. Like the idea of rationality, self-interest has acquired a special meaning in these discussions. It is perfectly possible to argue that a man in a traditional community who acknowledges a very wide range of kinship obligations and devotes much of his time and energy to promoting the well-being, security, and status of his relatives, his dependents, or his lord, is just as much actuated by self-interest as any Scrooge. The difference lies

6 See Louise A. Tilly, "The Food Riot as a Form of Political Conflict in France," *Journal of Interdisciplinary History*, II (1971), 23–57.

in the nature of the rewards that are sought, not in the degree of self-interest involved. It may also be argued that some traditional societies were so constituted as to put a high premium not only upon the pursuit of self-interest, but also upon a long-term calculation of advantage which in a different context might have gained the approval of Samuel Smiles. Among the Tiwi in northern Australia, for example, a man's status depended above all upon the number of his wives. No man could achieve high status in this way before his late forties, but he had to lay the foundation of his later success two decades earlier by forming links with powerful men who were willing to promise him female children born or as yet unborn as his future wives in return for present services. Twenty years is a long time to wait for an investment to mature, especially where there is a high risk that the premature death of infants, or an unfortunate run of male offspring, will make it impossible for the older man to fulfil his obligations.[7]

Whatever the justice of the prevailing stereotype of traditional societies, in the context of modernization, self-interest has come to mean the adoption of a calculus of advantage. In the calculus, the unit is the individual, or, at the widest, the nuclear family, and the accounting scale is pecuniary gain.

Tönnies, an early and extreme protagonist of the view that modern and traditional societies differ profoundly, wrote in *Gemeinschaft und Gesellschaft*: "The will to enrich himself makes the merchant unscrupulous and the type of egotistic, self-willed individual to whom all human beings except his nearest friends are only means and tools to his ends or purposes; he is the embodiment of Gesellschaft."[8] He thought the pressure toward atomistic individualism to be so acute that he added: "The family becomes an accidental form for the satisfaction of natural needs, neighbourhood and friendship are supplanted by special interest groups and conventional society life."[9] These attitudes eat like acid into the fabric of traditional society, destroying solidary groups. When this

7 "To become a really big man or even a minor figure among the elders, a Tiwi had to devote all his adult life to that goal. Careers were built up and influential positions gained not by executing spectacular coups at any one time, but by slow, devious maneuvering and dealing in influence throughout adulthood. Men in their early thirties invested their very small assets in the hope of large returns twenty years later." Wives, mothers, sisters, and daughters were all "investment funds in [a] career of influence seeking." C. W. M. Hart and Arnold R. Pilling, *The Tiwi of North Australia* (New York, 1960), 51, 52.
8 Ferdinand Tönnies (trans. and ed. Charles P. Loomis), *Community and Society* [*Gemeinschaft und Gesellschaft*] (East Lansing, 1957), 165.
9 *Ibid.*, 168.

happens, old values and attitudes are no longer internalized by the young, and the web of rights and obligations which binds together small traditional communities weakens and, in time, dissolves.

Other attributes of modernization may be inferred from its major characteristics. Social, occupational, and geographical mobility will tend to increase with the decline of ascriptive recruitment. Rights and obligations linked to kinship become less extensive and less easily enforceable, except perhaps within the nuclear family.[10] Structural differentiation at the institutional level parallels the specialization of individual roles. Again, modernization promotes the growth of towns, and in towns its attributes are more widespread, prominent, and pervasive than in the countryside. Its development fosters the spread of literacy and numeracy through a population.

There remain two aspects of modernization which are widely held to be important when assessing its relationship to industrialization in Western Europe. Both have received increased attention in recent years.

The first concerns the actions of the nation state. The close connection between rationality and bureaucratic method, which Weber frequently stressed, has already been remarked.[11] It is only one facet of the stimulus afforded by the state to modernizing tendencies. The state provides the sanction for the enforcement of contractual obligation. and the maintenance of order. Since it encourages the growth of a bureaucracy recruited by achievement rather than by ascription, it is apt to oppose particularistic interests, and to provide an administrative framework within which rational action can flourish. The bourgeois and the nation state are congenial to each other. Impediments to commerce, to the free movement of capital, to unrestricted discretion in the use of private property, and to the treatment of labor simply as a production factor, impediments which inhibit the growth of capitalism and which display a notable persistence in the face of change, can all be reduced to the vanishing point by a vigorous state acting in the bourgeois interest, which is also its own.[12]

Other forms of state action may also increase the momentum of

10 It may be as well to note that the prevalence of the extended family is one of several assumptions about the universal characteristics of traditional society which are disputable in the case of Western Europe.

11 See, e.g., Max Weber (trans. A. M. Handerson and Talcott Parsons; ed. Talcott Parsons), *The Theory of Social and Economic Organization* (New York, 1964), 329–341.

12 Such at least is the "pure type" of action by the state. It is, of course, unlikely to be paralleled exactly in any particular case.

modernization, which is further speeded as groups whose interests lie in accelerating change force an entry into the polity.[13] Taxation, for example, unless payment in kind or labor is accepted, forces the peasant into the market to raise cash. The maintenance of standing armies, like the growth of cities, enlarges the market for foodstuffs and textiles, and encourages specialization of economic function. Or, again, the actions of the state may undermine alternative and older institutional frameworks. The English Poor Law, for example, enshrined the view that if a man or a family fell upon evil times, responsibility for their support ultimately devolved upon the parish. It is evidence of the state's desire that all men who could work should do so, but it is also an acknowledgement of the responsibility of the state toward individuals in distress. Kinship ties and local custom were no longer the sole basis of all help and support in bad fortune. Nor was the lord of the manor expected to provide for his own in return for the services owed him by his men. Instead, the state created a statutory framework within which local communities were to make provision for the sick and needy.

Second, economic and social change produces tension not only between individuals, but also within them. For individuals to act rationally (always in the restricted sense described above), they must achieve rational control of affect and much greater autonomy than is needed or would be acceptable in a traditional society. In traditional society, authority is perceived as protective and nurturant. Hierarchical authority structures are acceptable as long as this holds true, and the values internalized by individuals legitimate the system. Affectual ties are strong and personal, and personal dependency does not involve severe conscious stresses in relation to authority figures. When, however, authority appears to be failing to fulfill its side of the bargain upon which a hierarchical structure of authority rests, hostility toward it, which was once successfully repressed, may surface. A competing set of values appropriate to individual autonomy may be internalized by a part of the population, and conflict between the old and new values will occur.[14] Institutional (social and economic) and internal (psychic)

13 It is sometimes argued that just as formal equality before the law is mandatory, so formal equality in political participation is ultimately inevitable, or at least that competing political groups should stand toward the polity much as competing firms do to the market. There is perhaps something of this in Burke's teaching about political party. The old parallel between party in the state and schism in the church was no longer acceptable.
14 On this aspect of modernization, see, e.g., Everett E. Hagen, *On the Theory of Social Change: How Economic Growth Begins* (Homewood, Ill., 1964); Fred Weinstein and Gerald M. Platt, *The Wish to be Free: Society, Psyche, and Value Change* (Berkeley, 1969).

changes both occur during modernization. If they get out of step with each other, tension and violence are likely to increase.[15]

Once any considerable number of men have ceased to internalize the values upon which traditional society rests, their behavior is certain to impede the smooth functioning of traditional authority and to call its legitimacy and its ability to protect and nurture further in question. Hence the belief that changes in the value systems of small groups of men, such as the early Calvinists, may have an importance in producing massive changes at a later date which might appear at first sight to be quite out of proportion to their number or political power. There is, of course, no reason why the later changes should necessarily follow the same pattern, for greater autonomy and control of affect may be achieved by internalizing value systems other than ascetic Protestantism. But the first successfully established alternative to the traditional ethic, if such it was, holds a special interest.

Not all analyses of modernization contain all of the elements described above. In part, this is an accident of chronology. Marx's analysis, for example, obviously could not be cast in a form which took account of the insights of Freud. Hence, psychic structural changes inevitably figure less prominently than those in social and economic structure. In part, it is a matter of terminology rather than substance. Unquestionably differences remain despite these two considerations, but there is at least tolerable unanimity that the several changes were closely interlocked and that they tended to reinforce each other. Latterly it has also been common to assume that an adequate understanding of modernization in Western Europe would entail *ipso facto* an understanding of the occurrence of the Industrial Revolution in England and its counterpart a little later on the continent.

In this view, the Industrial Revolution is a dramatic culmination to a long-gathering process of change, rather as the cylinder may be charged with a head of steam quite quickly but only if the water has long been heating. Geertz puts the matter succinctly. "In one sense, of course," he writes, "increasing per capita income *is* economic growth, not a mere index of it; but in another, it is clear that such increases are but one highly visible resultant of a complex process. . . . Though it may be true that, as an economic process, development is a dramatic,

15 On this argument, the attempt to impose new institutional forms by *force majeure* from the center not only offends local interests at the conscious level, but also stirs up large anxieties which are the harder for the individual to quell precisely because they are imperfectly accessible to him at the conscious level.

revolutionary change, as a broadly social process it fairly clearly is not. What looks like a quantum jump from a specifically economic point of view is, from a generally social one, merely the final expression in economic terms of a process which has been building up gradually over an extended period of time."[16]

This view is certainly plausible. The very concept of rationality as it has come to be used in the discussion of modernization is intimately related to the promotion of economic efficiency. All modernizing countries have enjoyed economic growth. The early stages of modernization produce, in Rostow's terminology, those changing propensities necessary for takeoff, after which takeoff itself occurs. Exponential economic growth gets under way. Real incomes rise. Material technology advances. Cities swell in size and population. Literacy becomes universal. As living standards rise, the death rate falls, presaging in its turn the control of fertility. Societies come to resemble more and more the late-twentieth century world.

It is my thesis in this essay that it is unwise to view the connection between the Industrial Revolution in England and the changes known as modernization in this manner. I shall argue that, although modernization may be a necessary condition for industrial revolution, it is not a sufficient condition; or, to put the same point in a different way, it is reasonable to argue that a society might become modernized without also becoming industrialized. I shall review in some detail what two major contemporary writers, Smith and Marx, had to say on this subject. It is convenient to do so because their account of the changes going on about them is a valuable corrective to some elements of the conventional wisdom about modernization and industrialization today. It is also a good base from which to explore further the evidence on which the competing explanations rest.

The *Wealth of Nations* might be described as the bible of modernizing man. Rationality and self-interest are made the guiding principles of action. No one has written more trenchantly and persuasively in their favor than Smith. He caught to perfection the capitalist ethic, as well as analyzing the advantages of a capitalist system in producing wealth:

16 Clifford Geertz, *Peddlers and Princes: Social Change and Economic Modernization in Two Indonesian Towns* (Chicago, 1968), 2.

... man has almost constant occasion for the help of his brethren, and it is vain for him to expect it from their benevolence only. He will be more likely to prevail if he can interest their self-love in his favour, and show them that it is for their own advantage to do for him what he requires of them. ... It is not from the benevolence of the butcher, the brewer, or the baker that we expect our dinner, but from their regard to their own interest. We address ourselves, not to their humanity but to their self-love, and never talk of our own necessities but of their advantages. Nobody but a beggar chooses to depend chiefly upon the benevolence of his fellow-citizens.[17]

Smith used a less technical and more telling prose than those who write of modernization today, but there is little in recent discussions of the topic which does not find a parallel in the *Wealth of Nations*.

Many later descriptions of the advantages of functional specificity in economic affairs and of the gains which flow from the division of labor refer to Smith's pinmakers. He was also insistent upon the importance of removing particularistic restrictions in the interest of higher overall efficiency. He advocated the abolition of the apprenticeship system. He opposed all regulations in restraint of trade, and legal incorporations. "The pretence that corporations are necessary for the better government of the trade is without any foundation. The real and effective discipline which is exercised over a workman is not that of his corporation but that of his customers."[18] He favored free trade in foodstuffs, including corn. The settlement laws were castigated: "There is scarce a poor man in England of forty years of age, I will venture to say, who has not in some part of his life felt himself most cruelly oppressed by this ill-contrived law of settlements."[19]

Adam Smith urged the fundamental importance of formal equality with great vigor. In a passage dealing with colonial trade, he finds its prosperity to be due above all to "that equal and impartial administration of justice which renders the rights of the meanest British subject respectable to the greatest, and which, by securing to every man the fruits of his own industry, gives the greatest and most effectual encouragement to every sort of industry";[20] a splendid text.

The *Wealth of Nations* also makes vividly clear the close connection

17 Adam Smith, "An Inquiry into the Nature and Causes of the Wealth of Nations," in *Great Books of the Western World* (Chicago, 1952), 7.
18 *Ibid.*, 56.
19 *Ibid.*, 61.
20 *Ibid.*, 264.

which Smith saw between modernization and firm, ubiquitous, reliable government. "Thirdly, and lastly," he remarks in a chapter entitled "How the Commerce of the Towns Contributed to the Improvement of the Country," "commerce and manufactures gradually introduced order and good government, and with them the liberty and security of individuals, among the inhabitants of the country, who had before lived almost in a continual state of war with their neighbours and of servile dependency upon their superiors. This, though it has been the least observed, is by far the most important of all their effects."[21] This chapter is one of the most interesting in the whole work, containing an account of the relationship between feudal law and medieval property and manners; a vignette of the redoubtable Cameron of Lochiel who in the mid-eighteenth century still exercised "the highest criminal jurisdiction" over his people "with great equity, though without any of the formalities of justice";[22] and an analysis of the way in which surplus income is disposed of in a country lacking commerce and manufactures —echoed more than a century later in Weber's discussion of the disposal of surpluses where "an expansion and refinement of everyday wants has not taken place."[23] There is even a passage in which Smith's diatribes upon the iniquities of the wealthy and powerful have a Marxian sting. Both believed that their follies and greed must bring about a revolution, though they had very different revolutions in mind.

> A revolution of the greatest importance to the public happiness was in this manner brought about by two different orders of people who had not the least intention to serve the public. To gratify the most childish vanity was the sole motive of the great proprietors. The merchants and artificers, much less ridiculous, acted merely from a view to their own interest, and in pursuit of their own pedlar principle of turning a penny wherever a penny was to be got. Neither of them had either knowledge or foresight of that great revolution which the folly of the one, and the industry of the other, was gradually bringing about.[24]

The proprietors and merchants were not alone in their ignorance of an impending revolution, for Smith himself was unaware of the immense changes already in train when the *Wealth of Nations* was written. Indeed, the implication of the arguments he used would rule

21   *Ibid.*, 175–176.
22   *Ibid.*, 177.
23   Weber, *Social and Economic Organization*, 189.
24   Smith, *Wealth of Nations*, 179.

out the possibility of rapid and sustained economic growth. The great revolution of which he wrote was an economic revolution, and was brought about by the group of changes now called modernization, but it was not an *industrial revolution* as that term has come to be used. If one were to characterize the difference between the two revolutions in a single phrase, one might say that whereas a defining characteristic of an industrial revolution is exponential economic growth, the expected outcome of modernization in Smith's view was asymptotic growth.

He believed that economic growth had been continuous during much of the same period as that in which the chief features of modern England took shape. "Since the time of Henry VIII the wealth and revenue of the country have been continually increasing, and, in the course of their progress, their pace seems rather to have been gradually accelerated, than retarded. They seem not only to have been going on, but to have been going on faster and faster. The wages of labor have been continually increasing during the same period, and in the greater part of the different branches of trade and manufactures the profits of stock have been diminishing."[25] This is a more optimistic picture of English economic history than would be thought orthodox today, but it did not lead Smith to an equally optimistic assessment of the future.

His doubts sprang in part from his analysis of the limitations upon the profitable employment of capital, and in part from his views on population trends. Like many of his contemporaries, he read, in recent Dutch experience, lessons about the future of other countries. Holland he held to be a richer country than England and one in which wage rates were higher, but the rate of interest lower than in any other country. "The government there borrows at two per cent, and private people of good credit at three."[26] Comparable rates in England were three and four per cent; in France higher still. Relative abundance of capital seeking profitable employment kept interest rates very low in Holland (and explained the large Dutch holdings in English and French funds); its relative scarcity meant much higher rates in Scotland and France. In general, he observed that high wages accompanied low interest rates, as in Holland, and *vice versa* as in France. Exceptionally, in colonies of recent settlement, both might be high together, although this happy state could not last long. But both might also be low, and Smith envisaged this as the most likely state toward which an economy might move. "In a country which had acquired that full complement of riches

25 *Ibid.*, 38.
26 *Ibid.*

which the nature of its soil and climate, and its situation with respect to other countries, allow it to acquire; which could, therefore, advance no further, and which was not going backwards, both the wages of labor and the profits of stock would probably be very low."[27]

The profits of stock would be low in this limiting case because investment opportunities had been exhausted. Wages would also tend to low because, as Smith put it in a passage which foreshadowed in part the views of Malthus: "Every species of animals naturally multiplies in proportion to the means of their subsistence."[28] A country might be wealthy but no longer growing in wealth. "If in such a country the wages of labour had ever been more than sufficient to maintain the labourer, and to enable him to bring up a family, the competition of the labourers and the interest of the masters would soon reduce them to this lowest rate which is consistent with common humanity."[29] Labor does best during the middle stages of modernization in Smith's analysis, because for a time capital finds the opportunity for fair profit while simultaneously labor may be relatively scarce.

> It is in the progressive state, while the society is advancing to the further acquisition, rather than when it has acquired its full complement of riches, that the condition of the labouring poor, of the great body of the people, seems to be the happiest and most comfortable. It is hard in the stationary, and miserable in the declining state. The progressive state is in reality the cheerful and hearty state to all the different orders of the society. The stationary is dull; the declining, melancholy.[30]

As modernization grew more complete, the prospects for both capital and labor would dim. The most favorable outcome that could be readily envisaged was one in which the material necessities of laboring men were set by social convention at a level well above that of bare subsistence. The least favorable might be very bleak. Both were equally consonant with what is now called modernization. Both David Ricardo, a generation later, and Marx after a further half-century, shared Smith's doubts about the prospect for the real wages of working men. The wages fund doctrine leaves little room for hope on this score. Yet, by definition, if real wages fail to rise, and *a fortiori* if they fall, industrialization is not taking place. A secular rise in real income per head is more a utopian ideal than an object for practical endeavor if economies

27 *Ibid.*, 40.
28 *Ibid.*, 34.
29 *Ibid.*, 30.
30 *Ibid.*, 34.

develop during modernization in the way Smith adumbrated—and his views on the matter were echoed by most of his successors until late in the following century. Marx, for instance was firm in his retention of Ricardo's argument on this point. "The value of labour-power is determined by the value of the necessaries of life habitually required by the average labourer. The quantity of these necessaries is known at any given epoch of a given society, and can therefore be treated as a constant magnitude."[31]

The course of events for many decades after the publication of the *Wealth of Nations* contained little to shake the convictions of those who doubted that the lot of working men could be greatly ameliorated. It is ironic, in view of the doctrine which links industrialization to rising real income per head, that there is clearer evidence for rising real wages in England in the first half of the eighteenth century and the second half of the nineteenth than for the intervening period during which the Industrial Revolution is usually supposed to have occurred. To save the phenomena, if rising real incomes are to be a defining characteristic of industrialization, their appearance must be conceded to be a heavily lagged effect.

It is clear enough why it was that Smith was mistaken in ruling out any hope of industrialization (in the sense the term is used in this essay). He failed to foresee the phenomenal productive powers which the new forms of fixed investment made possible. It was inventions like the steam engine, the coke-fired blast furnace, and the railway which proved him wrong in time, rather than some flaw in his logic or failure to perceive the nature of the modernization process, unless indeed this last is taken to imply the sort of technological advance which actually took place.

By Marx's time, the productive power of the new machines was already a dominant feature of the economic scene. This obliged him to treat the future prospects of man very differently from Smith, quite apart from any differences which might have sprung from their different attitudes to the modernization process in general. Factory industry appeared to Marx to be creating both greater misery and greater scope for future improvement than was conceivable without it. "Fanatically bent on making value expand itself, he [the capitalist] ruthlessly forces the human race to produce for production's sake; he thus forces the

31 Karl Marx (trans. from 3rd German ed. by Samuel Moore and Edward Aveling; ed. Friedrich Engels; rev. according to 4th German ed. by E. Untermann), *Capital: A Critical Analysis of Capitalist Production* (New York, 1906), 568.

development of the productive powers of society, and creates those material conditions, which alone can form the real basis of a higher form of society, a society in which the full and free development of every individual forms the ruling principle." [32] Meanwhile, productive potential was being perverted because of the way wealth was being dissipated: "the extraordinary productiveness of modern industry... allows of the unproductive employment of a larger and larger part of the working class, and the consequent reproduction, on a constantly extending scale, of the ancient domestic slaves under the name of a servant class, including men-servants, women-servants, lackeys, etc." [33]

Marx wrote *Capital* at a time when real wages were at the start of a period of steady and substantial growth. Had he written, say, twenty years later, he might have been tempted to apply to the later nineteenth century an observation he made about the fifteenth and early eighteenth centuries: "under special stimulus to enrichment, such as the opening of new markets, or of new spheres for the outlay of capital in consequence of newly developed social wants, etc., the scale of accumulation may be suddenly extended—[and]—the demand for labourers may exceed the supply, and, therefore, wages may rise." [34] Later in the chapter in which this passage occurs, however, Marx gives reasons for supposing that such a situation must prove temporary because of the basic defects of the capitalist system. [35]

In fact, real wages have risen steadily in the century since the publication of *Capital*, with only intermittent checks, and the assumption that this may be expected to continue, is deeply rooted in popular attitudes and in academic analysis (the prevailing definition of industrialization reflects this assumption). Over the same period during which real wages have been rising, mortality rates in urban areas, a measure which Marx sometimes used as a proxy for misery and degradation, have turned strongly downward; there has been a shift in the structure of aggregate demand which has combined with social preferences to reduce the numbers in domestic service drastically; the era of high mass consumption has dawned; "mixed" economies have become common. [36]

32 *Ibid.*, 649.
33 *Ibid.*, 487.
34 *Ibid.*, 672.
35 *Ibid.*, 680.
36 The possibilities latent in the last of these developments is suggested by Marx himself, although it was still too early for him to assess its longer term significance. In discussing the effects of the Factory Acts of 1850 and 1853, he wrote: "Their wonderful development [that of the industries affected by the Acts] from 1853 to 1860, hand-in-

Marx had the advantage over Smith in being able to observe very clearly that production *could* grow exponentially rather than tending to level off to some asymptote reached when the modernization process had exhausted the openings for profitable investment. He saw, in the tension between exponential growth in productive capacity and the asymptotic tendency of real wages among the vast majority of mankind, the certainty of violent, revolutionary change. Today, as far distant in time from *Capital* as *Capital* was from the *Wealth of Nations*, we can see that the secular trend of real wages is no more bound to be asymptotic than that of total production, but that, on the contrary, the two (when growth in total production is measured *per caput*) have marched closely together across the graphs of the last century.

With the benefit of hindsight, it may be said, the linkage between modernization and full-blown industrialization is evident, however it may have seemed to Smith at the onset of the Industrial Revolution or to Marx part-way through it. But hindsight is not always clear, and its benefit is sometimes questionable. In a rather trivial sense, since modernization was taking place in England from the sixteenth century onwards (Smith, Marx, Weber, and many lesser men are in substantial agreement here although their descriptive vocabularies differ), and was followed by the Industrial Revolution, it may be true that Smith's analysis was mistaken. But this is to say only that what happened, happened. We know that modernization *may* be followed by industrialization, but not that it *must*, or even that such a sequence of events is likely.[37]

Marx's account of the transition from handicraft industry to large-scale power-driven factory industry is interesting in this connection, since in his view the crucial change came before the use of inanimate sources of power on a large scale. He distinguished between tools and machines, the one characteristic of manufacture (handicraft industry), the other of modern industry. "The machine proper . . . is a mechanism that, after being set in motion, performs with its tools the same operations that were formerly done by the workman with similar tools.

---

hand with the physical and moral regeneration of the factory workers, struck the most purblind." Marx, *Capital*, 323–324.

37 The concatenation of changes which comprise the Industrial Revolution are a good example of what Hayek had in mind in writing: "Many of the greatest things man has achieved are not the result of consciously directed thought, and still less the product of a deliberately co-ordinated effort of many individuals, but of a process in which the individual plays a part which he can never fully understand," Friedrich August von Hayek, *The Counter-Revolution of Science: Studies on the Abuse of Reason* (New York, 1964), 84. The act of comprehension is almost as taxing as that of creation.

Whether the motive power is derived from man, or from some other machine, makes no difference in this respect. From the moment that the tool proper is taken from man, and fitted into a mechanism, a machine takes the place of a mere implement. The difference strikes one at once, even in those cases where man himself continues to be the prime mover."[38] Again, "The machine, which is the starting point of the industrial revolution, supersedes the workman, who handles a single tool, by a mechanism operating with a number of tools, and set in motion by a single motive power, whatever the form of that power may be."[39] The distinction between animate and inanimate sources of power Marx held to be unimportant. "The steam engine itself, such as it was at its invention, during the manufacturing period at the close of the seventeenth century, and such as it continued to be down to 1780, did not give rise to any industrial revolution. It was, on the contrary, the invention of machines that made a revolution in the form of steam-engines necessary."[40]

In a sense, the essence of the modernization/industrialization question lies in this last sentence. As rationality spreads and markets broaden, productivity in many branches of industry will increase by the division of labor and the adoption of machinery. If the "right" invention inevitably appears to match every opportunity as it emerges, the smallest gains will tend to be cumulative. Marx's view of the introduction of the steam engine by factory industry is reminiscent of Voltaire's aphorism about God—if He had not existed, He would have had to be invented. Rostow takes a similar line.[41] Smith vividly described how this process might become institutionalized. Having noted how many machines had been designed by workers to save themselves labor, he continues: "Many improvements have been made by the ingenuity of the makers of machines, when to make them became the business of a peculiar trade; and some by that of those who are called philosophers or men of speculation, whose trade it is not to do anything, but to observe everything; and who, upon that account, are often capable of combining together the powers of the most distant and dissimilar objects."[42]

38 Marx, *Capital*, 408.
39 *Ibid.*, 410.
40 *Ibid.*, 409–410.
41 "The appropriate general proposition concerning the composition of innovations seems to be that necessity is the mother of invention." Rostow, *Economic Growth*, 83.
42 Smith, *Wealth of Nations*, 5.

If, however, technological advance were a more wayward and circumstantial matter, and there were no automatic response to opportunity, it is incautious to assume that the issue can be passed over so lightly. It is interesting that Rostow takes exception to Schumpeter's discussion of innovation, quoting a passage which bears repeating:

> It might be thought that innovation can never be anything else but an effort to cope with a given economic situation. In a sense this is true. For a given innovation to become possible, there must always be some "objective needs" to be satisfied and some "objective conditions"; but they rarely, if ever, uniquely determine what kind of innovation will satisfy them, and as a rule they can be satisfied in many different ways. Most important of all, they may remain unsatisfied for an indefinite time, which shows that they are not in themselves sufficient to produce an innovation.[43]

Ironically, the same passage in *Capital*, from which Marx's observations about tools, machinery, and the steam engine were drawn, contains an aside which might suggest a very different conclusion from that which Marx drew. He refers to the drainage of the Haarlemmermeer by steam pump in 1836–37, noting that the machinery used the same principle as an ordinary pump and differed only in that it was driven by "cyclopean steam-engines."[44] In a footnote he describes the earlier history of drainage in Holland.

> It was partly the want of streams with a good fall on them, and partly their battle with a superabundance of water in other respects which compelled the Dutch to resort to wind as a motive power. The windmill itself they got from Germany, where its invention was the origin of a pretty squabble between the nobles, priests, and the emperor, as to which of those three the wind "belonged." The air makes bondage, was the cry in Germany, at the same time that the wind was making Holland free. What it reduced to bondage in this case, was not the Dutchman, but the land for Dutchmen.[45]

The perennial drainage problem which has plagued Dutch history is technically similar to the problem of evacuating water from coal mines, for which the Newcomen engine was developed in England. In both

---

43 Joseph A. Schumpeter, *Business Cycles: A Theoretical, Historical, and Statistical Analysis of the Capitalist Process* (New York, 1939), I, 85n.
44 Marx, *Capital*, 409.
45 *Ibid.*, 409n.

cases, a basic factor of production was in danger of destruction (or at least of becoming inaccessible) unless huge volumes of water could be pumped away. That the steam engine represents a better solution than the windmill to the drainage problem in Holland is clear from the eagerness with which it was adopted at the Haarlemmermeer and elsewhere, but that it would have been developed independently in Holland is highly doubtful, even though more was at stake for Holland than for England, and Holland was perhaps a more fully modernized country than England in the early eighteenth century.

If it is true that certain important technological innovations first introduced in the eighteenth century, such as the steam engine and the coke-fed blast furnace, were the product of special, local circumstances;[46] and if it is also true that without them, productivity, handicapped by a lack of power and precision in the available machinery, could have risen only moderately, then the connection between modernization and industrialization appears much more a matter of happy coincidence than of ineluctable necessity. It is not what was common to all modernizing countries, but what was peculiar to England which then appears important. And what is explained is not simply why the Industrial Revolution occurred in England earlier than elsewhere, but why it occurred at all.

The two conditions which must be satisfied if this conclusion is to follow are plausible but not conclusively demonstrable. It is likely on general grounds that a very large part of the total gain in productivity during the Industrial Revolution sprang from technological advances.[47] It is also reasonable to suppose that the relative scarcities of important raw materials in England, combined with local factor endowment, served both to produce an unusual range of problems at an early stage in industrial expansion and also to permit solutions whose long-term implications were not apparent at their first adoption. I have discussed these circumstances and their outcome elsewhere,[48] and wish in this

46   See E. A. Wrigley, "The Supply of Raw Materials in the Industrial Revolution," *Economic History Review*, XV (1962), 1–16.

47   For the class of reasons discussed, for example, by Robert M. Solow, "Technical Change and the Aggregate Production Function," *Review of Economics and Statistics*, XXXIX (1957), 312–320.

48   See n. 46, above.

essay to concentrate mainly on giving a context to the English experience by commenting on events elsewhere in Western Europe. However, it may be useful to refer briefly to those peculiarities of English economic life which had a bearing on the development of the steam engine and a new technology of iron production.

Shortage of wood made England increasingly dependent on coal for domestic and industrial fuel from the late sixteenth century, and, until well into the nineteenth century, English coal production dwarfed that of continental Europe. The coal industry's growth involved severe difficulties from the start, connected above all with mine drainage as the pits went deeper. Immense pains were taken to overcome them. Three-fourths of all patents issued between 1561 and 1668 are said to have been related to the coal industry's problems in some degree, and one-seventh was taken up with drainage. The engines of Savery and Newcomen were late entrants into the competition to find an answer to this problem. By the early eighteenth century, Newcomen engines had been developed to the point where they were reliable and necessary adjuncts to coal production, at once essential to its continued expansion and unusable without a local supply of coal. James Watt's refinement of the new machine made it the means of revolutionizing transport and transforming production in industry after industry as the nineteenth century drew on.[49]

The fuel problem also loomed large in iron production. In the first three-quarters of the eighteenth century, iron production made little progress in England due to a lack of charcoal or an acceptable substitute. In France at the same time, iron production, using traditional methods, expanded more rapidly and eventually surpassed English levels substantially. It was clear to many men that coal or coke might provide a good solution to the problem of finding a charcoal substitute, but it proved very hard to produce iron of acceptable quality in this way because of the difficulty of keeping the chemical impurities in the iron sufficiently low. Once the trick was learned, however, old limitations

49 On the question of patents, see Stephen F. Mason, *A History of the Sciences: Main Currents of Scientific Thought* (London, 1953), 217. Levasseur made an interesting calculation to drive home the significance of the steam engine in extending man's productive powers. He noted that, on the assumption that the amount of work done by one steam horse-power was equal to that of twenty-one men, France had at its disposal just over one million slaves of a new mechanical kind in 1840. By the middle 1880s, the figure had risen to 98 million, or two and one-half slaves for every inhabitant of France. Emile Levasseur, *La population française: Histoire de la population avant 1789 et démographie de la France comparée à celle des autres nations au XIXè siècle* (Paris, 1892), III, 74.

upon the scale of iron production disappeared. Mineral sources of heat and power, unlike the vegetable and animal alternatives which they supplanted, could be tapped in larger and larger quantities without driving up the marginal costs of production. Industry at long last escaped from the limitations under which it had labored as long as it was dependent upon the productivity of the land. Inanimate sources of heat and power offered great advantages over animate sources for this reason.

The steam engine and the coke-fired blast furnace were the result of a long defensive struggle against intractable production difficulties. They did not occur when production was rising unusually fast. In the second case, production was barely holding its own when the crucial innovations were made. This makes a contrast with the course of change in the cotton industry, where the burst of innovations occurred at a time of rising production and bright prospects. The water frame and spinning jenny came into use in the 1770s (the patents were dated 1769 and 1770) at a time when cotton production was already growing fast. Retained imports of raw cotton had doubled in the previous quarter century.[50] They were the result of a clear opportunity to expand rather than the wish to avoid contraction, and they presaged a period of much more hectic growth. The cotton industry during this period progressed in a manner which conforms well to Smith's view of "the progressive state." Considerable growth is clearly possible in this state and is linked to modernization, but for an industrial revolution to occur, there must be a switch to a new energy source.

The power requirements of the new textile machines were so modest that the steam engine was no more than a useful alternative to a waterfall for many years. The overshot wheel provided all the power that was needed to drive them. But there came a time when greater power was needed and unused waterfalls with a sufficient head were few and remote. Even in the textile industry, and still more in industrial production at large, it is reasonable to assume that the factory would not have become the predominant unit of production without the new technology of coal, steam, and iron. The unexampled and continuous growth in production per head which fascinated Marx's generation was based upon it.[51]

---

50 Phyllis Deane and W. A. Cole, *British Economic Growth, 1688–1959: Trends and Structure* (Cambridge, 1962), 51.

51 Jevons published a work which reflects this interest and the new attitude to the creation of wealth very well at almost exactly the same time as *Capital*. W. Stanley

If it were always a case of "Cometh the hour, cometh the engine," it would matter little how the new technology first came into being, since the need for a cheap, reliable source of energy to magnify the productive power of the new machines would have ensured its development. If, on the contrary, technological advance in a prescientific age is far from automatic, whatever the "objective" possibilities of the time— if Schumpeter's view is more just than Rostow's—if the development of power sources for textile machinery might have stopped short with water power as Dutch drainage did with the windmill, then the particular course of events in England will repay close attention. So, too, will the circumstances of other European countries at the same time, for they suggest other possibilities within the general framework of modernization.

Smith wrote not only of the relative abundance which was attainable in the progressive state, but also of stationary and declining states in which the lot of men was far less enviable. And it appears from the context of his remarks that he thought that a country could be modernized and yet find itself in one of the two latter states as easily as in the progressive. Europe in the eighteenth century affords examples of all three and also of more mixed conditions. Comparison with continental Europe offers some indirect warrant for thinking that England was fortunate to have remained in a progressive state.

Smith appears to have believed that Holland was in what he called a stationary state, having moved close to the asymptote which represented the full extent of growth possible in the circumstances of the day. The principal evidence for this was the prevailing rate at which money could be borrowed on good credit, and he found it necessary to remark that there was no good reason to suppose that business in Holland had actually declined, fearing that his readers would draw this inference.[52] In his view, Holland was the country with the highest real income per head of any in Europe, but was, for that reason, the more likely to be at or close to the limit of growth, rather than being poised for a continuing surge of expansion. That Holland had reached a high degree of rationality in economic affairs seems indisputable. Nor was this just an urban phenomenon, leaving the countryside largely untouched. A very telling example of the suffusion of the countryside by advanced forms of

Jevons, *The Coal Question: An Inquiry Concerning the Progress of the Nation, and the Probable Exhaustion of our Coal-Mines* (London, 1865).
52   Smith, *Wealth of Nations*, 38.

economic organization is to be found in Roessingh's recent analysis of a set of tax records relating to the Veluwe in 1749.[53]

The Veluwe lies in central Holland south of the Zuider Zee. It had never attained the degree of commercial or industrial development found in the west of Holland, and particularly in the province of Holland itself. It was an agricultural area with no large town, whose soils were at best of moderate quality. Yet Roessingh's study shows that even small settlements from 400 inhabitants upward almost invariably had a village shop (at a time when shops were still rare in England in places of similar size), a tailor, a shoemaker, and very often a weaver and baker, as well. All were frequently found in much smaller villages, too, and the hierarchical pattern of service function by settlement size was very well ordered. This was an economy in which division of labor had been pushed very far; in which money and the market entered into the lives even of small men to a degree which supported shops in small villages and caused wives to cease baking at home. The villages of the Veluwe were far removed from the type of communities which Tönnies had in mind in describing the nature of *Gemeinschaft*, even though theirs was largely an agricultural economy in a strictly rural setting. The Veluwe was part of an economy which had been modernized but not industrialized. Such an economy does not necessarily mean steadily rising real incomes, nor does it imply a move towards industrialization. When rationality prevails and men's actions are informed by self-interest, there must be gains in efficiency, but there is no certain and permanent rise in living standards for the bulk of the population.

At much the same time that the Veluwe census was taken, in another part of the Low Countries—in Belgian Flanders—the local economy was about to enter into what Smith might have called a declining state, as the work of Deprez and Mendels has shown.[54] They describe the instability of an economy, already substantially modernized, which becomes heavily dependent upon cottage industry to supplement income from agriculture. What begins as a useful addition to farming income comes to be, for many men, their prime or sole means of support. Population growth accelerates when checks upon early marriage

53   H. K. Roessingh, "Village and Hamlet in a Sandy Region of the Netherlands in the Middle of the Eighteenth Century," *Acta Historiae Neerlandica*, IV (1970), 105–129.

54   P. Deprez (trans. Margaret Hilton), "The Demographic Development of Flanders in the Eighteenth Century," in D. V. Glass and D. E. C. Eversley (eds.), *Population in History: Essays in Historical Demography* (Chicago, 1965), 608–630. Mendels' work is summarized briefly in Franklin F. Mendels, "Industrialization and Population Pressure in Eighteenth Century Flanders," *Journal of Economic History*, XXXI (1971), 269–271.

and high fertility, which are more powerful in a landholding community, lose their force. With the labor force growing more rapidly than opportunities for profitable employment, real incomes fall and the bitterly impoverished population is pushed down toward the lowest levels of subsistence. The lives of most men in the Vieuxbourg area, where conditions were especially bad, were indeed "melancholy," to use Smith's adjective for the declining state, by the end of the eighteenth century. In the Twente region of the province of Overijssel in east Holland, the declining, or at best stationary, state supervened about 1750. As in Flanders, the local linen industry proved unable to expand its markets as quickly as was needed to keep pace with the growth of the rural industrial population.[55] The economic history of early modern Europe contains many examples of areas at various stages along the road to modernization where change was accompanied by falling real incomes per head.[56] Eighteenth-century Holland represents as a whole a relatively happy outcome to this challenge in that real wages were maintained at a fairly high level.[57] Rationality in economic life neither led to a takeoff, nor plunged the population into misery.

Smith would not have been surprised at events in Flanders and elsewhere. Like Malthus and many later writers, including Marx, he saw dangers to living standards in rapid population growth and was inclined to regard population growth as dependent upon economic conditions. If the opportunities for employment grew, the labor supply could be relied upon to increase commensurately and was only too likely to increase more than commensurately. Marx expressed a view about what determines wage levels which is, in substance, the same as that of Smith or Malthus, although he had a special reason for taking a somber view of their secular trend. On the former point he wrote. "The value of labour-power is determined, as in the case of every other commodity, by the labour-time necessary for the production, and

55 B. H. Slicher van Bath, *Een samenleving onder spanning; geschiedenis van het platteland in Overijssel* (Assen, 1957). His conclusions are summarized in J. A. Faber, et al., "Population Changes and Economic Developments in the Netherlands: A Historical Survey," *Afdeling Agrarische Geschiedenis Bijdragen* (Wageningen, 1965), XII, 47–113, esp. 72–89.
56 Braun's study of an upland Swiss area is an example of the type of change which can easily produce this result. Rudolf Braun, *Industrialisierung und Volksleben: die Veränderung der Lebensformen in einem ländlichen Industriegebiet vor 1800* (Zurich, 1960).
57 It also illustrates a point which can hardly be made too strongly—that economic fortunes were at least as much a matter of region as of country in early modern Europe. They remained so during the early stages of the Industrial Revolution. I have traced one example of this in E. A. Wrigley, *Industrial Growth and Population Change* (Cambridge, 1961).

consequently also the reproduction, of this special article. . . . Given the individual, the production of labour-power consists in his reproduction of himself or his maintenance. . . . in other words, the value of labour-power is the value of the means of subsistence necessary for the maintenance of the labourer." [58] Convention may, however, play a part in determining the subsistence level.

> His natural wants, such as food, clothing, fuel, and housing, vary according to the climatic and other physical conditions of his country. On the other hand, the number and extent of his so-called necessary wants, as also the modes of satisfying them, are themselves the product of historical development, and depend therefore to a great extent on the degree of civilisation of a country, more particularly on the conditions under which, and consequently on the habits and degree of comfort in which, the class of free labourers has been formed. In contradistinction therefore to the case of other commodities, there enters into the determination of the value of labour-power a historical and moral element. Nevertheless, in a given country, at a given period, the average quantity of the means of subsistence necessary for the labourer is practically known. [59]

This was very much Smith's view, too. He felt the disquiet to which Malthus was later to give fuller expression, although his doubts were tempered by his appreciation of the complexity of the process of growth, which gave some ground for optimism. Nevertheless, if population is sensitive to economic stimuli and grows readily when conditions improve (for example, because young people marry when wheat is cheap), and if the rate at which population can grow exceeds the rate at which the economy can expand, then there is little hope of increasing subsistence wages set at some conventional standard, and a pressing fear that a volatile population growth may cause the conventional standard to be eroded. There was no warrant in past experience for expecting an economy to grow steadily at, say, 3 per cent per annum, a rate which would ensure that production grew more rapidly than population, and so enable real incomes to rise in spite of growing numbers.

By Marx's day, it had become clear that a rapid and sustained growth in industrial production was possible, but in his analysis, labor, by one of the crucial paradoxes of the capitalist mode of production, is

58 Marx, *Capital*, 189–190.
59 *Ibid.*, 190.

actually worse off as a result, both in income and in the general nature and conditions of work. His analysis depends upon his insistence that each historic mode of production has its own special population laws.[60] In a capitalist society, the industrial reserve army grows. Its relative size determines wage levels, and "The fact that the means of production, and the productiveness of labour, increase more rapidly than the productive population, expresses itself, therefore, capitalistically in the inverse form that the labouring population always increases more rapidly than the conditions under which capital can employ this increase for its own self-expansion."[61]

Given that over-rapid population growth may be a cause of economic distress (as it seems to have been in England in the late sixteenth and early seventeenth century), it is of interest that England in the second half of the eighteenth century was perhaps in greater danger than France or Holland, the two other countries in which modernization had progressed furthest.[62] The threat to wages posed by population growth had been increasing in most of Europe in the later eighteenth century. Ireland had embarked on a period of her history which brings to mind the process which Geertz calls agricultural involution, which "resembles nothing else so much as treading water. Higher-level densities are offset by greater labour inputs into the same productive system, but output per head (or per mouth) remains more or less constant."[63] The pool grows larger, but the numbers treading water in it increase at least as quickly.[64] Many other countries, especially in eastern and southern Europe, where population growth rates were often high, would eventually have met a fate like that which devastated Ireland, but for the safety valves afforded by industrialization in Western Europe and the possibility of emigrating to countries of European settlement outside Europe. But in France, there were signs that rationality was beginning to affect reproductive behavior.

60   *Ibid.*, 692–693.
61   *Ibid.*, 708.
62   In Holland, population increased hardly at all in the eighteenth century. In 1700, the total lay between 1.85 and 1.95 million; in 1795, 2.08 million (Faber, *Afdeling*, XII, 110). In France, the growth was faster but much less fast than that in England. The French population rose from 19.3 to 26.3 million between 1700 and 1789 (Marcel R. Reinhard, et al., *Histoire générale de la population mondiale* [Paris, 1968; 3rd ed.], 252, 683). The population of England and Wales grew from c. 5.5 to 9.2 million between 1700 and 1800.
63   Clifford Geertz, *Agricultural Involution: The Process of Ecological Change in Indonesia* (Berkeley, 1963), 78.
64   *Ibid.*, 95.

Perhaps it is symbolically appropriate that the first group which is known to have adopted effective and conscious family limitation as part of their habit of life should have been the bourgeoisie of Geneva, the city of Calvin. This pattern of behavior was firmly established by the end of the seventeenth century.[65] A century later it was growing common throughout much of France. Characteristically, it seems to have begun in small towns before the surrounding countryside was affected, but very early in the nineteenth century there were several large areas in which family limitation was widespread among peasant populations.[66] In consequence, French population growth was much more modest in the nineteenth century than that of any other major European state. By the end of the century, this had become a matter for the keenest regret among many French writers, an attitude still evident in the work of recent French scholars.[67] If the Industrial Revolution had not occurred, however, France might have been the envy of Europe. French population trends were much safer than English in the economic world which Smith depicted. The principles of rationality and self-interest which inform the entire range of changes during modernization point to fertility control within marriage as surely as to the division of labor or to the principle of universalistic criteria for group membership.

The process of modernization may also have affected fertility levels in other countries earlier than in England.[68] It may prove to be the case

65 Louis Henry, *Anciennes familles genevoises: étude démographique, XVIe-XXe siècle* (Paris, 1956), 77-78, 94-110, 127-142.

66 There is an excellent brief review of early modern French demographic history in Pierre Goubert, "Historical Demography and the Reinterpretation of Early Modern French History: A Research Review," *Journal of Interdisciplinary History*, I (1970), 37-48. Antoinette Chamoux and Cécile Dauphin, "La contraception avant la Révolution française. L'exemple de Châtillon-sur-Seine," *Annales, E.S.C.*, XXIV (1969), 662-684. Etienne van de Walle of the Office of Population Research, Princeton University, tells me that the large-scale study of nineteenth-century fertility in progress in that Office shows that by about 1830, when marital fertility was already low in parts of the south-west and Normandy, there was in those areas a very marked association between low marital fertility and early marriage—a very "rational" pattern of behavior in the sense that ability to limit family size within marriage removes what would otherwise be a telling "rational" argument against early marriage. There is some discussion of this point for a later period in his article, "Marriage and Marital Fertility," *Daedalus*, XCVII (1968), 486-501.

67 See, for example, Alfred Sauvy, *General Theory of Population* (London, 1969), 272-282.

68 I have found some evidence of family limitation in Colyton, Devon, in the second half of the seventeenth century, but it is not yet possible to say how widespread this was. And all trace of it had disappeared in Colyton by the middle decades of the eighteenth century. See E. A. Wrigley, "Family Limitation in Pre-Industrial England," *Economic History Review*, XIX (1966), 82-109.

that in parts of Holland there was restriction of family size at an early date. Van der Woude's tabulations for certain settlements in the province of Holland show that household size was unusually small in the late seventeenth and eighteenth centuries, and the number of children per family somewhat lower than in England.[69] This was an area deeply involved in commerce, with a high proportion of the population literate, perhaps the most thoroughly modernized part of that country which contemporaries regarded as the furthest advanced in modernization. Dutch church registers do not easily lend themselves to family reconstitution so that clear-cut confirmation of low marital fertility is hard to obtain, but it is at least possible that here, as in Geneva, rationality produced a lowering of fertility in marriage among some elements in the population. There is also evidence that a substantial proportion of men and women never married. Postponement or avoidance of marriage is an equally effective "rational" strategy (although it may also occur for other reasons). Early in the nineteenth century, a tendency toward modern patterns of marital fertility appeared among the native-born in New England.[70] It was well established half a century before the same pattern appeared in England.

Population growth in England accelerated sharply in the mid-eighteenth century and remained at a high level until late in the nineteenth, at or a little over 1 per cent per annum. If incomes were not eventually to suffer as a result, production had to increase at least as fast as the population. To Smith, the chance of tripling the national product in a century (roughly the scale of increase needed merely to offset population growth) would have seemed slight; and time for a solution was short when growth was so rapid. Over-rapid population growth brings great dangers to a modernizing society, although in an industrializing society, population growth may even confer benefits. It was England's good fortune that the Industrial Revolution rescued her from

69 A. M. van der Woude, "De omvang en samenstelling van de huishouding in Nederland in het verleden," *Afdeling Agrarische Geschiedenis* (1970), XV, 202–241.

70 See, e.g., Peter R. Uhlenberg, "A Study of Cohort Life Cycles: Cohorts of Native Born Massachusetts Women, 1830–1920," *Population Studies*, XXIII (1969), 407–420, esp. Tables 1 and 2. Evidence of family limitation among small groups within the settled American population may be found in Robert V. Wells, "Family Size and Fertility Control in Eighteenth Century America: A Study of Quaker Families," *Population Studies*, XXV (1971), 73–82. There is inconclusive but suggestive evidence that marital fertility fell at the end of the eighteenth century among high-status Dutch settlers in the Hudson valley in Alice P. Kenney, "Patricians and Plebians in Colonial Albany," *Halve Maen: Quarterly Magazine of the Dutch Colonial Period in America*, XLV (1970–71), 1: 7–8, 14; 2: 9–11, 13; 3: 9–11; 4: 13–14; XLVI (1971), 1: 13–15.

what must otherwise have been a period of great stress due to the pace of population increase.

Smith regarded investment in land as the surest way of increasing national wealth. "The capital employed in agriculture, therefore, not only puts into motion a greater quantity of productive labour than any equal capital employed in manufactures, but in proportion, too, to the quantity of productive labour which it employs, it adds a much greater value to the annual produce of the land and labour of the country, to the real wealth and revenue of its inhabitants. Of all the ways in which a capital can be employed, it is by far the most advantageous to society."[71] The extent of the growth in industrial production was, in his view, geared to agricultural expansion. But land was in virtually fixed supply and the increases in production attainable from land in farms were limited and usually secured only over a long period. Therefore growth in general must be limited, or, in the terminology I have used in this essay, asymptotic. Modern industry based on the steam engine, a new iron technology, and the organization of production in factories, came just in time to save the day. Whether the further development of the sources of increased productivity familiar to Smith could have achieved the same success is highly doubtful. The Industrial Revolution represented a break in the working out of modernizing tendencies in Europe, a break which ultimately generalized and extended the scope of modernization while at the same time modifying it, but which was initially ill-matched with it.

Capital is, in a sense, a commentary on the severity of the tensions which were produced by the uneasy marriage of industrialization and modernization, a marriage in which the former proved to be the salvation of the latter in England by giving it a vastly larger economic base and freeing it from restrictions which had earlier seemed inescapable. But the price was high. Marx made an attempt to categorize the lessons to be learned from the turmoil of the first half of the nineteenth century in England, and to glean from this experience an insight into the future. His message was clear. The marriage was intolerable and must be dissolved if the benefits made possible by industrialization (but denied to the masses by the capitalist system set in a bourgeois state) were ever to be distributed equitably. The marriage proved more durable than Marx expected, and it became the object of widespread emulation. As time passed, the characters of the two partners merged into each other,

71 Smith, *Wealth of Nations,* 157.

and the early difficulties faded from memory. What had seemed inconceivable to Smith and intolerable to Marx developed into an acceptable commonplace. National product could rise without apparent limit, and was so divided as to assure most men of rising real incomes.

Some of the differences between the gradual development of modernization and the novel changes produced by the Industrial Revolution are epitomized in the contrast between old and new urban growth in England. London grew steadily throughout the period of modernization in England from the sixteenth century onwards. By the end of the eighteenth, it was already a big city with a population close to one million. London's development was relatively smooth and continuous. The city grew no faster in the nineteenth than in the seventeenth century. Already in 1700 very complex arrangements were needed to sustain it, and the London market helped to cause notable changes in areas at some distance from London—in the agriculture of Fen-edge villages in Cambridgeshire, for example, or in those Leicestershire villages which became the home of the framework knitting industry. The growth of London was made possible by the economic and social changes of modernization, which were in turn fostered by it.[72] Defoe's London at the beginning of the eighteenth century, like Dicken's London in the mid-nineteenth, might be termed modernized, but not industrialized (there was, of course, a very large employment in industry, but the production units were usually tiny, often the home itself). Literacy was higher than elsewhere in England,[73] and the economic and social functioning of the city conformed well to what would be expected from a checklist of modernization—the chief concomitants of rationality and self-interest were eminently visible, while some of the most perturbing results of sheer size became less serious toward the end of the eighteenth century. Mortality rates, for example, had fallen considerably from the peak reached in the early decades of the century.

In contrast to the pattern of city growth in London, the large urban sprawls which unrolled across the industrial north and midlands from the end of the eighteenth century might almost be described as industrial but not modern. In these areas, levels of literacy were often very low, as poor as in the most backward rural areas of the country, and

72 See E. A. Wrigley, "A Simple Model of London's Importance in Changing English Society and Economy," *Past and Present*, XXXVII (1967), 44–70.
73 This is evident from the materials assembled by R. S. Schofield at the Cambridge Group for the History of Population and Social Structure. Schofield hopes to publish the results of his analysis of this material shortly.

mortality rates frequently very high. Even the free play of the market and the universal use of money as a means of exchange were threatened by the spread of truck systems of payment and the tying of employees to the company shop. Consumption standards were low and of limited scope. Tight-knit industrial and mining villages were almost solely of one class and there were few visible "betters" whose patterns of consumption could be aped. Rationality and self-interest had small room to flourish among men and women in the areas of working-class housing which grew up in knots round the factory or the pithead. This was a far cry from the capitalism of myriad small producers and consumers. It is not purely fanciful to see in communities of this type as many of the features which are held to go with *Gemeinschaft* as with *Gesellschaft*.[74] Industrialization brought with it major regressive features judged by the measuring rods of modernization.

In time this could be seen as a case of *reculer pour mieux sauter*, but it is hardly surprising that it was seldom seen in this way at the time. In hindsight, the magnitude of contemporary hazards and uncertainties tends to be lost to view. All one-piece theories of modernization/ industrialization, such as the analogy with the takeoff of an airplane, bear too heavily the marks of *ex post facto* summary to do justice to the Industrial Revolution. There is much to be learned from both Smith and Marx about the surprising and uncertain course taken by events. The fact that neither was right in the long run is not a good reason for ignoring their arguments. It is quite possible for a man to have, say, a one-in-fifty chance of hitting the jackpot and yet still win it. The relationship between modernization and industrialization cannot be reduced to simple odds, of course. Perhaps the analogy is misleading, but it will have served a useful purpose if it underlines the absence of any inevitability about the transition from a modernized but preindustrial economy to the postindustrial world.

74 Much of this has remained and is reflected in descriptions of the life of the industrial working classes in the recent past. See, for example, Richard Hoggart, *The Uses of Literacy: Aspects of Working-Class Life, With Special Reference to Publications and Entertainments* (London, 1967).

Franklin F. Mendels

Social Mobility and
Phases of Industrialization

The study of historical patterns of social mobility inevitably leads to questions about its determinants and to the search for correlations between mobility and industrialization. This paper is not based on any new empirical research on social mobility. Neither can it pretend to be based on an exhaustive reading of the extant literature. Rather, it focuses on the process of industrialization to provide some thoughts on social mobility during the passage of Western societies from the pre-industrial to the industrial age. Included here in social mobility are occupational, status and geographical, and inter- as well as intra-generational mobility. The discussion covers any of these three facets of social mobility when appropriate. A last caveat: this paper includes a typology of industrialization which is not fully and rigorously developed. Rather, the typology is used loosely with the sole purpose of emphasizing certain differences between phases or types of industrialization which are relevant to the study and understanding of social mobility in its various aspects.

The concept of industrialization usually refers to a dichotomy between traditional and modern society and to a more or less drawn-out transition from the former to the latter. For the purpose of analyzing the interactions between industrial change and mobility, it is useful first to recall how social mobility operates in pre-industrial societies. Second, it seems essential to take a close look at the process of industrialization itself and distinguish in it several phases (or types). Finally, it would be one-sided and

Franklin F. Mendels is Associate Professor of History at the University of Maryland Baltimore County.

This is a revised version of a paper I was asked to prepare for presentation at the Mathematical Social Science Board Conference on International Comparisons of Social Mobility in Past Societies, 1972. I have benefited from the comments and suggestions of Rondo Cameron, Paul Hohenberg, Hartmut Kaelble, Hans Medick, Iris Mendels, and Jürgen Schlumbohm. The ideas expressed in the first part of the article are a by-product of long discussions with Lutz K. Berkner about our joint work on "fertility and family law in Western Europe." Work for this paper has been supported by U.S.P.H.S. Grant HD 5586 and a grant under the Ford and Rockefeller Foundations Program in Support of Social Science and Legal Research on Population Policy. Of course, I alone am responsible for the opinions expressed here.

perhaps misleading to consider industrialization and economic development only as exogenous causal factors with respect to social mobility. Industrial development in Western countries was itself shaped in many ways by the stratification within respective countries, by the system of values of their various strata, and by the possibilities for the movement of individuals and groups— movement from employment in low-efficiency, low-earnings, or low-status occupations to employment in occupations with higher efficiency, earnings, or status; or movement from undifferentiated, unspecialized work to the kind of tasks needed in the factory system. Not all societies were endowed with the social and political structure which made such movements possible. To some extent, this structure adapted itself to economic forces and opportunities, but national or regional traditions, or the forces of vested interests, were sometimes persistent enough to slow down or postpone structural adaptation to a rapidly changing environment.

If in the study of social mobility we started from the work of Kuznets and others, we would define the epoch of modern economic growth (or modern industrialization) as one characterized by a "sustained increase in income per capita . . . most often accompanied by an increase in population . . . and by sweeping structural changes. The latter included a reallocation of resources toward non-agricultural activities (industry and services), a massive urbanization of the population, and changes in the relative economic position of groups defined by employment status, attachment to various industries, and level of per capita income."[1] At its own level of abstraction, this is an excellent definition. It means that a functional prerequisite of modern economic growth is a mobility which permits an initially rural, peasant agricultural society to transform itself over time into one where most people live in cities and work in industry and services.

Unfortunately, to look at change in this manner does not help uncover underlying mechanisms with any precision. A given rate of *net* occupational mobility between two dates may conceal much larger and more complex gross flows in and out of occupations. Similarly, the rural-urban transition of the early phases of industrialization resulted from much larger migration flows than would

[1] Simon Kuznets, *Modern Economic Growth* (New Haven, 1966), 1. The complete definition given by Kuznets is not relevant here.

appear from merely looking at the changing share of the population that was urbanized. As Wrigley has shown, the growth of London from 7 to 11 percent of the English population between 1650 and 1750 implies that the survivors of at least 17 percent of all the births taking place in the country eventually moved to London. If one could take account of the large movement of return migration, this figure would be even higher. Why such large gross flows were necessary to generate much smaller net changes is explained by the negative natural increase of cities, itself the result of the high urban mortality which prevailed in all European towns until the development of modern hygiene. For instance, the age of continuous growth by natural increase did not begin in Nottingham until 1740.[2] Similarly, the observed decline of the agricultural and the rise of the industrial labor force cannot be attributed to mobility alone on *a priori* grounds. It could have taken place without mobility by the simple effect of differential replacement rates between agriculturalists and industrial workers. As for the rise of services, that could have taken place through the succession by the numerous sons and daughters of the service workers of each generation. This is not what happened. The growing number of vacancies in industry, in the white collar positions, in public and private bureaucracies, and in the professions, was taken up to a large extent by the offspring of other occupational and status groups.[3]

Recent and current historical studies of social mobility during industrialization try to ascertain, by following the mobility pat-

2 Otis D. Duncan, "Methodological Issues in the Analysis of Social Mobility," in Neil J. Smelser and Seymour M. Lipset (eds.), *Social Structure and Mobility in Economic Development* (Chicago, 1966), 51. E. A. Wrigley, "A Simple Model of London's Importance in Changing English Society and Economy, 1650–1750," *Past &Present*, 37 (1967), 44–70. Wrigley's partly theoretical computations are confirmed by the experience of the town of Cardington, 45 miles from London. R. S. Schofield, "Age-Specific Mobility in an Eighteenth-Century Rural English Parish," *Annales de Démographie Historique, 1970* (Paris, 1971), 271. Jonathan D. Chambers, "Population Change in a Provincial Town. Nottingham 1700–1800," in David V. Glass and David E. C. Eversley (eds.), *Population in History* (Chicago, 1965), 334–353; Adna Ferrin Weber, *The Growth of Cities in the Nineteenth Century* (New York, 1899), 230ff; Louis Chevalier, *La formation de la population parisienne au XIXe siècle* (Paris, 1950), 48.
3 A mathematical treatment can be found in Judah Matras, "Differential Fertility, Intergenerational Occupational Mobility, and Change in the Occupational Distribution: Some Elementary Interrelationships," *Population Studies*, XV (1961), 187–197. See also Nathan Keyfitz, "Individual Mobility in a Stationary Population," *Population Studies*, XXVII (1973), 335–352.

terns of well-defined groups during well-defined periods, precisely the manner by which the new vacancies were being filled.[4] Since they carefully measure the regional and temporal variations in the rates and ranges of various types of mobility, the vision of industrialization which is exemplified by the definition quoted above is not congruent with the level of analysis needed in the new studies of mobility. I will propose here a taxonomy of industrialization and suggest for each phase (or type) actual or plausible relationships between selected aspects of social mobility and certain economic forces.

In order to enhance one's understanding of the effect of industrialization on social mobility, consider how, by contrast, social mobility operated in a pre-industrial society. One's grasp of the mechanisms at work will be tighter if one imagines an ideal-type "medieval" society predominantly made up of a homogeneous peasantry. There are some craftsmen, churchmen, soldiers, and men of government, but their small numbers are fixed by guild restrictions or other statutory norms.[5] This mythical society is peaceful and placid, so that great redistributions of land or status which result from plunder, murder, war, epidemics, famine, riots, or mass migration do not occur. The land available for agriculture is abundant but entirely settled and used, and is transmitted hereditarily, for there is no land market, or leasing of land by one peasant to another. It appears that in this mythical medieval society status and occupational and geographical mobility work hand in hand with the inheritance system, the population's net rate of reproduction, and its family structure. One can illustrate this from the demographic pattern. Assume that families have many children surviving to adulthood—as determined by some combination of fertility and mortality—but only one heir to the father's

4 Stephan Thernstrom, *Poverty and Progress* (Cambridge, Mass., 1964); the essays in Stephan Thernstrom and Richard Sennett (eds.), *Nineteenth-Century Cities* (New Haven, 1969); Michel Papy, "Professions et mobilité à Oloron sous la Monarchie Censitaire d'après les listes de recrutement militaire," *Revue d'histoire économique et sociale,* XLIX (1971), 225–264; P. E. Razzell, "Statistics and English Historical Sociology," in R. M. Hartwell (ed.), *The Industrial Revolution* (Oxford, 1970), 101–120. The common methodology is described in Thernstrom, "Reflections on the New Urban History," in Felix Gilbert and Stephen R. Graubard (eds.), *Historical Studies Today* (New York, 1972), 320–336.

5 See Lutz K. Berkner and Franklin F. Mendels, "Inheritance Systems, Family Structure, and Demographic Patterns in Western Europe (1700–1900)," in Charles Tilly and E. A. Wrigley (eds.), *Historical Studies of Fertility* (forthcoming).

farm, occupation, and status: then all the children but one, the heir, will experience mobility.

Figure 1 shows all the possibilities for non-heirs in a modern setting where non-agricultural employment is not rigidly constrained. Thus, in thirteenth-century Weston (Lincolnshire) where land partibility was limited, out of sixty-eight sons, nine entered the church and twenty-six (38 percent) emigrated from the village. In the neighboring village of Moulton, where partibility prevailed, the percentage of departures was only 23 percent. But was not mortality so high in a medieval village that replacement rates rarely surpassed 1.0? Data for 1270 show that the average Weston family produced 1.86 live adult sons and Moulton families produced 2.5. English replacement rates did fall below 1.0 in the period 1348–1450, but that was an exceptional time of plague and suffering.[6] Postan has explicitly made the link between replacement rates and mobility through opportunity for young men to find land. "When men were so plentiful, and land so scarce, the normal advancement of men by succession was denied to many—perhaps most—of the young people."[7]

Suppose, on the one hand, that extended families are the norm, while replacement rates are high. The non-heirs stay on the farm with the inferior status of celibate helper, except for those who move out, marry an heir, or obtain an occupation in a craft, in the church, or in the army. If, on the other hand, nuclear families are the norm, then the heir hires servants and workers instead of his unmarried kin to help on the farm. These servants and workers are themselves non-heirs from other peasant lineages. The loss of status that non-heirs suffer in comparison with their own father's is probably more serious if they have to hire themselves out as servants and laborers than if they stay celibate on the ancestral farm as in the case of the extended family. Moreover, geographical mobility is higher since there is a crossing of village limits to find positions. One can see that in this type of society the predominant status mobility flow for the largest section of the

6 H. E. Hallam, "Some Thirteenth-Century Censuses," *Economic History Review*, X (1958), 340–361. Sylvia Thrupp, "The Problem of Replacement Rates in Late Medieval English Population," *ibid.*, XVIII (1965), 101–119. T. H. Hollingsworth, *Historical Demography* (Ithaca, 1969), 378–379.

7 M. M. Postan, *The Cambridge Economic History of Europe,* (Cambridge, 1966, 2d ed.), I, 564.

Fig. 1 Career Paths for Farmers' Children

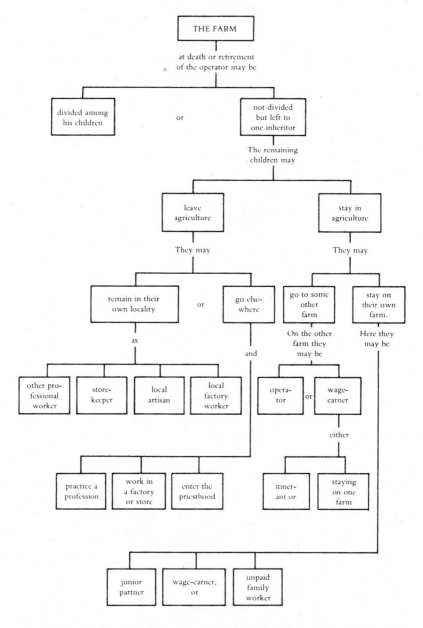

SOURCE: Nathan Keyfitz, "Population Problems," in Marcel Rioux and Yves Martin (eds.), *French-Canadian Society* (Toronto, 1964), I, 225; reprinted by permission of McClelland and Stewart, Ltd., Toronto, and the Carleton Library Board.

population, the peasantry, is downward. Chances of status improvement exist for the peasantry but are confined to the replenishment of the ranks of the church and army and to marriage with an heir. The higher the net reproduction rate, the stronger the downward flow.

If partible inheritance prevails, however, all the male offspring split the land at each generation. Male geographical mobility is constrained.[8] All of the sons stay in the village and acquire the father's occupation and status of a German *Bauer*, a Flemish *landsman,* an English yeoman, or a French *laboureur.* The prevailing norm of family organization determines whether farms are actually split or not by the division of property. Partible inheritance does not result in splitting of farms in the (relatively rare) case where all the heirs stay together as joint households. Fragmentation takes place if families are nuclear. A downward trend of status mobility is experienced to the extent that nuclear families are formed in the context of a high net rate of reproduction, since farms eventually become very small. However, if all lineages reproduce themselves at the same rate, the contraction of holding size depresses the income of all the peasants proportionately, without affecting their relative position.

In order to accommodate a rapidly growing population, the society may split into a class of heirs and one of non-heirs, thereby

---

8 In reality, the range of variation in inheritance systems is much broader than the opposition presented here between strict partibility and strict impartibility. Moreover, some additional possibilities are neglected, for instance the variation of retirement customs. In some cases the father handed over the land to his heir at the time of the latter's marriage in exchange for a written promise of support. In others, inheritance only occurred after the father's death. See Berkner, "The Stem Family and the Developmental Cycle of the Peasant Household: An Eighteenth-Century Austrian Example," *American Historical Review,* LXXVII (1972), 398–418. In some places, it was the custom to send the children off as servants of other households, perhaps temporarily. This fact introduces another dimension to the relationships between family structure and mobility. See Schofield, "Age-Specific Mobility," 261–271; Peter Laslett, *The World we have lost* (London, 1965), 14ff; Peter Laslett and John Harrison, "Clayworth and Cogenhoe," *Historical Essays 1600–1750, presented to David Ogg* (London, 1964), 170. For extensive discussions of inheritance systems in relation to family structure or demographic patterns, see, among others, Berkner and Mendels, "Inheritance Systems"; G. C. Homans, *English Villagers in the Thirteenth Century* (Cambridge, Mass., 1942), 109–222; Rosamond Jane Faith, "Peasant Families and Inheritance Customs in Medieval England," *Agricultural History Review,* XIV (1966), 77–95; Philip J. Greven, Jr., *Four Generations: Population, Land, and Family in Colonial Andover, Massachusetts* (Ithaca, 1970); H. J. Habakkuk, "Family Structure and Economic Change in Nineteenth-Century Europe," *Journal of Economic History,* XV (1955), 1–12.

generating a distinct social stratification. Or it may preserve a fairly homogeneous peasant class at the cost of depressing the incomes of all. As Smith observed, "How property is divided among heirs is always one of the determinants of class structure, powerful in proportion as other ways to wealth are closed. When completely closed, what a man inherits must fix his class position permanently and perhaps even that of his descendants through several generations. This situation was approximated in most parts of rural Japan in the seventeenth century."[9]

The pace at which class structure shapes itself depends on demographic determinants. The reasoning presented here assumes that the latter are given from the start, as well as the inheritance practices and family structure, an assumption only used for expository purposes. One must realize that these three data in fact interact. We simply do not know that any one set of them is more stable or at least more "given," thus more determining, than the others.[10]

The model which has been developed here is overly simple and its assumptions constraining. However, it is useful in the sense that relaxing its underlying premises is somewhat analogous to reading descriptions of social and economic changes that historians give of European countries emerging from the Dark Ages. New land is cleared in Europe or conquered overseas. Agricultural technology permits a better utilization of the existing land. Industrial occupations as well as positions in the tertiary sector of the economy are opened up. Cities grow, commodity markets expand, and a market in land is established. For instance, next to Weston and Moulton in Lincolnshire, the village of Spalding had deviated considerably from the ideal type as early as the thirteenth century. Out of 180 freemen, 25 percent bore the names of trades or professions. Most of the land was fragmented into tiny holdings and 20 percent of the 426 tenants lived on bought land. Many people settled in cottages along the river banks or the market place, and it appears that "commercial and industrial factors were

9 Thomas C. Smith, *Agrarian Origins of Modern Japan* (Stanford, Cal., 1959), 37.
10 The choice of an exogenous and determining variable is somewhat arbitrary but often seems related to one's relative ignorance. The more superficial one's understanding of a variable is, the more likely one is to treat it as given and determining.

more important in deciding the social structure of Spalding than inheritance customs."[11]

These changes have one effect in common, namely, to disengage occupational, status, and geographical mobility processes from the mechanism by which land is obtained, improved, increased, and passed along to the next generation. Indeed, it is very hard to find in a country such as France a small area in which the importance of inheritance rules is not mitigated, in early modern times, by the existence of leaseholds, by a land market, by nearby rural industries, let alone by the presence of a growing town. Even apparently isolated Pyrenean valleys, such as the valleys of the Ariège near Foix, the Bigorre, or the Valley of Aure, with their abundant sources of water power, provided a fertile ground for iron and textile industries.[12] This is not to say that the family-inheritance-population links cease to operate; only that they operate in a much larger network of interacting forces and therefore lose most of their determining power. It would therefore be an enormous task to construct a single model of mobility for an industrializing society. Presented instead are some thoughts on how the processes of mobility were linked with economic change according to the phase or type of industrialization in which an economy was engaged.

Well before the Industrial Revolution, various regions of Europe experienced an unprecedented growth in manufacturing. This type of "industrialization," however, was still remote from what is usually meant by the term. In particular, it was not carried out in factories and with machines coordinated to one source of power. There was nothing that prefigured the assembly line, yet it was not merely a growth of handicrafts for local markets. This causes some semantic ambiguity and has led me to define a phase of "proto-industrialization."[13] A number of features characterizes this phase and separates it from other subsequent phases of indus-

---

11   Hallam, "Some Thirteenth-Century Censuses," 348. Paul R. Hyams, "The Origins of a Peasant Land Market in England," *Economic History Review*, XXIII (1970), 18–31.

12   In eighteenth-century Flanders, inheritance law was far less important to explain what happened than market forces: Mendels, "Agriculture and Peasant Industry in Eighteenth-Century Flanders," in William N. Parker and E. L. Jones (eds.), *European Peasants and Their Markets* (Princeton, 1975), 179–204. Michel Chevalier, *La vie humaine dans les Pyrénées ariégoises,* (Paris, 1956).

13   Mendels, "Proto-industrialization: The First Phase of the Process of Industrialization," *Journal of Economic History,* XXXII (1972), 241–261.

trialization. On the one hand, the industrial role of cities was confined to a rather small share of manufacturing employment. One could thus say that there was industrialization without cognate urbanization. On the other hand, it was in the cities that the final stages of various production processes were carried out, e.g., those which were most intensive in the use of highly skilled craftsmen commanding high wages. The cities also gathered the men of enterprise who "put out" the work to be done by the peasants of the outlying districts or by urban craftsmen, or who purchased the finished goods sold by independent self-employed peasants at the weekly market and organized their sale to other regions or countries. Towns traded in agricultural goods and accommodated the *rentiers,* the professional men, and the men of government. And of course all these functions created employment opportunities for domestic servants and shopkeepers.

The growth of cities and the opportunities thus created for upward social mobility within them, as well as for movement into the city from the surrounding countryside, were small during this phase in comparison with what was to come later. But, as we have seen, the fact that growth was sluggish did not preclude a sizable fraction of the surrounding rural population from moving to the city anyway. Undoubtedly, many of these migrants were pushed out rather than pulled in; they simply joined the ranks of the vagrants and beggars and came to the cities because the charitable institutions and asylums were there. But, as capital requirements in both trade and industry were very small, and as the level of skills required for success in business and industrial ventures did not go far beyond literacy, both capital and skills could be acquired in a few years. Therefore, artisans with some spirit of enterprise could become merchant-manufacturers more easily than in the early seventeenth, and certainly more easily than in the late nineteenth century.[14]

If we now look at the situation in the countryside during this period, what is characteristic of the regions which are launched on the path of proto-industrialization is the domination of strong forces favoring downward social mobility. The introduction of new opportunities for land-saving occupations in the village considerably modified the mechanisms through which wealth and

14   See Dorothy Marshall, "La structure sociale de l'Angleterre du dix-huitième siècle," in Roland Mousnier (ed.), *Problèmes de stratification sociale* (Paris, 1968), 101–116.

status were passed on from one generation to the next. A cottage industry made it possible for families to survive in the countryside on very small holdings of land, since the produce of that land could be supplemented by another source of sustenance. This might have led to improved standards of living. But some demographic studies show that areas which turned to cottage industry tended to attract immigration, had earlier and more marriages, and had higher fertility than other rural areas. And there are many regions of Europe where an impressive growth of this type of manufacturing was accompanied by equally impressive poverty. This seems to have been the case among the peasants in the interior of Brittany, in Bas-Maine, the Beauvaisis, the interior of Flanders, Limburg, Overijssel, Ulster, and many other regions. In these European societies, where status was closely associated with ownership or control over landed property, if, from generation to generation, an increasing percentage of families did not have enough land to support themselves—although often too much to be called landless—downward status mobility would result. Furthermore, this loss of land was compounded in some areas by the loss of control over the tools of their industry by peasants who previously had owned them. This was another step downward on a path which ultimately led to a total dependence on wages and the labor market. [15]

Another process led in the same direction. Agricultural progress in regions of commercial farming was as characteristic of the phase of proto-industrialization as was the growth of cottage industry in areas of subsistence farming. The form of agricultural progress in this phase had certain effects on social mobility. The consolidation of plots and the appropriation of common lands resulted in pushing many of those who were already at the lower rungs further down to the ranks of landless wage earners. This did not necessarily mean a loss of income or employment. On the contrary, since the process of "enclosures" was accompanied, in-

15 Mendels. "Proto-industrialization," 249–253; G. E. Mingay, *Enclosure and the Small Farmer in the Age of the Industrial Revolution* (London, 1968), Karlheinz Blaschke, "Soziale Gliederung und Entwicklung der sächsischen Landbevölkerung im 16. bis 18. Jahrhundert," *Zeitschrift für Agrargeschichte und Agrarsoziologie,* IV (1956), 144–155; Kenneth Lockridge, "Land, Population, and the Evolution of New England Society, 1630–1790," *Past & Present,* 39 (1968), 62–80; Pierre Léon, *Economies et sociétés pré-industrielles 1650–1780* II (Paris, 1970), II, 330–346. On the loss of control over tools, Paul Mantoux, *The Industrial Revolution in the Eighteenth Century* (London, 1961, rev. ed.), 64–65.

deed stimulated, by increased demand for agricultural products, and since the new rotation techniques then introduced tended to be labor-intensive or to require at least temporary increases in labor demand for hedging, etc., the newly created agricultural wage earners could find employment easily in the countryside—so they did not *have to* flock to the cities.[16] But they had become wage earners, nevertheless, and this was perceived as lower status.

A different facet of social mobility, namely migration, was also characteristically affected by proto-industrialization. One economic change in this phase was the increased interaction between agriculture and manufacturing in the countryside. The divergence which has been observed between the areas of subsistence farming and those of commercial agriculture gave rise to increased efficiency, and not only through the normal effects of division of labor and specialization. The subsistence farming areas exported labor, their surplus resource, to the commercial farming areas. As demand for labor in farming was highly seasonal, only a small fraction of the laborers hired for the summer were needed for the rest of the year on the commercial farms. It was easiest for commercial farms to hire workers for only a few weeks when there existed nearby an area which could export them. The growth of cottage industry in subsistence farming areas, by promoting the settlement in some areas of a dense population, helped the development of commercial farming. The development of rural industry near an area with seasonal agricultural labor needs made it unnecessary to use the gangs of migrant laborers that annually descended from the hills, mountains, or poor lands of Europe to the rich fertile plains.[17] One could instead tap the large local supplies by way of short-distance migration.

Since there is a shortage of rigorous empirical studies of social mobility during this phase of industrialization, the picture I have been drawing of the relations between mobility and economic change remains hypothetical. The hypothesis can be summarized

16 Chambers, "Enclosure and Labour Supply in the Industrial Revolution," in E. L. Jones (ed.), *Agriculture and Economic Growth in England, 1650–1815* (London, 1967), 94–127.
17 Roger Béteille. "Les migrations saisonnières en France sous le Premier Empire. Essai de Synthèse," *Revue d'histoire moderne et contemporaine,* XVII (1970), 424–441; Mendels, "Industrialization and Population Pressure in Eighteenth-Century Flanders," unpub. diss. (University of Wisconsin, 1970), 109ff; Arthur Redford, *Labour Migration in England 1800–1850* (Manchester, 1964, rev. ed.), 3–6, 141–149; Abel Châtelain, "Les migrations temporaires françaises au XIXe siècle," *Annales de démographie historique, 1967* (Paris, 1967), 9–28.

in the statement that as work constantly alternated between agriculture and manufacturing, the peculiar sort of occupational mobility which resulted had no parallel in terms of status mobility, but proto-industrialization promoted increases in both upward and downward status mobility from different causes. Finally, by helping the settlement of labor close to where agriculture needed it seasonally, it tended to reduce the need for the seasonal immigration of manpower from remote areas. Was proto-industrialization in turn affected by prevailing modes of social mobility? Did mobility facilitate the process of proto-industrialization?

Landes, Kemp, and Perkin have assigned a determining role to social stratification and mobility.[18] At a general level it is argued that more flexible definitions of class and a higher degree of mobility have facilitated the process of industrialization in England. Conversely, it is said that the comparative *ease* with which successful French businessmen used their new wealth to climb up and out of the business world partly explains French backwardness. The same role has been assigned to the existence of a very large and open *hidalgo* class in Spain. Finally, when one considers that mobility may have even declined in England during the crucial decades preceding its industrial revolution, it seems that the argument that comparative ease of upward mobility into a privileged, old-regime upper class facilitated economic progress by providing achievement incentives is dubious at a general level. What remains, however, is that England was a country where the nobility had no legal definition or privileges, and where up and down movements between the aristocracy and the merchant class were comparatively frequent. The actual practice of primogeniture among the upper levels of English society meant that the younger sons of English nobles commonly had to work for a living. In France the nobility avoided division of the land as well, but titles and such privileges as tax exemption were passed down even to the non-heirs. Moreover the rules of *dérogeance* placed a strong deterrent in the way of younger sons going into trade and industry (except long distance trade, glass making and mining) since it would entail a loss of highly valued status and privileges. The incentives to purchase an office in the Church, army, or bureaucracy

18 David Landes, *The Unbound Prometheus* (Cambridge, 1969); Tom Kemp, *Industrialization in Nineteenth-Century Europe* (London, 1969); Harold Perkin, *The Origins of Modern English Society, 1780–1880* (London, 1969).

were all the stronger, and this reduced the flow of skills and capital into trade and industry.[19]

We can see the results of these social values on the development of agriculture. The possession of a country estate was a prerequisite to social prestige, but to make it into a profitable possession by careful personal supervision would be less rewarding than engaging in "conspicuous consumption" in the neighboring town, in Paris, or in Versailles. This meant that the immediate aim and long run policy of many French landlords was to squeeze as much surplus from the peasantry as was possible, thus removing any incentive on the part of the latter to improve yields. The manner in which taxes were assessed in this period had the same depressing effect on the peasantry insofar as the burden of the *taille* (from which nobles, clergy, and many towns were exempt) was distributed by the villagers in accordance with apparent wealth. The tax system, in other words, added its effects to the value system by reinforcing the strict compartmentalization of French society.[20] These differences between French and English society first appeared long before the beginnings of industrialization. Their persistence in the eighteenth century is the result of political forces, so that it would be fair to say that these differences played the role of an exogenous variable in the process of economic change.

Many of the characteristics of proto-industrialization (such as the continued importance of rural industries) did not disappear with the end of this phase and the beginning of the next. Nevertheless, it is comparatively easy to locate the coming of the second phase of industrialization, for the defining novelty of that new phase was the introduction of the factory system and the new industrial organization which it entailed.[21] In the phase of industrial history which preceded the introduction of the factory system, the

19 Lawrence Stone, "Social Mobility in England, 1500–1700," *Past & Present*, 33 (1966), 16–55; Alexis de Tocqueville (ed. J.-P. Mayer), *L'ancien régime et la Révolution* (Paris, 1964); Landes, *Prometheus,* 67, 129; Habakkuk, "England," in Albert Goodwin (ed.), *The European Nobility in the Eighteenth Century* (New York, 1967, rev. ed.), 1–21; Joan Thirsk, "Younger Sons in the Seventeenth Century," *History,* LIV (1969), 358–377; R. B. Grassby, "Social Status and Commercial Enterprise under Louis XIV," *Economic History Review,* XIV (1961), 19–38.

20 Tocqueville, *L'ancien régime,* 170, 209.

21 For a discussion of the processes which led to the Industrial Revolution and the manner in which proto-industrialization paved the way for further changes, see Mendels, "Proto-industrialization," 241–247.

growing number of households engaged in industrial work had not yet become fully specialized. Typically, agriculture and industry had complemented each other on each farm, and the family household along with its servants remained the focus of production and consumption as well as the fundamental unit of decision-making in family life. The creation of full-time, centralized, and specialized employment now caused disturbances in the household. Specialization and division of labor first meant the end of the traditional alternation of tasks between agriculture and industry. It also meant the separation of the workplace from home, and, sooner or later, the separation of family members during their working hours. To the extent that factory work demanded more attentiveness than dexterity or strength, a large fraction of the factory labor force could be constituted by children.[22]

Whether the introduction of the factory system facilitated upward social mobility is part of a larger debate, with an extensive literature, on the social consequences of the Industrial Revolution. First, that wages were often higher in factories than in the domestic system does not prove much. Rents and food prices were higher in the cities, and income from factory work could not be supplemented as easily with other sources as could rural domestic work with wages earned from harvest work or from the produce of one's own plot. Moreover, the wages had to be higher in the factories to compensate workers for the drudgery of coordinated and disciplined tasks. For this seems to have been the most detestable part of factory work: the regularity and monotony involved in it. From the means that had to be used in the early days by the factory masters, it appears that this kind of industrial organization was most undesirable for the workers. There are cases when the recruitment of the labor force was achieved through the penitentiary system.[23]

Second, the mechanization of a given industrial process naturally meant severe downward pressure on the earnings of those industrial workers who were eventually replaced or displaced by it. Since the factory system was not introduced in all in-

22 Neil J. Smelser, *Social Change in the Industrial Revolution* (Chicago, 1959), 180–312.
23 Sidney Pollard, *The Genesis of Modern Management* (Baltimore, 1965, 2d ed.), 189–231; the penitentiary in Ghent, Belgium, was turned over to textile manufacturers after the end of the eighteenth century. See also Roger Portal, "Serfs in the Urals Iron Foundries in the Eighteenth Century," in Val Lorwin (ed.), *Labor and Working Conditions in Modern Europe* (New York, 1967), 17–30.

dustries or processes at the same time and pace, not all categories of workers were affected in this manner at the same time either. The story of the shifting relations between the status and earnings of spinners and weavers, as spinning and weaving were modernized in a piecemeal fashion, has often been told.[24] This phenomenon was repeated in several industries during this phase.

Third, the separation of the family in different places of employment could result in the disintegration of the authority of the head of household, especially if his wife or children could earn a wage in the factory that could match or surpass his own. This was the case for the cotton handloom weavers during their period of decline. Nevertheless, it must also be recalled that the early textile factories sometimes hired entire families and, in such cases, the relative position of family members was maintained.[25]

Fourth, a large part of the first generation of factory workers was made up not of déclassé skilled artisans but of rural landless laborers. Was it downward mobility for the landless son of a small Irish peasant to end up in the factory after some years spent as summer harvest labor and in casual winter work?[26] It is therefore impossible to generalize on the balance of forces which led to upward or downward status mobility for the working class in this complex, revolutionary phase of industrialization. Specific groups experienced gains or losses in their status and income due to economic and technological forces which varied according to time, place, and occupation.

However, more can be said about other types of mobility. The rise of the factory system was accompanied by rapid urbanization and the growth of such new industrial centers as Barmen, Roubaix, and Manchester. Older cities also grew through the immigration of wage laborers, servants, craftsmen, and unskilled industrial workers. Furthermore, somewhat more definite statements can be made in this phase about status mobility for the middle and high levels of society. Skilled artisans as well as shopkeepers were then most favorably affected by the prevailing economic trends. This was a phase when skilled artisans were needed among

24 Mantoux, *Industrial Revolution*, 189–310; Landes, *Prometheus*, 84–87.
25 Smelser, *Social Change*, 188.
26 See Thernstrom, "Notes on the Historical Study of Social Mobility," *Comparative Studies in History and Society*, X (1968), 166, 168; Eric E. Lampard, "The Social Impact of the Industrial Revolution," in Melvin Kranzberg and C. W. Pursell, Jr. (eds.), *Technology in Western Civilization* (New York, 1967), I, 315–316.

the factory labor force in supervisory positions and for the non-repetitive tasks of maintaining and repairing tools and machinery. Few skilled artisans were yet replaced and downgraded by machine work in these early years. Those who were downgraded were among the unskilled ones, whose tasks had begun to be simulated by the still simple machines.[27] There were, moreover, numerous artisans during this phase who could enter the managerial or entrepreneurial ranks in their own lifetime. It was an age of unprecedented opportunities for those already endowed with skills, capital, or entrepreneurship. And the amounts of skill and capital needed were still such that they could be accumulated by individuals over a few years.[28]

Social mobility patterns, in turn, had an effect on the possibilities of industrialization under the factory system. The French "land reform" of the revolutionary period provides a good example of such mechanisms when it is compared with the effect of the German land reforms of the first half of the nineteenth century. The French land reform reinforced the control of the peasantry over the land it cultivated. This can be set against the disappearance of the peasantry in England and Germany. Here, peasants were finally able to gain personal freedom, but had to purchase it by surrendering a certain fraction of the land over which they previously had control. For many it meant descent into the ranks of the landless; whatever land remained in their hands was insufficient for sustenance, and they were likely to sell it in order to move to the city or to areas where rural wage labor was in demand. Meanwhile, those who were initially better off were able to consolidate and augment their holdings by purchasing at low prices the land that fell on the market in this manner.[29] Here is an example of the exogenous and causal effect of mobility patterns on industrialization for there is no doubt that the paths taken by "land

27 There are exceptions, like the wool croppers. See E. P. Thompson, *The Making of the English Working Class* (New York, 1966, 2d ed.), 521–533.

28 Herbert G. Gutman, "The Reality of the Rags-to-Riches 'Myth': The Case of the Paterson, New Jersey, Locomotive, Iron, and Machinery Manufacturers, 1830–1880," *Nineteenth-Century Cities,* 98–125; Eric J. Hobsbawm, *The Age of Revolution* (New York, 1964), 218–237.

29 Kemp, *Industrialization,* 81–118; Werner Conze, "Agrarian Reform in Central Europe," in G. S. Métraux and François Crouzet (eds.), *The Nineteenth-Century World* (New York, 1963), 86–103. Wolfgang Köllmann, "Les mouvements migratoires pendant la période d'industrialisation de la Rhénanie-Westphalie," *Annales de Démographie Historique, 1971* (Paris, 1972), 91–120.

reform" in France and Germany resulted more from political struggles than from previous industrialization. The effects of these struggles on the pace at which factory industrialization proceeded must have been important. The French peasantry was not pushed as strongly into the labor market, agricultural or industrial, as it would have been otherwise. Many of the French peasants, however, did not hold enough land to subsist on agriculture alone, so they complemented their incomes with the product of their rural manufacturing. As long as they stayed on the land and drew some income from it, their manufacturing wage rate, actual or implicit, could remain lower than the subsistence wage rate of urban workers who had no such complement. This helped to slow down the pace of factory-industrialization in France. Furthermore, the effect of the land reforms was not solely felt through the supply of labor: the poor but solidly established peasantry did not provide the modern industrial sector with a mass market for its products. It was not only that much was produced locally, but also that patterns of demand among the peasantry must have been less favorable for the growth of mass-produced consumer goods than would be the case among an urban population.[30]

The next phase (or type) of industrialization to consider is one where producers' goods are predominant in output or employment, or in shaping the growth of a particular locality. This phase, which can also be called the age of steel, was characterized by the rise of heavy industry as the leading sector. Advanced countries of Western Europe entered into it during the second half of the nineteenth century, although its chronological as well as conceptual borders with the previous phase are blurred. It must have induced a number of important changes in the processes of social mobility.

First, the development of heavy industry considerably increased fixed capital requirements over the previous phase. The more complex machinery also demanded much higher levels of technical skills among broad sections of the labor force; perhaps among the operators, but surely among those who designed and maintained them. As such industries now benefited from economies of scale, the advantage passed to the big industrial concerns whose administrations in turn created an unprecedented de-

---

30 Landes, *Prometheus,* 127–138, 187–192.

mand for white-collar employees. The considerable progress of engineering had an impact on the countryside as well as the cities. It was in this period that certain technical problems involved in attempting to mechanize the traditional industries were finally solved, as, for example, in wool combing. This determined the progressive but now irreversible decline of a number of handicrafts which had hitherto been protected from technological unemployment by their intricate nature. The demise of these last remnants of the old manufacturing system had a great impact. The disappearance of handicrafts from the countryside and the continued expansion of factory employment opportunities sharply increased the pace of rural depopulation. As this was also a phase when railroads were being built, large-scale population movements were being facilitated. But they created serious shortages in the countryside—the big farms could no longer rely on the summer work of the former peasant-craftsmen, who were now emigrating permanently. Mechanical reapers and other labor-saving machinery had to be introduced to replace them. I have selected the characteristics of this phase which strike the eye for their novelty. One must keep in mind that the continuing development of cities did also help the number and prosperity of shopkeepers as well as those in the building trades and other small-scale enterprises, all of which continued quantitatively to be of great importance in national economies.[31]

Thus, on the one hand, in view of the much increased capital requirements of new factories, this was no longer the age of individual entrepreneurs. Spectacular rises in business were more likely to need the mustering of scattered sources of capital in joint-stock companies or through the intermediation of financial institutions. Both the corporation and the bank were at the source of the creation of a large class of professional and clerical white-collar employees. As the capital accumulation necessary for in-

31   Philippe Pinchemel, *Structures sociales et dépopulation rurale dans les campagnes picardes de 1836 à 1936* (Paris, 1957), 106–120; John Saville, *Rural Depopulation in England and Wales, 1850–1950* (London, 1957), 20–30. E. J. T. Collins, "Labour Supply and Demand in European Agriculture, in E. L. Jones and S. J. Woolf (eds.), *Agrarian Change and Economic Development* (London, 1969), 61–94; Paul M. Hohenberg, "Change in Rural France in the Period of Industrialization, 1830–1914," *Journal of Economic History*, XXXII (1972), 227–231; T. J. Markovitch, "The Dominant Sectors of French Industry," in Rondo Cameron (ed.), with the assistance of F. Mendels and J. Ward, *Essays in French Economic History* (Homewood, Ill., 1970), 237–240.

dustrial success reached beyond the means of individuals, it is not surprising that a certain closing of opportunities for individual advancement through industrial or commercial success has been observed.[32] It resulted also from the rising technical complexity of most sectors of the economy which manifested itself among the managerial ranks of industry and in the development of large bureaucracies. On the other hand, there were enough areas left to small-scale enterprise; once more, it is hard on a priori grounds to make any general prediction.

A crucial novelty of this age with respect to the optimum path for social advancement was the importance of formal education. In the first, revolutionary phase of the Industrial Revolution in England, there initially had been a decline in literacy but jobs were being created which did not need literacy. The rising literacy of the 1830s may well have "led merely to a decline in mobility because the new jobs were not such as to absorb the literate in any case, in contrast, for example, to the creation of the vast clerk class at the end of the nineteenth century."[33] Indeed it is in this phase of industrialization that primary education first became a prerequisite for employment in a large section of the labor force, among the skilled factory workers as well as the growing army of white-collar workers. On the one hand, education opened up new avenues for social ascent because large corporations had a growing need for engineers, draftsmen, accountants, lawyers, etc. More generally, formal education facilitated inter-generational status improvements by opening rewarding careers to graduates of educational institutions whose entrance requirements were becoming, at least formally, blind to family origins. On the other hand, the bureaucratization of economic activity must have modified mobility patterns by curbing intra-generational mobility. Formal education acquired during youth, if it led to a recognized diploma, would place the laureate at the bottom of a hierarchical scale which

---

32   Perkin, *Modern English Society,* 424–428; Charlotte Erickson, *British Industrialists: Steel and Hosiery, 1850–1950* (Cambridge, 1959), 12, 56, 93, 129, cited in Perkin, *Modern English Society,* 425; Irene D. Neu and Frances W. Gregory, "The American Industrial Elite in the 1870s: Their Social Origins," in William Miller (ed.), *Men in Business* (New York, 1962), 193–211.

33   M. Sanderson, "Literacy and Social Mobility in the Industrial Revolution in England," *Past & Present,* 56 (1972), 102; Carlo M. Cipolla, *Literacy and Development in the West* (Baltimore, 1969), 62–99; Lenore O'Boyle, "The Problem of an Excess of Educated Men in Western Europe, 1800–1850," *Journal of Modern History,* XLII (1970), 471–495.

he would ascend with seniority. Formal education acquired at an early stage now strongly determined the life pattern of income and promotion for an increasing number of people.[34]

Cross-national comparisons, once more, show that social institutions could have had important effects on patterns of industrialization. The English economy experienced some setbacks in this period while the German and American economies were pulling ahead. Landes has assigned a large share of responsibility for English retardation to an educational system which failed to provide the economy with the needed skills, contrary to the German case. The English continued to rely much longer on the acquisition of skills by individuals through experience and on recruitment by patronage. The more rigid and authoritarian style of social interaction and stratification which prevailed in Germany nonetheless led to the creation of a schooling system and pattern of recruitment more favorable for rapid economic expansion. And yet it could hardly be said that it was previous backwardness in England which had in any sense prepared the way by bringing with it a schooling system of the German type. The creation of this school system can be traced back to the late eighteenth century. It must be ranked as an independent and exogenous event with largely unanticipated effects. The remarkable fluidity of English social stratification in the first two phases of industrialization undoubtedly contributed to the flourishing of industrial enterprise through individual initiatives. But this kind of mobility was no longer sufficient to promote industrial development under the economic conditions prevailing in this phase of industrialization.[35]

The last phase of industrial history began when the movement toward urban-industrial concentration was reversed in the late nineteenth century in Europe as well as in America. The rise of new sources of energy, petroleum and electricity, and the perfecting of the internal combustion engine contributed to a modification of the balance of costs and benefits of urban-industrial concentration at nodal points. The automobile and truck allowed a new flexibility not afforded by the railroad system. The use of electricity in industry also slowed down the trend toward

34 Hobsbawm, *The Age of Revolution*, 229.
35 Landes, *Prometheus*, 339ff, 348; O'Boyle, "An Excess of Educated Men," 485. See Margaret Scotford-Morton, "Some English and French Notions of Democracy in Education," *Archives Européennes de Sociologie*, VIII (1967), 152–161.

concentration which the steam engine had imparted.[36] The decentralization of industry was thus accompanied by the suburbanization of cities. Most of the economic forces which determined patterns of social mobility in the previous phase continued to operate in this new one as well. What had been said about the importance of education continued to be true. But the declining benefits of concentration could have been linked to new patterns of mobility. As the new industries, employing the largest proportion of highly skilled workers and employees, settled in the suburbs or the countryside (e.g., Princeton and Hightstown, New Jersey), rapid economic growth modified the social structure of the city itself. Upward mobility was accompanied by emigration from the city. The service industries, the banks, and the headquarters of many national corporations first remained in the center of the city, but the emergence of a new technology of communications rapidly diminished the advantages of central location for them as well.

The centrifugal forces characteristic of this phase also meant that countries where such forces were not given free rein, or where others counteracted them strongly, experienced economic difficulties. It is true that postwar French growth has been rapid, but one may justly wonder how much more rapid it would have been if a number of customs and institutions had not prevented the decentralization of the secondary and tertiary sectors instead of promoting the continued growth of Paris and its suburbs.[37] It has been a part of the national tradition of government and social life of that country for a long time that almost every initiative flows from the capital, leaving little power in the hands of localities. One result has been that migration to Paris has been a necessary means of upward social mobility. Whereas in another phase of industrialization this was a force promoting modernization (but it did not operate strongly then in France because of a peculiar rural social structure), its perpetuation in the contemporary world is an anachronistic force which causes a great misallocation of resources.

36 William N. Parker, "Economic Development in Historical Perspective," in Nathan Rosenberg (ed.), *The Economics of Technological Change,* (Baltimore, 1971), 137–147; Alexander Gerschenkron, "City Economies—Then and Now," in Oscar Handlin and John Burchard (eds.), *The Historian and the City* (Cambridge, Mass., 1963), 46–72; Eric Lampard, "The History of Cities in the Economically Advanced Areas," *Economic Development and Cultural Change,* III (1955), 124–126.
37 J. F. Gravier, *Paris et le désert français* (Paris, 1947); Tocqueville, *Ancien Régime,* 98–158.

This is an example of the persistence of a social pattern through several phases of industrialization, pointing to the need to consider national styles of social stratification and mobility as independent variables, not only as variables determined by economic development. Crozier's analyses of French society show how certain permanent traits in the national tradition of group or class interactions have affected the manner in which change and innovation could be introduced in that country throughout its modern history.[38] He argues that, on the one hand, there have been high barriers to mobility and communication between any levels of French society, class to class, profession to profession, or stratum to stratum within an occupation. On the other hand, there has been a high degree of egalitarianism within each of these levels, and much esprit de corps and camaraderie which make it possible to balance the strong centralizing tendencies. These characteristics and their multiple ramifications compose what he calls the "bureaucratic" system of social organization, entailing a certain pattern of social mobility and also explaining certain peculiarities of French economic history. The responsibility to innovate is left in the hands of the centralized authority of the state or the remote central headquarters of the company, at any rate not in the hands of those who are most directly affected by the innovation. The latter resist innovation which would disturb the social equilibrium prevailing at their level by leading to the promotion of some and the demotion of others. Although this style of social organization does not deter inventiveness, it does not provide a fertile ground for its practical application and therefore tends to prevent continuous change. When innovations are adopted by the force of blatant necessity, they are introduced from above, in a radical and sudden manner, and with considerable delays. An example would be the introduction of the railroad in France, postponed for several years by conflicts among vested interests until the legislature finally passed a law in 1842 outlining in a grand master plan the whole French network and the relations between the state and private enterprise.[39]

38 Michel Crozier, Le phénomène bureaucratique (Paris, 1971, 2d ed.), 247–347. For related aspects of French social structure, see Edmond Goblot, La barrière et le niveau (Paris, 1967, 2d ed.), 1–40; Jesse R. Pitts, "Continuity and Change in Bourgeois France," in Stanley Hoffmann et al., In Search of France (Cambridge, Mass., 1963), 235–304.
39 Arthur L. Dunham, La révolution industrielle en France (1815–1848) (Paris, 1953), 41–72.

What can an economic historian offer to those who undertake monographic studies or syntheses of social mobility during industrialization? Not much in terms of specific predictions. First, social mobility patterns are not unilaterally determined by what happens in industry or in the economy; on the contrary, the two mutually affect each other. Second, the interactions between mobility and economic change vary according to the type or phase in which a given local, regional, or national economy finds itself. Third, various kinds of mobility in a given period result from a number of economic changes, not all of which operate in the same direction. On theoretical and a priori grounds alone, therefore, there is little that can be said. Even for pre-industrial societies, which, in contrast, seem simpler to understand, predictions on the course of mobility can be made only for such particular economic and social structures that very few societies satisfy the conditions under which a model of mobility can be constructed at all. Only empirical research can reveal the course of mobility during industrialization in a given time and place.

On the other hand, an economic historian can certainly offer insights into some of the causative links which have operated in specific contexts, as I have done, for instance, for the phase of proto-industrialization. Focusing on the growth, persistence, transformations, and ultimate demise of rural (and urban) artisans reminds one that much is lost by assuming that industrialization is a linear process, and that comparing the two end points of that process should yield insights into social structure and mobility during the period examined. And yet, even though there is abundant information available on the artisan industries, modern economic historians themselves have failed to give them the place they deserve in abstract models and generalizations. Thus, students of mobility should not be blamed first if they experience difficulties in relating their findings to the dominant paradigms of economic history. A systematic and analytical economic history of artisan industries would be one step in bridging a gap.

Joel Mokyr

Industrialization and Poverty in Ireland and the Netherlands

the Netherlands A comparative study of Ireland and the Netherlands in the first half of the nineteenth century may appear far-fetched. The differences seem overwhelming. Economically, the Netherlands, although long past its glorious golden age, was still a prosperous country. It could rely on a wealthy and efficient agricultural sector, an important colonial empire, a large maritime sector, and a well-developed and highly monetized commercial structure.[1] Ireland, on the other hand, was regarded by contemporaries as one of Europe's poorest and most underdeveloped regions, and modern historians have not produced much evidence to the contrary.[2] Politically, too, the differences were great. Ireland's history after the Union with Great Britain in 1800 is one of bitterness and alienation, even though large-scale insurrections

Joel Mokyr is Associate Professor of Economics at Northwestern University. He is the author of *Industrialization in the Low Countries* (New Haven, 1976).

The research for this article was financed by the National Science Foundation Grant SOC 78-06710. Excellent research assistance by Michael Waks and Paul Zawa is acknowledged. The comments and suggestions of Louis Cain, Stanley Engerman, Cormac Ó'Gráda, Gavin Wright, and Harold R. C. Wright are gratefully appreciated.

1 Nineteenth-century Dutch agricultural history is essentially a *terra incognita* and is in need of thorough investigation. That Dutch agriculture was among the world's most advanced is likely to be modified but not reversed. Mokyr, *Industrialization in the Low Countries, 1795–1850* (New Haven, 1976), 5–6, 198–199; Zeger Willem Sneller, "Anderhalve Eeuw in Vogelvlucht, Part I: 1795–1880," in Sneller (ed.), *Geschiedenis van de Nederlandschen Landbouw, 1795–1940* (Groningen, 1943). To illustrate the significance of the colonial empire, the total East Indian goods auctioned off in the Netherlands between 1830 and 1850 amounted to 451 million guilders, of which about 215 million entered the Dutch treasury directly. For a fascinating description of the economic aspects of the Dutch empire in Indonesia, see H. Baudet and C. Fasseur, "Koloniale Bedrijvigheid," in J. H. Van Stuijvenberg (ed.), *De Economische Geschiedenis van Nederland* (Groningen, 1977).

2 For accounts of some knowledgeable travellers and well-informed contemporaries see Nicholas Mansergh, *The Irish Question, 1840–1921* (London, 1975; 3rd ed.), 37–75. The French agricultural economist Leonce de Lavergne wrote in 1855, "The agricultural history of Ireland . . . is as lamentable as those of England and Scotland are brilliant." Lavergne, *The Rural Economy of England, Scotland, and Ireland* (Edinburgh, 1855), 343. For a brief but useful overview of the consensus of present-day historians on Irish backwardness and poverty, see the essays in Louis Cullen (ed.), *The Formation of the Irish Economy* (Cork, 1969). My own computations indicate that Irish national income per capita may have been on the order of 60% of national income in Great Britain. This figure may seem high until one recalls that income per capita in real terms had been rising very slowly if at all in Great Britain before the 1840s.

were absent after 1798. The government and the established church were foreign to the majority of the people. Landownership was concentrated in the hands of a small class of landlords, many of whom were indifferent to the details of agricultural production and the fate of their tenants, and were often absent from their estates. In the Netherlands, after the restoration of 1813, one is struck by the comparative absence of deep conflicts, and the country earned a well-deserved reputation for languidness.[3]

Nonetheless, the two countries share two important features which merit comparison. First, both were seriously affected by the great famine of 1845–1850. Although no country went through a cataclysm like Ireland did, the Netherlands was more seriously affected than other Western European economies. This sheds a curious light on the differences listed above: why would a poor country like Ireland and an apparently wealthy country like the Netherlands undergo similar fates? Second, neither Ireland nor the Netherlands underwent much industrialization in the first half of the nineteenth century. What little industrialization that did take place occurred in small enclaves which were atypical of the rest of the economy: the Lagan Valley around Belfast in Ireland, and the areas of Twente and North Brabant in the Netherlands. Although their immediate neighbours underwent profound transformations, the Irish and the Dutch economies taken as a whole were both comparatively stagnant in the first half of the nineteenth century, even though they were then at different *levels* of development. Did the similar results come about from different or similar causes despite the striking dissimilarities between the two economies?

POVERTY AND CRISIS IN IRELAND AND THE NETHERLANDS   Economic historians today know that, although nineteenth-century industrialization did in most cases imply economic growth, economic growth did not necessarily mean an increase in the day to day consumption of the vast bulk of the population, let alone an increase in "economic welfare." The evidence suggests that the hypothesis of no drastic changes in living standards before 1850

3   The only exception to this calm may have been the response to the Belgian secession in 1830. Even in this case, however, the conflict between William I and his Parliament was late and brief. See E. H. Kossmann, *De Lage Landen, 1780–1940* (Amsterdam, 1976), 110–113, 124.

cannot be rejected. The benefits of the industrial revolution accrued largely to the third generation, whereas the first two generations paid the price and forewent the benefits. It might be tempting to conclude—following a fashionable stream in modern social thought—that industrialization was at best a mixed blessing, and that, by implication, economies which for one reason or another escaped it, were fortunate.[4]

Such a conclusion is totally unwarranted, for two reasons. First, as Gerschenkron and others have noted, those economies which started the industrialization process later often experienced a more costly and traumatic spurt, and thus probably paid a higher price for their industrialization, though the later date makes welfare comparisons meaningless. Although this consideration may be relevant to Eastern and Central Europe, it hardly applies to the Netherlands—which industrialized late but without any of the side-effects predicted by the Gerschenkronian framework—or to Ireland.[5]

Second, although economic growth during the first fifty years of the industrial revolution may not have raised the overall level of consumption on average, it changed the life of those who lived through it by gradually eliminating the great subsistence crises and catastrophes which struck Europe before and in the early stages of the industrial revolution. To state the issue in different terms, it is possible to redefine the concept of poverty in preindustrial and early industrial Europe. Although real income per capita, properly corrected for externalities and nonpecuniary items, remains a sound measure for many purposes, it is clearly insufficient. One reason, widely mentioned in the literature, is that a rise in income per capita, when accompanied by an increase in the inequality of income distribution, may do little to alleviate

4 M. W. Flinn, "Trends in Real Wages 1750–1850," *Economic History Review*, XXIV (1972), 65–80; Mokyr and N. Eugene Savin, "Some Econometric Problems in the Standard of Living Controversy," *Journal of European Economic History*, forthcoming; G. N. Von Tunzelmann, "Trends in Real Wages, 1750–1850, Revisited," *Economic History Review*, XXXII (1979), 33–49. For some evidence on living standards in other areas of early industrialization, see Mokyr, "Growing Up and the Industrial Revolution in Europe," *Explorations in Economic History*, XIII (1976), 392–393.

5 Alexander Gerschenkron, *Economic Backwardness in Historical Perspective* (Cambridge, Mass., 1962). The Dutch case is conveniently overlooked by Richard Roehl in his application of Gerschenkron's model to countries other than those in which Gerschenkron was primarily interested. See Roehl, "French Industrialization: A Reconsideration," *Explorations in Economic History*, XIII (1976), 233–281.

the poverty of the vast majority of the population. Even correcting for inequality may not, however, capture all the elements of poverty. As an alternative to the traditional measures, therefore, I suggest a new measure: poverty is higher, when the probability of a random individual at a random point in time dropping beneath subsistence is higher. The severity and frequency of subsistence crises thus become a strategic element in the measurement of poverty, and the elimination of these crises from the European scene is an indication of the disappearance of poverty by this absolute definition.

A few observations about this new measure are in order. First, the objection that the minimum of subsistence is not directly observed with much accuracy can be ignored. Income per capita, not to mention externalities, is not observed with much accuracy either. But death rates are available for many countries, and sharp increases in death rates ("excess mortality") can be associated with subsistence crises. Second, the new measure does correlate positively with the traditional measures of poverty. Poverty as defined above will fall, all other things equal, with a rise in income per capita and fall with an increase in equality. But it contains more information since it also takes into account the variance over time of income, as well as interactions between the variance over time and the cross-sectional variance at any given point of time. For instance, if we compare a case in which a crisis wipes out 10 percent of everyone's income to a case in which a disaster reduces national income by 10 percent by wiping out the income of the poorest 30 percent, the economy in the latter case would be considered to be poorer. Or consider two cases in which the poorest 30 percent of the population lose all their income. In one case the remaining 70 percent divert resources to prevent the worst from happening, whereas in the other case the mechanisms of poor relief fail in their task, or the government does not overcome the inherent "free rider" problems plaguing disaster relief efforts. The latter economy, according to our definition, would be said to be poorer.

Subsistence crises were becoming gradually rarer in nineteenth-century Europe. The crisis of 1816–17 struck the majority of the Western economies, and caused widespread increases in death rates as well as declines in birth and marriage statistics. All the same, the notion advanced by Post that 1816–17 was the "last subsistence crisis of the Western world" is open to criticism. The crisis of 1845–1850 was not confined to "restricted areas," and, although not as universal as that of 1816–17, was widespread. Thirty years of economic development and modernization had taken place in the Western world between the two disasters. Yet the 1845–1850 crisis should not be dismissed. As Post notes, "the steepness of the rise in the number of deaths is a more accurate indicator [of the severity of a subsistence crisis] . . . a rise in death rates signals a decline in biological well-being." In the entire region for which he was able to find information, Post concludes that death rates rose by about 9 percent in 1817, and then fell by slightly less than 7 percent the following year. By comparison, if we take average death rates from 1841 to 1845 as a crude approximation for the norm, we find that death rates in 1846 fell by 4 percent in Austria but rose the following year to 48 percent over the norm, and stayed at 37 percent above the norm in 1848. In France, the figures are respectively, 2.2 percent, 5.3 percent, and 4.0 percent above the norm, but in 1849 the death rate rose to 20.7 percent above normal. In Germany death rates are 4.2 percent above norm in 1846, 8.8 percent in 1847, and 11.5 percent in 1848. In Scandinavia, too, death rates were considerably higher in the late 1840s than average. However, the worst-hit countries in Europe were Ireland and the Netherlands.[6]

The great famine of 1845–1850 was without doubt the most traumatic event of modern Irish history. By the first half of the nineteenth century Ireland's consumption of potatoes had become astounding and the destruction of the staple crop in the 1840s inflicted upon the Irish the greatest natural demographic disaster of modern European history. A few statistics convey the dimensions of the disaster. Between 1846 and 1851 about 1.5 million famine-related casualties occurred in Ireland out of a population of about 8.3 million. Of these, about 1.1 million deaths were directly attributable to the famine (i.e., would not have occurred otherwise) and another 400,000 were "averted" births resulting from the sharply reduced birth and marriage rates during the great famine.[7]

6 John D. Post, *The Last Great Subsistence Crisis in the Western World* (Baltimore, 1977), 27, 108, 112–114. B. P. Mitchell, *European Historical Statistics 1750–1970* (London, 1975).
7 Total output of potatoes in a normal prefamine year was about 15 million tons, of which about 7 million was consumed directly by humans. More than half the population

The potato blight in the Netherlands has not received anything like the attention given to the Irish famine. This oversight is not justified even though the order of magnitude of the disaster was different in the two countries. Only two articles can be found in the literature that provide some details on the "hungry forties" in the Netherlands. Bergman suggests that the press and the government hushed up the extent of the disaster, so that literary sources are comparatively scarce. Therefore in order to get some idea of how extensive the disaster was, we have to rely on statistical evidence. The demographic data for the Netherlands for this period are considerably better than for Ireland, so that it is a fairly simple exercise to estimate the demographic impact of the potato famine in the Netherlands.[8]

The demographic dimensions of the famine in the Netherlands are represented in Table 1. The table presents the actual crude birth and death rates, and the gross population growth rates defined as the difference between births and deaths (ignoring migration). The values in parentheses are t-values which measure the intensity of the deviation of the observed rates for 1846–1849 from the normal rate in terms of the standard deviation. The normal rates are the average rates of birth, death, and natural growth for those countries in which these series were not subject to a time trend which was significant at least at the 10 percent level. When the trend was significant the normal rate was the rate

---

consumed an adult male equivalent of 12 lbs. a day, whereas another 22% consumed a male equivalent of 8 lbs. a day. A pound of potatoes yields about 346 calories and, when consumed with milk, provides all essential ingredients of an unbalanced but healthy diet. For details on the Irish diet see for instance K. H. Connell, *The Population of Ireland, 1750–1845* (Oxford, 1950), 121–162. For extensive evidence on the quantities of potatoes consumed see P. M. Austin Bourke, "The Use of the Potato Crop in Prefamine Ireland," *Journal of the Statistical and Social Inquiry Society of Ireland*, XXI (1968), 75–76. For details on the death estimates see Mokyr, "The Deadly Fungus: An Economic investigation into the Short-Term Demographic Impact of the Irish Famine, 1846–1851," in Julian Simon (ed.), *Research in Population Economics*, II, forthcoming.

8 Very little attention is paid to the famine in the Netherlands in general works dealing with nineteenth-century Dutch economic history, but the demographic aspects are covered in detail by E. W. Hofstee, *De Demografische Ontwikkeling van Nederland in de Eerste Helft van de 19ᵉ Eeuw* (Wageningen, 1977). M. Bergman, "The Potato Blight in the Netherlands and its Social Consequences, 1845–47," *International Review of Social History*, XII (1967), 390–431. Frida Terlouw, "De Aardappelziekte in Nederland in 1845 en Volgende Jaren," *Economisch en Sociaal-Historisch Jaarboek*, XXXIV (1971), 261–308. Terlouw's paper was written in 1950.

Table 1 Birth, Death, and Population Growth Rates, 1846–1849
In percentages (t-statistics in parentheses)

PROVINCE	1846			1847			1848			1849		
	BIRTH RATE	DEATH RATE	GROWTH RATE	BIRTH RATE	DEATH RATE	GROWTH RATE	BIRTH RATE	DEATH RATE	GROWTH RATE	BIRTH RATE	DEATH RATE	GROWTH RATE
North-Brabant	2.70 (-3.27)	2.33 (.15)	.36 (-1.83)	2.55 (-4.12)	2.48 (.90)	.07 (-2.76)	2.55 (-4.12)	2.51 (1.06)	.04 (-2.86)	2.99 (-1.50)	2.34 (.21)	.65 (-.93)
Gelderland	2.92 (-2.38)	2.40 (.95)	.51 (-2.00)	2.65 (-3.73)	2.51 (1.58)	.14 (-3.18)	2.96 (-2.12)	2.68 (2.54)	.29 (-2.72)	3.31 (-.35)	2.46 (1.26)	.85 (-.92)
South Holland	3.76 (-1.52)	3.51 (1.66)	.25 (-1.84)	3.55 (-2.58)	3.73 (2.58)	-.19 (-2.98)	3.64 (-2.13)	3.69 (2.41)	-.05 (-2.63)	4.05 (-.08)	4.72 (6.63)	-.67 (-4.23)
North Holland	3.88 (.27)	3.83 (1.44)	.04 (-1.07)	3.23 (-2.59)	4.41 (2.99)	-1.18 (-3.85)	3.52 (-1.29)	3.64 (.91)	-.12 (-1.44)	3.94 (.54)	3.98 (1.85)	-.04 (-1.28)
Zeeland	4.08 (-.37)	4.18 (2.45)	-.10 (-1.99)	3.50 (-2.49)	3.98 (2.02)	-.49 (-2.71)	3.61 (-2.01)	3.31 (.51)	.30 (-1.24)	4.18 (-.15)	3.19 (.27)	.99 (.05)
Utrecht	3.22 (-2.01)	2.93 (.48)	.28 (-1.78)	2.98 (-2.89)	3.40 (2.04)	-.43 (-3.60)	3.14 (-2.27)	3.40 (2.04)	-.26 (-3.16)	3.53 (-.84)	4.41 (5.39)	-.87 (-4.75)
Friesland	3.03 (-1.98)	2.72 (.74)	.31 (-1.24)	2.89 (-2.69)	2.87 (1.01)	.02 (-1.68)	2.90 (-2.64)	2.82 (.92)	.08 (-1.59)	3.62 (.99)	2.65 (.62)	.98 (-.24)
Overijssel	3.06 (-1.57)	2.75 (1.36)	.31 (-1.88)	3.00 (-1.80)	2.95 (2.41)	.05 (-2.65)	2.94 (-2.07)	2.89 (2.10)	.05 (-2.66)	3.46 (.14)	2.92 (2.24)	.54 (-1.19)
Groningen	3.16 (-1.24)	2.58 (.49)	.58 (-.80)	2.76 (-3.13)	3.00 (1.28)	-.24 (-2.04)	2.80 (-2.95)	2.95 (1.18)	-.15 (-1.90)	3.66 (1.09)	2.81 (.91)	.85 (-.39)
Drenthe	2.94 (-1.01)	2.94 (2.87)	0 (-2.99)	2.70 (-2.08)	3.02 (3.16)	-.33 (-3.86)	2.93 (-.97)	2.70 (1.99)	.23 (-2.38)	3.30 (.78)	2.97 (2.96)	.33 (-2.11)
Total Netherlands	3.34 (-1.85)	3.06 (1.60)	.28 (-2.15)	3.02 (-3.76)	3.29 (2.68)	-.27 (-3.99)	3.19 (-2.73)	3.13 (1.93)	.06 (-2.91)	3.64 (-.12)	3.37 (3.06)	.27 (-2.21)
Belgium	2.76 (-2.96)	2.49 (.12)	.27 (-2.52)	2.72 (-3.12)	2.77 (1.89)	-.05 (-3.75)	2.76 (-2.80)	2.48 (.06)	.28 (-2.48)	3.04 (-1.10)	2.77 (1.89)	.27 (-2.52)

predicted by extrapolating the trend.[9] The t-values are readily converted to probabilities for these rates occurring in a random population. With 29 degrees of freedom, the probability of randomness is 5 percent for t = 1.70, 1 percent for t = 2.46, and 0.5 percent for t = 2.75.

Table 1 demonstrates that the difference in excess mortality between the Netherlands and Belgium is striking. Although both countries experienced a severe slowdown in population growth, the t-statistics of the mortality rates are considerably higher in the Netherlands for all four years. Within the Netherlands, the two northern clay provinces of Groningen and Friesland were least affected by the famine.[10] The diluvial provinces of the northeast and the alluvial maritime provinces were hit severely, but Zeeland and North Holland recovered before the rest of the country. The southern sandy soil province of North Brabant displayed a pattern similar to Belgium, namely a large reduction in birth rates but moderate excess mortality rates.[11] The extraordinarily high mortality rates in Utrecht and south Holland in 1849 are explained in part by the cholera epidemic. The computations ignore any effect of different age structures among the observed populations.

If we assume that in the absence of the famine birth and death rates would have remained normal, then the total number of famine casualties in the Netherlands was about 126,000, of which more than 60,000 were excess deaths and the rest "averted births."[12] Ireland's casualties were thus fifteen times larger than the Netherlands in absolute terms. Since the Irish population was three times that of the Netherlands, the impact of the famine measured in terms of excess mortality was five times as severe in Ireland. It seems tempting to relate this difference to the different

9   In these cases the denominator was the standard error of the predicted value which is equal to SE$[1 + 1/n + (\overline{X} - X)^2/\Sigma x^2]^{1/2}$ where SE is the standard error of the regression, n the number of observations, and X a series of integers 1, 2 . . . 31.

10   These figures are to be contrasted with Bergman's suggestion that the clay provinces in the north were the most heavily affected by the famine, a conclusion based only on the fact that in both Groningen and Friesland population fell in 1847. Bergman, "Potato Blight," 403–404.

11   An objection to these findings is that many cases of infant mortality occurring in the first months of life may have led to a failure to report either birth or death, biasing the decline in birth rates upward and the rise in death rates downward.

12   In order to preserve comparability, all casualty computations assume that 1841 rates are representative of "normal" rates, since 1841 is the only year for which Irish prefamine birth and death rates are known.

dependencies on potatoes: the normal prefamine crop in the Netherlands was about 14 million hectolitres, or 962,000 tons, which in per capita terms is about one fifth of the prefamine Irish potato harvest. However, a direct relation between dependence on potatoes (as measured by potato output per capita) and famine-related deaths is not warranted. Per capita production of potatoes in the Netherlands was about .32 tons or 12.8 bushels. In Belgium the figure is .34 tons or 13.6 bushels. The destruction of potatoes in Belgium in 1845 was more complete than in the Netherlands in the same year and about as devastating as the following year in Ireland. And yet total Belgian excess deaths from 1846 to 1849 were only about 48,000. Total population losses were more than double that figure, but the steep decline in birth rates must in part be attributed to the demise of the Belgian cottage industry, which had been ailing for decades and the plight of which reached a crisis stage in 1845.[13]

't may be thought that the extraordinary death figures in the lat̲ ̲o40s reflect in part the cholera epidemic which struck Europe in 1848 and 1849 rather than starvation. Cholera struck both Ireland and the Netherlands and definitely increased excess mortality in those two years. The impact of cholera was not large enough, how ̲̲er, to account for more than a fraction of the ⌐xcess mortality of 1848 and 1849. In Ireland the total number of persons who succumbed to cholera from 1848 to 1850 was estimated at 34,426 by the 1851 census, a figure which is thought to be exaggerated. For the Netherlands, Hofstee has recently employed data provided by Evers, the nineteenth-century Dutch demographer, to produce a breakdown of excess mortality in the years 1846–1849 between starvation and cholera. Hofstee estimates that out of a total of 75,235 excess deaths, 22,078 or 29.3

---

13 Bergman, "Potato Blight," 394; Terlouw, "Aardappelziekte," 270. The Dutch harvested about 24% of their crop in 1845, while the Belgians got only 12.7% of the normal crop. Cf. Bergman, "Potato Blight," 394 and G. Jacquemyns, "Histoire de la Crise Économique des Flanders, 1845–50," *Academie Royale de Belgique, Mémoires*, XXVI (1929), 254–255. In 1846 the tables are turned: the Dutch harvest was less than 34% of their normal potato harvest, while the Belgian harvest was about two thirds of its normal level. But the rye crop appears to have failed more in Belgium than in the Netherlands. Belgian excess deaths are estimated from *Statistique Générale de la Belgique, Exposé de la Situation du Royaume (1841–50)* (Brussels, 1852), 4, 5, 21, 27. Belgian population in 1845 was 4.3 million, the Netherlands 3.0 million. (Earlier and smaller mortality peaks in Dutch death rates in 1822 and 1826–27 were absent in Belgium.) Mokyr, *Industrialization*, 237–258.

percent died of cholera. Unfortunately Hofstee's calculations are biased toward overestimating the number of excess deaths caused by cholera as opposed to starvation. It is incorrect to assume that *all* cholera deaths should be subtracted from the total excess mortality figures, since that assumes that *none* of the cholera victims would have died otherwise. More serious is his neglect of the possibility of interaction between the epidemic and the famine. Ordinarily, only about 50 percent of all cholera cases are fatal, but a famished population was likely to be more vulnerable.[14]

It is also enlightening to look briefly at the case of Scotland which, like Ireland and the Netherlands, was heavily dependent on potatoes for the subsistence of the lower classes. Whereas Scotland was severely hit by famine, the demographic impact was not nearly so calamitous as in Ireland or even in the Netherlands. Scottish aggregate demographic statistics seem hardly affected by the subsistence crises of either 1816–17 or 1845–1850. Although the Highlands and the Hebrides were more heavily dependent on potatoes than other regions, most of the mortality was in Glasgow and the Lowland rural areas, whereas the Highlands and Western Islands escaped relatively lightly. Famine proper killed few people, and although there was a high incidence of typhus and cholera, the other diseases often associated with famine, such as malaria and dysentery, were comparatively rare, and overall mortality rates remained low.[15]

14   *The Census of Ireland for the Year 1851, pt. 5: Tables of Death* (1856), II, 661 in Great Britain, Parliamentary Papers, XXX. William P. MacArthur, "Medical History of the Famine," in R. Dudley Edwards and T. Desmond Williams (eds.), *The Great Famine: Studies in Irish History, 1845–52* (New York, 1957), 307. Hofstee, *Demografische Ontwikkeling*, 212. Hofstee's source is J. C. G. Evers, *Bijdrage tot de Bevolkingsleer van Nederland* (The Hague, 1882), 76. Evers himself expressed some healthy skepticism on the reliability of the data during epidemics and notes (69) that there was evidence of physicians being mistaken in counting the number of cholera victims in 1849. It is not clear whether Evers thought that the data were too low or too high, although his subsequent remark that "there is a reduction in the victims of infectious disease (after 1870) which is only ostensible" seems to indicate the latter. The possible interaction between the epidemic and the famine is recognized by S. H. Cousens, "The Regional Variation in Mortality During the Great Irish Famine," *Proceedings of the Royal Irish Academy*, LXIII (1963), 143.

15   M. W. Flinn et al., *Scottish Population History* (Cambridge, 1977), 423–426. Annual vital statistics for Scotland are unavailable, but if these disasters had been truly acute, the decennial average annual population growth rates would have reflected it. These rates are; 1801–11: 1.16%; 1811–21: 1.41%; 1821–31: 1.22%; 1831–41: .99%; 1841–51: .98%. *Ibid.*, 302. Population in the Highland counties actually declined between 1841 and 1851, as it did in the two following decades in which there was no famine. The very rapid increase in the population of the western Lowland counties between 1841 and 1851 (1.58% per annum) suggests heavy internal migration.

Information on mortality rates in the late 1840s suggests that subsistence crises survived in many areas of Europe until at least the middle of the nineteenth century. By our definition of poverty we can establish a crude ranking of European economies for this period. As one would have expected, Ireland was extremely poor. More surprising is that Ireland found itself in the unexpected company of the Netherlands, which shared with it—although to a lesser degree—the dubious honor of preserving preindustrial poverty. Belgium and Scotland, which were by comparison more industrialized, seemed far less affected by the harvest failures. Was this a coincidence? If not, as I argue later, we should investigate the reasons behind the industrial failure experienced by Ireland and the Netherlands if we are to come to grips with the histories of these two economies in the nineteenth century.

THE FAILURE TO INDUSTRIALIZE   In assessing the reasons behind the slow and late industrialization in Ireland and the Netherlands, one is struck by a notable feature of physical geography: neither country possesses large amounts of the two natural resources which played such a central role in the industrial revolutions of the nineteenth century—iron and coal. It is tempting to infer that geographical factors were the primary determinants of the locational patterns of the industrial revolution. For instance, Ó'Tuathaigh has written recently:

> Ireland's economic problems in those decades [the first half of the nineteenth century] were similar to those being encountered in certain areas within Britain and throughout Western Europe as the industrial revolution traced its pattern of economic growth. Regions hitherto prosperous began to decay and new centres of industry, wealth and population arose with staggering rapidity. This dramatic change in the balance of regional economic activity owed its origins to the supply and use of the natural resources of industrial expansion; it was a function of the location of the sources of industrial power and energy.

Similar views have been expressed concerning the Netherlands. Recent writing by Bos and Griffiths place a large emphasis on the role of raw materials and transportation costs.[16]

16 Gearóid O'Tuathaigh, *Ireland Before the Famine, 1798–1848* (Dublin, 1972), 119. R. W. J. M. Bos, "Van Periferie naar Centrum; Enige Kanttekeningen bij de Nederlandse Industriële Ontwikkeling in de Negentiende Eeuw," *Economie*, XL (1976), 181–205; Rich-

In principle, fuel and material costs could have helped to determine the timing, location, and intensity of the industrial revolution. However, before we can draw definite conclusions in this respect, it is necessary to ask *how large* the effect of fuel and material price was. As it turns out, their overall effect on industrialization was of the second order. Lower production costs, for whatever reason, were the single most important element behind the adoption of new and capital intensive techniques. The relative importance of expensive raw materials and expensive labor can be compared by looking at the cost structure of manufacturing as a whole. For instance, if we were to compare an industrial sector in two countries, the appropriate variables would be the cost differences of raw materials and labor, and the respective shares of the two inputs in the total cost bill (including normal profits). To carry out the comparison correctly, input-output tables would be required since we are asking questions about an economy as a whole, not one particular industry. The average price of coal in Dublin and Belfast was approximately 50–100 percent higher than the average price in Britain, and perhaps as much as four times as high as the price of coal at pithead. The potential for an advantage is thus obvious, but ultimately the cost differential depends on the share of fuel costs in total production costs.

As noted above, these shares cannot easily be computed for the level of the economy or even the manufacturing sector as a whole. Looking at particular industries for which cost data happen to be available may be misleading. All the same, the shares estimated from firm records show that without exception the share of fuel costs in Ireland was less than 5 percent. Kane computes that for the British cotton industry as a whole, coal accounted only for 1.08 percent of total costs in 1833. A Leeds woolen manufacturer spent only .4 percent of the value of output on coal, so that if the firm were to be transplanted to Ireland, fuel costs would have risen to a little over 2 percent. At the Mulholland flax mill in Belfast, coal cost 13s. per ton in the mid 1830s, almost exactly four times the price in Leeds so that fuel amounted to

ard Griffiths, *Industrial Retardation in the Netherlands, 1830–1850,* forthcoming. I am indebted to Griffiths for allowing me to see extracts of his manuscript. For a similar view see William N. Parker, "European Industry, 1500–1850," in Peter Burke (ed.), *The New Cambridge Modern History,* forthcoming.

£3,042 a year, or about 3.8 percent of total value of output. In the cotton industry, fuel costs typically amounted to 2.7 percent. All other things equal, such marginal differences could have been crucial in the determination of industrialization processes. But other things were not equal. Wages in Belfast—a comparatively high wage area—were significantly lower than in England, so that total costs in Belfast were in fact lower than in England.[17]

In any event, the fuel cost differential and the proportion of fuel costs to total costs do not provide an accurate estimate of the difference in total costs caused by the absence of large amounts of cheap coal. The latter depends on the former. In economies like Ireland and the Netherlands, where fuel was expensive, one would expect fuel-saving techniques to be used, and goods that required low fuel intensities to be manufactured. Furthermore, since in both countries coal was more expensive compared to peat than in other countries, peat was widely used as a substitute for coal. The most obvious place for this substitution was the home, but one should not underestimate the industrial potential of peat. It is tempting, but entirely fallacious, to conclude from the fact that peat did not *actually* play a crucial role in the industrial revolution that under no circumstances could it have done so. Once the "counterfactual" possibility is recognized, the "indispensability theory" of coal will join the American railroads in the graveyard of mythical *sine qua nons*.

The economic significance of peat for Ireland was vast. For one thing, there was a lot of it. In the middle of the nineteenth century, about 2.8 million acres, or one seventh of Ireland's total surface, was covered by peatbogs. As late as 1920 there were still 4 billion tons of turf (250 times the annual fuel requirement of

17 Robert Kane, *The Industrial Resources of Ireland* (Dublin, 1845); *Second Report of the Commissioner Appointed to Consider and Recommend a General System of Railways in Ireland*, in Great Britain, Parliamentary Papers, XXXV (1837–38); T. W. Freeman, *Pre-Famine Ireland* (Manchester, 1957); Cormac Ó'Gráda, "Irish Bogs," private communication. The fuel cost for the Mulholland mill is an upper bound as it is computed on the assumption that the machines were employed year-round. An interesting example of the fallacy of blaming raw materials' prices for the failure to industrialize rapidly is provided by the *Report of the 1830 Select Committee on the State of the Poor in Ireland.* The committee concluded that the coal duty raised the price of coal and thus "prevented the increase of manufactures," and that repeal of the coal duty would be of major importance to the development of Irish industry. See Great Britain, Parliamentary Papers, VII (1830), 16. The coal duty was repealed in the following year with no noticeable effects on the Irish economy.

Ireland). Second, peat digging was often part of the land recla-
mation process, so that the fuel thus extracted was jointly produced with land reclaimed. Peat was dug at the surface, by hand,
so that its price was determined by the level of wages—which
was very low in prefamine Ireland. The main difficulty after
cutting was drying, which had to be done under some kind of
cover. Although some peat was available in practically every
county of Ireland, the richest deposits were concentrated in relatively remote areas. In some of the more developed regions,
earlier usage had in many places depleted the best turbaries. As
a result, large quantities of turf were shipped within Ireland,
although the average distances were not large.[18]

The use of peat as a fuel in Ireland was widespread, and
extended into a large number of industries. Peat lends itself to
coking, and the coke thus produced is about equal to coal coke
in calorific content and only slightly inferior to wood charcoal.
Although simple dried turf has only about half the caloric content
of average bituminous coal, there is a price at which it becomes
profitable to switch from coal to peat. It is not possible to compute
that price precisely because of varying qualities of both fuels, but
at a ratio of 3:1 between the price of a ton of coal and a ton of
peat this "switch point" was definitely passed. Since the price of
a ton of peat was about 3s.6d., it paid to switch to peat when the
price of coal exceeded about 11–12s. The steamships on the Shan-
non, for instance, switched to peat in the 1830s thereby cutting
fuel costs by 50 percent, and there is widespread evidence of peat
being used as fuel to drive steam engines. It is less known that on
the continent peat was even used as a fuel in the metallurgical
industry. In France, Prussia, Bavaria, and Bohemia, peat was used
both in smelting and in puddling.[19]

In addition, conditions in Ireland were conducive to the use
of water power. A large and relatively steady rainfall, mild win-
ters, and considerable variability in elevation provided the basic
ingredients for this form of energy. In a somewhat heroic calculation, Kane estimates the daily potential of water power at 3
million horsepower a day. This number is a theoretical upper

18 Connell, "The Colonization of Waste Land in Ireland, 1780–1845," *Economic History
Review*, III (1950), 55; Freeman, *Pre-Famine Ireland*, 8, 99.
19 A pound of peat yields about 6,000 B.T.U.'s, whereas coal yields between 12,000
and 14,000 B.T.U.'s.

limit, but it illustrates the economic possibilities inherent in water power. Finally, it may be worth mentioning that Ireland did have *some* coal (producing about 120,000 tons a year), vast supplies of culm, excellent stone, marble, and slate quarries, and some small-scale but prosperous exploitation of non-ferrous metals, mainly copper and lead.[20]

Consider now the Netherlands. The causal connection between high labor costs and the tardiness of Dutch industrialization could seemingly be extended to raw material costs. But labor and the availability of natural resources are substitutes at the level of the economy even if they are not substitutes at the level of the firm. Cheap labor could produce more and cheaper roads, canals, ships, harbor works, railroads, and trans-shipment and loading equipment. All of these could greatly—although never completely—offset the disadvantages of the absence of mineral wealth. By using extensive data on *prices* of fuel, for example, Griffiths does not prove that raw materials' prices were necessarily a factor of great importance in explaining Dutch industrial backwardness. The high price of coal in the Netherlands reflects in part the fundamental problem of the Dutch economy: high wages. Mineral resources at pithead were a primary resource, to be sure, but actual prices paid by users were determined largely by the prices of other inputs. In addition, as in Ireland, the proportion of fuel costs in total costs in the Netherlands was small. Griffiths presents some cost structure tables in which fuel costs in the textile industry amounted to 6.9 percent (in bleaching), and 5.9 percent (calico printing). In the Leyden foundry, the proportion of fuel costs in total costs was far higher at around 25 percent. But in a more integrated firm, like the Fijenoord machine tool firm in Rotterdam, the share of fuel costs in total costs (including profits) was about 3.6 percent for the period from 1830 to 1850.[21]

The availability of resources has been used as an explanation of the divergent development of Belgium and the Netherlands. Bos's argument that "the geographical position of the Belgian cotton industry in an area of low wages *as well as the indispensable coal* provided it with a better point of departure than Twente" is

20 Kane, *Industrial Resources*, 73–78. The importance of water power is illustrated in detail in H. D. Gribbon, *The History of Water Power in Ulster* (Belfast, 1969). Culm is dust of coals of poor quality, used in the preparation of lime.
21 All figures computed from Griffiths, *Industrial Retardation*.

incomplete. Although probably better located than Twente, Belgium's textile industries did not owe their early development to their favorable access to resources. More fundamentally, why did Dutch textile industry develop first in the remote areas of cheap labor rather than in, say, Zeeland or Friesland where access to Belgian or British coal was easier than in Twente? In any event, it is clear that the Netherlands benefited as much as Belgium from Belgian mineral deposits. As early as 1832, when the relations between the two nations following the Belgian secession of 1830 left much to be desired, the Netherlands imported 123,000 tons of Belgian coal.[22]

The dismal image of a country devoid of resources and thus doomed to lack an industrial sector is also exaggerated for the Netherlands. In a recent paper De Zeeuw has once again drawn attention to that basic fact. Using an ingenious accounting sheet of energy production and consumption, De Zeeuw maintains that cheap energy was an essential element in Dutch prosperity during the "Golden Age." Cheap energy was derived first and foremost from cheap peat, found in abundance in various regions in the Netherlands, and from wind power.[23]

Why then did an economy that in the seventeenth century was able to take advantage of an exceptional opportunity provided by the combination of wind, peat, and water fail to utilize these resources in the nineteenth century? True, the heavy exploitation of peat in the sixteenth and seventeenth centuries led to some exhaustion of the reserves, resulting in a rise in peat prices. But there were still large reserves of peat in the nineteenth century,

---

22 Bos, "Van Periferie naar centrum," 144–145 (my translation, italics supplied). The coal used in Ghent came from the Borinage, the western coal producing area in Belgium. Before the completion of the canal between Pommeroeul and Antoing (1826), the coal had to be transported through the Mons-Condé canal and was subject to French tools and tariffs, and to long delays. A direct connection between Ghent and the North Sea (the Ghent-Terneuzen canal) was completed even later, in 1829. The locational superiority of East Flanders compared with the Dutch maritime provinces is thus far from obvious. For further arguments against the resource location arguments in the Dutch-Belgium contexts, see Mokyr, *Industrialization*, 204–208.

23 J. W. De Zeeuw, "Peat and the Dutch Golden Age: The Historical Meaning of Energy Attainability," *A.A.G. Bijdragen*, XXI (1978), 3–31. De Zeeuw adds that peat could play the role it did largely because the Netherlands had the additional advantage of a good system of waterways. On the wide-ranging uses of peat in the Netherlands, see P. Van Schaik, "De Economische Betekenis van de Turfwinning in Nederland," *Economisch en Sociaal-Historisch Jaarboek*, XXXII (1968–69), 141–205.

and as late as 1840, 3,600 billion kilocalories, or 60 percent of total energy consumption in the Netherlands, came from peat—in spite of the rise in peat prices and the decline in the price of imported coal. The number of windmills in the nineteenth century was probably three times larger than in the seventeenth. The failure of the Dutch economy to industrialize can hardly be explained by the absence of energy sources alone, although these factors probably did reinforce trends that existed in the Dutch economy for other reasons.[24]

Although the a priori plausibility of "geographical determinism" is not in doubt, the same cannot be said for the theories inspired by the work of Frank on Latin America.[25] The "core vs. periphery" framework of colonialism has been applied to Ireland by Hechter, who summarizes his "internal colonialism" model as follows:

> According to this [the internal colonialism] model, structural inequalities between the regions should increase, as the periphery develops in a dependent mode. Individuals of the core culture are expected to dominate high prestige roles in the social structure of the peripheral regions . . . The bulk of the peripheral population will be confined to subordinate positions in the social structure. In sum, a cultural division of labor will tend to arise. . . . The findings tended to support the predictions of the internal colonial model, at least with respect to Wales, Scotland, and Ireland. Specifically, the expectations of the diffusion model [the alternative model against which the internal colonialism model is tested] were not upheld with respect to long term trends in aggregate regional inequalities. Industrialization did not diffuse into the peripheral areas in the same form as it had developed in the core. When industrialization did penetrate the periphery, it was in a dependent mode. . . . Regional economic inequalities persisted despite industrialization: the per capita income of the Celtic industrial countries has been lower than those of comparably industrial English countries for over a century.[26]

24 De Zeeuw, "Peat," 14.
25 André Gunder Frank, *Capitalism and Underdevelopment in Latin America* (New York, 1969; rev. ed.).
26 Michael Hechter, "Regional Inequality and National Integration: The Case of the British Isles," *Journal of Social History*, V (1971), 96–117; idem, *Internal Colonialism: The Celtic Fringe in British National Development, 1536–1966* (Berkeley, 1975). For the quotation see *ibid.*, 344–345.

Hechter's theory deals only marginally with economic differences, although much of his evidence is drawn from economic facts. No one can doubt that the cultural and political relations between Ireland and Britain were asymmetrical, and that the Irish were coerced into many policies that they might not have adopted by themselves. But can these policies truly be held responsible for Irish poverty in the nineteenth century? Hechter, following the nationalist economic historians writing in the 1920s and O'Brien in particular, squarely places the blame on the Union and the ensuing economic unification with Great Britain. The Union, Hechter maintains, implied that Ireland was forced into a specialization pattern in agricultural products, since Irish comparative advantage was in agriculture, thus denying Ireland the fruits of industrialization. This line of reasoning cannot be accepted in the simple form presented by Hechter. It simply will not do to maintain that Irish industry "could not withstand competition" with Britain; the question "why" is immediately begged. In short, whatever it was that made Ireland underdeveloped, also made it the "periphery" to England's core. Hechter is unable to specify precisely how trade between the "core" and the "periphery" resulted in a deepening and perpetuation of income differentials between regions. Interregional trade, similar to trade between nations or, for that matter, to trade between individuals, usually resulted in gains for both sides, compared to a situation in which no trade took place. As a first approximation, then, trade with Britain was likely to have resulted in higher incomes in Ireland. It probably also resulted in higher real incomes in Great Britain, but why should that matter to the Irish?[27]

The same framework is adopted by Bos, who argues that the

27 George O'Brien, *The Economic History of Ireland from the Union to the Famine* (London, 1921). Hechter, *Internal Colonialism*, 92. Whether Ireland actually had a comparative disadvantage in manufacturing, is unclear. There are considerable difficulties in applying the static concepts of comparative advantage to long run industrialization. For a similar statement in a different context, see Gavin Wright, *The Political Economy of the Cotton South* (New York, 1978), 111–112. From a different point of view, one could arrive at Hechter's conclusions by maintaining that an independent Ireland would have set up protective tariffs to protect its "infant industries." Whether this would have significantly accelerated industrialization is unclear. Even less clear is whether industrialization at considerable costs in terms of allocative efficiency (and thus income) would ultimately have been "better" for Ireland. It is possible that the outflow of labor from Ireland would have been much smaller in the counteractual world of an independent Ireland.

Netherlands in the first half of the nineteenth century failed to industrialize because the country found itself on the periphery of industrialized Britain. How the British managed to reduce the Netherlands to this sorry state is not explained, which makes Bos's framework even less plausible than Hechter's, which can at least rely on an indisputable situation of political domination between England and the "Celtic fringe." Later in the nineteenth century, Bos believes, British "market power" crumbled and the Netherlands moved away from its peripheral location because "the German customs union, and afterward the German Empire developed into an industrial power of the first rank due to a deliberate industrialization policy." If anything, this story turns the core vs. periphery theory upside down: Germany's industrialization should have turned the Netherlands even more into a "dependency," specializing in producing inputs for German industry (e.g. dock facilities in Rotterdam) rather than have provided a condition for economic development in it. Thus, Bos's own facts demonstrate the absurdity of the entire framework: whereas Britain's and Belgium's industrialization turned Holland into a "periphery," Germany's industrialization allegedly restored it to the "core." Clearly, there is little operational content to the core-periphery dichotomy, and the value of the concept as a tool in historical analysis must so far be considered doubtful.[28]

Other theories have been put forward to explain the retardation of the Irish and Dutch economies, but it would go beyond the scope of this article to discuss them in detail. The presumed absence or presence of demand for industrial goods—often claimed to be a strategic factor—is in reality a far more complex issue than has previously been thought. The comparison between Ireland and the Netherlands does indicate the basic problem with the various demand theories. If the Netherlands, with a small economy and neighbors protected by high tariff barriers, failed

28 Bos, "Van Periferie naar Centrum," 196–199; idem, Brits-Nederlandse Handel en Scheepvaart, 1870–1914, unpub. Ph.D. diss. (Catholic University of Tilburg, 1978), 100–110, 305–316. Bos employs a nebulous concept of "market power" which apparently is not used by him in its conventional meaning. It is defined rather as "large supply relative to demand" which resulted from the fact that the Netherlands was a small open economy and Britain a large one. Bos realizes that prices were set competitively, but fails to see that competitive pricing is inconsistent with his notion of "market power." Ibid., 308. The absence of a formal model in Bos's analysis is regrettable.

to industrialize because of too small markets, why did Ireland—which had access to the large British market—fail as well? [29]

More serious are the attempts to explain individual paths of economic development in terms of aggregate differences in tastes. One need not interpret the differences in tastes to mean that there were nations that preferred less income to more income. Rather, economic growth is often paid for in terms of more risk, less leisure, and more saving. If there were international or interregional differences in the rate of time preference (i.e., the willingness to postpone present consumption in order to consume more in the future), the degree of risk aversion, or the intensity of leisure preference, such differences could and would explain divergent paths of industrialization. Unfortunately, since utility functions are not directly observed in any form, such hypotheses must remain speculative at this time. [30]

How, then, is one to explain the slowness of the Irish and Dutch economies to modernize? As Karl Marx, Max Hartwell, and W. Arthur Lewis would all agree, the "engine" that pushed industrialization forward was profits. Higher profits meant more investment, either directly by means of retained earning, or indirectly by allowing the firm to borrow against its future income, with present earnings as a means of convincing potential lenders of the prospects for future profits. Since the Dutch labor force was comparatively expensive, its industry did not generate sufficient profits compared with, say, Belgium or Bohemia. The comparison with Ireland then yields a paradox: Irish labor was cheap; probably cheaper than anywhere in Western Europe. If the model emphasizing the crucial role of labor supply is realistic, how does one reconcile it with Ireland's failure to industrialize? The answer is simple: the inverse relationship between the rate of capital accumulation and the wage level holds, like all economic relationships, strictly *ceteris paribus*. As soon as we realize that other things were not equal, historical causal relationships will become more complex, and apparent paradoxes will arise. [31]

---

29 For an examination of various versions of this argument, see Mokyr, "Demand vs. Supply in the Industrial Revolution," *Journal of Economic History*, XXXVII (1977), 981–1008.

30 Bertram Hutchinson, "On the Study of Non-economic Factors in Irish Economic Development," *Economic and Social Review*, I (1970), 509–529.

31 For a fuller statement of this relationship, see Mokyr, "Growing Up."

The central assumption behind the above-mentioned model is that labor is immobile. For the case of the Low Countries, this assumption is not unrealistic. It is in fact surprising that during the sixteen years that the Netherlands and Belgium were united into one political unit, so few Belgians emigrated to Holland in spite of the large wage differentials. The total number of persons immigrating into the Netherlands before 1850 was small although not negligible: about 2,000 a year in the 1830s and 4,300 a year in the 1840s. The effect of immigration on what little industrialization occurred was probably significant. In many industries foreign labor appears to have played a big role. Nonetheless, the number of immigrants was too small to reverse the fate of the Dutch economy, especially since death rates among the German immigrants were extremely high—Malthus referred to Holland as "the grave of Germany." Consequently, in the Low Countries the characteristics of the labor force determined the parameters of the accumulation process: the cheaper the labor force, the higher the profits, and thus the larger the funds available for capital formation.[32]

Once the assumption of labor immobility is relaxed, this model requires modification. The positive effect that a cheap labor force has on the rate of capital accumulation could in part be negated by labor emigrating, while at the same time high wage countries could overcome their handicap by importing cheap labor. Ireland, although it had a cheap labor force, was part of a labor market which extended far beyond its borders. Instead of building up its own industrial sector, Ireland simply provided cheap labor to economies overseas which consequently could en-

---

32 Hofstee, *Demografische Ontwikkeling*, 48–49, Table 10, 167–168. Hofstee estimates that from 1815 to 1829 net immigration into the Netherlands was far higher and amounted to 5,174 per year. This last figure seems dubious. The net immigration figures are estimated residually by subtracting the population of 1815 and the births between 1815 and 1829 from the 1829 population figure and adding the deaths figures. This calculation depends crucially on Hofstee's *assumption* that the degree of undercounting in the 1815 census is not only small but negligible. Even a small error in the census will lead to large errors in the estimated number of migrants. A few easy calculations show that if the 1815 census undercounted Dutch population by as little as 1%, net immigration as estimated by Hofstee would be lower by 26%. Such a sensitivity of the data to minor errors in a census which is widely maintained to have been deficient prevents us from accepting Hofstee's migration figures for the earlier period. On foreign labor see I. J. Brugmans, *De Arbeidende Klasse in Nederland in de 19e Eeuw* (Utrecht, 1971), 88–91. Thomas R. Malthus, *An Essay on the Principle of Population* (London, 1826; 6th ed.), I, 322n.

joy higher profits and faster capital formation. In other words, Ireland industrialized, but unfortunately for the Irish, its industrialization took place outside its borders: in northwest England, the Scottish Lowlands, and New England.

The emigration data speak for themselves. Until 1845, Ireland was the only country in Europe which was experiencing an outmigration large enough to have had a significant impact on its demographic equilibrium. Connell has estimated that between 1780 and the Great Famine, about 1.75 million Irish migrated overseas. From 1821 to 1841, net outmigration averaged .68 percent annually, reducing the annual rate of population increase from a possible 1.6 percent (the difference between birth and death rates) to an actual .92 percent. By 1851, the number of persons of Irish birth residing in Great Britain was 734,000. Most of these people lived in big industrial cities, and there can be little doubt that the Irish migration was of the utmost importance for the progress of the industrial revolution in Great Britain, although economic historians have paid less attention to that fact than contemporaries. The unusually large dimension of Irish emigration is one reason why Ireland, unlike Belgium or Switzerland, was unable to take advantage of a cheap labor force.[33]

Most of the questions surrounding Irish backwardness in the

---

33 Connell, *Population of Ireland*, 27; Mokyr, "Poverty and Population," 30–31; *Census of Great Britain, Population Tables*, ci, in Great Britain, Parliamentary Papers, LXXXVIII (1852–53); George Cornewall Lewis, "Report on the State of the Irish Poor in Great Britain," 429–474 (Appendix G to the *Reports of the Commissioners for Inquiring into the Condition of the Poorer Classes in Ireland*) in Great Britain, Parliamentary Papers, XXXIV (1836).

The historical reality was more complex than this simple model will allow. The wages of unskilled labor remained low in Ireland mainly because emigration lowered the quality of the labor force and removed those workers who were in the upper end of the distribution of initiative, resourcefulness, and energy. The emigrants were a self-selected group who would have otherwise constituted the backbone of an Irish industrial entrepreneurship and proletariat. The wage differentials as far as skilled workers were concerned were far smaller. In 1824, for instance, Dublin wages of skilled workers were as high or higher than in London, which by itself already had higher than average wages for England. E. R. R. Green, "Industrial Decline in the Nineteenth Century," in Cullen (ed.), *Formation*, 96. In 1830 skilled brewers at Guinness's were paid between 13s. and 16s. weekly, whereas Dublin gardeners and other skilled workers were paid around 12s. per week. One businessman sighed that the wages of skilled artisans were "out of all proportion" in Ireland. Cf. *Report of the Select Committee on the State of the Poor in Ireland*, Great Britain, Parliamentary Papers, VII (1830). Kane concludes from a considerable amount of evidence that "skilled labour . . . is certainly dearer in this country [Ireland] than in Great Britain, whilst unskilled labour is much cheaper." Kane, *Industrial Resources*, 397–402.

nineteenth century remain open. Why did so many thousands choose to emigrate rather than stay in Ireland and help to establish an industrial sector there? With the notable exception of the Belfast linen industry, the few industries which did exist in Ireland in the first quarter of the nineteenth century—cotton, wool, silk, provisions, tanneries, coachmaking, glassworks, rope-walks— subsequently declined. What is needed at this stage is a far-reaching analysis of the structure of the nineteenth-century Irish economy and society, an ambitious project which cannot be attempted here. The important point to be emphasized here is that, whatever the other obstacles hindering the accumulation of capital in Ireland, cheap labor could do little to offset these disadvantages.[34]

INDUSTRIAL FAILURE AND THE PERSISTENCE OF SUBSISTENCE CRISES
The industrial revolution and the gradual disappearance of subsistence crises are two of the most striking features of the modern age. Were they related? It is reasonable to suggest that economic change and industrialization after 1750 were partly responsible for the gradual elimination of the great subsistence crises and thus reduced poverty in the sense used above, even if they did not do so in the traditional sense.

One plausible scenario is as follows: consider a country in the early stages of industrialization. In a normal year the surplus generated by the labor in the factories was used largely to generate more capital and more consumer goods for non-workers. In cases of severe crises, however, such surpluses were used to import and distribute the necessary foodstuffs to prevent the labor force and potential labor force of the factories from being wiped out. These interventions took various forms, such as direct government intervention, private famine relief with government encouragement and financial assistance, and purely voluntary poor relief by organizations and individuals. Furthermore, industrialization usually was accompanied by infrastructural development such as better transportation, retail networks, and so on, which were instrumental in sending the goods when and where they were needed to prevent starvation. Of course, industrialization in many places was preceded by the disappearance of demographic catas-

34 J. J. Webb, *Industrial Dublin Since 1698 and the Silk Industry in Dublin* (Dublin, 1913). Green, "Industrial Decline in the Nineteenth Century," in Cullen (ed.), *Formation*.

trophes. Other factors were clearly at work. All the same, it is plausible that there was a strong connection between the absence of economic change and continued susceptibility of an economy to disaster.

Economic development in eighteenth- and nineteenth-century Europe implied a gradual reduction in the probability of devastating subsistence crises for a number of reasons other than the simple increase in aggregate output. First and foremost, there was economic diversification. An increasing proportion of workers found their livelihood in occupations other than agriculture, less subject to natural disasters. Within agriculture, Europe's dependency on cereal crops for its basic carbohydrate intake was reduced: expanding production of sugar beets, maize, potatoes and other root crops, and rice meant a lower vulnerability of the basic food supply to any single event. Improved food processing methods, better preservation techniques, and cheaper storage facilities also meant that during the nineteenth century the cost of insuring oneself against harvest failure declined.[35]

More complex is whether commercialization of agriculture, i.e., increased inter- and intraregional trade in food products, reduced oscillations in food supply. Consider the case of an individual farmer (though the analysis holds just as well for a village or a small region). What is meant by commercialization is that a larger proportion of agricultural produce is sold at the market and a larger proportion of consumption is bought. For purposes of exposition only, assume that prior to commercialization the farmer was completely self-sufficient in food. Compare a self-sufficient farmer to a farmer consuming a basket of products, most of which are purchased in the market. The variance of the income of the self-sufficient farmer is by definition equal to the variance in agricultural output caused by external factors. For a typical farmer who sells most of his crop this identity is no longer true. When output falls due to harvest failure, agricultural prices rise, offsetting partially or completely the fall in income due to

---

[35] The larger quantities of food consumed in normal years also helped to reduce the peaks in mortality during famines. If people are better fed on a regular basis, their ability to withstand a given temporary reduction in their diet will be larger. H. J. Teuteberg, "The General Relationship Between Diet and Industrialization," in Elborg Foster and Robert Forster (eds.), *European Diet from Pre-Industrial to Modern Times* (New York, 1975), 61–109.

harvest failure. In this way, to use a technical term, the downward slope of the demand curve serves as an insurance policy. That is to say, when crops are small, agricultural prices are usually high, and the farmer may receive a higher money income than with good crops, although it is not obvious that he will be better off in real terms. It seems, however, that the worst risk of starvation in case of harvest failures are smaller than for the self-sufficient farmer. Although that is likely, one cannot conclude that the rise of the market economy *necessarily* reduces the risk to which farmers are exposed. The reason for this ambiguity is that the farmer in a market economy is now also subject to fluctuations which have nothing to do with his crop, but which are caused by perturbations in the nonagricultural sector or by fluctuations of harvests half a globe away. Such fluctuations would be perceived by farmers as movements *of* the demand curve. Nonetheless, it seems that these fluctuations typically were not as disastrous as major harvest failures.

Certainly, modernization replaced the risk of harvest failure with the risk of industrial unemployment during business cycle troughs. Yet there is not much evidence of widespread starvation and excess mortality during industrial depressions, although birth rates declined markedly during prolonged periods of unemployment. The deepest troughs in income patterns were thus eliminated, so that great disasters were by and large averted.

In both Ireland and the Netherlands, the slowness of economic change before 1850 was at least in part responsible for their vulnerability to famine. For Ireland, a better understanding of its vulnerability to the destruction of the potato harvest can be obtained from an analysis of the cross-sectional variation in the excess death rates within Ireland. The sample regression results presented in Table 2 demonstrate that excess death rates were higher in counties which had a lower proportion of workers in non-agricultural occupations, and in counties which had a lower income per capita. Literacy, the quality of housing, and the amount of livestock per capita (a proxy variable for the capital-labor ratio) were all negatively correlated with excess death rates.[36]

36 The regressions are based on a Generalized Least Squares procedure. Hence no values of R^2 are supplied, but the significance of the estimate can be read from the F-statistics. The critical value of $F_{(5, 26)}$ at the 1% level is 3.82.

Table 2   Regression Analysis of Excess Mortality in Ireland
(t–values in parentheses)

DEPENDENT VARIABLE[a]	REGRESSION NUMBER			
	1 ANNUAL AVERAGE EXCESS DEATH RATE	2 ANNUAL AVERAGE EXCESS DEATH RATE	3 ANNUAL AVERAGE EXCESS DEATH RATE	4 ANNUAL AVERAGE EXCESS DEATH RATE
Constant	.0787 (4.34)	.0073 (.29)	.0497 (1.76)	.0706 (3.22)
Income Per Capita	−.0041[b] (−3.42)			−.0026[c] (−2.34)
Housing Quality Index[d]		.0578 (2.11)	.0490 (2.01)	
Livestock Per Capita			−.0072 (−2.41)	
Percentage Small Farms	.0357 (2.65)	.0424 (2.81)	.0220 (1.37)	.0353 (2.32)
Literacy Rate	−.0933 (−2.45)	−.0621 (−1.67)	−.0613 (−1.93)	−.0637 (−1.70)
Percentage Non-Agricultural		−.0379 (−1.32)	−.0584 (−2.30)	
Rural Industry				−.0425 (−2.33)
Percentage Urban	.0534 (2.81)			
Rents Per Capita		−.0007 (−1.19)		
Index of Dependency on Potatoes[e]	.0065 (.21)			−.0281 (−1.19)
F (d.f.)	20.06 (5,26)	15.58 (5,26)	20.09 (5,26)	14.54 (5,26)
N	32	32	32	32

a   Definition of the Average Annual Excess Death Rate varies slightly from equation to equation.
b   Labor income only.
c   Total income.
d   Calculated in such a way that the index rises as quality deteriorates.
e   Measures used: percentage of land under cultivation under potatoes; potato acreage per capita.
SOURCE: Mokyr, "The Deadly Fungus," Table 8.

It may seem surprising that the excess death rates are apparently uncorrelated with the index measuring the degree of dependency on potatoes. The insignificance of the coefficients should be interpreted to mean that holding other variables such as income, urbanization, etc., constant, excess death rates during the famine were unaffected by the ratio of potato acreage to total population or to total land under cultivation. Some speculations which try to rationalize this unexpected result have been provided elsewhere. However, one cannot shake off the suspicion that fundamental data problems with the potato acreage variable lie at the heart of this seemingly incongruous result.[37]

The potato acreage data used for the regression presented in Table 2 were computed by Bourke from a constabulary survey conducted in 1846. In work currently in progress, I attempt to correct Bourke's series of county-by-county potato acreage for a number of inaccuracies and unnecessary simplifying assumptions, and to test whether these corrections change the conclusion that potato acreage was not significantly correlated with excess mortality during the famine years.[38]

Table 2 suggests that insofar as industrialization and modernization in agriculture had permeated Ireland, these forces acted as an antidote to the famine. Unfortunately, structural change in Ireland had only started to occur in a few small enclaves, mostly along a narrow strip on the east coast. Most of the counties in Munster, all of Connaught, and the central plains were barely or not affected, and thus extremely vulnerable to external shocks.[39]

The Dutch economy in the 1840s, although highly diversified and monetized, had developed rigidities often associated with

37 Mokyr, "Deadly Fungus."

38 P. M. Austin Bourke, "The Extent of the Potato Crop in Ireland at the Time of the Famine," *Journal of the Statistical and Social Inquiry Society of Ireland*, XX (1960), pt. III. 1–35; Mokyr, "Irish History with the Potato," unpub. paper, 1979.

39 An interesting view of Ireland as a dual economy along these lines is expressed by Patrick Lynch and John Vaisey, *Guinness's Brewery in the Irish Economy, 1759–1876* (Cambridge, 1960), 14–17. Lynch and Vaisey's views have been criticized as over-simplified. My own findings on Irish income per capita and vulnerability to famine are consistent with these criticisms. Rather than being a dual economy, Ireland was a continuum in which underdevelopment gradually became more severe as one moved westward. All the same, Lynch and Vaisey's emphasis on the low rate of monetization in the west is important, as monetization is a good indicator of the importance of production for the market.

declining economies. The top-heavy urban sector in the west was burdened by a large, semi-employed proletariat, whose fate depended on food prices, since nominal wages seem to have been insensitive to external economic forces. Furthermore, Dutch agriculture, as in large parts of Ireland, produced a cash crop for a remote outside market, whereas the rural proletariat lived off a subsistence crop. When the subsistence crops failed in the 1840s, the survival of the rural poor depended on the flexibility of the economy to divert resources from the cash economy to the subsistence sector.

A good example of how rigidities in a "sclerotic" economy offset the ostensible advantages of the high level of commercialization and income per capita is the nature of the Dutch poor relief system. While supporting a far higher proportion of the population than in any other economy, the Dutch poor relief system strove to reform the poor—retrain them, resettle them, and steer them to what was considered a productive life. Not only were such naive attempts usually doomed, but they also deprived the system from flexibility to meet emergencies such as the potato failure of the 1840s.[40]

At the same time in Scotland, government support, landlords, and other charities enabled most Highlanders affected by the famine to survive, although barely. The dependency of the Scottish Highlands on imported meal also must have lessened the impact of the potato blight. As has been argued above, commercialized economies, although not necessarily less poor in the usual sense of the word, were less vulnerable to disaster than self-sufficient ones. Flinn shows how the structural changes which occurred in Scotland in the preceding fifty years or so helped to absorb the shock and saved Scotland from a fate similar to Ireland's. The number of persons affected was relatively small, no doubt in part a result of industrialization. The Central Relief Board was able to distribute large amounts of food, and the worst stricken were able to survive through income provided by public

40   For an example of Dutch policies which attempted to reform the poor, see H. F. J. M. Van Den Eerenbeemt, "Het huwelijk tussen Filantropie en Economie: een Patriotse Illusie," *Economisch-en Sociaal-Historisch Jaarboek*, XXXV (1972), 28–64, XXXVIII (1975), 179–255, XXXIX (1976), 13–100. Total Dutch spending on poor relief from 1846 to 1849 shows a far blunter peak than similar spending in France. Frances Gouda, "Poverty and Poor Relief: the Netherlands and France, 1815–55," paper presented at the American Historical Association meeting (1978), Fig. 11.

works. Again, these resources must have come in part from the surplus produced by the modern sector. Finally, the Scots had at their disposal more accumulated savings which were drawn upon now that a rainy day had arrived.[41]

The general sluggishness with which Ireland and the Netherlands developed in the first half of the nineteenth century resulted in a failure on their part to eradicate a particularly heinous form of poverty: high excess mortality rates during so-called subsistence crises. Those Western economies which modernized during that period managed to muster enough resilience to weather severe scarcities and thus avoided the ordeal which Ireland and (to a lesser degree) the Netherlands underwent in the 1840s.

The similarities between the courses followed by the Irish and Dutch economies in the first half of the nineteenth century should not be overdrawn. The differences between the two dominate the similarities, and it was the differences which determined the further development of the two countries from 1850 to 1914. The two crucial differences between Ireland and the Netherlands, abstracting for the moment from large internal variations within each, were in the level of development of the agricultural sector and the survival of certain remnants of the golden age in the Netherlands, which had no counterpart in Ireland.

The Dutch agricultural sector was severely hit by the potato famine, and although the rural and urban poor, who depended on potatoes, could obtain little help from the modern sector, the bulk of the agricultural sector was sufficiently wealthy to allow the economy to recover rapidly and in the 1850s to start a slow but ultimately successful ascent toward industrial prosperity. As noted, the Dutch economy could still count on a colonial empire, a maritime sector, and a substantial class of *rentiers*—all in one way or another a heritage of a glorious past. None of these relics introduced much of a dynamic element into the Dutch economy. The famine in the late 1840s in the Netherlands was therefore

---

41 Scottish relief aid was organized by Sir Edward Pine Coffin who, despite his name, prevented mass starvation. Malcolm Gray, "The Highland Potato Famine of the 1840's," *Economic History Review*, VII (1955), 366. Other factors not directly attributable to the level of economic development were also at work in Scotland, such as landlord attitudes toward tenants, which were very different than in Ireland. Flinn, *Scottish Population History*, 434.

severe—more severe than in economies which had already undergone modernization. Yet, the Dutch economy was strong enough so that effects of the disaster were ultimately confined within tolerable limits and thus remained ephemeral. Dutch outmigration after the famine remained modest: between 1850 and 1880 an annual average of 1,560 persons left the Netherlands for the United States, too few to have an impact on those who stayed behind.

In Ireland matters stood differently. In the seven decades between the famine and the restoration of Irish independence, Irish history is unique: emigration and falling birth and marriage rates reduced the population of Ireland by 50 percent. Industrialization proceeded so slowly and in so few areas that Ireland was probably regressing in its relative position vis à vis the rest of Europe. One of the most challenging questions in Irish history still remains: to what extent was Ireland's failure to make much economic progress after the famine in comparison with the rest of Europe due to the disaster itself, as opposed to more deeply ingrained weaknesses in the Irish economy which themselves led to the enormity of the famine?

When harvest failures struck Ireland again in the late 1870s they hardly affected vital statistics at all. How is this fact reconciled with the lamentations about continued Irish backwardness after the famine? For one thing, the decline in population and the concomitant restructuring of agrarian society and land holding patterns after 1850 to some extent substituted for economic growth. More important, it should be realized that reduction of the vulnerability to famine depended on absolute, not comparative progress. The construction of a railroad network, the conversion of land from arable to pasturage, and the opening up of remote areas in the south and west to commercial agriculture eliminated the threat of high mortality even as Ireland was continually falling further and further behind compared to other Western European economies. Therefore, from 1850 on, it becomes impossible to approximate poverty from demographic data during a famine. Instead, income per capita, consumption levels, or other relative measures have to be used. These data show that Ireland stayed firmly entrenched in its position as the poorest economy of the areas, while the Dutch successfully entered the twentieth century as a prosperous nation.

Louise A. Tilly

The Food Riot as a Form
of Political Conflict in France   Food riots in France
since the seventeenth century can be most meaningfully explained not
in a simple economic formula of food shortage/hunger/riot, but within
a political context of changing governmental policy and in terms of
secular economic change in marketing arrangements of grain.

Food riots had several forms which show a definite change and development over time. The market riot, an urban version, was usually
aimed at bakers whose prices were too high or whose loaves were too
few, at city residents who were suspected of hoarding supplies of grain
in their houses, and at government officials who failed to act swiftly to
ease a food shortage.[1]

The *entrave* was the rural form of grain riot, in which wagons
or barges loaded with grain were forcibly prevented from leaving a locality. In isolated examples, at least, it can be traced to
the early seventeenth century. The market riot and the *entrave*
were polar opposites. The market riot was a sign that not enough
grain was available in a local urban marketplace. The *entrave* tried to
restrict the local grain supply to local consumption, and at reasonable
prices.

Taxation populaire, a form which emerged at the end of the seventeenth century, could occur at several levels, as described by Rose. His
first category is essentially what I have already labeled as the market
riot; the second concerns a "conscious political action against the authorities to secure the same end directly"; and the third was "*taxation
populaire*' itself . . . a disciplined measure implying an ordered sale and the
handing of proceeds to the proprietor."[2] The crowd would seize the
grain or flour, set a price recognized as the *just price* for the commodity
(and usually far below the current market price, sometimes remarkably
uniform from one riot to the next within a region),[3] sell the food, and

Louise A. Tilly is working on "A Social and Demographic History of the Working
Class of Milan, 1880–1914."

1 The market riot was traced back to the classical world by Nicolas Delamare in his
Traité de la Police (Paris, 1729; 3rd ed.), 4v. He was one of the grain commissioners
who served with the Paris police lieutenants at the end of the reign of Louis XIV. His
Traité was first published 1705–19, 3v. but citations for this essay are from the 3rd ed.
2 R. B. Rose, "Eighteenth Century Price Riots, the French Revolution and the Jacobin Maximum," *International Review of Social History*, IV (1959), 435, 438.
3 George Rudé, "La taxation populaire de mai 1775 à Paris et dans la région parisienne,"
Annales historiques de la Révolution française, XXVIII (1956), 177.

pay the owner. The *taxation populaire* could occur in a city marketplace and involve either bread or grain prices, or in a rural setting (*entrave*) as grain was sold off a wagon or barge.

The market riot was an old phenomenon in France, but the late seventeenth century saw a great increase of such riots, and of *entraves*, as well as the emergence of the new form of *taxation populaire*. The periodization of the increased incidence of food riots and the birth of the new form is important.[4] Widespread food riots, involving large numbers of people, but of relatively short duration, occurred in 1693/94, 1698, 1709/10, 1725, 1739/40, 1749, 1752, 1768, 1770, 1775, 1785, 1788/89, 1793, 1799, 1811/12, 1816/17, 1829/30, 1839/40, 1846/47, and the last few in 1853/54. All of these years were times of high grain prices, but the secular price movements between the end of the seventeenth century and mid–nineteenth were quite diverse. The period starts at a declining price phase; after 1720 or thereabouts started the long upward movement of the eighteenth century. A downturn began after 1815, continuing until 1850. This long temporal perspective suggests that the emergence and growth in importance of the food riot had no connection with the long-term trends of prices, although short-term price peaks accompanied all riots.

After the searing subsistence crises of the turn of the seventeenth to eighteenth centuries (1693/94, 1698, and 1709/10), there was a measurable decline in the effect of hunger on mortality in France.[5] Although

---

4 Abbott Payson Usher, *The History of the Grain Trade in France, 1400–1710* (Cambridge, Mass., 1913), remarks on the few documented grain riots before the mid-seventeenth century. In general, historical documentation of grain riots is sparse before the end of that century. Either there were few of them, or they were not considered worth mentioning. My impression that food riots increased in number is based on reading the following *general* works: Ernest Lavisse, *Histoire de France depuis les origines jusqu'à la Révolution* (Paris, 1910–11); Hippolyte Taine, *Les origines de la France contemporaine* (Paris, 1930; 32nd ed.). For regional studies of the seventeenth century: Emmanuel LeRoy Ladurie, *Les paysans de Languedoc* (Paris, 1964), 2v.; Pierre Goubert, *Beauvais et le Beauvaisis de 1660 à 1730* (Paris, 1960); Marc Venard, *Bourgeois et paysans du XVIIe siècle* (Paris, 1957); Gaston Roupnel, *La ville et la campagne au XVIIe siècle* (Paris, 1955); Pierre de St. Jacob, *Les paysans de la Bourgogne du Nord au dernier siècle de l'Ancien Régime* (Paris, 1960); Pierre Deyon, *Amiens, Capitale provinciale: Étude sur la société urbaine au 17e siècle* (Paris, 1967); René Baehrel, *Une croissance: La Basse–Provence rurale (fin du XVIe siècle–1789)* (Paris, 1961). For works focusing on the turn of the century: A. M. de Boislisle (ed.), *Correspondence des controleurs generaux des finances avec les intendants des provinces* (Paris, 1879), 3v.; René Lehoreau (ed. François Lebrun), *Cérémonial de l'Eglise d'Angers, 1672–1727* (Paris, 1967); Guy Lemarchand, "Crises économiques et atmosphere sociale en milieu urbain sous Louis XIV," *Revue d'histoire moderne et contemporaine*, XIV (1967), 244–265. For the eighteenth and nineteenth centuries, other detailed works are cited below.

5 Jean Meuvret, "Les crises de subsistences et la démographie de la France d'Ancien

there were periods of high food prices in the eighteenth century, demographic effects were less severe than earlier. An even further decline in both the intensity of price variation and of food-shortage-linked death occurred in the nineteenth century. The killing subsistence crises ended over a century before the last food riots—which continued to erupt during a period when, as far as starvation and misery went, life was improving.[6] Trends in population growth and agricultural productivity confirm this. Both of these curves were in downward or stagnant phases from the late seventeenth century to 1720; then there was a slow upward movement of population with agricultural productivity generally ahead of population growth.

The large-scale political and economic changes which I believe were crucial to the increased importance of the food riot as a form of political conflict were: (1) a two-directional movement in French political arrangements first toward political centralization and concentration on the national level of policy decisions concerning economic matters, then toward a modification of the traditional paternalistic economic policy; and (2) the formation of a national market, also under the influence of state action. The movement of enlarging markets corresponded with the emergence of Paris as a price-maker—even for distant markets—at the end of the seventeenth century.[7] In the absence of population growth in the seventeenth century, the trend to larger markets was a consequence of Bourbon financial and political policy. The fiscal nature of the tax system (erected in the seventeenth century against popular protest) went to support both royal ambitions in foreign policy and the overgrown bureaucracy which was needed to collect taxes.[8] Increased efficiency in tax collection drove peasants into the market—they had to sell much of their crop in order to pay taxes—and transformed many of them into buyers of food, with money earned by specialized

---

Régime," *Population*, I (1946), 643–650. See also Goubert, *Beauvais*, and LeRoy Ladurie, *Les Paysans de Languedoc*.

6 A recent article by Jean Meuvret, "Les oscillations des prix des céréales aux XVIIe siècles en Angleterre et dans les pays du Bassin parisien," *Revue d'histoire moderne et contemporaine*, XVI (1969), 543, remarks "the threatened populations made all the more noise since they were not completely wiped out."

7 André Rémond, *Études sur la circulation marchande en France aux XVIIIe et XIXe siècles* (Paris, 1956), 26, sees the frequency of eighteenth century crises and ensuing social problems as forcing a national policy of road-building and removal of hindrances to internal commerce.

8 Jean Meuvret, "Circuits d'échanges et travail rural dans la France du XVIIe siècle," in *Studi in onori di Armando Sapori* (Milan, n.d.), II, 1129–1142, emphasizes the effect of cities in drawing rural areas into the market economy.

farming or participation in rural industry.[9] The consequences of the heightened fiscal demands of the centralized state were both a growth in the number of buyers of food who were sensitive to price fluctuations and the increased movement of grain.

The popular reaction to these changes in governmental organization and policy took the form of food riots. Thompson's model of a moral economy of the poor becoming prominent in the period of the dismantling of the paternalistic economy and the transition to *laissez-faire* applies equally well to France as to eighteenth-century England.[10] The same legitimizing notions of justice which drove the tax rebels described by LeRoy Ladurie in seventeenth-century Languedoc moved the market rioters, who attracted more and more government attention after the 1690s. These men and women executed a rude justice, based upon a system of market regulations that endeavored to protect consumers by trying to force the government to act in the traditional ways or by themselves acting in the government's place. The emergence of the food riot marked the nationalization and politicization of the problem of subsistence, and was based on a conscious popular model of how the economy should work.

The location of the riots resulted from market expansion and the accompanying strains. They did not generally occur where prices were the highest, but erupted in productive areas from which the grain was drained by metropolitan, military, or overseas demand, and in large cities, where the continuing influx of food was a constant preoccupation and a source of intense anxiety in years of shortage. In any given year, prices were likely to be highest where the harvest was severely reduced or had failed. Areas which had good or normal crops, if they were at all accessible, were immediately tapped by merchants from Paris or other large cities, or by the military suppliers. Prices in these areas were driven up by commercial activity, which in turn reduced local supplies. This was the background to the rioting in productive areas, especially along their waterways or on their borders. It follows that as grain commerce increased and involved larger areas and longer distances, more protest could be expected, especially of the *entrave* type.

9 Goubert, *Beauvais, passim,* and also "The French Peasantry of the Seventeenth Century: A Regional Example," in Trevor Aston (ed.), *Crisis in Europe, 1560–1660* (New York, 1967), esp. 164–171.
10 Edward P. Thompson, "The Moral Economy of the English Crowd in the Eighteenth Century," *Past and Present,* L (1971), 71–136; *idem., The Making of the English Working Class* (London, 1964), 63–64.

The following pages contain, first, a discussion of the two large-scale transformations in the polity and economy of France which were accompanied by the emergence and growth of the food riot as a form of political conflict—the modification and eventual removal of paternalistic economic controls by government and the formation of a national market in grains; second, an application of Thompson's concept of a moral economy to the French case; and, third, case studies of the timing, form, and location of a series of food riots from the early eighteenth to mid-nineteenth centuries which illustrate the effects of these transformations and popular reaction to them.

EVOLUTION OF GOVERNMENT POLICY ON SUBSISTENCE   Traditionally, the government intervened in two ways with regard to matters of subsistence. It regulated markets and it controlled commerce.

The grain market regulatory system, which was gradually changed in the seventeenth century, and abolished toward the end of the eighteenth, was basically the medieval system, oriented toward protecting the consumer and preventing hoarding, speculation, and untoward profit. It required that all grain be sold in open markets, with bakers and merchants free to buy grain only after small buyers were supplied. In many markets, at least to about 1715, individuals still bought their subsistence in the form of grain, which was then milled and baked for them. Official market measurers checked the quantities. Once it was offered for sale at a stated price, the grain had to be kept in the market-place until sold, but for no more than three successive market days; on the fourth day it could be sold at a forced reduction in price. Standing wheat was not to be bought or sold, nor was grain to be held in granaries except on the farms that produced it, or in the home of the actual consumer. In times of shortage, administrative pressures were applied to cajole or force peasants and large farmers with stored wheat to put their grain on the market. For cereals, keeping a sufficient supply in sight and on sale was the main goal of market regulation. The enforcement of these regulations was originally a local responsibility, resting with local magistrates; but in 1667 the royal office of lieutenant of police for the city of Paris was established and given this task. The office was instituted in all major cities after 1699.[11]

11   A very useful state-of-the-question article was written over sixty years ago by Joseph Letaconnoux, "La Question des subsistances et du commerce des grains en France au XVIIIe siècle," *Revue d'histoire moderne et contemporaine*, VIII (1906–07), 409–445. My description of market controls is derived from R. B. Rose, "The French Revolution and

A similarly complex net of rules dealt with the supply of and price of bread. Within each city, the price of bread was "fixed" in terms of the price of wheat, and was to be sold at that price on all markets; it was not arbitrarily set at an ideal "just price." Prices were posted regularly for each weight and quality of bread, and no baker could sell his bread at another price. At first, the price of bread had been kept constant, and the weight of the loaf was reduced when costs went up. By the sixteenth century, this was no longer generally the case (in Paris, the change occurred by the 1430s), and bread prices themselves were allowed to move. In periods of extremely high grain prices, however, the proportional price formula was sometimes abandoned, as in 1693, in Paris, when the size of the loaf was reduced to minimize the apparent increase of bread prices. Officials did not overly press bakers who were unofficially reducing the size of the loaf and giving short weight.[12]

The centralizing political trend of the seventeenth century had its economic counterpart in mercantilism. Rothkrug describes mercantilism as the extension of the regulation of economic activity from commune to state. The crown supplanted local authority in one area after another. Royal officials took over the administration of traditional local laws and made them serve the needs of the state. The process of royal economic intervention has been described as "nothing but state-making—not state-making in a narrow sense but state-making and national-economy-making at the same time."[13] The sixteenth-century

---

the Grain Supply: Nationalization Pamphlets in the John Rylands Library," The John Rylands Library, *Bulletin*, XXXIX (1956–57), 175; Usher, *History of the Grain Trade*; Raymond de Roover, "The Concept of the Just Price: Theory and Economic Policy," *Journal of Economic History*, XVIII (1958), 418–434, 438–439; Jean Meuvret, "Le commerce des grains et des farines à Paris et les marchands parisiens à l'époque de Louis XIV," *Revue d'histoire moderne et contemporaine*, III (1956), 169–203.

12 Bread policy is described in Jean Meuvret, "Les prix des grains à Paris au XVe siècle et les origines de la mercuriale," Société historique et archéologique de Paris et de l'Ile-de-France, *Mémoires*, XI (1960), 286; Micheline Baulant-Duchaillat and Jean Meuvret, *Prix des céréales extraits de la mercuriale de Paris (1520–1698)* (Paris, 1960), I, 2–8. Joseph Letaconnoux, *Les subsistances et le commerce des grains en Bretagne au XVIIIe siècle* (Paris, 1894), 105–106, describes bread-pricing in Brittany. For eighteenth century Paris, see Léon Cahen, "L'approvisionnement en pain de Paris au XVIIIe siècle et la question de la boulangerie," *Revue d'histoire économique et sociale*, XIV (1962), 458–472, and Jacques Godechot, *La prise de la Bastille* (Paris, 1965), 87–91. Examples of flexible enforcement of regulations in Jacques St. Germain, *La Reynie et la police au Grand Siècle d'après des nombreux documents inédits* (Paris, 1962), 278–279; Boislisle, *Correspondence*, II, 145, 549; and Guy Lemarchand, "Les troubles de subsistances dans la Généralité de Rouen (seconde moitié du XVIIIe siècle)," *Annales historiques de la Révolution française*, XXXV (1963), 411.

13 Lionel Rothkrug, *The Opposition to Louis XIV: The Political and Social Origins of the*

monarchs attempted, and the seventeenth-century Bourbons succeeded in implementing centralized economic regulation and establishing a bureaucracy to carry it out.

This is not to claim that economic absolutism had any more concrete reality than political absolutism. Among the important restraints on the possibility of centralization of economic controls, especially of the grain trade, were the limitations of the bureaucracy and financial realities arising from national priorities.

The rickety, many-layered nature of the old regime administration is well known. The *intendant*, and other new officers, such as the lieutenant of police, took over prerogatives formerly held by local or provincial officers, but the old offices and their holders were not eliminated. The result, therefore, was far from even.

Constant frictions permeated the various layers of the bureaucracy and the courts throughout the seventeenth and eighteenth centuries. Conflicts between the *parlements* and the royal power are a prime example. Turgot wrote bitterly about the *parlements* which opposed his reforms:

> the regulations are an excuse for the magistrates in time of shortage to make a show of their paternal solicitude and to portray themselves as protectors of the people ... thus it is, authority is always precious to those who exercise it.[14]

There were also more strictly administrative conflicts of which those in Paris are the best documented. Despite his official role as regulator of markets, the police lieutenant of Paris still had to struggle in 1694 against the Provost of Merchants and the city hall for the predominance of royal officers over municipal.[15] It was only after this struggle that the office of police lieutenant was established in all cities, and it was still later that Delamare's manual for police officers was published, suggesting a long lag in the achievement of royal control of the police.

French Enlightenment (Princeton, 1965), 21, and Gustav Schmoller, *The Mercantile System* (1896), quoted in C. H. Wilson, "Trade, Society and the State," Ch. VIII in *The Cambridge Economic History of Europe* (Cambridge, 1967), IV, 573.

14 Anne Robert Jacques Turgot, *Oeuvres*, cited in Georges Afanassiev, *Le commerce des céréales en France au dix-huitième siècle* (Paris, 1894). This translation and all others are by L. Tilly. Léon Biollay, *Le Pacte de Famine et les operations sur les grains au XVIIIe siècle* (Paris, 1885), 267–274, attributes parlementary opposition to free trade in Burgundy to the realization that the *parlementaires* themselves would be among the first victims of popular ire.

15 St. Germain, *La Reynie*, 274.

Considerable personal independence and leeway in the actions of royal administrators, no matter what the official policy, made matters worse. In city after city the men on the spot, faced with the threat of disorder, would ignore regulations when they seemed too strict, or else would make regulations contrary to official policy when they felt them needed.

The French bureaucracy was neither effectively controlled from the center nor honestly run. The administration of old regime France did not have the skill to carry out either the old regulatory system, given the increased scale of enforcement on the national level, or the principle of free trade in grains, because of the persistence of localism, confused lines of authority, and the possibility of free play of opinions among administrators. Under these conditions, popular suspicion of administrators as speculators and popular efforts to sway officers by violence are both very understandable. Installed primarily to collect taxes, the bureaucracy was unable to cope with the problems arising from the enlarging market, the promotion of which was national policy. Thus, in a sense, the subsistence riots were a continuation of an anti-bureaucratic, anti-centralizing revolt.

The national priorities which royal policy established were also a serious constraint on any rationalization of the bureaucracy in the old regime. The question of doing away with offices and dues was a financial question as well as one of combating vested interests. As long as war and the pursuit of national or dynastic glory consumed the attention and financial resources of the state, there were severe limitations in how far economic and political reforms could go. Yet these very national policies (and the successful if inefficient imposition of taxes to support them) had the effect of enlarging the market.

One entire volume of Delamare's *Traité de la Police* is devoted to administrative problems arising from subsistence and marketing. He summed up the challenge: "Public security is never more threatened than in those periods when there is no bread, or when bread is difficult to obtain."[16] The regulated market system worked best in years of normal prices. As the French monarchy became more centralized, it not only gave formerly local powers to royal officers, as shown above, but also began to change the traditional market and commercial regulatory policies. This evolution of royal policy regarding grain is best seen in terms of the questions of (1) fixing commodity prices, (2) freedom of commerce, (3) requisitions, and (4) public granaries.

16　*Traité*, III, 828.

The question of commodity price-fixing and what it meant is complex. As de Roover has shown, even in scholastic economic theory, the "just price was simply the market price."[17] Although reasonable prices for food were the primary goal, even in the medieval period emphasis was placed in normal times on enforcing competition rather than price-fixing. When a dearth of grains caused rocketing prices for bread, however, strict regulations were invoked, but usually not price-setting for grain.

Delamare's chronology of royal attempts at price-fixing over the entire realm shows that, after 1500, there is no case of such attempts by the royal power. In 1709, grain price-fixing was discussed at length in the king's council and among administrators. Delamare prints a questionnaire regarding grain price-setting which local administrators were asked to fill out. His own answers, and his summary of the answers of others, were all decisively against such a policy. The controller general concluded that price-fixing:

> was still considered by the most experienced magistrates to be a measure impossible to carry out and subject to very great inconveniences; it is forcing men to act against their own interests, and they will find 100 ways to elude it.[18]

The old regime monarchic administration was too insubstantial to enforce national price-fixing. In fact, the only successful experiment with this policy in modern France was the Jacobin Maximum, when political terror and urban rationing accompanied price fixing. Even Napoleon's largely demagogic move to establish a maximum in 1812 was never applied in much of France and had to be annulled as the supply of grain being brought to market dried up in response.[19] The threat was real that farmers would simply refuse to bring their grain to market or else sell it in black markets. The debated national grain price-

---

17   de Roover, "Concept of Just Price," 429–430.
18   *Traité*, III, 922–934. Quote from controller general in Boislisle, *Correspondence*, III, 402.
19   Albert Mathiez, "Les restrictions alimentaires en l'an II," *Revue d'histoire économique et sociale*, XIV (1926), 42; Albert Chabert, *Essai sur les mouvements des prix en France de 1798 à 1820* (Paris, 1945), 390–391. Napoleon was acutely aware of the political importance of the price of bread in Paris, and said, "The government is there, and soldiers don't like to shoot at women, who with infants on their backs, come to shout in front of bakeries," cited in Jean Tulard, *La préfecture de police sous la monarchie de juillet suivi d'un inventaire sommaire et d'extraits des rapports de la Préfecture de police conservés aux Archives nationales* (Paris, 1964), 97. Tulard also describes bread price-setting based on grain cost under the July monarchy, 98.

fixing of 1709 never took place, and there are only two other cases in the period of the Revolution and First Empire.

On the local level, officials occasionally set grain prices even in the seventeenth and eighteenth centuries. In 1649, during one of the Fronde crises, the Parlement tried to set the price of grain in Paris. For Beauvais, Goubert finds only one case of official price setting of wheat, in 1709, and speaks of grain prices as "always free." And in Brittany in 1724, some police officers, believing that they were authorized to do so, fixed a maximum price on grain, an action which was soon annulled by the *intendant*.[20] The price of bread continued to be fixed, in proportion to the price of wheat and rye, in markets all over France. Yet, especially in the period of Physiocratic influence on grain policy, this kind of regulation, as well as other market regulations, was not strongly enforced. From Brittany in 1773 came a complaint that bread "était marchandé" and did not have a fixed price.[21] It is clear, however, that ordinary people often claimed that price-fixing of both bread and grain was a duty of local magistrates.

Commerce in grains was the main area in which the eighteenth century saw major changes. Controls on trade could be of several sorts: (1) actual declarations forbidding movement of grain out of a territory (royal officers tried to claim this as their duty, but various parlements, especially that of Normandy, disputed this—the correspondence of the *intendants* show them occasionally issuing such orders in the late seventeenth century, but more often a system of licences issued by them was used to *control* quantities moved; (2) regulations on who could take part in the grain trade—there was no change in this policy until 1763–64, as all merchants were required to be registered according to a declaration in 1699 (this document repeated traditional prohibitions), and various categories of men, including large farmers, nobles, royal officers, and the principal municipal officers were prohibited from trading in grain;[22] (3) strict enforcement of market regulations requiring that all grain be sold in public markets, and in general

20 Mme. Cubells, "Le Parlement de Paris pendant la Fronde," *XVIIe siècle*, 35 (1957), 193–194; Goubert, *Beauvais*, 368; Letaconnoux, *Bretagne*, 63.
21 *Ibid.*, 113. See also Robert Darnton, "Le Lieutenant de police J. P. Lenoir, la Guerre des farines et l'approvisionnement de Paris à la veille de la Révolution," *Revue d'histoire moderne et contemporaine*, XVI (1969), 611–624. Lenoir says in this memoir (622) that after 1775, even after the fall of Turgot and his own return to the police lieutenancy, the price of bread was regulated "naturally" and no longer formally set by police ordinance.
22 J. F. Rivière, *Précis historique et critique de la legislation française sur le commerce des céréales et des mesures d'administration prises dans les temps de cherté* (Paris, 1859), is the chief source of this chronology; see also Delamare, *Traité*, III, 615 ff.

making wholesale marketing very difficult and legally almost impossible. Therefore, although there was much talk of freeing commerce around the turn of the century, the commercial system was only slightly modified in that licenses had been substituted for an outright prohibition of trade movement. This was in contrast to the definite refusal to condone price setting.

The critiques of Boisguilbert and Vauban attributed the problems of French agriculture at the end of the seventeenth century to the system of regulated commerce in grains, and their ideas were partially and tentatively adopted in eighteenth-century administrative practice. The continuation of internal duties and market regulations, however, greatly limited the significance of the various decrees ordering the absolute liberty of circulation of grains. It is fair to say, nevertheless, that in law and administrative practice, free internal trade of grains had been a matter of discussion, with agreement in general terms on its desirability, for years before the appearance of Physiocratic theories, which called for the complete elimination of limits on who could trade, the removal of market regulations, and the extension of freedom to external trade. The decrees of 1763 and 1764 declared freedom of transport of grains throughout the kingdom and abroad, and opened the trade to anyone, without need of registration. These decrees were abrogated in 1770, as were Turgot's similar actions in 1774 and 1775, because of a combination of forces: bad harvests, popular opposition (including riots), and parlementary objections.

It was not until 1791 that the Legislative Assembly made free trade in grains, internal and external, the policy of revolutionary France, but even then the debate was far from over. In Lyons, and then in Paris, governmental intervention to guarantee cheap food for all became part of the Jacobin program, and the ensuing Maximum was repealed only in An III. The oscillation of public policy throughout the eighteenth century was due to genuine differences of opinion as to the proper degree and nature of state economic activity.

The fall of the Jacobins led to the triumph of economic liberalism, insofar as commerce in grain goes, but later years saw renewed discussion of price maximums on wheat (1812) and sliding scale export regulations. Remnants of market regulation lingered, and in the 1850s liberal propagandists were still heading their works with quotations from Turgot and urging Napoleon III to end the remaining haphazard controls.[23]

23 Victor Emion, *Legislation, jurisprudence et usages du commerce du céréales* (Paris, n.d.,
2—J.I.H.

Under the catchall heading of "requisitions" are included investigation of supplies, attempts to force grain onto markets, and buying and "dumping" grain in an attempt to lower price levels. When it became clear that a harvest was inadequate and prices started to rise, in the late seventeenth century royal officials set about finding out just how much grain was stored in their areas by actually visiting large farms and granaries. Sometimes not only officials were involved in this process, as seen by an *arrêt* of September 1693, which provided that throughout France "persons of probity" were to visit farms, abbeys, and houses to inventory stocks.[24] Generally, however, it was the royal officers who had the responsibility to make the visits, and this was a transfer to them of a duty which municipal officers had carried out in an earlier period. This transfer from local to royal officials took place during the seventeenth century. Of course, Paris is the clearest case of this transfer; elsewhere jurisdictional conflicts continued in the eighteenth century. The royal commissioners traveled to grain-producing areas and, using the broad powers granted them by the king, forcibly opened stores of wheat, determined quantities, and ordered them to be taken to market.

When all else failed, an expedient used by the monarchy and its officials to bring prices down was that of buying grain on their own account and either selling it below market price, usually secretly, or distributing it to the poorest consumers. Both Louis XIV's instructions to the Dauphin and Colbert's letters of the same period show this kind of energetic royal intervention in the famine of 1662. In 1698–99 and 1709–10, there were no purchases abroad on the king's account, as there were in 1662, 1684, and 1693–94, probably because of wartime financial problems.[25] However, in those years some *intendants* and even some royal commissioners secretly bought grain and took it to market to sell at loss prices. Some cities practiced similar methods for subsidizing the poor. In Aix, where bread prices were perennially high because they were pegged to expensive local wheat prices, although cheaper wheat was imported, it was the city that sold emergency grain from abroad to

---

but preface dated 1854), 13. See also Rivière, *Précis*, which quotes Turgot on the title page: "It is by commerce alone and by free commerce, that the inequality of harvests can be corrected."

24 Delamare, *Traité*, III, 870.

25 1662 events in Paul Bondois, "La misère sous Louis XIV. La disette de 1662," *Revue d'histoire économique et sociale*, XII (1924), 61–62; later period in Biollay, *Le Pacte de Famine*, 36–37. See also Gustave Bord, *Le Pacte de Famine: Histoire-Légende* (Paris, 1887), 36–37.

citizens at below-market price, and even below its cost to the city.[26] This policy was again tried in 1789, for the first time in years, as the monarchy bought grain abroad and sent it to other major cities as well as to Paris.[27]

Crucial to any project of governmental buying of grain, aside from its financing and honest administration, was the availability of granaries and storage places for wheat. Unlike the Italian cities, which had successful storage schemes, public granaries were not widespread in France. Lyons led in establishing a Chambre d'Abondance (an outgrowth of earlier granary programs) to store grain as well as to feed the poor (1643). Other French cities later experimented with similar plans. Colbert, after the experience of 1662, when the king's wheat was stored in the galleries of the Louvre, tried to persuade Parisian merchants to establish semi-public granaries. Nothing came of this because of opposition from the powerful merchants, but, in 1684, the crown borrowed 10 million livres to subsidize public granaries, one of the few non-military financial obligations incurred by it during the old regime. Military needs still came first, however, and the earmarked funds were absorbed in the Dutch war. The proposal to establish a city granary in Paris in 1709 foundered partly on conflicting claims of officers, and partly on the unwillingness of merchants. Later, in the eighteenth century, the use of granaries was promoted in periods when regulation was official policy, and abandoned when notions of free trade dominated.[28]

FORMATION OF NATIONAL MARKET   The second large-scale transformation which was linked to the increased importance of grain riots, most importantly to the location of such riots, was the expansion of local markets and the movement toward a formation of a national market. In his discussion of the English corn market, Gras argues that the concept of a metropolitan market should be substituted for that of a national market. He writes, "The conception of national economy which hitherto has been unchallenged, owes its position to the old and in many ways pardonable confusion between politics and economics."[29]

26 Baehrel, Une croissance, 61.

27 Biollay, Le Pacte de Famine, 67–68. See also Léon Cahen, "Le Pacte de Famine et les spéculations sur les blés," Revue historique, CLII (1926), 32–43.

28 Granary policies are discussed in St. Germain, La Reynie, 264; E. V. Hamilton, "Origin and Growth of the National Debt in France and England," in Studi in onore di Gino Luzzatto, II (Milan, 1950), 249; Rivière, Précis, 130; Biollay, Le Pacte de Famine, 40; Afanassiev, Le commerce des céréales, 392.

29 Norman Scott Gras, The Evolution of the English Corn Market from the Twelfth to the Eighteenth Century (New York, 1967), viii, also 95–99.

In the sense that Paris was the administrative capital for the centralized royal bureaucracy in the seventeenth century, the effect of Paris in enlarging markets was also the result of political developments. Precisely because I am emphasizing economic and political consequences of enlarged marketing of commodities, the term national market seems useful.

Military demands were also crucial. In fact, the demands of the army, the instrument of dynastic ambitions, provided an earlier influence on marketing arrangements than did the growth of cities. Military needs for food for men and animals, and also for the draft animals and wagons which were employed for the internal movement of grains, often had a disturbing effect on the distribution of available food supplies. Cities smaller than the capital, such as Lyons and Rouen, also exerted powerful demands on the grain-growing areas, sometimes in competition with Paris. Meuvret has described the parasitism of seventeenth-century cities in relation to the countryside;[30] the parasites also included the court, the bureaucracy, and the army. The third force acting to broaden the market was export overseas. This can be seen in Languedoc in 1630, 1645, and 1651, when the profitability of exports to Spain led large farmers and merchants to try to move grains out of the province and into ships headed toward Catalonia.[31] Similar effects can be seen in the eighteenth and nineteenth centuries for the Atlantic ports of Nantes, Bordeaux, and La Rochelle.

Despite different terminology and a broader application of the term national market, my evidence resembles that of Gras in demonstrating the emergence of Paris as a price-making center for a large area, and the increased importance of wholesaling merchants. The final paragraphs in this section will compare my findings to Labrousse's picture of the local markets in grains which were caused by the expense and difficulty of transport.

One way to show the emerging role of Paris as a price-maker, even for distant markets which had little or no trade with it, is by comparisons of wheat price series over long periods.[32] If the differential between

30 Meuvret, "Circuits d'échanges," 1141.
31 LeRoy Ladurie, Les paysans de Languedoc, 1, 448–449.
32 Wheat prices are used despite the fact that bread made of rye, or wheat and rye mixed, was the normal diet of ordinary people through most of my period. Scholars have generally paid first attention to wheat prices, and there are not the long published time series for rye that there are for wheat. C. E. Labrousse, Esquisse du mouvement des prix et des revenus en France au XVIIIe siècle (Paris, 1933), I, 5, justifies his emphasis on wheat prices this way, "The importance placed on it [the price of wheat] corresponds to its importance in the national market as 'product of exchange,' as an index of the fluctuations of the

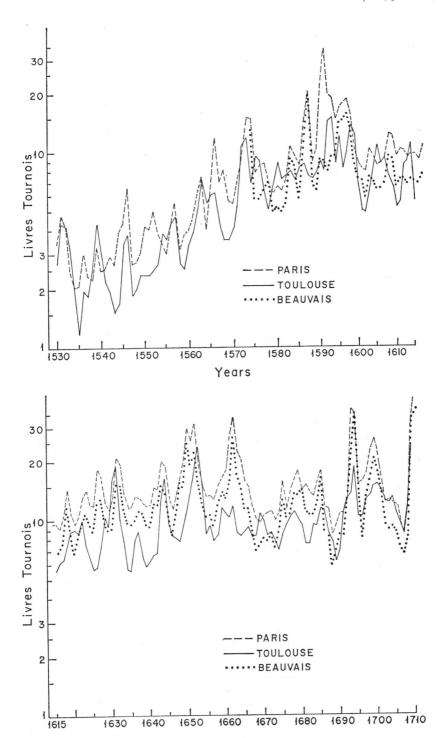

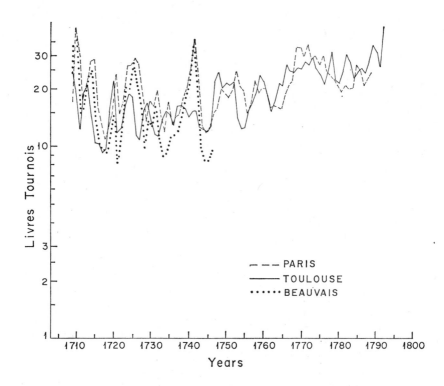

the two prices narrows (that is, the ratio between the prices moves toward 1.0), and the two prices and the cyclical movement of the two series tend to vary more simultaneously over time, strong evidence of the emergence of a national market exists. Fortunately, long series for major cities are available in nominal prices; they make possible a graphic and quantified presentation.[33] I have worked out a graph of

---

whole group of grains to which it is tightly correlated, rather than to its role in popular consumption," and I have followed this emphasis. Later studies, such as Goubert's, have confirmed the correlation between wheat and rye prices. Meuvret's recent article, "Oscillations des prix des céréales," 540–541, 552, points out that increases in the price of rye were proportionately stronger than those of wheat, reflecting increased consumption of the less expensive grain in response to higher wheat prices.

33 Thanks are due for methodological advice on this section to Charles Tilly and Emmanuel LeRoy Ladurie. The prices for Paris, Micheline Baulant, "Les prix des grains à Paris de 1431 à 1788," *Annales. E. S. C.*, XXIII (1968), 520–540; for Toulouse, Georges et Geneviève Frêche, *Les Prix des grains, des vins, et des legumes à Toulouse (1486–1868). Extraits des mercuriales suivis d'une bibliographie d'histoire des prix* (Paris, 1967); for Beauvais, Goubert, *Beauvais*, I, 401–405. The Beauvais prices are harvest year prices rather than calendar year prices as are the Paris and Toulouse prices, but Goubert's graphed comparison of harvest and calendar year prices shows that differences minimal for are

Paris and Toulouse wheat prices from 1530 to 1788, and Beauvais from 1574 to 1746, all expressed in *livres tournois* per *sétier*, the measure of Paris. The three curves, plotted on semi-log paper, show the familiar price peaks and irregular short cycles. From visual examination of the graph, the Paris/Toulouse (distant market) price curves, in the first half of the period, not only seem to vary according to different climatic and marketing systems, but the prices themselves are far apart. At the end of the seventeenth century, however, the prices converge and the difference between prices in the two markets is reduced. Although there are a few years around 1740 when price differences are very marked, after about 1745 the two curves move together, with very similar prices. As often as not Toulouse is higher than Paris. Beauvais and Paris (nearby markets) move together from about 1600.

Table I   Mean Prices and Standard Deviations from the Means

PERIOD	ARITHMETIC MEAN			STANDARD DEVIATION		
	PARIS	TOULOUSE	BEAUVAIS	PARIS	TOULOUSE	BEAUVAIS
1530–1549	3.17	2.60	—	1.12	0.97	—
1550–1599	9.63	6.93	—	6.21	3.12	—
1574–1599	—	—	9.21	—	—	3.98
1600–1649	12.41	8.29	9.68	3.34	2.88	2.70
1650–1699	16.46	10.57	12.69	6.53	3.36	6.47
1700–1746	—	—	14.79	—	—	7.14
1700–1749	18.16	14.56	—	6.97	3.85	—
1750–1788	17.37	17.56	—	5.00	4.27	—

Some straightforward statistical analyses confirm and refine the visual impressions given by the curves. First, the mean prices for each of the three markets and their standard deviations indicate the long trends and the extent of variability in prices from year to year. The means rise consistently from half-century to half-century, with the surprising exception that average prices in Paris drop slightly after 1750. Until that

study of long cycles, 372. See also René Baehrel, "L'exemple d'un exemple," *Annales. E. S. C.*, IX (1954), 213–214. The Beauvais curve has the added interest of being a proxy for Amiens, in the commercial grain-growing area of Picardy, as Deyon has shown in *Amiens*, 45–47. His comparison of price curves for Amiens and Beauvais (unfortunately he does not give the numbers on which the Amiens curve is based) show that although Beauvais was not an important commercial market and Amiens was, their prices were similar and varied together throughout the seventeenth century. From this I conclude that we can fairly say that Paris was making prices in Picardy as well as the Beauvaisis from about 1600, at least.

point, Parisian prices were consistently higher than those of the other two markets; the eighteenth century brought a marked convergence of the three series. The government policy of reducing marketing and commercial controls seems to have succeeded in bringing Parisian grain prices into the same range as those of distant Toulouse. We lack figures for the nearby market of Beauvais after 1746, but the pull of the Paris market most likely brought its average prices up. Baulant has observed this phenomena in the closer markets of Pontoise and Rozoy-en-Brie.[34]

The standard deviations show that on the whole prices varied more from year to year in Paris than in Beauvais, and, especially, more than in Toulouse. Relative to the mean price level, the century from 1650 to 1749 brought exceptional variability into the prices of Paris and Beauvais. Again, the market settled down to some extent in the years after 1749.

Table II Mean Deviation of Price Ratio from 1.0

PERIOD	PARIS : TOULOUSE	PARIS : BEAUVAIS
1530–1549	.38	—
1550–1599	.48	—
1574–1599	—	.47
1600–1649	.59	.29
1650–1699	.59	.29
1700–1746	—	.30
1700–1749	.30	—
1750–1788	.17	—

The mean deviations of the Paris:Toulouse and Paris:Beauvais price ratios from 1.0 measure more directly the extent of similarity from year to year. They show a distinct widening of the gap between Paris and Toulouse in the seventeenth century, followed by an even more decisive rapprochement in the eighteenth. Paris and Beauvais, on the other hand, experience relatively similar prices, year in, year out, from early in the seventeenth century. Both the means and the ratios, then, show a market based on Paris first making prices in nearby cities like Beauvais and then, in the eighteenth century, wielding its influence as far away as Toulouse.

34 Baulant, *Les prix des grains*, 521–522; Labrousse, *Esquisse*, I, 106–113, price table for fourteen generalities and Paris, 1756–1790. Labrousse's average prices for the Generality of Paris are higher in this period than those of the city of Paris. The Generality of Amiens also had higher prices than Paris in ten of the thirty-five years from 1756 to 1790.

This does not mean, however, that all the year-to-year fluctuations depended on events in the capital. The computation of correlations and regression coefficients for Paris: Toulouse and Paris: Beauvais make that clear. The prices of all three markets already had a strong tendency to fluctuate together (reflected by correlation coefficients in the vicinity of .6) in the sixteenth century. But during the time of the Fronde, and again in the 1740s, Toulouse and Paris oscillated in rather different rhythms. Climatic variations are probably important here. LeRoy Ladurie has made it clear that in Languedoc the subsistence crises before and during the Fronde were considerably milder than in the Beauvaisis and Paris; that is partly because the dry spells which reduced the northern harvests in those years were within the normal range of the arid South.[35] The acute but short-term effects of the sieges of Paris during the Fronde were probably not felt in Toulouse. In 1740 there again was a severe local dearth in northern France which appears to have affected prices in Toulouse relatively little.

Table III Correlation and Regression Coefficients for Prices

PERIOD	PARIS : TOULOUSE			PARIS : BEAUVAIS		
	r_{pt}	a_{pt}	b_{pt}	r_{pb}	a_{pb}	b_{pb}
1530–1549	.623	.872	.544	—	—	—
1550–1599	.688	3.606	.346	—	—	—
1574–1599	—	—	—	.579	4.63	.349
1600–1649	.485	3.104	.418	.377	6.17	.284
1650–1699	.605	5.435	.312	.917	− 2.26	.909
1700–1746	—	—	—	.876	− 1.10	.874
1700–1749	.365	10.91	.201	—	—	—
1750–1788	.609	10.91	.521	—	—	—

Paris and Beauvais experienced much more similar climatic conditions, but there were still some differences between them. The correlation between their prices was already high in the sixteenth century. It dropped during the period from 1600 to 1649, when the highly localized effects of the Fronde on Paris (documented by Goubert) probably affected the correlation. But after 1650 the correlation and regression coefficients for Beauvais: Paris show them to be so closely related as to be essentially the same price system. I conclude that both the graph of price curves and the quantitative measures of price comparisons with close and distant markets show that Paris by the end of the eighteenth

35 LeRoy Ladurie, *Les paysans de Languedoc*, I, 449–450.

century was a price-making center for a large area, but that movement in this direction had begun one hundred years before in the case of the distant market, Toulouse, and long before that for the neighboring market, Beauvais.

An indirect evidence of the growth of a national market is provided by the increased presence of merchants specializing in storing grain and moving it long distances. In England, the growing importance of the "corn middlemen," the engrossing merchant, and the *regrator*, is cited by Gras as evidence of the evolution of the metropolitan market in the sixteenth century. Fisher, writing of the period 1540–1640, also re-marked that London, in contrast to smaller cities, relied on middlemen for its supplies: "a large and increasing proportion of the capital's food passed, not through the common market places, but through the hands of the free retailers. . . ."[36]

In the case of France, there are no new descriptive professional words to use as evidence, but we do see in the seventeenth century that the local *blatier* trade was supplemented by merchants who specialized in handling larger quantities of grain over longer distances, and who often bought and sold outside of the regulated marketplace. In times of dearth, the *blatiers* and the merchants "became the enemy."[37] The chief way in which these men can be recognized is that during a shortage, the illegal character of their activity—buying at farms and granaries, buying by sample, and storing grain—attracted criticism and accusations from people who supported the traditional regulatory system.

In contrast to this, Arthur Young, the British agriculturist, saw the *accapareurs* as playing a useful and beneficial role in preventing starvation by storing wheat when it could be bought cheaply and bringing it out to sell when supplies were short.[38] Similarly, the greedy merchant, the *spéculateur*, and the *accapareur*, stripped of these value-laden titles, look to modern eyes very much like wholesale merchants. This is not to deny that their activities often hurt consumers in the short run. They did, and as long as the government was committed to consumer protection, much of its action tended to limit wholesaling activity.

36 Gras, *Evolution*, 198–199, and F. J. Fisher, "The Development of the London Food Market, 1540–1640," in E. M. Carus-Wilson (ed.), *Essays in Economic History* (London, 1954), I, 146.

37 Germain Martin, "Les famines de 1693 et 1709 et la spéculation sur les blés," Comité des Travaux historiques et scientifiques, Section des Sciences économiques et sociales, *Bulletin* (1908), 161.

38 Robert Latouche, "Le prix du blé à Grenoble," *Revue d'histoire économique*, XX (1932), 347. Lemarchand, "Troubles de subsistences," 410, writes that for ordinary people, the *accapareur* was the "gros négócient en grains."

But these merchants existed despite popular and governmental dis-approval; they are very evident in the second half of the seventeenth century, and, as government controls were reduced, they became even more important. Delamare's accounts of the various subsistence crises from the 1660s again and again mention the operations of merchants acting in their own interests rather than in those of the public.[39] It is clear that *accapareur* and wholesaler are synonyms. The confusion of words is similar to the situation in sixteenth-century England. "[City officials] found it difficult to distinguish between harmless direct buying and forestalling. County justices occasionally made themselves a nuis-ance by their efforts to protect rural consumers."[40] It seems to be equally difficult for historians to mark the dividing line between hoarders, speculators, and wholesale merchants. It is risky to judge by the testi-mony of contemporaries whose outlook was colored by a conviction that profits from trade in food must necessarily be limited.

The trend I have described of the movement toward a national mar-ket as early as the end of the seventeenth century runs counter to that noted by Labrousse. He emphasizes the imperfect and local markets which operated even after the mid-eighteenth century in France. In order to illustrate the limited usefulness for his purposes of local price series he compares prices of several groups of distant markets for rela-tively short periods (1744–1763 and 1756–1770). His graphs show ex-treme localization of prices, that the prices do not vary together, and that the direction of movement is also quite different.[41] Because I have compared prices over a much longer period, my graph and tables show that Paris' role as a price-maker for even a distant market, Toulouse, emerges strikingly after the end of the seventeenth century.

Labrousse argued that the enormous costs of transporting grain

39 Delamare, *Traité*, III, 829–830.
40 Fisher, "Development," 150. According to Littré's *Dictionnaire de la langue française*, the usage of *spéculer* in the sense of taking advantage of price changes in buying and selling commodities emerged in the eighteenth century; in the seventeenth, "spéculer, c'était méditer sur la metaphysique."
41 Labrousse, *Esquisse*, I, 5–9. See also Jean Meuvret, "La géographie des céréales et les anciennes économies européenes: prix méditerranéans, prix continentaux, prix atlan-tiques à la fin du XVII siècle," *Revista de Economia* (1951), 63–69. Meuvret demonstrates geographically-determined market regions, but his regional price comparisons are limited to the last quarter of the seventeenth century, because, he explains, "By extending the effort to a later period, one risks seeing the specific character of the mechanisms one wishes to analyze evaporate" (64). He implies by this that regional markets were less definable after 1700, which fits my findings.

led to a "weak . . . circulation of grains."[42] The cost of transport became less important to the price of wheat in periods of price increases, but, at the end of the eighteenth century, when the transportation network was most developed and other hindrances on trade most reduced, the profitable shipment of grain between the zones of high and low prices proved impossible.[43]

Although it is true that the northern and northeastern areas where wheat prices were usually low could not profitably ship to Roussillon and Provence (Labrousse's example) in the eighteenth century, the continued existence of regional markets does not vitiate a strong movement toward a national market and increased circulation of grain, especially in years of harvest failure. Provence, where prices were high, bought grain in years of dearth (and also in normal years as its own agriculture turned away from staples production) from Italy and North Africa.[44] In the case of Strasbourg in 1770–1771, the concerned city did not attempt to get grain from far off Marseilles, but concentrated on the closer German cities in the Rhine valley.[45] There was no trade connection between some of the high and low price areas, not because of high transportation costs, but because there existed closer foreign markets or French markets only slightly more distant than normal supply areas which could offer emergency supplies at acceptable costs. These costs were not always rational by modern economic standards, but they were accepted. The evidence shows that grain moved.[46] In contrast to

42 Labrousse, *Esquisse*, I, 124. For comparison with the English case, see C. W. J. Granger and C. M. Elliott, "A Fresh Look at Wheat Prices in the Eighteenth Century," *Economic History Review*, XX (1967), 257–262. Granger and Elliott use spectral analysis of grain price series over a long period to prove that regional markets had largely disappeared by the eighteenth century. T. S. Ashton argues in his *Economic History of England: the Eighteenth Century* (London, 1955), 86, that even before transportation improvements, wheat was commonly carried over long distances and market autonomy had disappeared.
43 Labrousse, *Esquisse*, I, 123–124. Following Labrousse, Chabert, *Essai*, I, 21–22, also emphasizes limitations on markets arising from transportation difficulties, and the great spread in price differentials for the period 1798–1820. See also Octave Festy, *L'Agriculture pendant la Révolution française: Les conditions de production et de récolte des céréales* (Paris, 1947), 88–89. Meuvret, in "Oscillations des prix des céréales," 548, recognizes the role of long-term market evolution in pointing out that although long cycles of price rise were accompanied by less severe price oscillations than in periods of price decline, this does not hold for the sixteenth century; he writes "Other factors were operating, from century to century, factors which we could provisionally sum up in a formula of a gradual development of grain commerce. . . ."
44 Baehrel, *Une croissance*, 78 and *passim*.
45 Yves Lemoigne, "Population and Provisions in Strasbourg in the Eighteenth Century," in Jeffrey Kaplow (ed.), *New Perspectives on the French Revolution: Readings in Historical Sociology* (New York, 1965), 61–62.
46 Fisher, "Developments," 150, writes for England, "Curiously enough the diffi-

Labrousse's picture of the impossibility of trade between high and low price regions in France, in years of high prices and shortages merchants did go beyond their usual supply areas. The cumulative effect of this process was grouped regional markets, enlarged markets, and increased movement of grain. The mechanism of this larger market was not, I suggest, in long links between distant markets, but in an interlocking web with ties that were only somewhat longer than those of the century before, but with a cumulative effect that is illustrated by the role of Paris as price-maker, even for Toulouse. This suggestion can be tested by a study of trade partners and routes for low and high-price years, as well as comparisons of local price series, both of which studies are beyond the scope of this paper. The local comparisons that had no part in Labrousse's study of long and short cycles of aggregate price movement would correct what I suspect is a wrong impression from his work of extremely local and imperfect markets and lack of circulation of grains.[47]

THE MORAL ECONOMY   Thompson's "moral economy of the poor" served to legitimate popular reactionary violence by appealing to traditional rights and customs. He sees the moral economy as a popular alternative when eighteenth-century governments changed the orientation of their national economic policy.[48] Thompson describes two

---

culties of land carriage do not seem to have impressed contemporaries. They were simply accepted to a degree which historians, debauched by the standards of a pampered age, are apt to forget. ..." Rémond, *Etudes sur la circulation marchande*, 38, writes "The considerations of distance, of the intrinsic values of the transported merchandise, of the pressing need for such and such a product surely influenced its level (and especially in the case of grain transport) but not in a mathematical sense." Rémond also emphasizes the importance of commercial connections between distant cities to the level of transport prices (89).

47   There are several lapses in the logic of Labrousse's argument on the lack of national market and his exclusive reliance on a national aggregate price series which is an unweighted average of the average yearly prices of fourteen generalities and the city of Paris. See *Esquisse*, I, 102n, 16–18, 63–85. If grain markets were so local, what can an unweighted average of them mean? Labrousse states that it is wheat's "importance in the national market as a product of exchange" (5) that explains the attention he pays to wheat prices.

48   Thompson's argument, summarized here, appears in the unpublished paper cited above, fn. 10. Natalie Z. Davis, in *Strikes and Salvation in Lyon* (forthcoming), argues that there was a felt "right of rebeine" (revolt) in sixteenth-century Lyons, which although vaguer than Thompson's moral economy, played the same role in legitimizing revolt. There was a similar vague justification for market riots of the seventeenth century and earlier which was based on the claim that the monarch, and by extension, municipal governments, had an obligation to see that food at reasonable price was available to all,

major alternative models for a national economy in eighteenth-century England. The older was the paternalistic, in which widespread government controls were invoked to protect consumers. Opposition to this policy came from economic theorists and practical men who believed that such controls hindered the growth of large-scale commerce and industry, growth which became accepted as a goal by important groups in society and eventually in government. Thompson calls the second model "laissez-faire." It removed overt moral assumptions from economic theory and action and posited an unregulated but self-adjusting market which would, in the case of grain, distribute supplies geographically and temporally (that is, throughout the harvest year) by means of the free play of competition. High prices in years of shortage, according to this model, were necessary to reduce consumption and adjust it to supply.

As has been shown above, there was no simple and swift change-over of economic arrangements in France from paternalism to *laissez-faire*. There *was* a long, slow process of transformation of economic policy with small changes, much debate, and hesitant larger changes. Both market regulations and royal regulation of grain commerce were greatly reduced before 1791, when the Assembly officially ended both types of governmental intervention.

Given the pattern of changing economic theories and actions in which consumer protection was being de-emphasized, and given the emergence of a national market which meant longer shipments of grain, frequent distributional problems, and often higher prices for consumers in producing areas, it is not surprising that the grain riot became an important form of political pressure by ordinary people. Their justification was a theory of moral economy.

The moral economy, as defined by Thompson, is a traditional view of the social role of government and the proper economic roles of producers, consumers, merchants, and officials. Legitimation of popular violence in defense of these traditional concepts was actually sometimes strengthened by the leniency of local authorities and a general acceptance in the community. Thompson illustrates his model of the moral economy mostly with reference to popular price-setting. In France there were three basic assumptions about the government's role on which the action of grain rioters was based: The government

at all times. This was, after all, at base simply a popular statement of the consumer-protection which was accepted government policy and the theory behind market regulations. The moral economy, as an alternative model with a very specific content as to how government should act in reference to the commerce of grains and food prices, only appeared when governments stopped intervening in traditional ways.

should (1) keep bread prices low by controlling and regulating the sale of bread and by setting the price of grain, when necessary; (2) search out grain supplies, requisition them if necessary, or force them onto markets at reduced prices; (3) prevent the movement of grain outside an area unless local needs were satisfied at a reasonable price. These are all actions which governments had taken in the past, which were arrogated to the royal government in the seventeenth century, and about the continuation of which there was incessant debate.

FORM AND LOCATION OF RIOTS   The *form* of food riots in the eighteenth and nineteenth centuries (*entrave* and *taxation populaire*) was determined by the reduction of governmental intervention in grain commerce and marketing. As the government withdrew, the people, whether city dwellers who forced price-setting in their markets, or country dwellers who prevented movements of grain from their locality, rose to act in its place, or to force it to act. The *locale* of grain riots can be attributed to the interaction, one could say collision, between the third assumption, that grain should not be exported from a region when prices were high, and the government policy of free exchange. The ideal of the moral economy is the link by which the form and location of eighteenth and nineteenth century riots can be connected to large-scale economic and political transformations with which the periodization of the emergence of the grain riot coincides.

As the French government and its agents were seeking to equalize food supplies by encouraging commerce, refusing to fix grain prices, and failing to keep bread prices under control, the new form of *taxation populaire* was born. In 1694, a crowd in Rouen rioted outside the palace of the *parlement*, demanding that the price of bread be lowered. They claimed that in the two-week absence of the president, the bread price had increased one sol. Local officials, finding the price of wheat slightly reduced, lowered the price of bread, too, and the crowd was sufficiently appeased to leave, although some of its elements attacked the house of a grain merchant and others pillaged a baker's house. This was a kind of taxation under popular pressure. Several explanatory letters were sent off to Paris, indicating an anxiety on the part of the local officials to justify what they had done. In Lyons in 1699, as the city was negotiating a purchase of wheat at the current market price, a crowd of women protested that the bread price should be lowered.[49] In 1709, there was a

49 Boislisle, *Correspondence*, I, No. 1310, and No. 1829. The only reference I have found to *taxation populaire* before this period is in Michel Caillard, "Recherches sur les

taxation of the most direct kind in the Paris region, which was to be troubled by this kind of riot for over a century after. At La Ferté-sous-Jouarre, a Parisian merchant, trying to load his wheat onto a barge on the Marne, was stopped by a crowd. They demanded his wheat at three livres for a *bichet*; he fled, and the crowd, which included a variety of solid citizens, obtained the wheat.[50] Clearly they thought that justice was on their side in their attempt to stop grain from leaving their locality *and* in demanding that it be sold to them at a price they set. Also in 1709 in Abbéville, where military buying was affecting price levels, a placard addressed to the council said: "We are dying of hunger, we must absolutely order you to set prices on bread and grain or else we will break from our homes like enraged lions, weapons in one hand, fire in the other." Here there was evidently no riot, only a fierce demand for governmental action.[51]

Price-setting on bread and on grain was intermingled in the above examples. The most clear cases of *taxation populaire*, those of grains, almost always took place during an *entrave*, and will be discussed below. In a strict sense, only these should be considered as a new departure, and as the result of the interaction of reduced governmental intervention, increased market size, and the moral economy. With regard to bread, however, even though price-setting was still the custom, as long as it varied in proportion to wheat prices, and wheat prices were soaring, it did not satisfy people who had a simple idea that the government's role was to prevent starvation. The appropriate royal officers had to move swiftly and deftly to fend off the threat of riot under these circumstances. A contemporary, reporting on events in Roan in 1709, wrote, "At

---

soulèvements populaires in Basse Normandie (1620–1640) et spécialement sur la Révolte des Nu-pieds," in Michel Caillard, *et al.*, *A Travers la Normandie des XVIIe et XVIIIe siècles* (Caen, 1963), 38–39. There was one protest in Caen in 1630 against the export of grain, and one in 1631 which attacked bakers and merchants, took grain "au prix qu'ils voullaient," and forced officials to set a "normal" but uneconomic price on grains. The beginnings of Normandy's long struggle with problems of conflicting demand and grain distribution probably antedated the late seventeenth century period on which this paper focuses, and during which similar problems can be seen throughout France. Perhaps this was due to, on the one hand, Normandy's maritime economy, through which export trade demands were felt, and, on the other, its closeness to Paris and the wheat-growing Norman Vexin which bordered regions which were normal Paris supply regions. R. B. Rose, "Eighteenth Century Price Riots and Public Policy in England," *International Review of Social History*, VI (1961), 279, notes that the first price-fixing riot which he can find occurred in April 1693.

50 Jacques St. Germain, *La vie quotidiene en France à la fin du Grand Siècle* (Paris, 1965), 216.

51 Deyon, *Amiens*, 472.

one moment 16 thousand persons rose to get bread and killed one of the principal royal officers who was accused of not having taken the proper steps to calm the people."[52]

Even in connection with bread prices there are suggestions of a hardening of governmental attitudes about the wisdom of consumer protection, especially after 1750. Letaconnoux's work on Brittany led him to say, "If they intervened, it was above all to maintain order and security, to prevent riots which despite their efforts broke out . . . to prevent pillage . . . it was also for political reasons, to avoid being made responsible for the sufferings of the people."[53] Lemarchand, in a recent study of Normandy, remarks on the fear, horror, and exaggeration of authorities and their quickness to repress with force, especially after the mid-eighteenth century.[54] While at the turn of the century distributions of free bread and lowering the quality as well as the quantity of bread for a given price were expedients used by police authorities, in the Guerre de Farines of 1775 official attitudes were very different. The government answer was repression; there was no felt obligation to protect consumers. The Prince of Poix, who, as governor of Versailles, lowered the price of bread under pressure from a rioting crowd, was criticized in court circles for this "sotte manoeuvre." In Paris, although a riot was being born, the price of bread the next day was posted at one-half a sol higher. Police orders to bakers, once the riot had started, were that they were not to sell bread under the posted price. This policy of Turgot was opposed by the police lieutenant, who was forced to resign, and by the *parlement*, which petitioned the king to take measures "to lower the price of grains and of bread to a level proportionate to the means of the people."[55] The parish priests were ordered to preach free trade and remind their parishioners that "all confiscation of food, even if paid for, if it is at a price inferior to its value is a true theft, disapproved by divine and human law. . . ." Hardy, the Parisian bookseller and diarist, heard a sermon on this subject in Paris, and reported grumbling and protest among the listeners.[56]

There was a direct feedback to the problem of bread prices from

52 Lehoreau, *Cérémonial*, 194.
53 *Bretagne*, 55–56.
54 Guy Lemarchand, "Les troubles de subsistances dans la Généralité de Rouen (seconde moitié du XVIIIe siècle)," *Annales historiques de la Révolution française*, XXXV (1963), 413, 423.
55 Rudé, "La taxation populaire," 164. See also George Rudé, "La taxation populaire de mai 1775 en Picardie, en Normandie et dans le Beauvaisis," *Annales historiques de la Révolution française*, XXXIII (1961), 305–326; Darnton, "Le Lieutenant de police."
56 Rudé, "La taxation populaire" (1956), 165.

the popular position on grain price-setting. The reason for setting a controlled price on grain, after all, was to lower bread prices. A short-circuit of the theory plus resistant or insensitive authorities led to *taxation populaire* of bread; the eighteenth-century riot waves demanded interchangeably that the government should set grain prices and lower bread prices, especially during episodes of urban popular violence.

Taxation populaire also existed in the countryside, but it was usually associated with people acting in the place of government in two ways: They scoured the large farms looking for stores of grain, and they tried to prevent grain from leaving their locality.

Popular requisitions are a feature of the immediate pre-Revolutionary period. These processions of aroused peasants and village dwellers contain a strong suggestion of class conflict—poor against rich. Lemarchand cites several cases of marching against granaries in 1784 and 1789, and remarks on the fact that chateaux and monasteries as well as farms were attacked. "Thus, these popular risings, aimed firstly at seizing wheat wherever it could be found, ended by challenging the entire social system of the epoch, although the rioters were not fully conscious of this." Armed crowds, with banners and martial music, went into the Norman countryside to "taxer le grain chez le cultivateur."[57] Other raids on chateaux came from nearby regions of the west, Maine and Anjou. In the small Angevin towns of Baugé and Longué the Revolutionary militia led the chateau-searchers.[58]

Probably the most common form of popular violence about grain was still the *entrave*. There were some riots of the *entrave* type because of popular opposition to any export in a period of rising prices even in the early seventeenth century, when export controls were usually imposed by local officers, provincial magistrates, or, later, *intendants*. Earlier still, there was official opposition from local governments. Some cities even claimed a kind of "riparian rights" to a share of grain passing through their territory on canals or rivers, and also on roads. Claims of this sort were made by Amiens, Compiègne, Clermont-Ferrand, and Poitiers.[59]

By the end of the seventeenth century, the policy of most of the

---

57 "Troubles de subsistances," 413, 423.
58 Robert Triger, *L'Année 1789 au Mans et dans le Haut-Maine* (Mamers, 1889), 293; François Mourlot, *La fin de l'Ancien Régime dans la généralité de Caen (1787–1790)*, (Paris, 1913), 312; Daniel Solasseau, *Histoire de Baugé* (Baugé, 1960), 277–278. See also Richard Cobb, *Terreur et subsistances, 1793–1795* (Paris, 1964).
59 René Gandilhon, *La politique économique de Louis XI* (Paris, 1941), 150–151, 156.

intendants, as described above, was to keep channels open except in the worst situations. From Lyons, the *intendant* wrote in 1698:

> It is terrible and dangerous that the provinces isolate themselves this way, one from the other; it is the way for all to lack, for, at bottom, no one lacks; but however good orders can be given, they cannot be without inconvenience, nor can they produce the good effect that liberty of commerce produces infallibly.[60]

Popular clamor against export existed in all classes of the population. At Marans, through which grain passed to La Rochelle, "the principal inhabitants declared their solidarity, by public act, with all the pillage that might come in the future."[61] And from Moulins, the *intendant*, himself, wrote:

> Since, in this type of sedition there is some sort of memory of law, and public right is not completely violated ... what leads these unhappy people into error, it seems to me, is that they believe that the *arrêt* which forbade transport of grains outside the kingdom also forbade it from one province to another. ...

He therefore recommended light punishment for rioters.[62]

Turgot, in instituting his reforms, realized that people had to be persuaded of the benefits of free trade. He wrote, "It is absolutely necessary to put before the eyes of the public the details of the regulations which we are suppressing so that people know what is being done away with and realize its absurdity. ..."[63] The Guerre de Farines, which resulted from his policy, consisted largely of alarmed people putting into action the traditional policy of limiting exports from an area by themselves blocking movement of wagons or barges and selling grain at low prices to local residents. In Brittany, where there were many substantial farmers and merchants who were profiting from the grain trade, the *intendant* ordered the parish priests in 1787 to explain free trade from their pulpits.[64] But it was hard to persuade people to abandon fear for their local supply of food. Grain riots continued to occur until the 1850s when improvements in the communication and transportation network made possible quick shipments to balance supply and demand.

The incidence of the *entrave* grew with the increased circulation of

---

60 Lavisse, *Histoire de France*, VIII, pt. 1, 227.
61 Boislisle, *Correspondence*, III, No. 346 (incident in 1709).
62 *Ibid.*, I, No. 1873 (1699).
63 Rivière, *Précis*, 79.
64 Letaconnoux, *Bretagne*, 332.

grain—the transformation from local to national marketing. The location of the *entraves* was determined by the routes of the movement of grain and by special market demands from period to period.[65] The factors leading to increased and fluctuating demands on producing areas (discussed above) were the growth of city markets, military needs, and exports. To illustrate the interplay of these forces, I give more detailed descriptions of riot locations for three crisis periods for which documentation of riots is fairly full: 1709/10, 1816/17, and 1839/40.

CASE STUDIES OF RIOT PERIODS   The killing famine of 1709/10, which Delamare called the worst in history, followed the killing cold of the *"Grand hiver"* of 1709. Yet a reading of the sources indicates that there was at least one very important exceptional demand that had to be satisfied, and was, thus leading to all sorts of strains on the distribution of the available grain in France. This was the provisioning needs of the army in Flanders. The case of Burgundy and Champagne is best documented. Burgundy evidently saved more of its harvest than the area close to Paris, for in 1709/10 not only did supplies go to the capital, but also to the army and south to Lyons. St. Jacob states that "the dearth was less an affair of lack than of distribution."[66] Within the province, which was quickly tapped by the large military and urban consumers, smaller cities sought food and the countryside armed to prevent loss of vital supplies. "There was an open war with the peasants to get their grain," wrote a canon of Beaune. Officials and troops from Beaune only managed to get a good quantity of grain in the Auxois by armed force. Macon's purchases were stopped by peasant *entrave*. In Pontailler the grain which had been officially designated for movement to Lyons was seized and distributed at a set price. Similar violence was directed against grain boats elsewhere. The feelings of the Burgundians

65 Daniel Mornet, *Les Origines intellectuelles de la Révolution française, 1715–1787* (Paris, 1933), 444–445, lists about 100 "émeutes de pain" between 1715 and 1787. I mapped these for Mornet's three periods—1715–1747, 1748–1770, 1771–1787—and found that the riots were by no means randomly distributed. For the first two periods, over 50 per cent are in Brittany and Normandy. The increasing involvement of Brittany in the export of grain in the eighteenth century is one of the themes of Letaconnoux's *Bretagne*. In the third period, seven out of thirty-five events were in Brittany, ten more were in the western areas from which grain was exported through La Rochelle and Bordeaux. There were practically no riots in central, southwestern, or southeastern France. If we add the city of Lyons, and the Lyonnais, Champagne, Languedoc, and Alsace to the western areas listed above, we can account for over 90 per cent of the riots.
66 Germain Martin and Paul Martenot, "La Côte d'Or. (Etude d'économie rurale.)" Offprint from *Revue Bourguignonne*, XIX (1909), 312, and St. Jacob, *Les paysans de la Bourgogne du Nord*, 195.

were that "there is no justice if people die of hunger in Burgundy to feed the city of Lyons."[67] Lyon's demand was also considered excessive in the area closer to Lyons in 1709, when a rash of *entraves* took place in nearby villages.[68]

The northern area of Burgundy and Champagne were being tapped by Paris, and Delamare was concentrating his efforts to make the movement of grain easier in the area of Troyes-Chalons-St. Dizier-Vitry, much to the uneasiness of the inhabitants. He arrived at Troyes the day after a riot in which the houses of judges, and the Bureau de Recettes des Droits du Roy, had been attacked. Committed as he was to restoring rational trade through commercial regulation, Delamare declared at the marketplace that he had been sent by the king to help the people and restore plenty, and he persuaded a gathering crowd to disperse. At the border of Champagne and Brie, at Sezanne, there was another *entrave* in which police reported that although there was plenty of grain, people refused to see it sold and shipped.[69]

In the west, Brittany had had a better harvest than the rest of France, yet grain was stopped at Saint-Brieuc and Paimpol.[70] A list of the important riots of 1709 in Anjou shows that one was an *entrave* of wheat leaving Ponts-de-Cé for Nantes; the second, in Angers itself, was an *entrave* of wagons leaving for Laval, with violence continuing in a generalized attack on bakers; and the third was an *entrave* at Montejean of barges bound for Angers. The Ponts-de-Cé episode was notable because people insisted on buying part of the wheat which they had prevented from leaving and let the larger part proceed to Nantes. The reserved grain was distributed at a low price to the poor, as certified by their parish priests.[71] Finally, in the north, Normandy was, as was often the case, squeezed by extraordinary demands from Paris and the army. In both 1709 and 1710 large quantities of grains from the Caux and the Vexin were shipped off to Flanders for military needs. The riot that took place in Rouen in July 1709 was aimed most directly against the *intendant*, who, it was felt, had not acted promptly to assure the subsistence of Normandy.[72]

---

67 *Ibid.*, 190; Usher, *History of the Grain Trade*, 187.
68 Henri Hours, "Emeutes et émotions populaires dans les campagnes lyonnaises au XVIIIe siècle," *Cahiers d'histoire*, IX (1964), 139.
69 Delamare, *Traité*, III, 915–916.
70 Saint-Brieuc *entrave* in Letaconnoux, *Bretagne*, 328; Paimpol, Usher, *History of the Grain Trade*, 35.
71 Lehoreau, *Cérémonial*, 191–193.
72 Lemarchand, "Crises économiques," 253, 263.

This list of events was not selected in any way except to group them regionally, yet it is perfectly clear that every one of them was triggered by more movement of grain than people thought was right. Price differences were attractive enough to merchants to move grain, and Parisian and army demands were politically crucial enough for government to promote and protect that movement. Martin sums up the effect of large purchases: "Even if they acted in a strictly honest way, their [merchants'] purchases were so large that they caused a local shortage of grain and a certain price increase."[73] Riots erupted in those areas in which redistribution occurred.

An early challenge to the restored Bourbon government came with the bad harvest of 1816 and the ensuing wave of riots which has been described by Chabert and Marjolin. The latter emphasizes the royalist proclivities of the areas in which the early riots occurred, and concludes that these areas also supported the paternalistic economic policies of the old regime.[74] But paternalism regarding the commerce of grain had been largely abandoned by the old regime itself. The troubles started in Toulouse at the end of October. The harvest had been good in the Haute-Garonne, but grain was being shipped to Provence where it was needed. Grain barges were stopped by an angry population and the price fixed on grain in the market. In the Vendée, where the harvest had also been good, a group of *entraves* took place against grain headed for Bayonne. In 1816/17, almost all riots were *taxation populaire* of grain and *entraves*. There was a kind of ritualization of protest as the forms of popular violence over the movement of grain followed familiar scenarios. In place after place, familiar roles were filled by merchants and their shippers, enraged women and men armed with sticks and pitchforks who stopped the barges or wagons and "taxed the wheat." A kind of guerrilla theater—an acting out of ritualized protest—came into being.[75]

People thought that circumstances amply justified their action. "When you don't have any bread, who's afraid of prison?" was the shout heard in a village on the Orne. Officials found it quite natural also, for example, that the inhabitants of the Ille-et-Vilaine were aroused by purchases of grain by merchants from Bordeaux and Brittany.[76]

---

73   Martin, "Les famines de 1693 et 1709", 168.
74   Chabert, *Essai*, 406–416; Robert Marjolin, "Troubles provoqués en France par la disette de 1816–1817," *Revue d'histoire moderne*, VIII (1933), 426–427.
75   Paul Gonnet, "Esquisse de la crise économique en France de 1827 à 1832," *Revue d'histoire économique et sociale*, XXXIII (1955), 251, has an excellent description of a *taxation populaire* in 1829 which illustrates this ritualization of form.
76   Chabert, *Essai*, 408–409. See also Marjolin, "Troubles," 428, 431, 436.

Familiar areas became involved quickly, and Chabert's list of the locations most seriously affected by riots is to a large degree a traditional one: the Paris region, lower Normandy, Lyonnais, but with some new locations, the Nord, Borbonnais, and Bas-Poitou. Parisian demand can be seen in its own hinterland and Normandy. Shipments of wheat from Le Havre up the Seine had to be accompanied by troops. In the Paris region, Champagne, Burgundy, the Nivernais, and Orleanais, Marjolin describes a seemingly formless, furious "jacquerie descending on the markets, spreading through the country, pillaging farms, besieging cities, not fearing to attack the cities or attacking troops and throwing them back."[77] Despite the descriptive word "jacquerie," however, most of this violence took the form of *taxation populaire, entraves*, and requisitions, and took place in commercial wheat-growing areas in which extra heavy demand was distorting prices in the popular conception and putting grain into open view as it was shipped out. The Nord protests were along the Dunkerque canal, through which grain was moving to the interior. The Lyonnais experienced familiar troubles as, again, the area surrounding the city felt itself depleted of supplies by the demand of the city.

The west was involved as areas along the smaller rivers feeding the Loire became agitated. Redistribution within the west meant that a department like the Sarthe, which was not a major producing area, was called on to ship grain north to Alençon and Rouen, east to Chartres, and presumably on to Paris, with ensuing problems and popular violence.[78]

Marjolin's conclusion is that most of the violence occurred where harvests were good or normal and the inhabitants were aroused by the attempts to redistribute unequal supplies. Where there were real shortages, there were fewer riots, and more *taxation populaire*. Chabert agrees that the incidence of violence did not coincide with the regions of highest prices (which were the Haut- and Bas-Rhin, and the southeast). His explanation is that the areas most heavily involved were the most densely populated and the most industrialized, hence the most affected, following the Labroussian model, by the slowdown of industrial activity which rapidly followed a poor harvest.[79] More work has to be done on the 1816/17 wave of grain riots—especially in careful correlations of the incidence of violence with the economic structure of

77   *Ibid.*, 438; Chabert, *Essai*, 410–414.
78   Marjolin, "Troubles," 436.
79   Chabert, *Essai*, 414.

the departments where it occurred—since Chabert's own information shows many riots in commercial farming areas, which were heavily involved in grain-production, not industry. In the context of the long period I have been describing, however, the 1816/17 riots fall into the same pattern in that their location can be attributed by the pattern of distribution of grain and their form to a popular belief in the need for governmental intervention. When the government failed to act, popular violence tried to force it to do so, or the crowd acted in its place.

In the 1839/40 food riots, discussed and mapped by Levy-Leboyer, there is a decisive shift of location to the west.[80] The first wave, which actually started in December 1838, but reached its height in early 1839, was concentrated around the Atlantic ports of Brest, Nantes, and La Rochelle, through which grain was being shipped to English buyers. The same kind of export-spurred protest recurred late in 1839, after another mediocre harvest. Paris' demand and redistribution within the west shows up in the post-harvest 1839 protest, especially in Sarthe and Mayenne. South of the Loire, most of the incidents of popular violence were *entraves* (this was true throughout France, also; of sixty incidents classified according to type, thirty-nine were *entraves*)[81] on waterways leading to the Loire. Once on the river, some of the grain headed toward Paris via Orleans, some for the Atlantic ports. Roads north through Berry and Limousin witnessed numerous *entraves*.

Although the industrial crisis with which Levy-Leboyer is primarily concerned may have had some effect in mobilizing unemployed textile workers in the Norman and Breton *bocages*, the unemployment explanation does not hold for all of the cases described. Again the major influence was location in areas which were involved in larger market systems than they had been, and the form of protest in which *taxation populaire* was dominant, harking back to demands for a return to the paternalistic intervention of the government.

CONCLUSION   The food riots of the mid-seventeenth to mid-nineteenth centuries were the consequence of the nationalization and politicization of economic problems. They accompanied a shift of concerns about subsistence policy to the national political arena, and, in a sense, they continued the anti-tax, anti-centralizing revolts of the pre-Fronde

80 Maurice Lévy-Leboyer, *Las banques européenes dans la première moitié du XIX siècle* (Paris, 1964), also links unemployed textile workers with popular protest, 530–531n.
81 Barbara Herman, "Some Reflections on the Grain Riots in France, 1839–1840," seminar paper, Harvard University (January, 1967).

period because it was the growth of the centralized state, with its political goals and financial needs, which determined the large-scale changes in the economy, and the changed role of government in the economy.

The timing of the increased importance of food riots coincides with the growth of the market in response to the demands of the centralized state, its administration and court, and its political goals of foreign domination. The food riot grew even more common, and its shape became formalized as a consequence of the late eighteenth-century reduction of government intervention in the commerce of grain. The political consciousness of ordinary people was sharpened as they rioted, not only because they were hungry, but also because they thought that the government had an obligation to act in specific ways when faced by high food prices. The ideology of the moral economy, which recalled earlier government paternalism, was the popular justification for the *taxation populaire* and the *entrave*. The location of the riots, especially the riots in producing regions, resulted from the distribution problems which accompanied the emergence of a national market, and was complicated by an extraordinary demand from the army, administrative centers, and later by growing industrial cities and overseas export.

Backward-looking protest, in the form of grain riots which invoked paternalistic economic regulations, occurred in 1788 and during the Revolutionary years. A harbinger of modern social legislation, the Jacobin Maximum was also a reformulation of a principle that the old regime had already questioned and to some degree abandoned. Popular violence, *entraves*, and *taxation populaire*, continued throughout the transition from a paternalistic to a *laissez-faire* economy and the attainment of a national market. The market rioters were expressing a rough-and-ready ideology of controls, sanctioned by tradition. They were crying out in protest at being made to be the ones to pay the cost of a giant step in national economic development. And they were using the political tool of powerless people—popular violence. The achievement of political and economic integration—political participation for the popular classes and an efficient market—marked the end of the food riot in the mid-nineteenth century.

John Bohstedt and Dale E. Williams

The Diffusion of Riots: The Patterns of 1766, 1795, and 1801 in Devonshire

Why do riots spread? Why does a riot in one town seem to spark riots in others? Are riots contagious? The media in America and Britain have often referred to a "copycat" process at work in waves of riots, such as those in the summer of 1967 in the United States or in 1985 in Britain. Strictly speaking, contagion is a concept that sociologists have used to describe impulses from one individual to another, rather than from one group to another. Diffusion is the name given to the adoption of innovations by communities; its analysis is well established in many branches of social science—rural sociology, geography, economics, anthropology, and mass communication theory, to name but a few. Until about 1960, analysis of diffusion tended to focus on channels of communication as the key variable in the diffusion of innovations. Indeed, in some early studies of contagion in political events, contagion was assumed whenever events were contiguous in time and space.[1]

John Bohstedt is Associate Professor of History, University of Tennessee. He is the author of *Riots and Community Politics in England and Wales 1790–1810* (Cambridge, Mass., 1983). Dale E. Williams is law clerk, Louisiana State Supreme Court, and author of numerous articles on riots in England.

The authors are grateful for the comments of Andrew Charlesworth and Hew Joiner on a version of this paper given at the Social Science History Association Conference (1982). They are grateful to Thomas Hood and Thomas Bell for suggestions, and to Nicholas Billingham for allowing them to use his list of riots in Britain between 1750 and 1790. Quotations from Crown-copyright records in the Public Record Office appear by permission of the Controller of Her Majesty's Stationery Office; quotations from Crown-copyright records among the Fortescue lieutenancy papers in the Devon County Record Office appear by permission of the Keeper of the Public Records. Figures 1 and 4 are reproduced with the permission of the editors of *Past & Present* and the Harvard University Press, respectively.

1 Contagion: Albert Bandura, "Imitation," in David L. Sils (ed.), *International Encyclopedia of the Social Sciences* (New York, 1968), VII, 96–101; diffusion: Elihu Katz, Martin L. Levin, and Herbert Hamilton, "Traditions of Research on the Diffusion of Innovation," *American Sociological Review*, XXVIII (1963), 137–152; consensus: Torsten Hagerstrand, "The Diffusion of Innovations," *International Encyclopedia of the Social Sciences*, IV, 174–177. Cf. David L. Huff and James M. Lutz, "The Contagion of Political Unrest in Independent Black Africa," *Economic Geography*, L (1974), 352–367.

More recently, even imitative behavior has come to be seen not as a simple and mechanical process, but rather as a complex learning experience which is affected by motivations, including costs and gains, and situational contexts. At the same time, a more sophisticated understanding of diffusion has emerged, which sees the force of example as only one of a hierarchy of causes. From a sociological perspective, "the process of diffusion may be characterized as the (1) *acceptance*, (2) over *time*, (3) of some specific *item*—an idea or practice, (4) by individuals, groups, or other *adopting units*, linked (5) to specific *channels* of communication, (6) to a *social structure*, and (7) to a given system of values, or *culture*."[2] Historians might add an additional factor, a meaningful triggering event at the national level, or similar events at the local level, which had parallel effects in a number of communities.

Until the late 1960s, applications of diffusion theory to riots were rare. Even Rudé, in his classic *Crowd in History*, dealt with the spread of riots mostly by description, especially by maps. Recently, the geographical spread of riots has been analyzed more thoroughly for two reasons. Government officials have sought to control "epidemics" of riots in the United States and Britain. Historians have made increasingly sophisticated analyses of rioting. The notion of contagion is still a sensitive issue, given saturated media coverage and its imputed effects. Critics blamed the media for fanning the flames of riot in the United States in 1967 and in Britain in 1981, even though some careful analyses concluded that those charges could not be substantiated. But Murdock, although skeptical of the simplistic, common-sense version of the "copycat" effect, concludes that "it is more productive to explore the *interaction* between reporting and the riots, rather than to pose the question of media influence in 'either/or' terms."[3]

2 Katz, Levin, and Hamilton, "Traditions of Research," 240; Bandura, "Imitation," 98–99; Hagerstrand, "Diffusion," 177; Stephen Davies, *The Diffusion of Process Innovations* (Cambridge, 1979), 20.
3 Graham Murdock, "Reporting the Riots: Images and Impact," in John Benyon (ed.), *Scarman and After: Essays Reflecting on Lord Scarman's Report, the Riots and their Aftermath* (Oxford, 1984), 88. George Rudé, *The Crowd in History: A Study of Popular Disturbances in France and England 1730–1848* (New York, 1964), 151–152, 154. See also Eric J. Hobsbawn and Rudé, *Captain Swing* (New York, 1968), 209–220. The leading student of the historical geography of riots has been Andrew Charlesworth. See his "The Spatial Diffusion of Rural Protest: A Historical and Comparative Perspective of Rural Riots in

Analysts of diffusion now include not only information and ideology, but also the social structure which predisposes or inhibits participants from adopting innovations or patterns of behavior. Recent studies of social movements have recognized that it is not sufficient to analyze what is in rioters' minds, be it ideology or grievance or rumor; attention must be given to the social structure and organization which allows or prevents discontent from taking shape in behavior.[4]

For students of the history of riots, these findings suggest that contagion is not simple. In the first place, the stimulus of example works on crowds or communities rather than individuals. What needs to be explained is collective action, mobilization for complex, often ritualized social transactions, not merely individual reactions. Second, riots have costs—they are not free. They may also have gains, for rioters have had their successes. Food riots were not simply the work of excitable beasts—rather, simultaneously with the stimulus of example, crowds employed a rough calculus of costs and benefits: the chance of jail sentences, violent repression, and loss of jobs balanced against the chance to gain food at lower prices. Third, the stimulus of example is only one element in a hierarchy of "causes" which predispose members of a community to riot or to remain peaceful. For, if two towns riot, why does a third remain quiet? Food riot "epidemics" in eighteenth-century Devonshire provide a setting in which to study the operation of three different levels of causation, common responses to triggering factors, channels of communication, and social structure.

GENERAL STIMULI: HARDSHIP, OUTRAGE, EXAMPLE   The first level of causation includes motivations for riots which might be present

Nineteenth-Century Britain," *Environment and Planning. D: Society and Space* (1983), I, 251–263. In his analysis of the Brixton riots and other disturbances in 1981, Lord Scarman suggested that the media bore some responsibility for the escalation and for the "imitative element" of the riots without offering substantiating evidence. Lord Scarman, *The Brixton Disorders, 10–12 April 1981* (London, 1981), 111. For a critical analysis of other conservative criticism, see Howard Tumber, *Television and the Riots* (London, 1982), 7–11, 44–48.
4   Social structure: Cox and Demko, "Conflict Behavior"; Gary T. Marx and James L. Wood, "Strands of Theory and Research in Collective Behavior," *Annual Review of Sociology*, I (1975), 363–428; John D. McCarthy and Mayer N. Zald, "Resource Mobilization and Social Movements: A Partial Theory," *American Journal of Sociology*, LXXXII (1977), 1212–1241.

in many communities. The most important of these is hardship. All three of the epidemics of social disturbance in Devonshire that are analyzed in this article—1766, 1795/1796, and 1801—took place following harvest failures which resulted in steep rises in the price of bread grains. Workers in Devon were particularly vulnerable to such a rise in their cost of living. The county's chief industry, the manufacture of woolen cloth, was already being ousted from its seventeenth-century prominence by the competition of the Yorkshire trade, by the damage done to its foreign markets by eighteenth-century wars, by changing fashions, and by technological conservatism. What spirit there was in the western clothing trade was reserved for the quarrels which took place incessantly between employer and employee. Existing social divisions were made sharper by the segregation of the wealthy clothiers and skilled craftsmen from the poorly paid spinners and weavers. In Devon, the industry was divided among the wealthy and skilled, concentrated in the finishing trades in Exeter and Tiverton and the less affluent "country clothiers." In the first half of the century alone, serious violence occurred in 1717, 1720, 1725, 1729, and 1738. The level of violence in 1756 approached the level of 1766. The French wars at the end of the eighteenth century gave the industry its coup de grace.[5]

Broadly speaking, West Country agriculture was not likely to employ out-of-work miners, smelters, or cloth-workers. Agricultural holdings in many areas were small, husbandry techniques were backward, and the requisite labor was secured either from the proprietor's family or from wretchedly paid servants. Agriculture and industry in the West Country were neither coextensive nor particularly complementary. As the status of the master weaver declined, so did livelihoods which mixed manufacturing with husbandry.[6]

5 Devon: Edwin A. G. Clark, "The Estuarine Ports of the Exe and the Teign, with Special Reference to the Period 1660–1880: A Study in Historical Geography," unpub. Ph.D. diss. (Univ. of London, 1957), 367. The instances of early eighteenth-century violence are catalogued in David G. D. Isaac, "A Study of Popular Disturbances in Britain, 1714," unpub. Ph.D. diss. (Univ. of Edinburgh, 1963), 341–344; Jeremy N. Caple, "Popular Protest and Public Order in Eighteenth Century England: The Food Riots of 1756–7," unpub. M.A. thesis (Queen's University, 1978).

6 Agricultural holdings: William Marshall, *The Rural Economy of the West of England* (London, 1796), I, 106–107; II, 231; William Pitt, *General View of the Agriculture of the County of Worcester* (London, 1813), 290–293; mixed economy: R. Perry, "The Glouces-

Under these circumstances, the textile workers' wages stagnated or fell. Devon wage rates were among the lowest in England. In 1769, Arthur Young judged wages in the West to be far too low, and he was by no means a noted advocate of an improved standard of living for the lower orders. Colonel James Wolfe, sent to quell the riots in 1756, found the weavers "so oppressed, so poor and so wretched" that he believed that they would "hazard a knock on the pate for bread and clothes, and turn against the soldiers through sheer necessity." Agricultural wages, a fair indicator of relative labor market conditions, were only 7s. a week in 1795, compared with a national average of 8s. 11d. Later eighteenth-century observers described the condition of Devonshire's laboring families as poverty-stricken and degraded. Poor rates rose dramatically throughout Devon in the last half of the century; even so, Devon was in the lower third of all English counties in per capita poor relief in 1801.[7]

This economic vulnerability sometimes resulted in acute hardship. A motif of impending starvation runs through the popular unrest of both crises at the end of the century. Rioters at Exeter in 1795 said that "if they were to suffer they might as well be hung as starved, and they would run the risk of making their situation better, for worse cou'd not be." In 1801, the poor at Bideford cried, "We are starving alive," and a man in the Modbury crowd declared, "It is a hard matter to starve." An anonymous handbill at Beerferris in June 1800 protested, "We have been starving for 6 months." However, there is no direct literary evidence in contemporary newspapers and letters of people actually

tershire Woolen Industry in the 18th and 19th Centuries," unpub. Ph.D. diss. (Univ. of London, 1947), 111.

7 Falling wages: William G. Hoskins, *Industry, Trade and People in Exeter, 1688–1800* (Manchester, 1935), 56; Arthur Young, *A Six Weeks Tour through the Southern Counties of England and Wales* . . . (London, 1769; 2nd ed.), 340; Lt. Col. James Wolfe to his mother, 24 Oct. 1756, in Beckles Wilson, *The Life and Letters of James Wolfe* (London, 1909), 304–305; Arthur L. Bowley, "The Statistics of Wages in the United Kingdom during the Last Hundred Years. I: Agricultural Wages," *Journal of the Royal Statistical Society*, LXI (1898), 704–707. Gilboy's wage figures for the eighteenth century give a similar picture, although she warns that "money was perhaps the least part of the real earnings of the agricultural community" (Elizabeth W. Gilboy, *Wages in Eighteenth Century England* [Cambridge, Mass., 1934], 86). Poor rates: Hoskins, "The Farm Labourer through Four Centuries," in *idem* (ed.), *Old Devon* (Newton Abbot, 1966), 191; the per capita poor relief rank is calculated from Mark Blaug, "The Myth of the Old Poor Law and the Making of the New," *Journal of Economic History*, XXIII (1963), App. A.

dying of starvation, which one would certainly expect if such deaths were a widespread occurrence. Malnutrition, however, did contribute to outbreaks of disease.[8]

Hardship alone cannot explain the crises, for rioting did not take place at the points of highest prices, either in time or place. Evidence for 1766 indicates, on the contrary, that the onset of the riots coincided with a lowering of prices on the Mark Lane exchange, and that the end of the rioting sparked a dramatic increase (see Figures 1 and 2). The market towns of the north and west, for instance, generally reported higher prices but fewer riots than their counterparts to the south and east. Moreover, analysis of these and other riots has shown that it was not the poorest people who rioted but those at least one level above pauperism. Although the hard-pressed woolen workers certainly participated in riots, the highly prosperous dockyard workers were among the most formidable rioters in 1795 and 1801.

The second general factor that produced riots was the popular sense of injustice which arose from the conviction that farmers and merchants selfishly profited from community need. That sense of injustice was much more visible and articulate in Devon at the end of the century than it had been in 1766. In 1795 and 1801 crowds typically took the high moral ground of setting prices and did not simply seize food outright, whereas in 1766, although a few price-fixing riots occurred, generally the crowds simply grabbed food or attacked mills. In any case, even a popular sense of injustice is still too general an explanation to explain why some towns witnessed riots and others did not. It cannot be shown, nor can it be assumed, that the people of Newton and Ashburton, who rioted, felt more outraged than the people of Teignmouth and Chudleigh, who did not riot.

---

8 Exeter: Univ. of Nottingham, Portland Papers, PWF (hereafter PWF), 9847 Richard Eastcott, Jr., 28 Mar. 1795; Crediton: Pub. Rec. Off. (hereafter P.R.O.), Home Rec. Off. (hereafter H.O.), 42/34 Anonymous handbill, enclosed in George Bent, 5 Apr. 1795; Bideford: Devon Rec. Off. (hereafter D.R.O.), 1262M/L52 J. Willcock, 15 Apr. 1801; Modbury: D.R.O., 1262M/L60 Deposition of Francis G. Steer, 12 May 1801; Beerferris: P.R.O., H.O. 42/50 copy of paper posted at Beerferris (7 June 1800), in John N. Foote, enclosed in J. P. Carpenter, 22 June 1800. In 1766, high prices and short supplies produced only a slight demographic effect, but the effect was approximately the same in both rioting and non-rioting areas (Williams, "Were 'Hunger' Rioters Really Hungry? Some Demographic Evidence," *Past & Present*, 71 [1976], 70–75); malnutrition: *London Chronicle*, 9 Apr. 1795.

Fig. 1 Disturbances in 1766: Incidence and Frequency

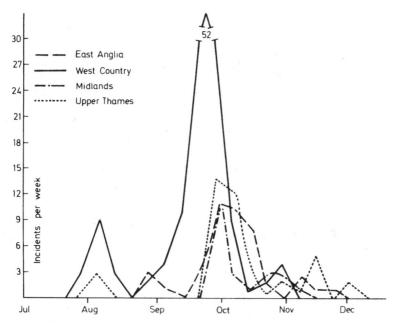

SOURCE: Williams, "English Hunger Riots in 1766," unpub. Ph.D. diss. (Univ. of Wales, 1978), 57.

The third general factor in our hierarchy is the force of example, or contagion. If contagion, or the force of example, were a sufficient explanation, rioting ought to radiate from a starting point, say Exeter, and move in all directions more or less evenly. Towns equidistant from Exeter ought to be equally susceptible. They were not, as can be seen from the maps in Figures 3, 4, and 5.

The impact of example was rarely recorded, but there are scraps of evidence which explicitly describe the path of "riot news." The news of a neighboring community's success in lowering prices through rioting might inspire townspeople to recalculate their own estimates of the probable gains and costs of a riot and thus increase their inclination to take direct action. In 1801, the Volunteer commander at Exmouth blamed unrest there on "the people who returned from Honiton market with the news

Fig. 2 Price and Volume of Wheat Sold at the Mark Lane Corn Exchange in London, August 1766—April 1767

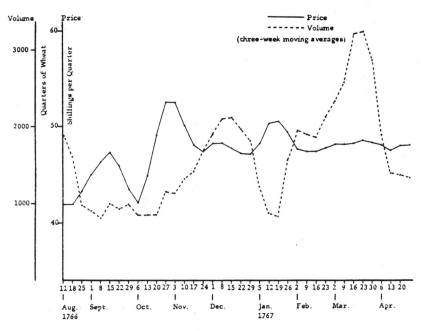

SOURCE: Corp. of London R.O., Mealweighers' Books.

of what had been done there." He believed that "the Exeter mob had instructed the people at Exmouth to demand wheat at 10s. and barley at 6s. the bushel. . . ." In 1801 a handbill told the people of Chudleigh to follow the example of Exeter and "to order the farmers to bring their corn to market at the same price as Exeter." At Modbury, there were rumors about the mid-April riots at Plymouth and Dock. Rioters at Fowey, in Cornwall, threatened to seek the help of the dreaded dockyard men, twenty-five miles away, if their demands were not met. The release of arrested rioters at Totnes was said to have intimidated witnesses of the Modbury riot, ten miles away. The Brixham crowd visited farmers with a price contract borrowed from neighboring Dartmouth. They carried a copy of the Dartmouth Articles and replied, when questioned, that "they followed the Dartmouth peo-

Fig. 3 The Spread of Riots in 1766

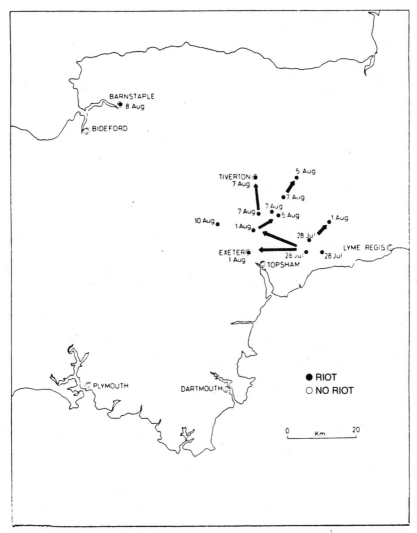

Fig. 4   Food Riots in Devon, 1766, 1795–1801

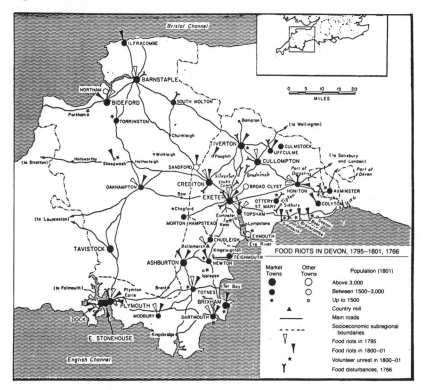

ple. . . ." The Dartmouth Articles were notorious: the *Exeter Flying Post* deemed it "prudent" not to print them, as they were "of too serious a nature to be inserted in a public newspaper." But a committee of twelve claiming to speak for the riotous workers of the dockyard hailed "the example of Dartmouth and Places adjacent, their Plan tends to PUBLIC GOOD."[9]

9   Volunteer commander at Exmouth: P.R.O., H.O. 42/61 James Coleridge, two letters of 19 Mar. 1801, enclosed in John G. Simcoe, 29 Mar. 1801; Chudleigh handbill: Clifford Papers, Ugbrooke House, Devon, General Correspondence, 1800–1813, Letters Miscellaneous, 1800–1804, George Burrington, 29 Mar. 1801; Modbury: P.R.O., H.O. 42/61 enclosure no. 1 (signature obliterated) in John P. Bastard, 18 Apr. 1801; Fowey: P.R.O., H.O. 42/61/725 Francis St. Aubyn, 16 Apr. 1801; Totnes: P.R.O., H.O. 42/62/359 (no. 11) Lord Fortescue, 10 May 1801; Brixham: D.R.O., 1262M/L52 Henry Studdy, 7 Apr. 1801; "Dartmouth Articles": *Exeter Flying Post*, 2 Apr. 1801; committee of twelve: P.R.O.,

Fig. 5 The Spread of Rioting in 1801

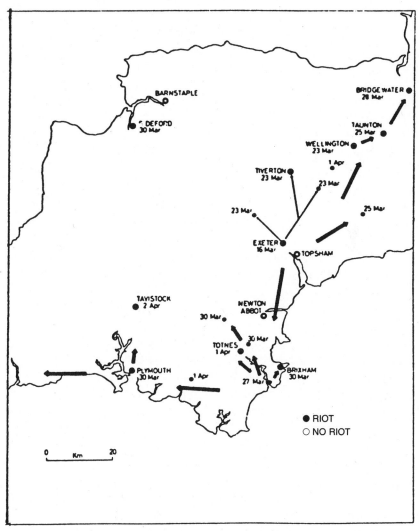

All three general factors—hardship, popular outrage, and example—clearly figured in riots but they do not completely

H.O. 42/61 printed handbill signed by William Johns and distributed at Dock, 4 Apr. 1801, enclosed in St. Aubyn and John Williams, 5 Apr. 1801.

explain them. For hunger, outrage, and temptation permeated the social atmosphere for many Devonians in 1766, 1795, and 1801. Yet only certain of them acted on these stimuli. Why did Cullompton and Crediton rise, for example, but not Tavistock and Torrington?

CHANNELS OF COMMUNICATION   Even a cursory inspection of the map of unrest suggests a second level of analysis—that of the geographical networks of riot (see Figure 4). Some communities were situated at nodes or intersections that ensured that they would receive more news of hardship and riots than the more isolated towns. The social and economic geography of Devon presents clear regional contrasts in the densities of social intercourse that help to explain the regional differences in the incidence of riots.

The distribution of the rioting falls naturally into three areas which correspond geographically, economically, and administratively to the three distinct subregions of Devon (see Figure 4). The economy of the first region, upland North and West Devon, was based on its clay and gravel soil, and was devoted primarily to stock raising, with an enclave of mixed corn and livestock farming in the Taw Valley around Barnstaple. Comprising half the territory of the county, Northwest Devon was thinly populated, with a density of only ninety persons per square mile. As might be expected in a pastoral area, the settlement pattern was one of scattered cottages and farmhouses. Outside the towns, the villages were "few and small."[10]

To the south, stretching in a crescent along the coast from Plymouth to the Teign River, lay the second subregion, the South Hams, a belt of red loam that was "not to be exceeded in richness and fertility by any [district] . . . perhaps in any part of England." This subregion was the breadbasket of Devon, although grain did not preclude cattle, especially around Plymouth.

The economy of the third subregion, East Devon, was dependent on its fertile loam soil, but also included the decaying woolen industry in Exeter, Crediton, and Tiverton, corn farming

10 Marshall, *Rural Economy*, I, 24; Joan Thirsk, "The Farming Regions of England," in *idem* (ed.), *The Agrarian History of England and Wales. IV, 1500–1640* (Cambridge, 1967), 71–78; Charles Vancouver, *General View of the Agriculture of the County of Devon* (London, 1808), 97, 400–401.

in the Exe valley, and an important dairy area in the eastern-most part of the county. More nuclear villages and denser population in the south and east reflected the differences in livelihood between these regions and Northwest Devon. The density of the population of South Devon was 205 persons per square mile, that of East Devon, 209. Each of the three regions contained about one third of Devon's total population, but South and East Devon each covered only half as much territory as Northwest Devon.[11]

The riot history of these areas in 1766, 1795, and 1800/1801 was distinctive. Northwest Devon had few riots in the period, and they were scattered in time and place. East Devon had more than three times as many riots in 1766 as did North Devon. East Devon and South Devon each had twice as many riots in 1795 as Northwest Devon and more than three times as many in 1800/1801, and they tended to be linked together in epidemics. To explain why this disparity existed sheds light on what kinds of communities rioted, and on the links between those communities.

The distribution of towns is an important factor in the riot experience of Devon's three subregions. Each of the three areas had thirteen market towns in 1800, but many of those in the northwest were small, and the five sizable market towns in the region were clustered in the northwest corner of the county. Hence there were considerable expanses of Northwest Devon that lacked even a medium-sized town of 1,500 people. South and East Devon, by contrast, had many more such good-sized market towns in half the area of Northwest Devon.

Perhaps the most important and distinctive feature of the towns was their function as markets or more generally, as nodes on various networks of social and economic intercourse. There is a close relationship between such market functions and the incidence of riots. Twenty-one (70 percent) of the thirty largest market towns in Devon had food riots in 1795 and 1801. Of the forty-two riots in those two crises, thirty-five (83 percent) took place in market towns. Obviously, riots that sought to force the sale of food occurred at marketplaces. Generally the rioters were iden-

---

11   South Hams: Robert Fraser, *A General View of the County of Devon* (London, 1794), 12, 20; Thomas Brice, *History of Exeter* (London, 1802), 182; East Devon: Vancouver, *General View,* 51–53; Hoskins, "The Ownership and Occupation of the Land in Devonshire 1650–1850," unpub. Ph.D. diss. (London Univ., 1938), 1–19; *idem, Devon,* (London, 1954), 96.

tified as people of the town, although in three cases people from the surrounding parishes participated in the rioting.

But also the market towns were the places where, in times of dearth, movement of food stuffs in and out must have contributed to the buildup of social tensions. Such traffic was visible and provocative; food was considered "exported" once it was shipped out of the neighborhood where it was grown. Locally, it mattered not whether the ultimate consumers were Frenchmen, Italians, Londoners, or English sailors.

In 1766, large-scale exportation of corn from Exeter and Barnstaple had helped touch off riots in midsummer at Exeter, Honiton, Barnstaple, and Tiverton. Consumers were particularly outraged because the export of corn was encouraged and even made profitable, not only by high prices on the Continent, but also by a governmental bounty on grain export that had negligently been left in place during the summer parliamentary recess. News of the royal proclamation against forestallers, regraters, and engrossers issued in September resulted in a rush to ship provisions out of the county. Any movement of wheat, bacon, or cheese became suspect and even provocative. For some months, the new starch mills at Lyme had been a major focus of resentment. It was said that the proprietors had exported large quantities of flour and bacon to France, and that the local scarcity and high prices were due largely to the operation of the mills. These accusations were, of course, denied by the proprietors, but, in mid-September, there were frequent rumors of mob attacks on mills and corn-traders in the district. Outside Exeter a crowd actually stopped a man taking a cart-load of dried peas to the nearby village of Wimple and forced him to return to the city. They brought him before a magistrate, who found that the man was breaking no law and endeavored to explain this fact to the crowd. But, later the same day, the crowd successfully turned back wagons which were transporting cheese to a neighboring fair at Newton Bushel.[12]

That same evening a crowd attacked the White Hart Inn in Exeter, where cheese was being collected apparently for shipment

---

12 A letter signed A FRIEND TO THE POOR stated the proprietors' case in the *Western Flying Post*, 13 Oct. 1766. A public statement by the proprietors was printed in the same issue.

to distant urban centers. A total of eleven hundredweights was taken and sold publicly. Order was restored but not before arrests of riot ringleaders, a rescue attempt, and a skirmish between mob and magistrates had occurred. In October, incidents were infrequent, sporadic, and nonviolent in nature. At Exeter in October a large crowd marched out to Exweeke Mill and dismantled its bolting machinery.[13]

A major cause of the disturbances had been the export of provisions from Exeter and Barnstaple to European and other destinations. In normal times, Devon was almost self-sufficient in foodstuffs. Hence, when the government declared an embargo on exports in late September, the Devon food situation improved and peace returned.

By the end of the eighteenth century, Devon's corn and cattle were increasingly shipped to regional and national markets, centering on distant towns like Bristol and London. These changes affected the South and East more than the Northwest. Northwest Devon's market towns were smaller, less economically differentiated, and not evenly distributed. Most of the grain there was consumed locally rather than exported, with the possible exception of the region around Barnstaple and Bideford (where there were riots). The agriculture of the South Hams and the Vale of Exeter, by contrast, was more commercially developed because of its proximity to the major urban areas of Exeter and Plymouth. Farms were larger, farmers had become more entrepreneurial, and dealers were more specialized and active. Dealers from Exeter and Plymouth, for example, were accused of driving up grain prices in the South Hams in 1800.[14]

Hence Exeter and East Devon were increasingly drawn into the market orbits of London and Bath, especially for dairy produce. This development encouraged a long-run tendency to con-

---

13   Taunton: *ibid.*, 20 Oct. 1766; Frome: *Felix Farley's Bristol Journal*, 25 Oct. 1766; *Western Flying Post*, 3 Nov. 1766; Exeter: *ibid.*, 27 Oct. 1766, *Jopson's Coventry Mercury*, 3 Nov. 1766; *Northampton Mercury*, 3 Nov. 1766; *Berrow's Worcester Journal*, 6 Nov. 1766. The crowd at Frome let the cheese wagon pass when the owner of the cheese declared on oath before a magistrate that the cheese was on its way to the Salisbury fair and was not for export. The crowd at Exeter did no further damage when the miller promised to supply the poor with wheat at 5s. per bushel.

14   The Plymouth market area did extend into Northwest Devon. Farmers, who became regrators (brokers) attended its markets from as far north as Ashwater. Accusations of Exeter and Plymouth dealers: P.R.O., H.O. 42/52 J.H. Rodd, 28 Oct. 1800.

vert fields from tillage to pasture, to the point that Marshall believed that the Vale of Exeter was no longer self-sufficient in grain, and hence was vulnerable in times of bad harvests. The popular judgment on such economic specialization was expressed in 1795 at Cullompton (in East Devon), where a threatening letter demanded a return from pasture to tillage and a mob declared that they would destroy all of the dairies in the neighborhood.[15]

That economic evolution, which increasingly placed agriculture in Devon at the disposal of distant urban consumers, was aggravated at the end of the century by strategic naval demands which strained Devon's capacity to produce food. With every French war of the eighteenth century, the naval dockyard at Plymouth Dock expanded. Greater Plymouth was the largest and fastest growing urban area in Devonshire. Its three chief towns, Plymouth, Plymouth Dock, and East Stonehouse, comprised a total of 43,194 persons by 1801, nearly one eighth of the county's population. That concentration of population, together with the provisioning of ships, meant that Plymouth drew food supplies overland from as far as thirty-five miles away. Both the demand for food and its price were further increased by specific strategic necessities, for example, naval and merchant ships waiting for convoy at Plymouth. In 1794, the fleet lay at anchor for months in Tor Bay, opposite Devon's primary cereal-producing region. These 25,000 extra mouths drained the coastal region of cattle, sheep, grain, and potatoes, and drew supplies from as far away as Worcester. The resulting local scarcity was blamed by the press for the riots there. The same factors were still at work when bad harvests in 1799/1800 led to national scarcity. In short, the conjuncture of all of these factors placed maximum pressure on South Devon.[16]

---

15 Market Economy: PWF 9847 Eastcott, 28 Mar. 1795; Clark, *The Ports of the Exe Estuary 1660–1860* (Exeter, 1960), 84; fields to tillage: Fraser, *General View*, 30; Marshall, *Rural Economy*, II, 109; threatening letter: PWF 298 letter from "a gentleman of fortune and respectability" to Nathaniel Battin, 30 June 1795. The establishment's concern over the need for more tillage was expressed at a meeting of an Exeter association about tithes (*Sherbourne and Yeovil Mercury*, 7 Dec. 1795), which was seconded and reiterated by the Devon Grand Jury (*ibid.*, 1 Apr. 1796). In 1800, a plan to try to compel more tillage was vetoed by the Lord Lieutenant (D.R.O., 1262M/L44 Lord Fortescue, 22 Sept. 1800).
16 Greater Plymouth: P.R.O., H.O. 42/61/725 St. Aubyn, 26 Apr. 1801; P.R.O., H.O. 42/62/359 (no. 11) Lord Fortescue, 10 May 1801; demand: D.R.O., 1262M/L52 Studdy, 7 Apr. 1801; fleet: *Exeter Flying Post*, 2 Apr. 1801.

Besides their strategic importance in the food marketing system, market towns were also nodes of communication. The maps of the spread of epidemics of riot in 1795 and 1801 demonstrate how those epidemics depended on trade routes (see Figures 4 and 5). It is significant that riotous towns like Colyton, Honiton, and Cullompton were located on the main arteries of communication between Exeter and London. Tiverton, Honiton, and Cullompton in East Devon were also on the main lines of communication with the textile districts of West Somerset. Axminster and Ottery, although similar in size and industrial character to the riotous towns, were off these main arteries and were somewhat less susceptible to the epidemic. In Northwest Devon, this relationship to the main routes may help to explain why rioting occurred in Okehampton and Ashburton, which were located on through roads, but not in Tavistock. Even if such networks of communication explain why Crediton and Modbury rioted, and Kingsbridge and Moreton Hampstead did not, they still do not account for the relative peace of Chudleigh and South Molton. For them, other explanations are necessary.[17]

On the whole, the differences in the density of population, the transportation networks, and the distribution of towns meant that Northwest and West Devon were much the most isolated of the three sections, and had fewer "receivers" and "transmitters" of the riot impulse.

Unrest also spread from one community to another along institutional networks, the most important being the Volunteers—local auxiliary militia units organized in the 1790s for home defense against riot and invasion. In September 1800, an Axminister Volunteer declared at a public house that he would be absolutely unwilling to protect the "damnation farmers" from a food riot. In December, those sentiments emerged in a wave of discontent that swept through the Volunteers of East Devon. Threatening handbills distributed at Tiverton seemed designed "to feel the pulse of the Volunteers." Several of the "old men" of the oldest Exeter corps of Volunteers turned in their arms saying that "they would not protect the Farmers." Two weeks later, handbills crit-

17   See Gilbert Sheldon, *From Trackway to Turnpike* (Oxford, 1928), for a map of the turnpike network of East Devon. Cf. John Cary, *Map of England* (London, 1794), which clearly shows the road and market town network on which Figure 4 is based. For the serge industry network, see Hoskins, *Industry, Trade and People*, 29.

ical of the farmers were delivered by the postman to the Volunteers along the East Devon road to Exeter; they were apparently
similar to those posted at Exmouth, which called on the Volunteers to meet "to consider the conduct of the farmers and to sign
a paper to be true to the cause." One such handbill urged the
Exmouth Volunteers to petition the magistrates for market regulation as the Sidmouth Volunteers had done. Disaffection was
spreading through the Volunteers, whether initiated by them or
by outsiders one cannot say. A Volunteer at Sidbury even declared
that a miller "should be hung up at his own door."[18]

The previous week Volunteers had led a riotous price-fixing
at nearby Branscombe after an anonymous letter to the parson
announced a "bond [pact], as to have better times" between the
"volunteers and inhabitants of this place." On the same day, a
crowd had gathered on the cliffs at neighboring Beer and tried to
force some of the Volunteers there to join them. Two Volunteers
were expelled from that corps for going with the Branscombe
mob. Lord Rolle believed a "certain sect" with "sinister purpose"
was at work to subvert the Volunteers. In the new year the
Exminster and Kenn Volunteers publicly repudiated an attempt
by "some evil-disposed persons to excite us to acts of Riot and
Outrage," and the Ottery Volunteers disavowed any connection
with threatening letters sent to the farmers and signed, "a Delegate
of the 1st Co. of Ottery Volunteers." At Lympstone (just across
the Exe from Exminster and Kenn, and within two miles of
Exmouth), handbills had appeared at the end of December urging
the Volunteers to meet "on particuler busnes [sic]." At the next
drill, a stormy confrontation occurred between the men and their
commander over the high prices of food, which ended in the
company's being "very much reduced" by the expulsion of the
dissidents. Certainly the Volunteers' unrest continued to increase:
across the county at Torrington the Volunteers were agitated
when an inflamatory letter was read to them from one of the East
Devon corps. In the wave of riots in March 1801, Volunteers

18 Axminster. Devon: Quart. Sess. Rolls, 1802 Papers, Deposition of John Liddon, 20
Sept. 1800; Tiverton: D.R.O., 1262M/L44 John B. Cholwich, 8 December 1800; Exeter:
D.R.O., 1262M/L44 Richard Eales, 3 December 1800; East Devonroad and Sidbury:
P.R.O., H.O. 42/55 Lord Rolle, 22 December 1800; Exmouth: P.R.O., H.O. 42/55 "The
Statement of the Rev. Marker . . . ," 22 Dec. 1800 (the petition and a copy of the Exmouth
notice are attached to Marker's statement).

took an active role at Exeter, Newton, Totnes, Dartmouth, and Brixham. The sparks flew across the Volunteer network by hand-bill and letter and by personal contact at field exercises or public houses.[19]

Communication also passed along other networks such as those of particular occupational groups (for example, clothwork-ers or sailors). Rarely were specific labor organizations observed in these riots. However, the prior solidarity of such occupational groups, together with the seasoning gained by collective action in labor disputes by woolcombers, sorters, fullers, weavers, and dockyard artisans provided a foundation for collective action on food prices. In 1766, groups of men in related clothing crafts in the country converged on the cheese stored at Exeter's White Hart Inn. In 1795, magistrates suspected that a society of wool-combers, sergemakers, and laborers at nearby Wellington, So-merset, had tried to instigate unrest by messages to their coun-terparts at Cullompton and Tiverton. The woolcombers and weavers were repeatedly blamed for the riots in that area, but there is only one piece of direct evidence of their participation in riots. At Uffculme (near Cullompton) in 1801, "the [workers' mutual insurance] clubs were and are divided; the riotous part took out the money and spent it," but the peaceful members of the woolcombers' Apron Society published a disclaimer of any intent to disturb the peace. In Plymouth, the dockyard workers' organization was also important in the unrest. Its chief objective was to cooperate with the other government dockyard workers to get higher wages, but the members also took part in the food rioting, issuing handbills and rescuing prisoners.[20]

Finally, there are indications that rioters created their own ad hoc means of organization and communication. Sometimes the

19 Branscombe: P.R.O., H.O. 42/55 Thomas Puddicombe, 21 Dec. 1800; Beer: D.R.O., 1262M/L46 copy of the evidence of Mr. Daniel French . . . Thomas Bidry . . . and John Wood (n.d. Dec. 1800); P.R.O., H.O. 42/55 Rolle, 24 Dec. 1800; 1262M/L46 Rolle, 28 Dec. 1800; repudiation: *Exeter Flying Post,* 8 Jan. 1801; *ibid.*, 1 Jan. 1801; Lympstone: D.R.O., 1262M/L48 Wakelin Welch, 4 Jan. 1801; Torrington: D.R.O., 1262M/L58 Rolle, 19 Jan. 1801; Exeter, Newton, Totnes, Dartmouth, and Brixham: Bohstedt, *Riots and Community Politics in England and Wales 1790–1810* (Cambridge, Mass., 1983), 38, 50.
20 Cullompton: D.R.O., 1262M/L44 Henry Skinner, 4 Sept. 1800; John Kennaway, 9 Sept. 1800; PWF 298 Letter from a "gentleman of fortune and respectability" to Battin, 30 June 1795; P.R.O., H.O. 42/61/351 Simcoe, 27 Mar. 1801; Uffculme: D.R.O., 1262M/L58 John Pearse Manley, 19 May 1801; Plymouth dockyard: Bohstedt, *Riots and Community Politics,* 56–57.

town crier was used to announce a riot. More frequently handbills called the people of a community or an area to assemble. Gentlemen reported other kinds of ad hoc communications; however, as a group they were generally suspicious of any evidence of "system" among the common people. For example, they reported that the leaders of the Modbury rioters met every night and corresponded with other societies, including one at Exeter. One informant reported that "they certainly correspond with people at a distance, particularly it is known that they were together one night last week till late and many letters were sent off next day." A magistrate described as "one of the most active and intelligent magistrates" of the county said that "it is well known though perhaps it would be difficult to give legal evidence of it, that men stiling themselves Delegates elected and appointed by the mob constantly communicate from Town to Town, and by this means carry intelligence from place to place, spread rumors of insurrection, and keep alive the spirit of discontent and uneasiness." His analysis was accepted by the Lord Lieutenant himself, but no further evidence has survived to sustain it.[21]

Evidence suggests that the networks themselves became more numerous and sophisticated between 1766 and the end of the century, thanks to the development of the capitalist market and communication system and the appearance of the Volunteer network, which did not exist in 1766. These developments, in turn, imply two things about the spread of riots. Spatially, the location of a town within the networks was an important factor in whether or not that community was riotous. Temporally, the development of economic and social networks by 1800 helps explain the contrast between the riots of 1766 and of 1795 through 1801. The riots in 1766 were sporadic—they arose quickly, were contained, and died away. The emergence of regional networks in the next generation may explain why the riots of 1795 and 1801 in Devon were part of widespread waves of rioting across the southwest of England, from Cornwall to Somerset.

SOCIAL STRUCTURE   A third level of analysis involves an examination of the social networks within the communities that

21 Newton: D.R.O., 1262M/L52 "Memo of riots at Modbury," n.d.; Ilfracombe: D.R.O., 1262M/L51 Roger Chappell and Robert Hulland, 7 Oct. 1801; Modbury: D.R.O., 1262M/L53 notes of the examination of witnesses by William Symons, Thomas Lane, and Foot, 5–6 May 1801; P.R.O., H.O. 42/61 enclosure no. 1 (signature obliterated) in Bastard, 18 Apr. 1801; magistrate: P.R.O., H.O. 42/61 William Tucker, 9 Apr. 1801.

rioted. The germs of hardship, outrage, and example found nourishment in some towns and not in others because of differences in the local networks that underlay the crowds' capacity for collective action. Hardship, outrage, and riot "news" did not *create* crowds out of free floating individuals. Rather, these factors were most likely to bring about riots by galvanizing networks of people *already* used to cooperating.

First, there was a clear tradition of riot in most of the riotous towns. In 1795 as in 1766, rioting began at Exeter and spread outward to Topsham, Honiton, and other textile towns. In 1795, Barnstaple and Bideford in the northwest and Plymouth and Dock in the southwest part of the county witnessed separate riots.

The pattern of the 1800/1801 riot epidemics replicates the geographical distribution of unrest in the previous generation. Exeter and Plymouth were the most riotous towns in Devon between 1750 and 1790, as in 1795 and 1801. The year 1800 saw only isolated outbreaks at Okehampton, Dock, and Ashburton. At the end of the year a series of incidents in southeast Devon found the Volunteers leading the violence. There was a lull until mid-March, when mobs began to assemble in Exeter to go out and visit the farmers. The towns around Exeter saw forced sales in the marketplace, as did Plymouth and Dock at the end of the month. Then, in the spring of 1801, between the riotous "poles" of Exeter and Plymouth, the towns along the south coast once more ignited, spilling crowds into the neighboring parishes to compel the farmers to comply with fixed-price agreements. The Northwest was also disturbed in April, although less violently so.

These recurrences suggest that a tradition of rioting existed in these particular places. The experience of successful rioting in the past could have been part of the collective mentality of a given community and increased its proclivity to riot when threats or opportunities appeared. Experience could have provided a stock of tactics or "consultants" on which to draw, and also could have provided expectations about the local balances of force and opinion.

In Devon, the surest predictor of riot in 1801 was riot in 1795. Of Devon's forty-five most populous parishes, thirteen had rioted in 1795, with 75 percent of those rioting again in 1800/1801. Of the thirty-two parishes that did not riot in 1795, less than 33 percent rioted in 1800/1801. It is clear from these data that a "tradition of rioting" can be used to predict future riots, but the question of what led to the development of such "traditions" remains.

There were several reasons for the emerging tradition. First, the towns that rioted were stable. They were growing slowly. Almost all of them grew less than 10 percent between the censuses of 1801 and 1811—well below the national average. Their stability would allow traditions and networks to endure. Second, their size was small enough so that most inhabitants might know each other but large enough to be distinctly differentiated from the rural hinterland. Except for Exeter and greater Plymouth, the riotous towns were almost all in the range of 1,500 to 6,000 people. Third, the riotous towns had high proportions of nonagricultural workers (especially in the decaying woolen towns.) By contrast, the towns that did not riot contained more agricultural workers. This economic differentiation underscores the fact that food riots were essentially a kind of rough haggling—a violent transformation of the routine market transactions and the implicit tensions between food vendors and consumers. Rural villagers, especially farm laborers, did not have to go to market because they could get their grain directly from the farmer, either by direct purchase in times of dearth or by pilferage.

Several other networks of collective action provided the sinews of habit and custom for riot. First, the woolen workers had a formidable tradition of tight organization and violent action in defense of their interests between 1700 and the 1760s—especially at Tiverton. The decay of the woolen industry undercut their bargaining power, but their militant traditions furnished tactical precedents and consultants for bread riots. The transition from workers' direct action to communal bread riots appears to be an example of the impact of deindustrialization on popular protest.

Second, many of the riotous towns were political boroughs with relatively large electorates ranging from a few hundred to several thousand voters. That size was enough to spawn intermittent popular political autonomy, exemplified, for instance, by the clubs of plebeian voters at Honiton and Okehampton, which joined together to sell their votes to the highest bidder.

Third, members of the Volunteers formed the nucleus for riots in Devon in 1801. Many of them participated in and led riots, and, in Exeter, they did so even in their uniforms. The

Brixham mob formed around the Volunteers, and even coerced their officers into taking them to visit local farmers and acting as their spokesmen and mediators. The irony is that the Volunteers had been created by the gentry and given an official constitutional role—as a force against invasion and as a potential militia to be called out against riot. When food prices soared, their bellies, and no doubt their families, told them they were ordinary consumers first and keepers of the peace a distant second.

Finally all of these networks among the rioters had vertical dimensions as well—that is, ties between the common people and the gentry that made riotous bargaining possible, fruitful, and therefore frequent.[22] The riotous towns had such networks; the non-riotous towns did not. In a few places, for example South Molton, Chudleigh, and Tavistock, both the generosity of Devon's leading peers in sending food to market and perhaps subtler social influences preserved the communities from the infection of riot.

Milgram and Toch have concluded that collective behavior cannot be studied in a laboratory setting because crowd action is the consequence of variables that are too complex to replicate there.[23] Chief among these variables is the historically conditioned experience not only of individuals but most importantly of crowds and whole communities. By the end of the century, crowd action in Devon was much more sophisticated tactically and more articulate ideologically than it had been in 1766. The events of 1766 were essentially a short-term response to immediate economic pressures. The crisis was short, the riotous epidemic was brief, and the official remedies were prompt. By the end of the century, the social networks of Devon were capable of supporting a more elaborate protocol of riot and an articulate ideology of grievances.

Any explanation of the spread of riots in Devon must be sought on at least three levels. At the most general level, the degree of hardship is a necessary but not sufficient explanation, for it does not explain who rioted nor when nor where. Likewise, ideologies of injustice were presumably shared by consumers in

22 See Bohstedt, *Riots and Community Politics,* 47–61, 68.
23 Stanley Milgram and Hans Toch, "Collective Behavior: Crowds and Social Movements," in Gardner Lindzey and Elliot Aronson (eds.), *The Handbook of Social Psychology* (Reading, Mass., 1969; 2nd ed.), IV, 582, 584.

both riotous and quiet towns. "Contagion"—the force of example, especially successful examples like the popular Dartmouth Articles—certainly contributed to the spread of riots. But hardship, outrage, and "contagion" must be set in a much richer context to explain why riots spread along some paths and not others.

At a second level, we have reconstructed the social and economic networks between towns that served as conduits to channel and intensify the stimuli of hardship, outrage, and example so as to affect certain towns more than others. Riots spread more in South and East Devon than in the Northwest, because the networks of roads and market towns in the South and East were both denser and more exposed to external market demands than the economy of the Northwest. The communication of the impulse to riot was further facilitated by the networks of Volunteers, especially in East Devon.

Finally, at a third level, some communities were more receptive to the riot "impulse" because their social structures permitted fruitful bargaining between crowds and magistrates that enabled rioters to succeed in lowering prices. "Horizontal" networks among the common people included local Volunteer Corps, political clubs, and the traditional solidarities of militant workers. "Vertical" networks between crowds and elites were created by varieties of social patronage. The stability and density of those networks, greater in the South and East, encouraged the evolution of local traditions of bargaining by riot in such towns as Exeter, Totnes, and Honiton.

Some of the seeds of riot fell on rock—where there was no medium of supportive networks—and so withered away. And some of the seeds fell among thorns—where they were choked by prudent charity from the gentry. And some of the seeds fell on fertile soil, and grew—supported by community networks—and yielded a great harvest of protest in times of dearth.

Gloria L. Main

Inequality in Early America: The Evidence from Probate Records of Massachusetts and Maryland

The distribution of wealth in America is highly unequal now and was even more unequal a hundred years ago. If the distribution of slaves in 1790 is a trustworthy guide, inequality, in the South at least, was already high in the earliest years of the Republic (see Table 1). A careful probing of the census data on wealth-holding for the years 1850, 1860, and 1870 persuaded one investigator that the distribution of wealth was highly *stable* as well as unequal. The relatively slight decline in inequality registered by a 1962 survey, he argues, was almost entirely attributable to such demographic factors as the aging of the general population, its geographical redistribution, and the virtual closing-off of foreign immigration.[1]

Because this limited but weighty evidence strongly suggests that the structure of wealth-holding in America may have long been frozen at a high level of inequality despite enormous economic and social change, one wonders whether the condition is somehow inevitable and therefore irreversible. One approach to the issue is to investigate the distribution of wealth in the more distant past to discover if, indeed, inequality has always been high. This essay first reviews existing studies for the period prior to 1860 and then introduces new evidence. The focus throughout is on the *course* of inequality over time. If it did change significantly, can the timing of such changes reveal their origins? The paper contributes both to the history of the distribution of wealth in America, and more ambitiously, toward an understanding of the nature of inequality itself.

Gloria L. Main is currently working on a book describing the changes in the wealth and standard of living of farmers in colonial Massachusetts and Maryland.

Members of the Columbia University Seminar in Early American History and Culture in 1974 and of the Cliometrics Conference at the University of Wisconsin, Madison in 1976 heard and commented on earlier versions of this article. The author wishes to thank them and, in addition, John McCusker, Richard Rapp, Jackson T. Main, James Shepherd, and anonymous reviewers of this Journal.

1 Lee Soltow, *Men and Wealth in the United States, 1850–1870* (New Haven, 1975), 60, 123, 177, 182, 183.

Table 1   Indices of Inequality in the American Past

RURAL AREAS OF THE NORTH	YEARS	DATA SOURCE	%SSTT	GINI
Chester Co., Pa.	1693	Tax Records	24½	.27
”	1715	”	26	.32
”	1730	”	29	.39
”	1748	”	29	.35
”	1760	”	30	.44
”	1782	”	34	.50
	1800–02	”	38	.56
Essex Co., Mass.[a]	1635–60	Probate Records	36	.54
”	1661–81	”	49	.62
Vermont Townships	1860	Census	38	.53
Tremeauleau Co., Wis.	1860	”	39	.48
CITIES OF THE NORTH				
Salem, Mass.	1635–60	Probate Records	31	.51
”	1661–81	”	59	.69
New York, N.Y.	1675	Tax Records	51	n.a.
”	1695	”	45	.60
”	1701	”	46	.59
”	1735	”	45	.55
”	1789	”	54	.67
”	1796	”	61	.72
Boston, Mass.	1687	”	47	.70
”	1771	”	63½	.73
”	1790	”	65	.79
”	1820	”	50	.65
”	1830	”	66	.78
”	1845	”	73	.91
”	1860	Census		.94
REGIONAL AGGREGATES				
Middle Colonies	1774	Probate Records		.51
New England	1774	”		.55–.62
South (Slaves)	1790	Census		.83
South (Slaves)	1860	”		.93
United States, North	1860	”		.81
”	1870	”		.82
United States, South	1860	”		.84
”	1870	”		.87
United States	1962	Survey, Households		.76(.79)[b]

a   Includes Salem.
b   Figure in parentheses adjusts for changes in definitions.
SOURCES: Chester Co., Pa.: James T. Lemon and Gary B. Nash, "The Distribution of Wealth in Eighteenth-Century America: a Century of Change in Chester County, Pennsylvania, 1693–1802," *Journal of Social History,* II (1968), 13; Essex Co. and Salem, Mass.: Donald Warner Koch, "Income Distribution and Political Structure in Seventeenth-Century Salem, Massachusetts," *Essex Institute Historical Collections,* CV

Table 1 summarizes the current literature on the distribution of wealth in America's past, using as measures of inequality two of the more commonly used indices: the size share of the top 10 percent of all potential wealth-holders, "SSTT," and the Gini coefficient of inequality.[2] The latter index ranges from 0.00 to 1.00 and measures the degree to which any distribution departs from absolute equality of wealth shares among all potential wealth-holders. The greater the level of inequality, the higher the value of the Gini coefficient. The size share of the richest decile is especially useful when the data sources omit or overlook those with little or no property, because it is particularly sensitive to changes in the wealth of the rich. As we shall see later, alterations in the relative fortunes of those at the top played a significant role in determining the level of inequality in the past.[3]

The evidence assembled in Table 1 suggests that inequality was generally lowest in simple farming communities, higher in

---

(1969), 57, 59; Vermont and Trempeauleau Co., Wis.: Merle Curti, *The Making of an American Community* (Stanford, 1959), 78; New York, N.Y.: 1676, Robert C. Ritchie, "The Duke's Province: A Study of Proprietary New York, 1664–1685," unpub. diss. (UCLA, 1972), 244; 1695, Joyce D. Goodfriend, " 'Too Great a Mixture of Nations': The Development of New York City Society in the Seventeenth Century," unpub. diss. (UCLA, 1975), 163; 1701–1796, Bruce M. Wilkenfeld, "The Social and Economic Structure of the City of New York, 1695–1796," unpub. diss. (Columbia Univ., 1973), 22, 58, 59, 80, 122, 158, 192; Boston, Mass.: 1681, 1771, James A. Henretta, "Economic Development and Social Structure in Colonial Boston," *William and Mary Quarterly*, XXII (1965), 80, 82; 1790; Alan Kulikoff, "The Progress of Inequality in Revolutionary Boston," *ibid.*, XXVIII (1971), 380; 1820, 1830, 1845, computed from grouped data in Lemuel Shattuck, *Report to the Committee of the City Council Appointed to Obtain the Census of Boston for the Year 1845 . . .* (Boston, 1846), 95; 1860, Soltow, "The Wealth, Income, and Social Class of Men in Large Northern Cities of the United States in 1860," in James D. Smith (ed.), *The Personal Distribution of Income and Wealth* (New York, 1975), 236; Middle Colonies and New England, 1774: Alice Hanson Jones, "Wealth Estimates for the New England Colonies about 1770," *Journal of Economic History*, XXXII (1972), 119; South (Slaves), 1790: Soltow, "Economic Inequality in the United States in the Period from 1790 to 1860," *ibid.*, (1971), 838; South (Slaves), 1860: Soltow, *Men and Wealth*, 136; United States, North and South, 1860 and 1870: *ibid.*, 103; United States, 1962: Dorothy S. Projector and Gertrude S. Weiss, *Survey of Financial Characteristics of Consumers* (Washington, D.C., 1966), 30; adjustment to these data for comparison with the 1860 census data, in Soltow, *Men and Wealth*, 183.

2 For mathematical explorations of inequality, two classical articles are Joseph E. Stiglitz, "The Distribution of Income and Wealth Among Individuals," *Econometrica*, XXXVII (1969), 382–399; Anthony B. Atkinson, "On the Measurement of Inequality," *Journal of Economic Theory*, II (1970), 244–263. A useful formula for computing Gini coefficients for grouped data may be found in Charles M. Dollar and Richard J. Jensen, *Historian's Guide to Statistics* (New York, 1971), 124.

3 See text below, 570, 581.

urban areas, lower in the colonial period, and much higher since then. The evidence is not wholly without ambiguity, however. The Chester County series, for instance, reveals some increases in concentration during the eighteenth century, but the tax base had also expanded in the meanwhile, encompassing a greater variety of property with each change in the statutes. A more significant contribution toward rising inequality in Chester County came with the appearance of several very wealthy individuals after the Revolution. The largest assessment there rose from £180 in 1748 to £5,298 in 1782 and again to $39,666, equivalent to £11,000 at 6 shillings to the dollar, in 1800–1802.[4]

Early probate records from Essex County, Massachusetts, exhibit levels of inequality similar to those found in the wealth censuses of Vermont townships and a frontier county in Wisconsin two centuries later. The growth of Salem, Essex's major port, substantially altered the distribution of wealth in the county's probate records, lending support to the notion that urbanization does contribute toward greater inequality.

Urbanization is a complex process and is itself a symptom of economic change. One would expect the distribution of wealth to vary somewhat from city to city according to its principal source of income and relative occupational structure, but inequality also varied within cities. The tax structure of colonial New York City, for instance, was less unequal than Boston's and grew even less concentrated between 1675 and 1735. Both cities experienced greater inequality after the Revolution, but Boston's tax data, on the whole, show a relatively narrow range of fluctuation until 1845. Both cities experienced strong surges in inequality between the tax lists of circa 1830 and 1845.[5]

Taxable wealth is not total wealth, and the difficulties in establishing the degree of comparability between tax lists over several years or between different jurisdictions make any conclusions

---

4 James T. Lemon and Gary B. Nash, "The Distribution of Wealth in Eighteenth-Century America: a Century of Change in Chester County, Pennsylvania, 1693–1802," *Journal of Social History*, II (1968), 11, 13.

5 The top 1% of taxable households in New York City owned 29% of private taxable wealth in 1828 and 40% in 1845. The equivalent group in Boston owned 33% in 1833 and 37% in 1848. Edward Pessen, *Riches, Class, and Power Before the Civil War* (Lexington, Mass., 1973), 33–34, 39.

based on them highly tentative.[6] If inequality rose *within* cities over time, however, the growth of inequality in the North sometime after the Revolution cannot be attributed solely to the growth of cities themselves. Urbanization and growing inequality are both products of the same underlying processes.

The story for the South features a different plot. The study of the 1850–1870 censuses referred to above bluntly attributes the higher levels of inequality there to the presence and consequences of slavery.[7] Since the Gini coefficient for inequality of slaveholding was already high in 1790, it seems that inequality in the colonial South rose with slavery and that the two are necessarily intertwined. Such a possibility demands investigation.

Table 1 furnishes the elements for plotting a profile over time of the level of inequality in the American past. The gaps between points are great, however, and there are very few points for the early colonial period. The need for more data, particularly in continuous series form, is readily apparent. Because of the relative absence of other sources, this need can be met only by probate records. Before proceeding, however, some description and discussion of their limitations is in order.

Inventories of estates list and evaluate in monetary terms the personal and, in New England, the landed possessions of deceased property holders, most of whom died intestate. Accounts of administration of probated estates, which survive for a substantial minority of them, often provide additional information such as the value of harvested crops, loans recovered, and debts paid. Obviously these records draw from a sharply restricted sector of society—deceased property holders who were mostly free white males in the older age brackets. Inherent biases due to age and wealth, therefore, may seriously distort the inventories' picture of society and its material possessions.[8]

---

6 By demonstrating the different assessment bases of the 1687 and 1771 tax schedules, for instance, G. B. Warden effectively destroyed their implication of a long-term trend toward greater concentration of wealth in colonial Boston. G. B. Warden, "Inequality and Instability in Eighteenth-Century Boston: A Reappraisal," *Journal of Interdisciplinary History*, VI (1976), 585–620. Warden's recalculations register a slight *decline* in the level of inequality for Boston between 1687 and 1771. *Ibid.*, 602.

7 Soltow, *Men and Wealth*, 133–134.

8 Early inventories of Maryland and Virginia valued personal property in pounds of tobacco. For a fuller description of these records, see Gloria L. Main, "Probate Records as a

The difficulties of correcting for these biases are considerable but not insuperable, and their burden should not outweigh in the reader's mind the priceless nature of the new information to be gained in the process. Successful studies based on them have begun to appear in print, their authors having grappled critically and substantively with the problems of bias.[9] Indeed, it may well be that historians have reserved for these records a sensitivity toward biased origins which might profitably be applied to more traditional sources.

Inferences about trends in the distribution of probate wealth will not require any adjustment of the data if the sources of bias remain constant. Recent work in Connecticut probate records demonstrates the validity of this statement. A rich variety of genealogical materials and town tax schedules enabled the author to determine the extent of probate coverage among adult males and the relative wealth of those missing, and to measure the distortion introduced by the lopsided age structure of adult decedents.[10] Table 2 reproduces from that study the mean personal wealth, deflated to current money circa 1700, the size shares of the top 10 percent of probated estates, and the estimates of these based on corrections for the living population of adult free men.

As the Hartford, Connecticut, study shows, the higher average age of the adult male decedents raised average wealth but did not affect the level of inequality. The distribution of values merely moved up the scale. The shape of the distribution of probate wealth, however, approximates that of the living population only so long as the missing propertyless are not too numerous. One must attempt to estimate the degree of coverage and gauge the proportion of young in order to adjust for missing estates. This

Source for Early American History," *William and Mary Quarterly*, XXXII (1975), 89–99. *Idem*, "The Correction of Biases in Colonial American Probate Records," *Historical Methods Newsletter* 8 (1974), 10–28; Daniel Scott Smith, "Underregistration and Bias in Probate Records: an Analysis of Data from Eighteenth-Century Hingham, Massachusetts," *William and Mary Quarterly*, XXXII (1975), 100–110.

9   Alice Hanson Jones pioneered the measurement and correction of biases in probate records in "Wealth Estimates for the American Middle Colonies, 1774," *Economic Development and Cultural Change*, XVIII (1970), 1–172; "Wealth Estimates for the New England Colonies about 1770," *Journal of Economic History*, XXXII (1972), 98–127.

10   Jackson T. Main, "The Distribution of Property in Colonial Connecticut," in James Kirby Martin (ed.), *The Human Dimension of Nation Making: Essays on Colonial and Revolutionary America* (Madison, 1976), 54–104.

Table 2 Average Personal Wealth[a] and the Size Share of the top
10% of Probated Estates and of Living Adult Males,
Hartford[b], 1650–1774

YEARS	AVERAGE ESTATE (£)	PER LIVING MAN (£)	SSTT, ESTATES (%)	SSTT, LIVING (%)
1650–1669	209	167	45	45½
1670–1679	170	126	48	43
1680–1689	145	87	47	47
1690–1699	146	109	49	43
1700–1709	134	109	47½	46
1710–1714	176	140	47	45
1715–1719	159	131	43½	43½
1720–1724	142	108	49	45½
1725–1729	124	115	37	42½
1730–1734	165	130	44	48
1735–1739	132	108	32	33
1740–1744	132	98	41	44
1745–1749	118	98	45	43
1750–1754	120	98	37	39
1755–1759	107	94	35	34
1760–1764	125	99	43½	47
1765–1769	203	174	45	48½
1770–1774	163	132	50	45½

a Personal wealth deflated to level of inventory prices c. 1700.
b .The Hartford probate district covered an area larger than the present-day county.
SOURCE: Jackson T. Main, "The Distribution of Property in Colonial Connecticut,"
88.

rough procedure will produce an adequate degree of comparability for probate data of diverse origins if one does not lean too heavily on small differences between sets.

Probate records are a principal source material for exploring the early history of the distribution of wealth in America. Inventories from Maryland and Massachusetts, supplemented by the data from Hartford, provide important new evidence for the seventeenth and eighteenth centuries, while published summaries of such records from nineteenth-century Massachusetts carry forward the story for that state. Federal and state censuses offer a valuable opportunity to test the effects on inequality in individual counties of Massachusetts of the growth of cities, manufacturing, and foreign immigration.

Table 3 summarizes the colonial and early national findings, showing the size shares of the top 10 percent, SSTT, and the Gini coefficients of inventoried estates of adult males in six coastal counties of Maryland from 1674 through 1719 and again during a four-year period at mid-century, 1750–1753.[11] Tax data from 1783 supply a limited comparison with the probate data and with the census data on slaveholding.[12]

Two large geographical areas of early Massachusetts are represented in the inventories of Suffolk and Hampshire Counties the populations of which constituted almost a third of the colony's total in 1690.[13] Although the probate records of Suffolk County actually begin as early as 1638, they are too few before 1650 to support inferences about the course of inequality in those early years. The table distinguishes between Boston and the rest of the county's towns, here grouped under the rubric, "Rural Suffolk." Much of Hampshire County remained exposed frontier throughout the years 1666 to 1719, but even by the middle of the eighteenth century, little change marked the personal belongings of the deceased male residents of this extensive farming region. The western part of Suffolk County was set off as Worcester County in 1721, and inventories of this region are represented in the table for the years after 1760.

Two sets of contrasts mark the early data: North versus South and urban versus rural. Although such contrasts will evoke

11   See note "a" to Table 3 about the geographical makeup of the six-county sample from Maryland. Menard, Harris, and Carr found no trend in the distribution of wealth in the inventories of their counties, two of which overlap with those of the present set. Their choice of measure for inequality, the distance between the median and the mean, did not permit the inclusion of their results in Table 1. Russell R. Menard, P. M. G. Harris, and Lois Green Carr, "Opportunity and Inequality: the Distribution of Wealth on the Lower Western Shore of Maryland, 1638–1705," *Maryland Historical Magazine*, LXIX (1974), 181.

12   Incomplete schedules for four of the six counties indicate a size share for the richest 10% of taxables, including those excused from payment, of about 60% of total taxable property, which included land, slaves, livestock, money, silverplate, and unspecified "other." Sixty percent is a conservative estimate of the true size share because I made no effort to link properties owned by the same person in separate districts, although Charles Carroll of Carrollton and John Ridgely were so conspicuous on the lists that I was able to identify and combine the values of their holdings for the lists I did examine. The method of noting down the largest values in each schedule and the summed assessments has only convenience and speed to recommend it. It forecloses any possibility of computing a Gini coefficient because it does not take account of the remainder of the distribution.

13   Evarts B. Greene and Virginia D. Harrington, *American Population Before the Federal Census of 1790* (New York, 1932; reprinted Gloucester, Mass., 1966), 19–21.

Table 3 Indices of Inequality among Inventoried Males, 1650–1788

	MARYLAND[a]		BOSTON		R. SUFFOLK[b]		HAMPSHIRE[c]		WORCESTER[d]	
YEARS	SSTT	GINI	SSTT	GINI	SSTT	GINI	SSTT	GINI	SSTT	GINI
1650–64	—	—							—	—
1665–69			.60	.73	.37	.50			—	—
1670–74	—	—	.64	.74	.37	.54	.30	.47	—	—
1675–79	.49	.60							—	—
1680–84	.51	.64	.59	.70	.38	.53	.38	.54	—	—
1685–89	.53	.61							—	—
1690–94	.55	.64	.46	.61	.34	.46	.37	.51	—	—
1695–99	.53	.66							—	—
1700–04	.56	.68	.50	.64	.36	.48	.35	.49	—	—
1705–09	.54	.65							—	—
1710–14	.65	.74	.55	.66	.33	.45	.38	.48	—	—
1715–19	.65	.74	.54	.68	.31	.44	.52	.58	—	—
1750–54	(.66)	.80)	.53	.67	.31	.46	.41	.54	—	—
1760–69	—	—	.53	.68	.38	.50	—	—	.39	.50
1782–88	(.60)[e]	—	.56	.72	.42	.53	—	—	.43	.55

a   Six counties only: Anne Arundel, Baltimore, Calvert, Charles, Kent, and Somerset. Boundary alterations took place periodically making somewhat imprecise the geographical area included in the jurisdiction of the six probate courts. Only personal wealth was included in the inventories of Maryland. Data for 1750–54 corrected for under-reporting. See appendix (available on request from the author) for details.
b   Rural Suffolk County originally stretched from the coast to the borders of Hampshire. The creation of Worcester County defined Suffolk's western border but excluded very few settlements in the process since most of this interior upland country remained empty until well into the eighteenth century. When Boston and its suburbs were set off as Suffolk County in the nineteenth century, the remainder of the old Suffolk County became Norfolk. "Rural Suffolk" is roughly contiguous with the latter.
c   Hampshire County included the entire Connecticut River valley from Suffield, Connecticut, northward until 1790 when Franklin County was established and 1830 when Hampden County was set off.
d   Worcester County was set off from Suffolk in 1721.
e   Taxable wealth in 1783 included both real and personal property. The schedules are on microfilm and are incomplete. Those analyzed for the present work were all the surviving schedules from the counties of Anne Arundel, Baltimore, Calvert, Kent, and Worcester (formerly part of Somerset County). None survived from Somerset and only one did so for Charles.
SOURCES: Maryland: *Inventories*, I–III, 43–60; *Ancounts*, I–IV, 27–32; miscellaneous will books, county records, and testamentary proceedings. All in Hall of Records, Annapolis. Tax Assessment Schedules, 1783: microfilm copy, Institute for Colonial Studies, SUNY-Stony Brook. Massachusetts: Suffolk County Probate Court Records, I–XXII, 50–54, microfilm copy, Institute for Colonial Studies, SUNY-Stony Brook; LXIII–LXXI, 81–87, manuscript notes, courtesy of Jackson T. Main. Hampshire County Probate Court Records, I–IV, 7–8, microfilm copy, Institute for Colonial Studies, SUNY-Stony Brook. Worcester County Probate Records, VIII–X, 18–21, manuscript notes, courtesy of Jackson T. Main.

no surprise among readers, their appearance at so early a date is clearly a matter of great interest and significance. The size share of the top 10 percent of male decedents in the relatively more urbanized Hartford district averaged about 45 percent of personal wealth, but the same decile in "Rural Suffolk" seldom reached as

high as 40 percent. Maryland's richest 10 percent, however, en-
grossed shares comparable to those of urban Boston's top decile.

Differences in the demographic structures of the regions
created the initial gap between the levels of inequality displayed by
the two agricultural regions, but the story grows more complicated with the passage of time. In order to probe these sectional
differences more fully, we will first examine the history of Maryland's wealth-holding patterns and then apply the implications of
that state's experience to the rest of the upper South.

MARYLAND   To a degree unknown in colonies to the north, and
perhaps as a case more comparable to that of the West Indies,
young males rather than family groups dominated white immigration into the Chesapeake for most of the years between settlement
and the virtual cessation of such movements after 1687.[14] The
heavy mortality sustained by new arrivals and the continuing
influx from abroad during much of the seventeenth century
created a population with rather bizarre characteristics: foreign-
born, heavily male, and concentrated in the 16 to 40 age group.
These characteristics did not subside until the formation of family
units in sufficient numbers eventually permitted population
growth through natural reproduction. Such a transition took place
in Maryland somewhere between 1690 and 1710 when fewer
young men came and more left, thus impelling the age distribution toward stability. A long depression in the European tobacco
market combined with improvement in labor opportunities in

14   The following description of the demographic history of Maryland rests on the work
of Carr, Harris, Menard, Walsh, and their colleagues on the St. Mary's City Commission
staff who have explored public records of every description in order to reconstruct the demographic experience of this colony. They are not responsible for any errors in my interpretation of their work. Lorena S. Walsh and Russell R. Menard, "Death in the
Chesapeake: Two Life Tables for Men in Early Colonial Maryland," *Maryland Historical
Magazine,* LXIX (1974), 211–227; Menard, "Immigration to the Chesapeake Colonies in
the Seventeenth Century: a Review Essay," *ibid.,* LXVIII (1973), 323–329. See also Wesley
Frank Craven, *White, Red and Black: The Seventeenth-Century Virginian* (Charlottesville,
1971), 1–37; Darrett B. Rutman and Anita H. Rutman, "Of Agues and Fevers: Malaria in
the Early Chesapeake," *William and Mary Quarterly,* XXXIII (1976), 31–60. On the dem-
ographic experience of the British West Indies in the seventeenth century, see Carl and
Roberta Bridenbaugh, *No Peace Beyond the Line: the English in the Caribbean, 1624–1690*
(New York, 1972), chs. 1 and 2; Richard S. Dunn, *Sugar and Slaves: the Rise of the Planter
Class in the English West Indies, 1624–1713* (Chapel Hill, 1972), chs. 8 and 9.

England to shut off the stream of immigration from the mother country, while out-migration to the flourishing new settlements of Pennsylvania during the middle 1690s and again after 1703 balanced the sex ratio by reducing the preponderance of young men in the population. Blacks, who had played only a minor role in Chesapeake demography until 1690, then began to grow rapidly in number as planters attempted to replace their vanishing labor supply.

Maryland's demographic history has relevance for our purposes because it goes far toward explaining the early high levels of inequality in the probate records—high by comparison with those of the rural North. The immigrant background of the overwhelming majority of white adults in Maryland during these years explains both their poverty and the greater weight enjoyed by the rather small number of men whose relative wealth and social prominence nominated them for positions of public responsibility and authority.[15] For the majority of the foreign-born, however, the years of servitude rendered in their youth prolonged the stage of legal dependence, shortening thereby the number of years during which accumulation out of current income could take place. Native-born residents, on the contrary, were thrice-blessed. They gained independence at an earlier age than their immigrant predecessors, tended to live longer, and, since the sex ratio was naturally balanced among them, wives were more readily available as the native-born replaced the immigrants. Thus proportionately more men were able to live longer working lives and enjoy their earnings earlier. Native-born fathers, by marrying younger and living longer, were better able to help their sons to make a start in life, thus extending the time horizon of the family by perpetuating the gains of one generation in the income potential of another.[16]

For the seventeenth century, then, the presence in the colony's population on the one hand of large numbers of freed servants born overseas and on the other of a very small group of men

15 Lois Green Carr and David William Jordan, *Maryland's Revolution of Government 1689–1692* (Ithaca, 1974), ch. 6 and the appendix, "Biographies of the Members of the Associators' Convention," 232–288.

16 References to grandchildren are uncommon in Maryland wills before 1700: Gloria L. Main, "Personal Wealth in Colonial America: Explorations in the Use of Probate Records from Maryland and Massachusetts, 1650–1720," unpub. diss. (Columbia Univ., 1972), 41.

of some means produced a relatively high level of inequality in Maryland's probate records. Other things being equal, the replacement of the former by a native-born population free of contract obligations and capable of enjoying the fruits of their own labor plus some of their parents' as well, should have tended to reduce inequality. On the contrary, the inventories show an increase in the size share of the richest 10 percent and in the Gini coefficient of inequality, particularly after 1710.[17]

A solution to the paradox of rising inequality in the face of declining proportions of immigrants and freed servants in the white population lies in the growth of great fortunes during these years despite the secular depression in the tobacco market. Valuable clues to the origin of this wealth lie in the inventoried assets themselves, because one characteristic common to the majority of personal estates worth £1,000 sterling or more is the involvement of their owners in mercantile and financial activities.[18] Occupational versatility, not specialization in tobacco culture, marked the careers of Maryland's richest men.[19]

Although the rapid growth of slavery in the Chesapeake during these years coincided with the emergence of great wealth, the latter permitted the former and was not caused by it. From the point of view of Maryland's economic elite, slaves as well as land

17 A moderate contraction in the probate coverage of free adult male decedents may have taken place during the decade after 1704, but it cannot explain this increase because the missing tended to come from the poorer ranks of society and their greater relative absence would decrease inequality rather than the reverse.

18 On the depression in tobacco output, see the export statistics in U.S. Bureau of the Census, *Historical Statistics of the United States, Colonial Times to 1970, Part 2* (Washington, D.C., 1975), 1189–1190. Tobacco production stagnated between 1697 and 1727 while population in the two Chesapeake colonies more than doubled in size. For a discussion of the sources of the depression in the market for tobacco, see Jacob M. Price, "The Economic Growth of the Chesapeake and the European Market, 1697–1775," *Journal of Economic History*, XXIV (1964), 496–511. Aubrey C. Land first pointed out the strong association between wealth and mercantile activity in the inventories of colonial Maryland planters in "Economic Base and Social Structure: the Northern Chesapeake in the Eighteenth Century," *Journal of Economic History*, XXV (1965), 647.

19 The variety of occupations pursued by Maryland's residents included many which, in the North, concentrated in cities or port towns. Earle's study shows how an extensive system of natural waterways, the ease of making roads over level, sandy soil, and an abundance of sturdy little horses enabled men pursuing "urban" occupations to spread out over the land in order to supervise their farming enterprises. Carville V. Earle, *The Evolution of a Tidewater Settlement System: All Hallow's Parish, Maryland, 1650–1783* (Chicago, 1975), ch. 5.

were merely investments of capital involving less risk than alternative but potentially more lucrative forms of economic activity.

Access to mercantile enterprise provided the key to great wealth in the South and slaves the means by which to preserve it. Most men, however, had to farm land in order to gain any income at all. The question of trends in landholding looms importantly in this agricultural society, but firm evidence on land use and ownership remains elusive. Leasing through some form of sharecropping provided many freed servants the wherewithal eventually to purchase their own acreages in the seventeenth century. Evidence from one Maryland parish suggests that the rate of tenancy probably rose in the Tidewater regions of the Chesapeake during the course of the eighteenth century as population growth placed greater pressure on the land despite substantial levels of emigration.[20]

The only colony-wide evidence on the pattern of landholding in the early Chesapeake comes from a Virginia quitrent roll of the year 1704. Of 5,501 individuals named on the roll, the top 10 percent owned approximately half the acreage included, but the number of free adult males owning no land is unknown. County militia lists supply an absolute minimum of 31 percent of all white adult males without land, but the true figure may be close to double that if the militia lists excluded as many as did those in Maryland.[21]

Depending on the estimated proportion of men owning on land at all, the top 10 percent of all potential land-holders in the Chesapeake owned half to two-thirds of the available acreage in the opening years of the eighteenth century. Eighty years later the landowning elite probably controlled about two-thirds of the

20 Menard, "From Servant to Freeholder: Status Mobility and Property Accumulation in Seventeenth-Century Maryland," *William and Mary Quarterly*, XXX (1973), 52. Earle, *All Hallow's Parish*, 206–207.
21 Thomas J. Wertenbaker, *The Planters of Colonial Virginia* (Princeton, 1922), appendix. A minimum estimate of white adult males without land comes from the membership figure for the militia: 7,972 minus 5,501 landowners equals 2,471, or 31% without land. Greene and Harrington, *American Population*, 149–150. A Maryland governor enumerated the "Christian" men and women in the colony in addition to white servants and slaves. His report of the size of the militia was fully one-fifth smaller than the number of "Christian" men and fewer than three-fifths of all white men in the colony. William Hand Browne, *et al* (eds.), *Maryland Archives*, XXV (Baltimore, 1905), 258.

land, given the proportion of landless men found in the tax schedules for Virginia in 1787: 48.5 percent of free males aged 16 and over in the state's Piedmont area and 57 percent in the old Tidewater section.[22] These figures approach the upper limit of the equivalent range in 1704 and lend support to the idea that the distribution of land in the colony as a whole altered little in the course of the century.

The level of inequality marking the distribution of both personal and real property in the Chesapeake was high around 1700 and bore a strong resemblance to the distribution of slaves in the 1790 census and to the distribution of wealth in the South in the census of 1860. Because Maryland's economy diversified in the nineteenth century, it ceased to conform to the rural southern pattern, and we will not follow the state's history further. Maryland's colonial experience does serve, however, to confirm our doubts about a pristine egalitarian past for at least that section of early America.

MASSACHUSETTS AND CONNECTICUT   We have argued that Maryland's distribution of wealth was more unequal than that of the rural areas of the North, at first because of continuing immigration of indentured servants, and then in even greater degree because of the expanding wealth of a few families. No such great change took place in New England, according to the probate data from two counties in Massachusetts and one large district in Connecticut.

The distribution of wealth in colonial New England seems to have remained stable under conditions of a rapidly growing population and with little gain in productivity per capita attributable to technological improvements. Expanding markets for their manufactures and shipping services permitted economic growth to raise the standard of living without also enhancing inequality.[23]

Despite poor farming conditions and rapid population growth, the New England economy proved flexible. The older towns exported their surplus young men to the port cities and the

---

22 Jackson T. Main, "The Distribution of Property in Post-Revolutionary Virginia," *Mississippi Valley Historical Review* XLI (1954), 243–248.
23 Shuttle-style shipping to myriads of small ports lowered the possibility for economies of scale and this may have placed a ceiling on the growth of individual fortunes.

frontier, where the founding of new towns proceeded apace after 1720.[24] Although such an out-migration undoubtedly served to suppress the level of inequality in the older settlements, a simultaneous restructuring of the occupational makeup of the labor force took place as well.[25] Sons of farmers combined farming with artisanal work or even specialized in the latter entirely, merely supplementing this income with the produce of a garden and a cow.

Trade abroad, then, had provided a diversity of occupational opportunity and enabled a multiplying population to live on shrinking units of land. Growing commercial competition with ports to the south, coupled with steadily advancing costs of farmland, may have increasingly troubled parts of New England as the eighteenth century wore on, but the degree of inequality in wealth-holding did not worsen.[26] On the contrary, it merely fluctuated within a rather narrow range. In Hartford, the corrected size share of the richest 10 percent peaked at 48 percent in the first half of the 1730s and again in the 1760s. It touched bottom at 33 percent in the second half of the 1730s and at 34 percent in 1755–1759. Such fluctuations resulted as much from accident as from real cause, since the timing of a rich man's death could place his estate in one five-year period rather than another: in 1734, for example, instead of 1735. Close examination of the probate evidence for New England simply will not support the thesis that some irresistible force levered open a widening gap between rich and poor.

NINETEENTH-CENTURY MASSACHUSETTS   Measured in terms of its distribution of probate wealth, society in eighteenth-century New England appears positively egalitarian compared to the degree of

24 Lois Kimball Mathews, *The Expansion of New England: The Spread of New England Settlement and Institutions to the Mississippi River 1620–1865* (Boston, 1909), ch. 4.

25 Jackson T. Main, "Distribution of Property in Colonial Connecticut," 89.

26 See Kenneth Lockridge, "Land, Population and the Evolution of New England Society, 1630–1790," *Past & Present,* 39 (1968), 62–80; Alan Kulikoff, "The Progress of Inequality in Revolutionary Boston," *William and Mary Quarterly,* XXVIII (1971), 392, 404, 409–411; James Henretta, "Economic Development and Social Structure in Colonial Boston," *ibid.,* XXII (1965), 88–92, *idem, The Evolution of American Society, 1700–1815: an Interdisciplinary Analysis* (Lexington, Mass., 1973), *passim.* G. B. Warden and Jacob Price treat this view with great skepticism: Warden, "Inequality and Instability in Boston," *Journal of Interdisciplinary History* VI (1976), 585–613; Jacob M. Price, "Quantifying Colonial America: A Comment on Nash and Warden," *ibid.,* 707–708.

inequality which one encounters in Massachusetts in the following century. Table 4 shows the corrected size shares of the richest 10 percent of Massachusetts estates and Gini coefficients of inequality for four time periods of three years each at intervals scattered throughout the nineteenth century. The unadjusted indices are given in Table 5.

The data in Table 4 required correction for differences in the rate of coverage of adult male decedents, since the years from 1859 to 1861 and after show sharp declines in the proportion of inventories to estimated deaths.[27] Because the corrections merely amplified differences already large, it seems reasonable to conclude that the sharp rise in inequality revealed there was a real

Table 4 Indices of Inequality among Inventoried Males, 1829–1891

COUNTY	1829–31		1859–61		1879–81		1889–91	
	SSTT	GINI	SSTT	GINI	SSTT	GINI	SSTT	GINI
Boston	.83	.86	.94	.95	.84	.90	.86	.91
Norfolk	.59	.69	.75	.82	.74	.81	.81	.85
Worcester	.50	.63	.57	.73	.66	.77	.69	.80
Barnstable	.52	.63	.56	.69	.94	.95	.61	.69
Berkshire	.40	.56	.69	.81	.64	.75	.61	.71
Bristol	.57	.68	.73	.80	.80	.85	.65	.75
Dukes	.32	.44	.45	.51	.62	.68	.43	.61
Essex	.73	.80	.65	.77	.82	.87	.68	.78
Franklin	.41	.56	.50	.66	.39	.57	.58	.69
Hampden	.67	.79	.47	.63	.72	.82	.71	.81
Hampshire	.44	.56	.57	.69	.72	.81	.38	.56
Middlesex	.57	.69	.60	.71	.78	.86	.70	.80
Nantucket	.64	.72	.47	.65	.31	.54	.81	.81
Plymouth	.40	.54	.45	.56	.54	.66	.62	.72
State	.70	.77	.74	.82	.80	.86	.75	.83

SOURCE: Bureau of Statistics of Labor, *Twenty-Fifth Annual Report* (Boston, 1895), 238–267; see also appendix to this article, available on request from the author.

27 An appendix gives the details. The correction procedure estimated the differences in the recording rates, adjusted for those whose estates were probated but not inventoried, and filled in as zeroes the remaining number of "missing." Because of space constraints a note on the methodology of the correction procedures does not appear with the article. Copies of this appendix are available on request from the author.

Table 5 Unadjusted Indices of Inequality among Inventoried Males, 1829–1891

COUNTY	1829–31		1859–61		1879–81		1889–91	
	SSTT	GINI	SSTT	GINI	SSTT	GINI	SSTT	GINI
Boston	.81	.83	.80	.86	.76	.83	.78	.84
Norfolk	.59	.69	.73	.80	.73	.79	.81	.84
Worcester	.49	.63	.51	.62	.61	.71	.63	.73
Barnstable	.52	.63	.56	.69	.94	.95	.61	.69
Berkshire	.40	.56	.64	.72	.62	.73	.61	.71
Bristol	.57	.68	.70	.77	.80	.85	.65	.75
Dukes	.32	.44	.45	.51	.62	.68	.43	.61
Essex	.73	.80	.60	.72	.80	.85	.65	.74
Franklin	.71	.56	.47	.59	.39	.57	.58	.69
Hampden	.55	.76	.43	.53	.69	.78	.68	.76
Hampshire	.44	.56	.55	.63	.70	.78	.38	.56
Middlesex	.57	.68	.60	.71	.71	.80	.69	.77
Nantucket	.64	.72	.47	.65	.31	.54	.81	.77
Plymouth	.40	.54	.45	.56	.54	.66	.62	.72
State	.67	.76	.70	.78	.77	.83	.74	.80

SOURCE: *Twenty-fifth Annual Report*, 238–267.

phenomenom. By 1830, therefore, Massachusetts had undergone a transformation in its distribution of wealth which resulted in an increase in the Gini coefficients from about .55–.62 to one of .77. By 1860, the index had again risen to .825. As a basis for comparison, the census data for the North that year yielded a coefficient of .81 and for Boston, .94 (see Table 1).

The major problem raised by the Massachusetts probate data is to explain the timing of that transformation in its distribution of wealth. The first step is to test the impact of demographic changes, for marked alterations in the makeup of the state's population did take place. However, the modifications of the age composition of the adult population actually militated *against* increases in inequality. The proportion of adult American males aged 20–29 declined from 41 percent in 1830 to 36 percent in 1860, and it continued to decline thereafter, dropping to 32 percent in 1900, and to 26 percent by 1970.[28] In short, shrinkages in the youngest and

28 Oscar Handlin, *Boston's Immigrants, 1790–1880: A Study in Acculturation* (Cambridge, Mass., 1959; rev. ed.), 242, 262; Frank L. Mott, "Portrait of an American Mill Town:

poorest age bracket could only have tended to lower the level of inequality.

But the growth of cities and of foreign immigration certainly exerted a contrary effect. The percentage of people living in cities, however, rose significantly *after* 1830, not before. Moreover, inequality *within* cities also jumped, *before,* as well as after, 1830. As to immigration, little occurred until after 1847, so it could not have caused either the initial increase in the concentration of wealth or the rise within the cities subsequent to 1830. The great waves of Irish and others only further supported a level of inequality already high.

The same conclusion emerges from a county-by-county analysis. Those counties whose populations contained the largest proportions of foreign-born did not uniformly exhibit the greatest degrees of concentration in probate wealth. Table 6 ranks the individual counties by their proportion of foreign-born in the year 1870, compares their levels of inequality a decade before and a decade after that year, and also lists other information, including the percentage population change between 1860 and 1880, the relative proportion of the population employed in manufacturing, and the size of manufacturing establishments as measured by their capital investment. Those counties with a fifth or more of their population born outside of the country showed considerable variation in their rates of growth, in the importance of manufacturing, and in the distribution of their probate wealth.

Immigration, urbanization, population growth, and manufacturing employment are obviously interrelated developments, and disentangling their effects on the level of inequality would require much more data and the application of sophisticated mathematical analysis. Certain observations might prove useful, nevertheless. First, foreign immigration wielded only minimal impact on inequality in areas showing levels which were already high. Second, manufacturing appears to have raised inequality

Demographic Response in Mid-Nineteenth Century Warren, Rhode Island," *Population Studies,* XXVI (1972), 147–157; Stephan Thernstrom, *The Other Bostonians: Poverty and Progress in the American Metropolis 1880–1970* (Cambridge, Mass., 1973), 33. The proportion of Boston's labor force in unskilled occupations grew from 13% in 1830 to 16% in 1840, but then vaulted to 30% in 1850 at the height of the Irish immigration. By 1860, however, it was already dropping, reaching 15% in 1880 and 12% in 1900. Peter Knights, *The Plain People of Boston* (New York, 1971), 84; Thernstrom, *Other Bostonians,* 272.

Table 6 Massachusetts Counties and Inequality, 1860 and 1880, Ranked by % Foreign–born

GINI 1860	COEFF. 1880	COUNTY	FOREIGN– BORN, %[a]	POPULATION GROWTH %[b]	WORKERS MANUFAC.[c]	CAPITAL PER ESTB.[d]
.63	.82	Hampden	26½	81½	216	32½
.71	.86	Middlesex	26	47	181	27
.73	.77	Worcester	24	42	221	16
.81	.75	Berkshire	23	25	143	20
.80	.85	Bristol	23	48	261	34
.77	.875	Essex	22	48	262	20
.82	.81	Norfolk	22	−12[e]	168	14½
.69	.81	Hampshire	20	25	139	15
.66	.57	Franklin	11	14½	96	11
.66	.66	Plymouth	10	14	181	9
.69	.95	Barnstable	6	−11	67	13
.65	.54	Nantucket	5	−39	54	6
.51	.68	Dukes	3	−3	30	10
.95	.90	Boston	34	101[e]	128	13

a   For the year 1870.
b   Between 1860 and 1880.
c   Average number of workers per 1,000 population, 1860 and 1880.
d $1,000's, average invested per manufacturing establishment, 1860 and 1880.
e   County boundaries redefined between two census dates.
SOURCES: Various federal census publications and Table 7.

most substantially in those counties into which it had newly pene-trated. The economies of Bristol, Essex, Hampden, and Middle-sex had based themselves on manufacturing early in the century, but the growth of manufacturing and of relatively large establish-ments reshaped the distribution of wealth only in those counties which had been previously dependent on agriculture: Worcester by 1860, and Berkshire and Hampshire by 1880.[29]

The shift out of agriculture appears to have been a crucial first step in the direction of rising inequality, but insufficient in itself. Manufacturing on a small scale appeared early in the eastern part of the state and in the older settlements of Connecticut with no visible effect on the distribution of wealth. The introduction of the factory system, or of heavy machinery, may have played the criti-cal roles of catalysts, but the relationship between the size of the

29   *The Census of Manufactures* (Washington, D.C., 1810) provides the earliest profile of county economies. Soltow, *Men and Wealth*, 10.

manufacturing sector, the capital investment per establishment, and the Gini coefficient of inequality in probate records of individual Massachusetts counties does not support any position which pins the tail on these particular donkeys. Essex County, for instance, waited until the 1840s to reorganize its shoe industry, yet the Gini coefficient in the probate records of that county was higher before than after this technological change had taken place.

A final and fundamental characteristic of the Massachusetts probate data is the dramatic increase in the relative frequency of very large estates over the course of the century. The gap between poor and rich appeared at the upper end of the distribution before it widened at the bottom. Although the definition of what constituted a "large" estate must be arbitrary, an examination of the "Rural Suffolk"/Norfolk inventories from 1750 to 1890 provides an illustration of the progression into higher classes of estate wealth over the years. Table 7 gives the frequency distributions as well as the total number of inventories in each period, their mean value in pounds both in current money and deflated to sterling, and two measures of inequality.

Norfolk County's distribution of wealth in successive time periods is characterized by a rising trend in inequality which accelerated in the forty years between the final data from the eighteenth century and the earliest for the nineteenth. Although the level of inequality continued to rise even further in the course of that century, the annual rate of increase in the size shares of the richest 10 percent of estates slowed in the second half as the central tendency of the distribution moved up out of the lower class values. Estates valued under £300 or $1,000 made up 43 percent of all the inventories in the eighteenth century but declined to just under 40 percent in 1830, 27 percent in 1860, and 20.5 percent in 1890. Although this decline in the poorer estates did curb the progressive increases in the level of inequality in Norfolk's inventories, the size share of the richest 10 percent leveled off after 1860, primarily because the growth in numbers of the largest fortunes had also leveled off.

The largest estates in colonial Boston had never reached as high as £20,000 sterling, or $66,667. Even estates of £5,000 sterling were rare there during the colonial period and virtually nonexistent in the rural inventories. By contrast, the first half of the nineteenth century witnessed a great advance in the numbers and

Table 7 Distribution of Total Estate Values in Rural Suffolk/Norfolk County (Males, %)

CLASSES IN $	EQUIVALENT IN £	1750–53	1763–69	1783–88	1829–31	1859–61	1889–91
Under 500	Under 150	20.9	21.85	24.5	26.5	15.1	10.6
500–999	150–299.7	22.7	21.1	18.4	13.2	11.6	9.9
1,000–4,999	300–1,499.7	53.5	48.15	48.2	38.8	39.4	46.5
5,000–9,999	1,500–2,999.7	2.9	6.7	6.4	12.3	13.7	14.65
10,000–24,999	3,000–7,499.7	—	2.2	2.1	5.5	10.6	9.4
25,000–49,999	7,500–14,999.7	—	—	0.35	1.8	4.1	4.3
50,000–99,999	15,000–29,999.7	—	—	—	1.4	2.5	1.4
100,000–199,999	30,000–59,999.7	—	—	—	0.5	2.1	1.7
200,000–299,999	60,000–89,999.7	—	—	—	—	0.4	0.3
300,000–399,999	90,000–119,999.7	—	—	—	—	—	0.2
400,000–499,999	120,000–149,999.7	—	—	—	—	0.2	—
500,000 and over	150,000 and over	—	—	—	—	0.4	1.2
Total Number Estates		172	270	280	219	518	587
Mean Value £ (current)		486	598	623	1442	4039	5669
Deflated £ (sterling)		376	464	417	966	2706	4394
Size Share Top 10%		31.0	38.0	42.4	59.5	72.9	80.8
Gini Coefficients		.456	.503	.532	.692	.796	.844

Deflators: 1750–53, 0.775; 1763–69, 0.775; 1782–88, 0.67; 1829–31, 0.67; 1859–61, 0.67; 1889–91, 0.775. Those for the eighteenth century are based on wholesale commodity price index numbers for the month of June, compiled by Ruth Crandall. Arthur H. Cole, *Wholesale Commodity Prices in the United States 1700–1861* (Cambridge, Mass., 1938), 118. Deflators for 1829–91 are based on wholesale commodity prices in Philadelphia, *Historical Statistics* (Washington, D.C., 1962), 116, and on the Warren and Pearson wholesale commodity price index, *ibid.*, 119.
SOURCE: Suffolk County Probate Records, C–CIV, CXIII–CXXI, CXXXI–CXXXVII; *Twenty-Fifth Annual Report*, 256–258.

wealth of those at the top. Whereas immigration and industrial development wielded their greatest impact on the level of inequality in the former agricultural counties, growth in the numbers of the very rich provided the all-important upward thrust in those areas where manufacturing and commerce had long served as the major sectors of employment.

Close attention to the history of the distribution of wealth in the probate records of three states has yielded valuable insights into the nature of inequality and its range of behavior. In the rural communities of the preindustrial Northeast, from colonial times to the Civil War, a relatively egalitarian distribution prevailed. Even those historically low levels of inequality, however, suggest that a natural floor existed beneath which inequality could not go. The effect of the life cycle on wealth accumulation is that men in their fifties and early sixties owned more property than men in their twenties.

For Maryland, and, by extension, for the South, the picture was different from the start. In the seventeenth century, immigration and disease combined to keep a major portion of the population in the younger and poorer age brackets. The practice of indenturing servants, which paid the transportation costs of this mass movement, placed a majority of these men further behind in the process of economic accumulation compared to even the poorest among the native-born. A few men of substance and connection migrated as well and, with their families, founded a small and not very opulent upper class whose life style differed little from their neighbors. Thus in the early South, a large class of poor and a small class of well-to-do characterized a society the wealth distribution of which was more unequal than in the rural North.

As the eighteenth century got well underway, a handful of Maryland planters who had hitherto been only well-to-do grew quite rich. The source of their new wealth lay not in raising tobacco, although that crop continued to offer steady employment for their capital, but in trade and money lending, "urban" activities which were dispersed over the countryside rather than centered in cities.

Colonial cities of the North exhibited greater levels of inequality than did their rural hinterlands, because opportunity, the sources of credit, and the mobile poor concentrated there. Although that level fluctuated with trade conditions, no long-term trend emerged before the Revolution. Viewed in the aggregate, the distribution of wealth in the colonial North proved stable, producing a size share for the richest 10 percent of about 45 percent and a Gini coefficient probably in the range of .55–.60.

Sometime after the Revolution cracks appeared in the picture of stability. In Massachusetts by 1830 the level of inequality as measured by the Gini coefficient had climbed by some twenty points. It would climb only a little further in the years thereafter despite the steady and rapid advance of industrial progress and its demographic accompaniments.

As in Maryland's case much earlier, the growth of wealth at the top rather than the expansion of the propertyless provided the impetus for Massachusetts' sudden jump in inequality. Whatever the source of that great new wealth, it was before the Industrial Revolution and before the great growth of the cities that the distribution of wealth in Massachusetts took what now appears an irreversible leap forward in the degree of its concentration.

Raymond A. Jonas

Peasants, Population, and Industry in France   Despite the best efforts of Gustave Courbet and Jean François Millet and of Emile Gillaumin and Pierre-Jakez Hélias, it was Edward A. Ross, an American sociologist, who supplied the most telling, not to mention amusing, evocation of the twilight years of rural society. When he discussed rural depopulation in turn-of-the-century America, he had no use for sentimental language; he preferred concrete, sober, and picturesque terms. For Ross, depopulated towns were "fished-out ponds, populated chiefly by bull-heads and suckers." Those individuals who remained were too stubborn or too foolish to leave. Towns and cities took the best of the rural populace, not the worst—a fact to be celebrated, not deplored. Depopulation was transparently a good thing because it revealed a dynamic society—one which was willing to take risks and one in which talent followed opportunity. The "World We Have Lost" did not merit sentimental evocation; it had simply outlived its usefulness.[1]

In France much gloomier language was used. The passing of peasant society was often remarked in utterly romantic terms. French culture evinced a preference for the rustic well before the rural exodus. As early as the eighteenth century, the French were fascinated with authentic rustic virtues, exemplified by the "cult" of Benjamin Franklin. These sentiments were deepened and introduced into the political culture of France after 1870 and have been exploited ever since—and not only by the Right. France's humiliating defeat in the Franco-Prussian War (1870–1871) became a symbol of its spiritual and political decline. Thus although

Raymond A. Jonas is Assistant Professor of History at the University of Washington.

The author is grateful to Christopher Johnson and David Pinkney for their thoughtful comments. Funding for this study was provided by the French Embassy to the United States in the form of a *Bourse Chateaubriand* and by the Graduate School and the Keller Fund of the Department of History at the University of Washington.

1   Ross, "Folk Depletion as a Cause of Rural Decline," *Publications of the American Sociological Society,* II (1917), 21–30.

rural depopulation signified progress in agricultural yields and in the distribution of labor out of the agricultural sector, in France depopulation was identified as a "problem" and cited as one of the root causes of that nation's weakness.

By the eve of World War I, the "clocher"—the church bell-tower which dominated the rural horizon—had become a symbol of "la France profonde." The future of France depended upon the preservation of a way of life that was linked to the countryside. The *clocher* stood in symbolic contrast to the decadence, as much moral as military or economic, that was invariably seen as a function of city life. Ardouin-Dumazet, a French traveler and chronicler, declared that "stopping the erosion of population from the countryside [is] the most grave social problem of the present hour." Employing language and concepts which received official sanction under the Vichy regime—and which lose some of their cloying sentimentality when translated—he warned that "If we do not succeed in bringing back to the villages [literally, back to the shadow of the *clocher*] some of those who have forsaken it . . . the debilitation of the French race will continue, becoming a calamity of the proportions of the great epidemics of the Middle Ages."[2] Ardouin-Dumazet believed that there was something essentially rural about the French "race," and that the vitality of the French nation depended upon maintaining close contact with the land.

By 1912, when Ardouin-Dumazet wrote of the perils of depopulation, much of the putative damage had already been done. *L'exode rural* had been the defining demographic feature of nineteenth-century France. The evocative term "rural exodus" was clearly a misnomer, given that few saw their exodus as an escape from bondage, and cities were far from fitting most definitions of a Promised Land. Yet it became conceptual shorthand

---

2 It still is. The dominant motif of François Mitterrand's "Force tranquille" campaign of 1981 was a hilltop village, dominated by a churchtower, silhouetted against a sky of blue, white, and red. It was the emotive equivalent of the Main Street USA motif used so effectively by the Ronald Reagan/George Bush campaign.

The term "erosion" is mine, but the metaphor is Ardouin-Dumazet's. He wrote, "le maintien sur le sol des populations des campagnes. . . ." Victor-Eugène Ardouin-Dumazet, *Petites industries rurales* (Paris, 1912), 1. On Vichy policy and attempts to halt rural depopulation, see Robert Paxton, *Vichy France: Old Guard and New Order* (New York, 1972).

for the rapid depletion of the rural population in France after mid-century.[3]

Like the original Exodus, for some it seemed that the rural exodus in France involved the fate of an entire people. World War I simply accelerated the uprooting that had been underway for more than two generations. And if it took compulsory education and the formative effect of military service to turn peasants into Frenchmen, the experience of rural industry meant that peasants—who, according to Weber's famous formula, had not yet become Frenchmen—were nonetheless ceasing to be peasants at an alarming rate in the nineteenth century.[4] If not fully French, what did these uprooted peasants become?

Many of them entered an ambiguous status—a social and cultural twilight—between the peasantry and the working class. The pervasiveness of rural industry in parts of France vulnerable to the exodus provided an alternative to urban migration, thus answering the prayers of those such as Ardouin-Dumazet who feared that rural depopulation would have a negative effect on the national character. Even if we do not share that concern, the example of the department of the Isère shows that rural industry fulfilled two important functions in late-nineteenth-century France: it served as a regional safety net, trapping the so-called

3 Garavel rejects the notion that city life exercised an irresistible appeal on the peasantry. See Jean Garavel, *Les Paysans de Morette* (Paris, 1948).

4 The literature on the history of population changes in France in the nineteenth century is not so vast as one might think, given the importance of demography as a kind of historical substratum in *Annales*-type social history. Charles-Marie Pouthas, *La population française au XIXe siècle* (Paris, 1971), is comprehensive but riddled with so many errors that Pouthas' conclusions are cast into doubt. See Paul G. Spagnoli, "The Demographic Work of Charles Pouthas," *Historical Methods Newsletter,* IV (1971), 126–140. Volumes 3 and 4 of *Histoire de la population française* (Paris, 1988) under the direction of Jacques Dupâquier have provided the systematic treatment the topic deserves. See also André Armengaud, *La Population française au XIXe siècle* (Paris, 1971); Abel Chatelain, *Les migrations temporaires en France, 1800–1970* (Paris, 1970). The Centre National de Recherche Scientifique is providing some of the raw material for careful population study in a series entitled *Paroisses et Communes de France; Dictionnaire d'histoire administrative et démographique,* under the general editorship of Jean-Pierre Bardet and Jacques Dupâquier. The data are not yet available in machine-readable form.

On the transformation of French peasants, see Eugen Weber, *Peasants into Frenchmen: The Modernization of Rural France, 1870–1914* (Stanford, 1976). The ambiguities in Weber's formula are highlighted in Charles Tilly, "Did the Cake of Custom Break?" in John Merriman (ed.), *Consciousness and Class Experience in Nineteenth-Century Europe* (New York, 1979), 17–44.

"floating population" of the countryside which would otherwise have been drawn into the current of the rural exodus; it also literally capitalized on the chronically underemployed and seasonally unemployed peasants and thereby initiated the transformation of peasants into workers.[5]

THE RURAL TEXTILE INDUSTRY IN THE ISÈRE   The Isère, like many other departments in the Lyon region, benefited directly from the expansion of Lyon's silk industry. Early in the nineteenth century, its silk merchants attempted to cut wages and to introduce new techniques for the production of silk. The skilled silkworkers (canuts) of Lyon resisted these initiatives and staged massive uprisings in 1831 and 1834. The silk merchants overcame these difficulties by circumventing them—they turned to cottage industry. Rural weavers shared neither the craft organization nor the militant traditions of the artisans of Lyon. Rural weavers did not seem to threaten the industrial peace of the silk industry, at least not initially.[6]

The department of the Isère, to the east and south of the city of Lyon, was one of the favored sites for the extension of rural weaving networks. However, cottage industry had its limits and disadvantages. For most peasants, farm work took precedence over weaving, making them a good deal less reliably productive than full-fledged workers who had no such division of loyalties between land and loom. One observer estimated that the productivity of a rural loom was at best one half the productivity of an urban loom. Thus the alternation between farm work and weaving, the very reason for the cheapness of the peasant-workers' labor, was also the reason for their limited productivity. Because

5 Although the term "floating population" typically indicates "persons without a settled place of residence," I use the term in a somewhat broader sense to include all those rendered vulnerable to the forces driving the rural exodus by a declining peasant economy—persons defenseless before the "current" of the rural exodus.
6 The extension of the silk industry ultimately facilitated the radicalization of politics in the Isère. The 1906 "general strike" against the silk patronat in the Isère involved thousands of workers who walked out of a dozen mills scattered across the Bas-Dauphiné. Socialist support and coordination of the strike were repaid in 1910 when voters in the Bas-Dauphiné elected three Socialist candidates. For the Lyon revolts of the 1830s see Fernand Rude, L'Insurrection lyonnaise de novembre 1831 (Paris, 1970); idem, Le Mouvement ouvrier à Lyon de 1827 à 1832 (Lyon, 1977); Robert Bezucha, The Lyon Uprising of 1834: Social and Political Conflict in the Early July Monarchy (Cambridge, Mass., 1974). One of France's few incidents of "Luddism" occurred in the Isère.

the rural weavers' allocation of their time to weaving, as opposed to farming, was inelastic, so was the volume of their production. In this manner, the domestic weavers' "indiscipline," in Foucault's sense of the word, was as much a problem to be remedied as the indiscipline of the silk workers of Lyon.[7]

Factory-based production could solve these problems, because factories provided a controlled setting—one designed for full-time work. Thus, the introduction of factories was not in the first instance a function of motorization and mechanization, but a means to control and regulate the productivity of the workers. Factories forced farming to conform to the routine of industry rather than the other way around; it made silk production orderly and dependable. The inspiration driving factory development was very much a matter of discipline; mechanization and inanimate power provided their own impetus later. The development of powered mechanical looms, which could not realistically be adapted for cottage use, accelerated the switch to factory-based production.[8] These processes, even though contemporaneous, were historically distinct.

Once entrepreneurs installed mechanical looms, new forces began to weigh against cottage industry. The decline of cottage industry was not simply the working out of the consequences of competition between efficient and inefficient producers. The switch to factory-based production obligated entrepreneurs to support expenses previously shouldered by the domestic weavers themselves. It is therefore little wonder that, during periodic contractions, silk merchants chose to shut down the putting-out networks first because of the higher fixed costs that their own looms represented. As one silk merchant explained in testimony before the Chamber of Deputies, "When an industrialist has both

7 For the textile industry, see Claude Fohlen, *L'Industrie textile au temps du Second Empire* (Paris, 1956); on the Lyon region, see Yves Lequin, *Les Ouvriers de la région lyonnaise (1848–1914)* (Lyon, 1977), 2 v. For the Dauphiné, see Pierre Léon, *La Naissance de la grande industrie en Dauphiné* (Paris, 1954). For a regional case study, see Elinor Ann Accampo, *Industrialization, Family Life, and Class Relations: Saint Chamond* (Berkeley, 1989). For estimates of the productivity of rural looms versus urban looms, see Ernst Pariset, *Histoire de la Fabrique Lyonnaise* (Lyon, 1901), 308. The classic statement of adaptation to factory discipline is provided by Edward P. Thompson in "Time, Work-Discipline and Industrial Capitalism," *Past & Present*, 38 (1967), 56–97. But see also Michel Foucault (trans. Alan Sheridan), *Discipline and Punishment: The Birth of the Prison* (New York, 1979).
8 Léon, *La naissance de la grande industrie*, 506.

factory weavers and domestic weavers, if the [amount of] work diminishes he stops the domestic weavers first."[9] No amount of self-exploitation could save rural weavers idled by entrepreneurs who had large investments to amortize. Thus, in good times domestic weaving throve alongside factory weaving because there was sufficient work to occupy everyone, but given the self-interest of entrepreneurs, shrinking markets had a disproportionately negative effect on domestic hand-loom weavers. Each market cycle relentlessly reduced the contingent of domestic weavers. Just as rising tides raise all ships, neap tides left domestic weavers stranded.

The distribution of the new factories constituted a unique feature of industry in the Isère and, from the perspective of settlement patterns, one of critical importance. Industry typically locates in industrial centers where supplies of labor, raw materials, and power, and access to transportation and markets, are assured. Manchester, England, is a classic case. Yet such a pattern could not be replicated in the Isère, which, like much of France even in the second half of the nineteenth century, was rural. The population of Grenoble, the departmental capital, remained below 60,000 throughout the nineteenth century. Because of the pervasiveness of small-scale farming, most of the Isère's population was distributed across the countryside. Factories could not concentrate in a single town because to do so would mean that demand would rapidly outstrip the limited local labor supply. Industrial concentration made no sense in a setting where labor was widely distributed—it would only make industry a hostage to labor shortage. Small-scale facilities flourished in an environment in which large factories were an ungainly and ill-adapted species. In 1850, the first factory to house hydraulically powered mechanical looms opened at Moirans, a town of barely 2,800 persons just south of Voiron.[10] In the years that followed, entre-

---

9 France, Assemblée Nationale, *Commission d'enquête sur l'industrie textile* (Paris, 1906), II, 18.

10 For population figures, see Bernard Bonnin et al., *Paroisses et Communes de France,* (Paris, 1983), XXXVIII, LXIX. For a discussion of the mutual affinity of rural industry and certain village types, see Philippe Pinchemel, *Structures sociales et dépopulation rurale dans les campagnes picardes de 1836 à 1936* (Paris, 1957), 82–86. On Moirans, see Philippe Vigier, *La Seconde république dans la région alpine: étude politique et sociale* (Paris, 1963), II, 45. For mills, their locations, and employee counts see, Archives departementales de l'Isère (hereafter ADI) 138 M Statistiques industrielles 3, 10, 11, 12, 13, 14, 15, 16.

preneurs established dozens of factories in the area between the plain east of Lyon and Voiron, two dozen kilometers northwest of Grenoble. They took care, in a territorial fashion worthy of competitors in the natural world, to maintain a respectable distance between themselves and their nearest rivals.

Although there was some concentration as cottage industry was absorbed into factories, the labor supply imposed practical limits on concentration. As a result, factories were dispersed and, by most measures, small. The expansion of the silk industry was typically achieved through the establishment of new sites rather than the enlargement or multiplication of mills at existing sites; the contraction of cottage industry continued apace. The ready availability of power in the Isère, in the form of rivers and streams to turn water wheels, facilitated this development. The dispersal of the mills meant that industrialization did not bring about rapid urbanization in the Isère. Instead, the silk industry was in effect "ruralized" as it conformed to the Isère's demographic contours, thereby inhibiting the processes of rural depopulation and urbanization by acting as a countervailing force.[11]

Several points emerge clearly from Figure 1. First, industrial development in the Isère followed a "ruralized" pattern—industry was distributed, not concentrated. Had it not been for a similarly broad distribution of waterways, the influence of labor distribution on industrial location would have been mitigated—greater concentration of industry would have been inevitable. A plentiful supply of "white coal," the energy trapped in the rivers and streams of the alpine foothills of the Isère, meant that there were few locations where both cheap energy and labor were not close at hand. Given the complementary distribution of labor and energy sources in the Isère, industrialization did not entail rapid urbanization.

Second, cottage industry continued, even if it did not thrive, in areas where conversion to water-powered looms was not feasible; for a time, cottage industry and factory weaving coexisted. Handlooms and mechanical looms operated in the same factory—literally side-by-side—until the 1890s. The silk industry in the Isère is a perfect example of a model wherein returns to scale are

---

11   This discussion is developed in much greater detail in Jonas, "The Red and the Green: Peasants, Industry, and Politics," unpub. ms. (University of Washington, 1991).

Fig. 1 Rural Handloom Weaving at its Apogee: Centers of Weaving in
the Isère, 1866

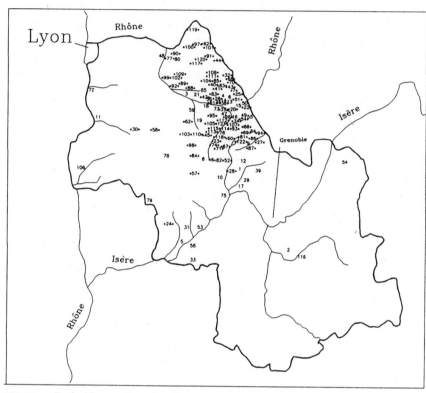

NOTE   Ranked by number of workers.
★ Centers of domestic weaving, all others are mill-based.

1 Voiron	19 Chateauvillain	65 St-Chef
2 Vizille	21 Ruy	72 Serezin
3 Jallieu	29 St-Jean-de-Moirans	73 Sainte-Blandine
4 Dolomieu	31 Chatte	75 Tullins
5 la Sône	33 Pont-en-Royans	76 Virieu
6 Corbelin	35 la Tour-du-Pin	78 la-Côte-St-André
8 Bevenais	36 Cessieu	79 St-Claire
9 St-Geoire	39 Coublevie	★38 St-Clair-de-la-Tour
10 Renage	46 Lemps	80 Crémieu
11 Vienne (nord)	47 St-André-le-Gaz	106 Roussillon
12 St-Nicholas-de-	48 Charvieu	116 St-Barthélémy
Macherin	49 la Folatière	★7 les Avenières
13 Bâtie-Montgascon	50 Aoste	★20 Fitilieu
14 Faverges	54 Allevard	★22 Romagnieu
15 Chimilin	55 Pont-de-Beauvoisin	★23 Chabons
16 les Abrets	56 St-Romans	★24 St-Antoine
17 Moirans	59 les Eparres	★25 Veyrins
18 Serezin	64 St-Jean-d'Avelanne	★26 Chapelle-de-la-Tour

Fig. 1   Continued

*27 St-Bueil	*67 Charavines	*97 Charette
*28 Rives	*68 Brangues	*98 Eydoche
*30 St-Jean-de-Bournay	*69 Montferrat	*99 Chamagnieu
*32 St-Victor-de- Morestel	*70 le Bouchage	*100 St-Baudille
*34 Charancieu	*71 Oyeu	*101 Bouvesse-Quirieu
*37 St-Didier-de-la-Tour	*74 Burcin	*102 Panossas
*40 Vézeronce	*77 Tignieu-Jameyzieu	*103 Flachères
*41 St-Sorlin	*95 Torchefelon	*104 Sermérieu
*42 Rochetoiron	*81 Paladru	*105 Biol
*43 Thuellin	*82 Colombe	*107 St-Ondras
*44 Creys	*83 Vignieu	*108 Arandon
*45 Bizonnes	*84 Longchenal	*109 Veyssilieu
*51 Granieu	*85 Morestel	*110 St-Didier-de- Bizonnes
*52 Apprieu	*86 St-Martin-de- Vauleserre	*111 Passins
*53 Têche-et-Beaulieu	*87 Merlas	*112 Panissage
*54 Pressins	*88 St-Savin	*113 Montrevel
*57 St-Geoire-en- Valdaine	*89 St-Marcel	*114 Chassignieu
*58 Chatonay	*90 St-Romain-de- Jalionas	*115 Chélieu
*60 le Pin		*117 Soleymieu
*61 St-Jean-de-Soudain	*91 Mepieu	*118 Blandin
*62 Montalieu-Vercieu	*92 Frontonas	*119 la Balme
*62 Badiniéres	*93 Valencogne	*120 Courtenay
*63 Curtin	*94 St-Albin-de- Vaulserre	*121 Doissin
*66 la Bfie-Divisin	*96 le Passage	*122 Bilieu

SOURCE   Archives départementales de l'Isère (hereafter ADI), 138 M 10 Situation industrielle, 1863–1868.

low. Thus, if French business culture conflated the concepts of *ferme* and *firme,* as Smith has pointed out, there were also practical linkages and limits to scale. Entrepreneurs in the Isère would have gained little simply by being larger. Indeed they stood to lose much since, as scale increased, they increased the chances that they would have to use wages to soften the relative inelasticity in the local labor supply—in effect, to bid with cash to persuade peasants to weave rather than farm.[12]

12 On some issues related to the persistence of cottage weaving, see Paule Bernard, "Un Exemple d'industrie dispersée en milieu rural. Deux vallées en bas-Dauphiné: la Bièvre et le Liers," *Revue de Géographie Alpine,* XL (1952), 133–157. For a fresh look at the debate over firm size, see John Vincent Nye, "Firm Size and Economic Backwardness: A New Look at the French Industrialization Debate," *Journal of Economic History,* XLVII (1987), 649–669. Smith has suggested that there is a third term linking and determining the dimensions of *ferme* and *firme,* namely, *famille.* Robert J. Smith, "Family History and the Rise and Fall of an Industrial Enterprise: Bouchayer-Viallet of Grenoble, 1870–1972,"

But even while it inhibited urbanization as a grand process, rural industry fostered the transformation of towns, villages, and even hamlets into "micro-urbs." The median textile commune had a regular population of about 1,500 persons, well below the (INSEE)-recognized boundary between urban and rural communes of 2,000 inhabitants. However, the population captured by the official census greatly underrepresented the workday population. The effective population of the industrial villages was inflated by hundreds with the arrival of millhands. For example, the "median" village of Coublevie, which had a population of just over 1,500 at the turn of the century, grew by as much as one third with the daily arrival of 600 workers. Charavine's population (960 in 1891) increased by a similar proportion when over 300 workers arrived to begin their day. In such villages and hamlets, population increased and decreased with tidal regularity—its rhythm determined by the mill, its size, and its schedule. Like modern cities, the population of these factory communes swelled daily with the regular arrival of "commuters" from surrounding farms.[13]

Thus even if they generally fell short of the "urban" classification, textile villages duplicated city life in some important respects. In textile communes, one household in two was a textile household; that is, one in two households included at least one textile worker. And whereas the typical textile household was headed by a worker of the land, one in three textile households was headed by an industrial worker. Here was a rural proletariat in intimate contact with peasant society.[14] In similar fashion, many others not directly linked to the textile industry owed their livelihood to it. Those in commerce and services depended on the patronage of textile workers and their families and understood that their fate was tied to that of the dominant local industry.

---

paper presented at the Western Society for French History (New Orleans, 1989). On questions of labor supply and French industry, see William Reddy, *The Rise of Market Culture: The Textile Trade and French Society* (Cambridge, 1984).

13 INSEE, L'Institut national de la statistique et des etudes economiques, recognizes urban communes as those having 2,000 inhabitants or more in the agglomerated settlement. The median case in 1891 was Coublevie, with 1,540 persons. ADI 123 M 6 recensement, 1891; AN F7 12785 Police générale.

14 ADI 123 M 61–62, 64, recensements, 1896. Based on the sample of the cantons of Pont-de-Beauvoisin, St-Geoire-en-Valdaine, and Virieu, which showed 615 textile households among 2,400 households overall, a ratio of one in four. Textile communes—villages and towns containing mills—in the same sample showed ratios as high as one textile household for every two households overall. See Table 1.

Textile mills created a vigorous hybrid social tissue, richer and more vascular—hardier too, for a time—than that traditionally associated with insular and inbred peasant society.

The insinuation of the silk industry into the existing pattern of rural life minimized the manifestations of change. However, the spread of rural industry meant that a rural economy that had been based largely upon agriculture took on a significant industrial dimension. The result was a "binary economy," at once dependent upon industry and agriculture but also independent to a degree from the vagaries of either.[15] This binary economy soon had noticeable social effects both at the level of individual households and at the regional level, where the industrial stimulus imposed a drag on the pace of the rural exodus and sometimes even reversed it.

Evidence drawn from census lists and represented in Figure 2 suggests that the silk industry was a barrier against rural depopulation. A study of the cumulative population change in all of the 560+ municipalities of the Isère shows the extent of the rural exodus. The median population decrease between mid-century and the eve of World War I was on the order of 30 percent.[16] In other words, the typical commune in the Isère in 1846 was one third smaller in 1911 than it had been in 1846. Such a decline would have ably supported Ardouin-Dumazet's assertions about population trends, if not his sentiments. However, the experience of textile communities was markedly different.[17]

15   On the binary economy in the twentieth century, see Harvey Franklin, "The Worker Peasant in Europe" in Teodor Shanin (ed.), *Peasants and Peasant Societies* (Harmondsworth, Eng., 1976), 98–102.

16   This figure is calculated from census data in ADI 123 M 3, 6, 8, 10, 51, 53–55, 57, 60; Bonnin et al., *Paroisses et Communes*, XXXVIII, LXIX.

17   How does one identify textile communes? This question is more difficult to answer than it may appear. First, the impact of the textile industry extended beyond the administrative limits of the commune, so any measure relying exclusively on the population figures of the communes with mills *alone* will undoubtedly fail to measure the impact of the industry on the surrounding communities. Second, there was some expansion but also considerable consolidation in the textile industry between 1846 and 1911. Many "textile communes" in 1866 were no longer so designated a generation later. Any valid measure must include communes which retained their identity as textile communes throughout the period. I therefore chose as a representative group the 32 communes which were centers of the textile industry in 1866 and remained so through subsequent decades. I then used a demographic contour map to describe the impact of industry on the surrounding areas. For a list of textile centers, see ADI 138 M, Statistiques industrielles 16, 162 M 3, 4, and 5, Industrie et travail.

Fig. 2   A Comparison of Cumulative Median Population Change in Textile Communes as against All Communes, 1846–1911

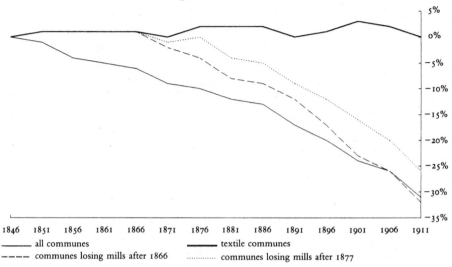

1846 1851 1856 1861 1866 1871 1876 1881 1886 1891 1896 1901 1906 1911
———— all communes   ———— textile communes
– – – – communes losing mills after 1866   .... communes losing mills after 1877

SOURCES   ADI 123 M 3, 6, 8, 10, 51, 53–55, 57, 60; Bernard Bonnin et al., *Paroisses et Communes de France* (Paris, 1983), XXXVIII, XXXIX.

The textile industry was a bulwark against the rural exodus, at least in the short run. Before 1900, the population in the textile communes was largely stable. In fact, during some periods of growth in the textile industry, the population of the textile communes increased. Only after 1900 were there signs of loss, for reasons explicable within the history of the silk industry, but even in 1911 the textile communes, collectively speaking, were no smaller than they were before mid-century. In the Isère, a department which suffered rural depopulation like few others, the silk industry provided effective oases in areas that would otherwise have been denuded by the rural exodus.

The effects of de-industrialization were rapid and brutal. Communes which lost textile mills rapidly took their place among the net-population losers; their aggregate population loss by 1911 was comparable to that for communes which had never had industry. Rural industry was a barrier, albeit temporary, to rural depopulation. And its influence often extended well beyond the mill towns themselves.

THE CONTOURS OF RURAL INDUSTRY   The women and, far less often, men who worked in the textile mills often traveled considerable distances between home and work. Some walked only from their town or village to a riverside mill. Others came from out-of-the-way farms and hamlets or more distant villages. For some workers the distances were so great that daily "commutes" were impossible. In order to attract these more remote workers—in effect, in order to enlarge the radius of the labor pool—employers built factory dormitories where workers lodged from Sunday night through Saturday.[18] In many cases workers sent their wages directly home, where they helped to support these more distant households. In this fashion the industry's economic and demographic consequences extended well beyond the limits of the textile commune.

The silk industry shaped the village economy in indirect ways, too. The production of manufactured goods stimulated demand for support services. For example, the shipment of goods imposed new burdens on transport facilities, calling for more hands to operate and maintain them and more workers to expedite the shipment of raw materials and finished products. New industry drew new workers; it also meant a new café or bakery.[19] It brought new clients to merchants and, after the Ferry laws regarding compulsory education in the 1880s, brought new pupils, the children of workers, to primary schools. Each worker employed by the textile mills increased the burden on the local infrastructure for goods and services. The establishment of a textile mill meant a more diverse and prosperous local economy, so that the relationship between industrial location and population, in growth as in decline, was mutually reinforcing. Since the textile

18   The story of the factory dormitories has yet to be told in detail. The most important study to date is Chatelain, "Les usines-internats et migrations féminines dans la région lyonnaise," *Revue d'histoire économique et sociale,* XLVIII (1970), 373–394. See also Joseph Jouanny, *Le Tissage de la soie en bas-dauphiné* (Grenoble, 1931), 55. One of the larger dormitories was in Renage. See AN C3021, *Enquête,* Renage, Montessuy, et Chomer. On dormitories in the department of the Ain, see Pierre Leroy-Beaulieu, "Les Ouvrières de la Fabrique," *Revue des Deux-Mondes,* XCVII (1872), 651.

For a worker's point of view on the dormitories, see Lucie Baud, "Les Tisseuses de soie de la région de Vizille," *Le Mouvement socialiste,* II (1908), 422. For a labor inspector's point of view, see Justin Godart, *Travailleurs et métiers lyonnais* (Lyon, 1909), 391.

19   Cafés were ubiquitous. They proliferated with the mills. In one village, it was noted, "a factory goes up and a café soon follows." As a result, "there is not a single hamlet which does not have its 'café de l'usine' . . .". Jouanny, *Tissage de la soie,* 131.

industry was scattered throughout the rural Isère, these effects were widely distributed, creating microregions of economic and demographic growth. Around these were areas without industry—communities often marked by crisis and population decline.

One way to delineate and measure these effects is to examine changes in the population in a new way. Prosperity exerted a powerful influence. It had its own specific gravity. If small, marginal farming households of the late nineteenth century were to resist the forces driving the rural exodus, they needed to seek out additional sources of income. As households adjusted their routines to send one or more members to work in the mills, or as they relocated, they produced observable shifts of population.

Figure 3 is a contour map, but it differs from standard contour maps which show variations in elevation. This map reveals not changes in the elevation of the land, but changes in the demographic contours of a region. Shifts in population between censuses reflected population growth and decline. These values were calculated for the more than 560 municipalities in the department of the Isère and then used to identify and circumscribe areas of population growth. Contour lines indicate areas of population stasis. Within these lines are areas of population growth; outside them are areas of decline. The result is a visual representation of a demographic landscape shaped by the peasant response to the silk industry.[20]

The Franco-Prussian War had occasioned the deepening of the cultural and political pessimism which Ardouin-Dumazet linked to population change. Between the conclusion of the war and the onset of the Long Depression in 1873, the silk industry of the Isère enjoyed unprecedented prosperity. Figure 3 shows the population of the Isère during that period of vigorous growth. One can rapidly identify regions of demographic expansion outside of the major urban centers of Lyon and Grenoble. The contours reveal several zones of population growth and, by inference, broadly based prosperity, including a Vizille-Grenoble-Voiron axis, a littoral along the Rhône, and many pockets along the

20 For an explanation of the technical aspects of contour map generation, see Jonas, "Visualizing Population in History: Surface Modeling Techniques in Demographic Analysis," *Historical Methods* (forthcoming). See E. Anthony Wrigley's *Population and History* (New York, 1969), 99. He imagines the use of contour-mapping techniques to explore economic regions.

Fig. 3 The Prosperity of the Early 1870s

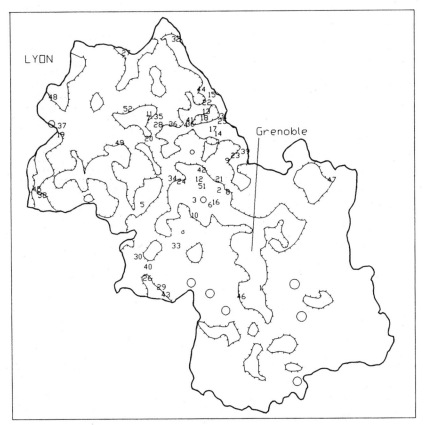

NOTE   Circumscribed areas denote population growth between 1872 and 1876.
SOURCES   ADI 138 M 16, *Statistiques industrielles,* 1877–80; ADI 123 M 3 Population;
Bonnin et al., *Paroisses et Communes,* XXXVIII, LXIX.

waterways in the interior of the department. Many of these areas
had no notable economic activity outside of farming and the
textile industry. Between the small agriculture for which these
regions were known and the prosperity of the silk industry, these
communities held their populations and, in fact, drew on the
population of less fortunate surrounding villages and hamlets. In
these areas, the rural exodus was arrested, even reversed.

Conversely, the alpine southeastern portion of the department shows pervasive population loss—it is here that the rural exodus continued without interruption. Outside of the domain of rural industry, the rural exodus continued unabated; within this territory, it was brought to a halt. Villages outside these areas were tributary to the villages where there was industrial growth. And limited local migration sometimes substituted for definitive rural exodus. Employing the language of Le Roy Ladurie in connection with Languedoc, we might call this expansion of the early 1870s the first phase of an economic and demographic "respiration."[21]

If prosperity "looks" like nothing so much as a broadly distributed growth, how might one visualize the demographic impact of economic recession? After 1870, the textile industry experienced two long economic cycles—two periods of prosperity followed by recession. The first began with the short boom after the Franco-Prussian War, when wages rose sharply as demand for labor increased (for the local demographic impact of that boom, see Figure 3). After the expansion of the early 1870s came the broader downturn marking the beginning of the Long Depression, which extended to 1896. A measure of prosperity returned during a second phase in the mid to late 1890s, the Belle Epoque. For the silk industry, however, this recovery soon faltered under the weight of foreign competition, especially from German and Swiss producers, and the closing of markets, notably the lucrative American market, behind tariff walls. Such events in the competitive environment cut deeply into French producers' share of a shrinking market. By comparing the contour maps in figures 3 and 4, it is possible to make inferences about the relationship between population and known economic factors—between economic prosperity, the presence of rural textile industry, and the movement of population. By the first decade of the twentieth century, the silk industry in France was suffering; much of the rural Isère was suffering with it.

Once again, population shifts reveal the contours of economic distress. Gone are the extensive regions of growth identified in the boom of the 1870s. The Vizille-Grenoble-Voiron axis was broken, and the belt along the Rhône littoral vanished, as

21 Emmanuel Le Roy Ladurie, *Les Paysans de Languedoc* (Paris, 1966).

Fig. 4 Localized Distress of the Silk Industry, 1901–1911

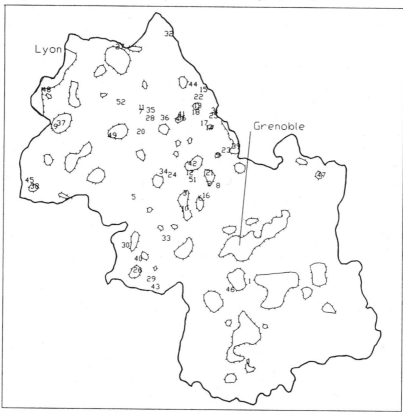

NOTE   Circumscribed areas denote population growth between 1901 and 1911.
SOURCES   ADI 123 M 8, 10; B. Bonnin et al., *Paroisses et Communes*, XXXVIII,
XXXIX.

did the zones of prosperity surrounding the textile communes along the interior waterways. The difficulties of the textile industry prompted individuals and entire households to vote with their feet. This exodus was the second part of the demographic "respiration." The population that had been drawn to the rural textile centers was driven away by the silk industry's distress. During the bleak years for the silk industry, some workers returned to farms; and there were signs of growth in the populations of regions adjacent to the mills. But many workers simply left.

The rural exodus—that "form of strike, individual and unremit-ting"—had resumed.[22] It had not been avoided, only postponed.

Who departed? Who remained behind? What impact did the resumption of the rural exodus—brought on by the crisis of the silk industry—have on the makeup of the rural community? Those workers who relied on wages from the silk industry rarely had somewhere else to go. They represented the marginal ele-ments of peasant society—attached to the land, but lacking suf-ficient land to live exclusively from its fruits. For them, the contraction of the silk industry meant the loss of the income which made it possible to make ends meet. We can learn "who left" and "who stayed" by looking at the makeup of households prior to the onset of the crisis after the turn of the century.

RURAL HOUSEHOLDS IN THE ISÈRE, 1896   The social changes in-duced by rural industry were not only vertical but horizontal—the silk industry influenced both the movement of persons across space and the social and gender relations within rural communi-ties. When wages from labor in silk mills postponed rural depo-pulation, a portion of rural society was, in effect, singled out for reprieve—notably the "marginal" rural households. Silk workers typically came from the marginal peasantry or from a rural work-ing-class or artisanal background—all elements of rural society "at risk" in the second half of the nineteenth century. These social elements would ultimately make up the belated rural exodus brought on by the contraction of the silk industry.

But the effect of the silk industry was also uneven in gender terms. It touched the feminine half of the population most directly because the introduction of mechanical looms made it physically easier for women to tend the looms, and by the 1860s at least two thirds of the silk workers were women. This feminization of the silk industry, in turn, led to a new sexual division of labor in rural households wherein women went to the mills and earned a wage, and men stayed at home and minded the farm or went off to their own place of work.

22 The formula belongs to Augé-Laribé, who insisted on the primacy of rural distress in any explanation of the phenomenon of the rural exodus. See Michel Augé-Laribé, *La politique agricole de la France de 1880 à 1940* (Paris, 1950), 102; Augé-Laribé, cited in Pierre Barral, "Aspects régionaux de l'agrarisme français avant 1930," *Mouvement social*, LXVII (1969), 10.

Corollary to the feminization of wage labor was the masculinization of agriculture. Insofar as this shift was a departure from the norm—agricultural and domestic tasks filled the workday of most women in peasant households—rural industry was more likely to attract persons from enterprising households prepared to renegotiate some features of conventional gender roles for the sake of the household. This adaptation was both cultural and economic and was potentiated by the need to earn more than farming alone would provide. In this sense, rural industry depended upon two forms of opportunism—the opportunism of entrepreneurs and of wage earners. Table 1, which shows the occupations of the heads of rural households in the Isère, helps to clarify these points.

I sampled every fifth household in three contiguous cantons—about 1,800 households in all—as reported in the 1896 census. I separated textile households from the sample as a whole in order to determine how they differed from other rural households. Textile households were defined as those households which had at least one member listed in the census rolls as a textile worker.[23]

What was the social background of the textile workers? For the sample population, the most common social background, as measured by the occupation of the head of household, was in agriculture (see Table 1). "Farmers"—a category including *cultivateurs, fermiers,* and *proprietaires-cultivateurs,* as well as *journaliers* and *domestiques-agricoles*—headed one half of all of the households in the sample.[24] Workers, artisans, and shopkeepers were also more or less common occupations for heads of households. A handful of household heads made their living in the liberal professions (1 percent) or business (1 percent), or as *rentiers* (2 percent).

The 615 textile households differed from the others in several ways.[25] Farmers were still the most important category among heads of textile households—46 percent versus 50 percent for the

23 The cantons were Pont-de-Beauvoisin, St-Geoire, and Virieu—the 1896 *recensements* for these cantons are found in ADI 123 M 61–62, and 64, respectively.
24 Vagaries in precision in reporting make it risky to treat these as reliable counts of discrete categories within the agricultural sector. And fragmentation of landholdings meant that some individuals belonged to more than one category—for example, *proprietaires-cultivateurs* sometimes doubled as *journaliers*—hence the catch-all rubric "farmers."
25 This evidence is a snapshot. It represents only one moment in the long history of the rural society of the.Isère.

Table 1 Occupation of Head of Household

	ALL HOUSEHOLDS		"TEXTILE" HOUSEHOLDS	
None	8%	(n = 148)	6%	(n = 37)
Farmer	50%	(n = 929)	46%	(n = 280)
Worker	16%	(n = 298)	35%	(n = 213)
Artisan	10%	(n = 178)	10%	(n = 59)
Shopkeeper	5%	(n = 96)	1%	(n = 9)
Civil Servant	4%	(n = 70)	1%	(n = 7)
Personal Service	2%	(n = 37)	1%	(n = 6)
Professional	1%	(n = 20)	0%	(n = 0)
Business Professional	1%	(n = 25)	0%	(n = 2)
Rentier	2%	(n = 45)	0%	(n = 2)
	1,846 cases		615 cases	

SOURCES   ADI 123 M 61–62, and 64 recensements.

general population, a plurality of cases but no longer a majority. "Worker" was the second most common occupation among heads of textile households, and some of them were textile workers themselves. This fact suggests that the silk industry relied on a rural industrial proletariat which had somewhat tenuous ties to the land. Taken together, peasant and worker backgrounds accounted for four fifths (81 percent) of the textile worker households, the only other significant groups being the artisanate (10 percent) and the unemployed (6 percent).

Overall, textile households present a less diversified social background than the general population, and their members were less well off. Although textile households were far from uniformly proletarian, the most significant difference between the textile households and the sample overall was the much stronger proletarian element in the textile households. Because the Isère was a rural department, only 16 percent of households overall were working-class households, but in areas of textile industry the great majority of working-class households were textile households (more than 70 percent in the sample).[26] Textile workers did not emerge from the world of the rural social elite of professionals, civil servants, and merchants. The vast majority of

26 The basis for assertions about areas of textile industry alluded to here is the sample of the censuses of Pont-de-Beauvoisin, St-Geoire, and Virieu.

textile workers were from farming and working-class backgrounds. The textile industry was a great resource for those very segments of the population which were most vulnerable to the forces driving the rural exodus—marginal peasants, rural workers, and the rural poor.

But if the textile households tended to be uniform in social terms, they presented a picture of great internal complexity, especially in their household strategies. Farms larger than ten hectares were rare in this part of the Isère. As a result, peasants could harvest only a bare minimum from the land. The best that they could expect was to "gather their own wheat and make their own wine; a few patches of buckwheat or truffles, some corn, a good batch of potatoes . . . that's all they ask of the soil." Such conditions drove peasants toward rural industry. But the silk industry was selective; its preference for women workers imposed a sexual division of labor on peasant households. Men remained on the farm, whereas life for women took a proletarian turn. When women worked at distant mills, they commuted weekly, leaving the farm in the men's hands until they returned on Saturday evening—a schedule which upset rural household routines and redefined conventional male/female roles. As soon as a factory was "erected nearby . . . the mother and the daughter [got] themselves hired: the father stay[ed] on the farm and work[ed] by himself; if he need[ed] help he hire[ed] a farm hand. Meals [were] summary: soup and vegetables; the man [had to] get his meals for himself. . . ."[27] The press of limited peasant resources—the press of the rural exodus itself—compelled peasants to rethink household strategies, even to the point of rethinking gender roles.

The rural exodus was not a simple linear process, an abrupt cleansing of the rural population, or a stripping of peasant society of its marginal elements. An organic metaphor for the decay of peasant society would be apt; peasant society even late in the nineteenth century was a complex organism, living symbiotically with rural industry. The rural exodus was symptomatic of the decay of peasant society from its apogee just before mid-century. It proceeded in a cyclical fashion as peasants were drawn into rural industry only to be expelled later; rural depopulation oc-

27 Jouanny, *Tissage de la soie*, 18, 20.

curred through a series of respiration-like movements, spread out over generations. Rural industry inserted pauses in this decline but failed to arrest it. As peasant society was coming to an end, rural industry momentarily gave it new life or, more darkly, prolonged its mortal contractions.

Most members of rural society far preferred to make an uncertain living from resources cobbled together—a marginal existence drawn from industry and agriculture—than to face the great uncertainty that a definitive exodus represented. The appeal of rural industry for the peasantry, a value very much a part of the wages that they earned, was derived from the promise of a future short of a definitive departure from the land and the abandonment of familiar surroundings and a familiar way of life. Peasants did not share Ardouin-Dumazet's national cultural pessimism—coming, as it did, out of a Catholic, conservative and, above all, bourgeois milieu—but they shared the belief that the worst possible outcome was the *dépaysement* of the *paysan*.

Consciously or not, rural industry throve on these fears and uncertainties when it conformed to the highly distributed pattern of the French population in the nineteenth century. As such small firm size represented a rational, even shrewd, adaptation to business opportunities in France—insofar as the distribution and expectations of labor shaped those opportunities. Mill managers profited from the peasants' preference for waged work, however poorly paid, to a definitive departure from the countryside. This adaptation paid dividends for businesses in the cities, where urban artisans were cowed into accepting wage scales near those prevalent in the countryside.[28]

The spread of rural industry, and the demographic respirations which the business cycles produced as a consequence, directly altered rural settlement patterns and the makeup of rural society. Rural industry captured a significant part of the rural working poor, those most vulnerable and therefore most likely to be swept up into the rural exodus. Ross was thus only partly right: the rural exodus was primarily a matter of resources or lack

28 Low wages inspired a strike among Lyon silk workers in 1903. Its unsatisfactory outcome led the Lyon Bourse du Travail to conclude that it would have to organize rural workers if it wanted to control conditions in Lyon. The 1906 general strike in the Isère was led by Charles Auda, a former rural weaver, Socialist, and undisputed leader of the Lyon Bourse du Travail. See AN F7 12785, police, 8 Apr. 1906.

thereof, and therefore not strictly a matter of character, of "bull-heads and suckers." Those peasants who ultimately left were at least as bullheaded as those whose resources permitted them to stay. But he was right in the sense that the lack of resources inspired ingenious, complex, and enterprising household strategies in response to the crisis of peasant society. Peasant society was impoverished when such strategies ultimately failed—when the withdrawal of rural industry left entire households little choice but belatedly to join the exodus.

Rural industry had drawn in poor and "marginal" peasants and the rural underemployed and unemployed, because it offered them a haven, an alternative to the admission of failure and migration. Although it seemed that the silk industry would anchor them in the countryside, it was a tether no less tenuous than the subsistence farm. Now their lives were subject to the caprices of international demand for silk. Contractions and consolidations were inevitable in an industry unusually prone to crisis in that it produced luxury goods for a notably mercurial market. For many, rural industry could only insert a "pause" in the rural exodus.

Rural industry prepared, even initiated, the transition from peasant to urban worker. Peasants were drawn to rural industry for what it represented to them in the form of wages and ultimately the preservation of their rural existence. Some peasants imagined that they would work only long enough to enlarge their farm, pay off their debts, or raise their children to working age, or until better times for farming arrived. But as they and, ultimately, their children became involved in rural industry, it became very difficult to withdraw—to revert to their former mode of existence.[29]

Rural industrial labor was part of a creative response to a conservative impulse—to preserve a rural way of life. In the event, however, it became a transformative experience. Peasants entered the mills but rarely found it possible to leave; nor could they afford to be indifferent to the possibility that the mills might leave them. Their fate, and the fate of the communities that grew up

29 I agree with Cottereau's criticism of the notion that industrial workers in France were merely uprooted peasants. My remarks represent an attempt to fill in the details of the transition from peasant to proletarian. See Alain Cottereau, "The Distinctiveness of Working-Class Cultures in France, 1848–1900," in Ira Katznelson and Aristide R. Zolberg (eds.), *Working Class Formation* (Princeton, 1986), 111–154.

around the mills, became bound up with that of the silk industry. When general economic conditions, new competition, and tariff wars provoked the inevitable contractions in the demand for silk goods, mills closed. Such events induced demographic spasms in the microurban villages and hamlets of rural industry. When they did, they sent semi-proletarianized peasants, not raw peasant recruits, into France's urban centers.

Michael B. Katz

Social Class in North American Urban History

Social class analysis is an old tradition in American social science. Late nineteenth-century American social commentary routinely assumed that two great classes, Capital and Labor, dominated American society. Not only academics, social critics, or spokesmen of the labor movement, but also representatives of business interests and government shared this perception. Indeed, the "development of a permanent working class," according to Furner, preoccupied many of the earliest professional social scientists, the founders of the American Social Science Association.[1]

The subsequent decline in the prominence of class as a topic accompanied a shift in the orientation of the social sciences, described by Furner as a turn from advocacy to objectivity. The early concentration on social class had emerged from the concern of social scientists with reform. Its founders wanted social science not only to understand society but also to change it. As a result, early social scientists challenged powerful interests, the representatives of which responded with attempts to expel the insurgents from university campuses—campaigns which resulted in the famous series of academic freedom cases in the late nineteenth and early twentieth centuries. In the end academic freedom, despite its early setbacks, triumphed, or so the story goes. Professors were free to speak and write about controversial issues without fear of reprisal. But they paid a price. They shifted their concerns away from reform and toward a complex, methodologically rig-

Michael B. Katz is Professor of Education, History, and Public Policy at the University of Pennsylvania. He is the author, with Mark Stern and Michael Doucet, of *The Social Organization of Early Industrial Capitalism,* forthcoming.

The research on which this article is based was supported by the Canada Council, Grant #75-1536 and 410-0265, and by the Center for the Study of Metropolitan Problems, National Institute of Mental Health, Grant #R) 1 MH 27850. The formulations grew out of my collaborative work with Michael Doucet and Mark Stern. For their helpful and perceptive comments on an earlier version of this essay I would like to thank Michael Frisch, David Hogan, Charles Rosenberg, Daniel Scott Smith, and Mark Stern.

0022-1953/81/020579-27 $02.50/0

1 Mary O. Furner, *Advocacy and Objectivity: A Crisis in the Professionalization of American Social Sciences, 1865–1901* (Lexington, 1975), 22.

orous emphasis on objective, value-free social analysis. Deploying objectivity as their guiding ideology, social scientists developed increasingly sophisticated ways of analyzing narrow and less explosive problems. As they became experts, they gained security and standing within universities, public life, and private enterprise.[2]

The virtual abandonment of social class analysis accompanied the movement from advocacy to objectivity; the study of social structure became the delineation of stratification rather than the explication of class. Misunderstanding its essential characteristics, social scientists have confused class with stratification, using the two interchangeably and carelessly. Frequently they have dismissed class analysis as simple-minded and reductionist.[3]

But the question is not merely methodological, nor is it one of the relative virtues of complexity—over simplicity and reductionism. It also is political. For class is a concept which rests on a perception that the social order is divided into conflicting groups, the differing interests of which derive from their fundamentally opposing relations to the production of material life.

The analysis of stratification, by contrast, has no theoretical core. Groups may be composed of any divisions which seem most appropriate, or which yield the most useful predictions on particular measures, such as self-evaluation, the rating of occupations through a survey of the population, income, or a standard scale of socioeconomic position. None has any theoretical basis. None offers any way of understanding the reasons that a social formation assumed a particular shape, why groups have different relations to each other, or how social structure relates to social change.

One reason for the weakness of stratification analysis lies in its reflection of a leading orientation within twentieth-century social science: what Haskell has termed interdependence. Haskell has argued that the development of the social sciences rested on a shift in the mode of causal attribution. As social scientists exchanged advocacy for objectivity, they also traded straightfor-

2 *Ibid.*
3 Charles Hunt Page, *Class and American Sociology: From Ward to Ross* (New York, 1940), 250; see 9n. below. An anonymous reviewer of a recent essay by myself and a colleague commented that if Karl Marx had had access to multivariate analysis, his work would have been much better.

ward, often superifical, explanations of social phenomena for an image of a world composed of interdependent variables interacting in a way that makes direct causal arguments inadequate. Underlying this point of view is a perception of a social order without a core, one in which conflict is neither endemic nor reasonable. Rather, conflict reflects a mis-perception, a failure of enlightenment, and an inability to grasp the essential harmony of interests in an interdependent world.[4]

Recent American history underscores the inadequacy of social theory which treats conflict as exceptional or pathological and which fails to realize the extent to which reform is a zero-sum process. Drawing on the failure of American social theory either to predict or explain the course of events very well, a growing body of criticism shows that the bankruptcy of social science stems from a combination of its narrow preoccupation with method and the inadequacy of its treatment of conflict and of class.

There are ironies: the social scientists and historians who deny the appropriateness of class as a category with which to study America and its past usually base their case upon either high rates of social mobility, the relative absence of class-conscious political movements, or the primacy of ethno-cultural identity. They fail to realize that none of these properly characterized the American historical experience or, in the case of sociologists, that their own discipline was founded upon the serious analysis of class.

Even historians more sympathetic to class analysis are guilty of ahistoricism. Ironically, Thernstrom, who delivered a stunning critique of ahistorical social science in his attack on Warner in the appendix to his brilliant *Poverty and Progress,* provides an especially prominent example.[5]

Despite his interests in mobility and his concern with the openness and justice of American society, Thernstrom nowhere offered a definition of class. Indeed, class as a concept is not found in the index to his work on the history of social mobility in Boston. His analysis there used the occupational categories com-

4 Thomas L. Haskell, *The Emergence of Professional Social Science: The American Social Science Association and the Nineteenth-Century Crisis of Authority* (Urbana, 1977).
5 Stephan Thernstrom, *Poverty and Progress: Social Mobility in a Nineteenth Century City* (Cambridge, Mass., 1974), 225–239.

mon in mid-twentieth century social science and defined movement across class lines as a transition between white- and blue-
collar occupations. However, no explanation was offered for the
appropriateness of this criterion of class division or of the difference between class and stratification. Why is the movement from
white to blue collar more important, or different, than the movement from unskilled to skilled worker? Wherein lies the difference, and how do the meanings of those movements alter over
time?[6]

Moreover, Thernstrom simply assumed that all men with a
blue-collar title were within the same class. Yet, his data did not
distinguish between wageworkers and proprietors or masters who
had the same occupational title. The shoemaker or carpenter who
acquired his own business but did not alter what he called himself
retained, in Thernstrom's universe (and in that of most other
historians of mobility), the same class position. Is this justifiable?
The answer requires the taking of a position about the nature of
social structure, and about the meaning of occupation, proprietorship, and their relations to each other.

The ahistoricism of social scientists and of some historians
does not exhaust the ironies in the contemporary historiography
of class. For the advocates of historical class analysis frequently
are not without responsibility for the sorry state of the subject in
North America. Rightly perceiving the implications of the quantitative fetish in social science and correctly understanding the
political implications of much contemporary historiography, too
many historians of the Left have rejected numerical analysis as
inherently biased. But this is a myopic and ahistorical point of
view. Marx emphasized the critical importance of a careful delineation of social structure, drew heavily on quantitative evidence,
and used the best empirical data available at the time that he
wrote. Instead of rejecting quantification, the Left should eman-
cipate it and return empirical social history to its origins.[7]

6 *Idem, The Other Bostonians: Poverty and Progress in the American Metropolis, 1880–1970*
(Cambridge, Mass., 1973).
7 Consider, for example, the following statement made by Marx and Friedrich Engels
in (ed. R. Pascal) *The German Ideology* (New York, 1939); "The premises from which we
begin are not arbitrary ones, not dogmas, but real premises from which abstraction can
only be made in the imagination. They are the real individuals, their activity and the
material conditions under which they live . . . These premises thus can be verified in a
purely empirical way" (6–7).

The modest amount of evidence presented in this article should make clear both that social class provides an appropriate organizing category with which to study North American historical experience and that class can be made an operational concept in a rough and imperfect, although nonetheless useful, way.

Class, as a term, appears often in North American history. Examples are discussions of the role of the working class in Jacksonian politics; the existence of an upper class in the late nineteenth-century; the role of the middle class in social reform; and the degree of social mobility between the working and the middle class. In the last case, class usually is defined in terms of white versus blue collar, a use implicit in much of the other writing on class as well. In this conception class is confused with stratification. It becomes synonymous with the divisions on a rank ordering of the population according to some variable, usually the assumed socioeconomic position of occupations or, sometimes, wealth or income.[8]

Class, however, should be distinguished sharply from stratification because class is an analytical category that refers to the social relationships which derive from the ways in which material life is reproduced. The confusion between class and stratification, it should be pointed out, is not the fault of historians alone. The interchangeable use of the terms has also been a feature of North American sociology since relatively early in the twentieth century. Indeed, it is from sociologists that historians have borrowed the terminology with which they describe the social order.[9]

Even if a definition of class can be agreed upon, important and difficult problems remain. For the proponent of class must be able to show that it provides a mode of explanation through which social structure and social behavior can be analyzed in a precise and significant way. Thus, the initial problem confronting

8 Many studies could be used to illustrate this point. Two examples are Edward Pessen, *Riches, Class and Power Before the Civil War* (Lexington, Mass., 1973); Thernstrom, *Poverty and Progress*. See also S. R. Mealing, "The Concept of Social Class and the Interpretation of Canadian History," *Canadian Historical Review*, XLVI (1965), 201–218. One of the few attempts to treat class precisely and in a way useful for historical research is R. S. Neale, *Class and Ideology in the Nineteenth Century* (London, 1972).
9 The confounding of class and stratification is evident in many works in American sociology. See, for instance, Seymour Martin Lipset and Reinhard Bendix, *Social Mobility in Industrial Society* (Berkeley, 1964).

anyone who wants to undertake the task of utilizing class analysis is operational. How is one to define class in a way that can be approached with historical data? The problem is no different from the one confronting contemporary social scientists who must search out the best index of the relations that they wish to employ. In both cases the most adequate, though far from perfect, indicator is occupation, and the first task becomes the classification of occupations according to a scheme which can be defended by theory rather than simply by the observed distinctions between different groups on measures such as income or social status.

The difficulty is, first, that occupation is an imprecise measure and, second, that it is the variable most frequently used in descriptive analyses of stratification. Thus, class analysis in practice is easy to confuse with the analysis of stratification. However, as Wright and Perrone observe:

> Class . . . is a way of looking at social structure entirely different from occupation. The term 'occupation' designates positions within the *technical* division of labor, i.e. an occupation represents a set of activities fulfilling certain technically defined functions. Class, on the other hand, designates positions within the *social* relations of production, i.e., it designates the social relationship between actors.[10]

One way to contrast the influence of class and occupation is by comparing their relative ability to account for aspects of social structure and social behavior. Wright and Perrone have done precisely this for contemporary America. Using categories representing theoretically derived class positions and stratified occupations, they have demonstrated that class has an independent influence on income and that returns of education to income differ within classes.[11]

Whether this independent influence of class is a feature of late twentieth-century society in which class divisions have hardened and opportunity dwindled, or whether it is a long-standing characteristic of North American life, remains an open question. The presumption is that aspects of North American class structure

---

10 Erik Olin Wright and Luca Perrone, "Marxist Class Categories and Income Inequality," *American Sociological Review*, XLII (1977), 35.

11 *Ibid.*, 32–55.

have been in place for a long time, at least since the mid-nineteenth century. The reason is that class structure derives from the way in which material life is reproduced, and the characteristic North American mode of production—capitalism—has been firmly established for at least a century and a half. Thus, a working hypothesis is that a class structure characteristic of capitalist social formations existed in mid-nineteenth-century North American cities. Before presenting evidence which supports this hypothesis, however, it is important to be clear about the definitions of class and capitalism.

Classes are the fundamental groups within a social structure; their identity is determined by the underlying property of a mode of production, a concept embracing the organization of both social and technical relations. Within each society, social, economic, and technological relations cluster together in distinctive ways. However, although they are distinctive, modes of production are not exclusive. One mode usually dominates a given time and place, but others, either lingering, older modes or new, ascendant ones, often will be found at the same time. Different historical eras derive much of their distinct identity from the coexistence of competing modes of production.[12]

Classes are groups of people who share a common relationship to a mode of production. Within a mode of production the cluster of social relations that unite people into classes have certain common properties. Ossowski listed four of them: (1) they are ordered vertically; (2) the interests of the classes are permanent; (3) people within them share a sense of class identity, although the awareness may take various forms; (4) classes are relatively isolated from each other. Individuals from different classes have minimal social contacts, and membership within them is relatively permanent.[13]

Despite these common properties, the class structure of any given society varies with the mode of production which generates it. In actuality the class structure in any given place often is extremely complex because it must be conceived in terms of parallel structures generated by the coexistence of different modes

12 My analysis of class is indebted to Anthony Giddens, *The Class Structure of the Advanced Societies* (London, 1973).
13 Stanislaw Ossowksi, *Class Structure in the Social Consciousness* (London, 1963), 134–136.

of production. The analytical problem and the potential for conflict both vary with the size and strength of the alternative modes. In Europe, for instance, the competition between feudal and capitalist modes of production is a classic example. In North America the absence of a feudal tradition eliminated for all practical purposes the conflict played out in Europe. Here the struggle waged in the late eighteenth and early nineteenth century took on a different form, and one not yet adequately analyzed by historians—the competition between capitalism and a mode of production was dominated jointly by independent yeomen farmers who produced primarily their own subsistence and independent artisans who produced goods for local consumption. These people did exist in the context of a metropolitan, market economy dominated by merchants, but the emergence of the essential features of capitalism were for a time checked by the abundance of land, the shortage of labor, and the ease with which men could establish themselves upon the land or in a trade.[14]

Two characteristics distinguish capitalism. "(1) Production is primarily oriented to the realization, or search for the realization, of profit accruing to privately owned capital. (2) This process is organized in terms of a market upon which commodities, including labor itself, are bought and sold according to standards of monetary exchange." Capitalism, in Dobb's words, was "not simply a system of production for the market . . . but a system under which labour-power had 'itself become a commodity' and was bought and sold on the market like any other object of exchange." These are the two basic components from which the class structure of capitalism derives.[15]

Capitalist society possesses two classes because most people share a common relation to both of its key aspects: the private ownership of capital and the sale of their labor as a commodity. Most of the people who sell their labor do not own capital, and those who own capital are the purchasers of labor. However, immense complications accompany any attempt to use this distinction to describe actual societies. The situation is most difficult today, given the rise of a non-owning managerial group and the

---

14 David Harvey, *Social Justice and the City* (Baltimore, 1973), 197–203; Marx, *Capital* (Moscow, 1954; orig. Eng. ed. 1887), V, 1: 716–724.
15 Giddens, *Class Structure*, 142; Maurice Dobb, *Studies in the Development of Capitalism* (New York, 1974; rev. ed.), 7.

expansion of white-collar work. In the mid-nineteenth century, however, neither managers nor bureaucrats yet existed in large enough numbers to create a serious difficulty for class analysis, and a good case (to be elaborated shortly) may be made for their inclusion within the capitalist or business class. The more difficult problem concerns artisans, independent proprietors who produced goods but did not employ labor. Usually, these are treated as a transitional class, a remnant of a social order replaced by capitalism. They are understood as part of the class structure of a mode of production which captialism replaced.

Thus, mid-nineteenth-century cities may have had three classes, a business and working class, reflecting ascendant forces, and an artisan class belonging to an older social order. Or it could be that by the mid-nineteenth-century industrial capitalism had established its hegemony so thoroughly that craftsmen by and large worked for wages, even prior to the mechanization of production. This is the situation that now appears to have been most likely.

The nature of occupational designations on censuses has made difficult the resolution of the artisan question. Men were listed by and large simply with an artisanal title: shoemaker, tailor, or carpenter. Rarely has it been possible, using only the census, to determine if they were masters or employees. However, using business directories, the manufacturing schedules of the census, and newspaper advertisements, it is possible to distinguish between the masters and journeymen with a high degree of accuracy.

The distinctions between them are the pivot of an occupational classification. First, I divided occupations into two classes: the business class and the working class. Within each class a number of groupings of individuals engaged in different sorts of work were identified. Some groups do not fit easily or properly into the class structure as defined here, notably women and men with agricultural occupations.

Because class derives from relations to the mode of production, it is necessary to determine class membership through the sort of work which a person performed. For it is the social relations that stem from the organization of work and the accumulation of wealth that cluster persons into classes. The only consistent measure of class is occupation. Thus, it is not possible to base it upon a measure other than occupation even though it is analytically important to distinguish between the two. As the data which follow show, most of the effect on important aspects of social structure commonly attributed to occupational strata can be accounted for, instead, by class. That is, the aggregation of people in different occupations into classes proves a powerful analytic technique. Despite variation among the occupations within classes, class itself remains a key influence on critical aspects of social behavior.

Yet, occupational title is an imperfect indicator. In many instances, it is not possible to ascertain exactly what sort of work a person did, or whether individuals were wage workers or proprietors, simply on the basis of occupation. Greater attention to sources which supplement the census, such as business directories, overcome some, although by no means all, of the ambiguity. However, despite its problems, occupation remains the best available indicator of the nature of an individual's work and, used carefully, yields reasonably reliable results.

The new occupational division has been used to analyze social structure in two nineteenth-century cities, Hamilton, Ontario, and Buffalo, New York. Hamilton, it should be noted, was a commercial city of about 14,000 people in 1851. Within twenty years it underwent significant industrialization, most notably during the 1860s. The leading industrial sector was the metal industry and very few textile goods were manufactured in the city. Industrialization was spurred by a number of factors, including a conscious policy adopted by city leaders who believed that the weakness of an economy based solely upon trade had contributed to the devastating impact of the depression of the late 1850s upon the city. By 1871 the city's population had grown to about 26,000 drawn mainly from England, Scotland, and Ireland, with a small American-born group and a small but increasing German community.[16]

As the terminus of the Erie Canal, Buffalo was an exceptionally prosperous city. Its rapidly increasing population had

---

16   A more complete account of Hamilton's industrialization, of the relevant contextual features in Buffalo, and of the notion of class presented here may be found in Katz, Michael J. Doucet, and Mark J. Stern, *The Social Organization of Early Industrial Capitalism: Themes in the North American Experience,* forthcoming.

reached about 60,000 by 1855. In that year ten railroads passed through the city; it was a launching point for travel to the west and an important center for the transshipment of goods between regions. Indeed, the city serviced a rich agricultural area. Although more of Buffalo's population than of Hamilton's were native born, the American city had a substantial proportion of immigrants. Its largest group, about 40 percent of the city's household heads, had been born in Germany rather than in Ireland.

These cities provide excellent contexts in which to test a conception of class. Each was primarily a commercially based capitalist city in the 1850s. By 1871 Hamilton had entered the era of early industrial capitalism (as had Buffalo, although we do not have census data from the city in that year). For a two-class model to be valid, it should characterize accurately each city's social structure prior to industrialization, and, in Hamilton, it should apply equally well to the early industrial period. Indeed, because the contention here is that a bifurcated and relatively rigid social structure emerged in the early stages of capitalist development and remained in place throughout its early history, there should be little fundamental difference in class structure during the commercial and early industrial periods of Hamilton's history.

It is not the contention of this article that the class model advanced here best characterizes North American society after the late nineteenth century. The creation of new forms of capital, the production of services in novel forms of bureaucratic organizations staffed by members of emerging occupations, the growth of a managerial sector divorced from ownership, the transformation in the meaning of clerical work, the growth of trade unions, and the invention of academically certified experts—all of these factors complicated the social structure and must be incorporated into any delineation of class structure after about 1880 or 1890. Nor is it the intention here to deny the existence of various divisions within classes, the complex nature of stratification, or the role of ethnicity. Similarly, I do not wish to appear to dismiss the role of consciousness, which is critical to any full analysis of class. However, the intent of this article is not to delineate the complex character of stratification or to explore class consciousness. Rather, it is to point to the social morphology of the commercial and early industrial era of North American cities and, particularly, to demonstrate a way to make class operational in historical research.[17]

There is, nonetheless, an underlying position on a controversial issue: namely, that the social relations which constitute the class structure assume an objective form. Class, certainly, is a relation, not a thing, but class relations affect the way in which people behave and the distribution of resources. For class does not represent a relation among equals. Its nature is, on the contrary, asymmetrical. Those who sell their labor power do not do so on a free market in which, unimpeded, they strike a bargain that serves their interests equally with those of their employers. Those with the power to buy and control labor have by far the greater power, and they use that power to appropriate a disproportionate share of scarce and desirable resources. Although this point seems elementary, it needs emphasis. For simple as it is, it constitutes the theoretical basis for the expectation that class will be reflected in the structure of inequality, that it has an objective embodiment, and that it exists even when it remains unacknowledged, obscured, or denied.[18]

The empirical case on which this argument about class is founded rests on a massive data base. For the city of Hamilton it consists of the entire manuscript censuses of the city for 1851, 1861, and 1871 put into machine-readable form. To these have been added the assessment rolls of 1852, 1861, 1871, and 1881. In addition, the data base includes the industrial censuses, newspaper listings, city directories, school records, jail records, credit ratings, and parish records. Individual records from different sources have been joined and people traced across time. The completed files thus provide detailed social, demographic, and economic data on the entire population of the city (14,000, 19,000, and 26,000 individuals) in each of the three census years and on the people who remained in the city between censuses.[19]

The data base from Buffalo consists of the entire population of the New York State Census of 1855 put into machine-readable

17 A detailed account of stratification and some data on class consciousness are included in *ibid*.

18 Ossowski, *Class Structure*, 149.

19 The data base is described in Katz, *The People of Hamilton, Canada West: Family and Class in a Mid-Nineteenth Century City* (Cambridge, Mass., 1975).

form. In order to identify master artisans, individuals were traced to the city directory for 1855. The file consists of about 60,000 individuals. The 1855 New York State Census includes property ownership, length of residence in the city, and an economic variable, value of dwelling inhabited. Using the latter figure dwelling value per capita has been computed for each household. This provides a reasonable economic ranking of households roughly comparable to the figure for total assessed wealth with which the population of Hamilton was rank ordered.[20]

To test the independent influence of class, occupations were grouped in four ways: (1) sixteen clusters based, first, upon class and, second, within classes, upon the sort of work performed; (2) the entire workforce divided into business and working classes only; (3) masters and skilled wage workers separately; (4) masters and skilled wage workers divided into twenty-one major trades. The distinction in this instance was between trades, not between masters and workers.[21]

It is not possible to give approximate ratios of masters to workers within trades. Not all of the non-proprietor blacksmiths, for instance, worked for master blacksmiths. Many worked for the railroad or foundries. The same is true in a variety of other trades as well. Thus, any attempt to use these figures to establish ratios within trades would be inaccurate. Overall, the ratio of masters and manufacturers to male skilled wageworkers in Hamilton in each year and in Buffalo hovered around 10 to 1 (Table 1).

The first important question to ask is this: was the distinction between classes greater than the distinctions between the occu-

20 I obtained the coded manuscript census of Buffalo from the archives of SUNY Buffalo. It was coded under the supervision of Laurence Glasco. Shonnie Finnegan, the university archivist, enabled me to gain access to the tapes.

21 The business class consists of those individuals who owned the means of production or those whose interests and aspirations identified them with the owners. Thus, the groups are professionals and rentiers; agents and merchants (vendors of commodities); proprietors of service establishments and semi-professionals (vendors of services); business employees; government employees and masters and manufacturers. The working class consists of four groups: skilled workers (people with an artisanal title); transport workers; "other working class" (peddlers, waiters, huxters, and so on); and laborers. The two least satisfactory groups are government employees and "other working class," which proved to be quite heterogeneous categories composed of persons whose stated occupation did not precisely identify the sort of work that they did or their place within this scheme.

Table 1   Class and Occupational Structure: Hamilton, Ontario, 1851, 1861, and 1871

	NUMBER			PERCENT OF WORKFORCE		
	1851	1861	1871	1851	1861	1871
Business-Class						
Prof. and Rentier	179.	225	195	3.5	3.7	2.2
Agent and Merchant	239	371	475	4.6	6.1	5.4
Service and Semi-Prof.	97	158	188	1.9	2.6	2.1
Business Employee	270	402	772	5.2	6.7	8.7
Gov't Employee	86	110	183	1.7	1.8	2.1
Master and Manufacturer	225	306	441	4.4	5.1	5.0
Sub-Total				21.3	26.0	25.5
Working-Class						
Skilled Worker	1,653	1,632	3,256	32.0	27.1	36.8
Transport Worker	198	233	358	3.8	3.9	4.0
Other Working Class	175	224	285	3.4	3.7	3.2
Laborer	725	899	1,148	14.0	14.9	13.0
Sub-Total				53.2	49.6	57.0
Other						
Female Domestic	983	981	804	19.0	16.3	9.1
Other Female Worker	210	300	580	4.1	5.0	6.6
Agricultural Proprietor	67	74	82	1.3	1.2	0.9
Agricultural Non-Proprietor	—	—	2	—	—	0.0
Unclassifiable	56	118	79	1.1	2.0	0.9
Sub-Total				25.5	24.5	17.5
Total	5,163	6,033	8,848			

SOURCE: Canadian Manuscript Censuses 1851, 1861, 1871

pational groups within them? To answer this question an analysis of variance was performed. The F-ratio which it produced compares the distribution within and between categories. If the F-ratio is significant (by the standards employed here if the odds were no more than 1 in 100 that the results could have occurred by chance), then the differences between the groups were greater than those within them.

For either city to have been dominated by two classes, the distinction between classes on critical measures had to be greater than the differences within them. Similarly, the distinctions between masters and skilled wageworkers had to be significant; the distinctions between trades with no separation of masters and workmen should not have been. This in fact was the situation in both Hamilton and Buffalo.

As an example, take economic rank. In general, the relations between economic rank and the various occupational groupings were stable throughout the transition from commercially based to industrial capitalism (Table 2). The F-ratio was significant in three out of the four occupational groupings. It was not significant for individual trades, which shows that little variation in economic rank divided trades when masters and employees were not separated from each other. This is critical evidence for the contention that the two groups should be distinguished from each other. That case is bolstered by the very high and significant F-ratio in the comparison of masters and skilled wage workers separated into two groups and compared solely with each other. Thus, it was relation to the ownership of productive enterprises rather than membership in a specific trade which most strongly affected the determination of economic rank. Likewise, the high and significant F-ratio for the two classes shows that class by itself had an independent influence on economic rank.

Although the F-ratio is higher in the class than in the occupational analysis, it is not possible to conclude on this basis that class was more influential than occupation in accounting for economic rank. The reason is that the number of cells in the table on which the analysis is based—the degrees of freedom—differ in each of the comparisons, and the degrees of freedom affect the size and significance of the F-ratios. In order to overcome this limitation and arrive at an estimate of the comparative explanatory power of class and occupation it was necessary to use a different statistic, the eta. The eta squared (e^2) represents the amount of

Table 2 F-Ratio Between Class, Occupation, and Economic Rank: Hamilton, Ontario, 1851, 1861, and 1871

	DEGREES OF FREEDOM						F-RATIO		
	1851		1861		1871		1851	1861	1871
16 Occupational Groups	14	1,937	14	2,731	14	4,284	20.2**	31.5**	18.2**
Masters and Skilled Workers	1	825	1	1,027	1	1,840	79.5**	50.6**	59.3**
21 Trades	20	806	20	1,028	20	1,821	1.1	1.1	1.0
Business and Working Class	1	137	1	2,363	1	3,855	133.6**	165.5**	122.8**

SOURCE: Canadian Manuscript Censuses 1851, 1861, and 1871; assessment rolls Hamilton, Ontario, 1852, 1861, and 1871.
** = Significant at .01 or lower

variation in a dependent variable accounted for by an independent variable.

In both Hamilton and Buffalo, the majority of the variation in economic rank attributable to occupation was accounted for by class (Table 3). In Hamilton in 1871 the sixteen occupational categories accounted for 24 percent of the variation in economic rank between individuals. Class, however, as measured by the two-class model, by itself accounted for 18 percent, or 75 percent of the variation seemingly attributable to occupation. In Buffalo in 1855, the sixteen occupational categories accounted for 11 percent, and the two-class model, by itself, for 9 percent, or 82 percent of the former. This means that in both cities most of the individual variation that seemed to stem from occupational position was the product of class. Although significant differences in wealth separated the sixteen occupational groups, most of those differences stemmed from the position of those occupational groups within the class structure.

The distinction between the business and working class was not altered by the life cycle. The working class was not composed primarily of young men who later left it. Although there were differences in age between masters and wage workers, they were much smaller than the distinctions between the groups on other measures, such as economic rank, servant employment, or length of residence in the city. They do not point to a wholesale movement of men out of working-class jobs as they aged. Indeed, the

Table 3 Eta and Eta Squared for Relation Between Occupation, Class, and Economic Rank: Hamilton, Ontario, 1871, and Buffalo, New York, 1855

	E	E^2	F	SIGN.
Hamilton				
16 Occupational Categories	.493	.243	98.327	.00005
2 Classes	.425	.181	473.734	.00005
Buffalo				
16 Occupational Categories	.330	.109	147.471	.00005
2 Classes	.302	.091	605.396	.00005

SOURCES: Hamilton (See Table 2); Buffalo, Manuscript of New York State Census of 1855. Economic Rank in Hamilton = Log Total Assessed Value; Buffalo, Log of Dwelling Value/Capita

mean age of the men in various sorts of work was similar, with the exception of clerks who often were young.

When only adult workers (as opposed to all people in an occupation) are considered, the presence of large numbers of skilled wage workers who headed households and did not become masters stands out unmistakably. Younger men usually did not start their working lives as masters or proprietors, although a small proportion did become proprietors later in life. However, these appear to have been disproportionately the sons of masters and manufacturers. (In Hamilton between 1851 and 1861, 13 percent, and in the next decade 15 percent, of skilled workers who remained within the city—a distinct and atypically prosperous group—became owners.)[22]

By contrast, the sons of the business class dominated the ranks of the business employees, the point at which many of them began their careers. Clerical jobs served agents and merchants much as the skilled trades served the masters and manufacturers: as entering points and training grounds for their sons. In this way the life cycle itself relfected and did not contradict the class relations in this nineteenth-century city.[23]

If class position were primarily a result of social origins, then demographic factors—age, ethnicity, and marital status—should have been able to explain relatively little of the variation in class membership. This, in fact, was the case (Table 4). In a multivariate analysis trying to account for class membership in 1871, these factors accounted for only 6 percent of the variation. Some categories of the variables, nonetheless, were particularly influential, for instance an age of less than twenty or Irish Catholic birth, both of which promoted working-class membership. But, overall, the influence of these factors was small. Class simply was not a demographic matter. Nor was this situation unique to Hamilton. Comparable analyses of Buffalo produced similar results.[24]

22 Of the sons of masters and manufacturers 28% living at home were themselves masters and manufacturers compared to 10% of the sons of skilled wage workers.

23 The proportion of business employees among the sons of various groups dwelling at home was: professionals and rentiers, 25%; agents and merchants, 55%; business employees, 72%; government employees, 46%; masters and manufacturers, 16%; skilled wage workers, 9%.

24 The technique used was multiple classification analysis. The probability of membership in the business class doubled from 18% for men under the age of 20 to 36% for those at least 40, but most of the rise first occurred among men in their twenties and evened out

Table 4 Multiple Classification Analysis of Class Membership in Business and Working Class in Hamilton, Ontario, 1871: Summary Statistics

	CLASS MEMBERSHIP ETA/BETA
Factor Variables	
Age	.07/.03
Ethnicity	.18/.20
Marital Status	.03/.03
Persistence Since 1851	.11/.05
Persistence Since 1861	.12/.09
R^2	6.0

SOURCE: See Table 2

However, the nature of the class structure must not be oversimplified. Consider, for instance, the masters and manufacturers in Hamilton, a group with a rate of downward mobility far exceeding that in any other business–class category. Between 1851 and 1861, 27 percent and in the next decade 43 percent moved downward into the ranks of skilled wage workers.

Did downward mobility occur randomly, or did some characteristics distinguish those masters who retained from those who lost their position? To answer the question, the masters and wage workers were divided into four groups: those who moved from skilled wage worker to master; those who dropped from master to skilled wage worker; those who remained skilled wage workers; and those who remained masters. There were no significant differences in age between any of these groups.

However, there were differences in economic rank. Those who moved either into or out of the ranks of masters were less well-to-do than those who remained masters throughout the decade, but more well-off than those who remained wage workers. The mobile masters formed a distinct stratum of marginal, petty producers, much like the group identified in Edinburgh in the

---

after the age of 30. The likelihood that an Irish Catholic man would be in the working class was 92%. Next came English Anglicans, 61%. The distinctions among other ethnic groups were minor.

same period by Gray. Note, however, that the mobile masters were themselves substantially more well-to-do than those who remained artisans. Clearly, they were an unstable intermediate group.[25]

Thus, the four groups of masters and wage workers did not differ in age; they did differ in economic well-being. The other major dimension on which they should be compared is specific occupation. Were some types of work more unstable or more promising than others? Although men within some trades were more likely than others to be masters or workers, it was the distinction in their wealth, and by implication in the size of their operation, rather than in the nature of the work that they did that separated the men who remained masters from those whose experience was more fluid or who remained within the working class.[26]

Given the fluidity of the masters and the fact that one group within the business class—business employees—had a distinctly lower economic position than the others, it might be asked why the two-class model is emphasized. Would it not make more sense to interject a middle class? The answer is no, on various grounds. In part, the reason is theoretical. Class expresses a relationship to the means of production, a relationship in which the notion of "middle" is inappropriate. Whatever their wealth, masters and manufacturers within Hamilton and Buffalo shared a relation similar to that of other proprietors. They owned private enterprises and employed wage labor.[27]

However, the patterns of mobility do show that although the boundaries between classes were relatively distinct, the experience of a small segment of the population led them to cross that boundary at relatively frequent intervals. Whether the small proprietors who drifted occasionally into the ranks of wage labor

25 R. Q. Gray, *The Labour Aristocracy in Victorian Edinburgh* (Oxford, 1976), 132–134. In 1871 the proportions of men traced since 1861 in the bottom 20 economic percentiles were: non-mobile wage workers, 27%; men who moved from wage workers to master or manufacturer, 9%; men who dropped from master-manufacturer to wage worker, 8%.
26 There were some minor patterns. Movement into the ranks of masters was a little more likely in the building trades, and plumbers seemed to retain their position as masters especially well.
27 The proportions of various occupational groups in the top 20 economic ranks were: professionals and rentiers, 60%; agents and merchants, 45%; masters and manufacturers, 37%; business employees, 22%; skilled wage workers, 10%.

saw themselves as business or working class remains an elusive and important question, at present without answer.

The other problematic group consists of the business employees. In view of late nineteenth- and twentieth-century connotations of clerical work, it appears ludicrous to include them within the business class. However, circumstances differed in the mid-nineteenth century, prior to the feminization of office work, the development of complex organizational bureaucracies, or the widespread existence of department stores and supermarkets. In that period clerical work had a different meaning. Empirically, as noted, sons of men within the business class often began their working lives within clerical occupations, and the mobility of men out of clerical work and into proprietorship was quite high. For many men clerical work was the initial phase in a commercial career.

Clerks were paid a salary, not a wage. This was a crucial distinction at the time. It indicated that they could expect work throughout an entire year and did not experience the seasonal fluctuations to which men paid daily wages were subject. The irregularity of employment which marked the experience of wage workers was not a feature of their lives. [28]

The case for including nineteenth-century clerks within the business class has been made convincingly, I think, by Braverman. "The place of the handful of clerks in the early industrial enterprise—and there were generally fewer than a half dozen in even the largest firms—was semi-managerial," wrote Braverman. In various studies, clerks emerge as, "assistant manager, retainer, confidant, management trainee, and prospective son-in-law." Of course, Braverman notes, "the condition and prospects of life" of many clerks hardly exceeded "those of dock workers." Overall, however, "in terms of function, authority, pay, tenure of employment . . . prospects, not to mention status and even dress, the clerks stood much closer to the employer than to factory labor." [29]

---

28 In this connection, it is important to observe that in his survey of wages and the cost of living in Massachusetts in 1875, Carroll Wright made the distinction between wage and salary workers the basis of his division of the population. Massachusetts Bureau of Statistics of Labor, *Sixth Annual Report* (1875).

29 Harry Braverman, *Labor and Monopoly Capital: The Degradation of Work in the Twentieth Century* (New York, 1974), 293–294.

Class is not only reflected in occupation or wealth. It also infil-trates thought, feeling, and behavior. Class, in short, is very much a cultural matter. The problem is that the precise delineation of the interior of human experience in past times and its associa-tion with the divisions employed here is difficult, a methodolog-ical problem to which there is not yet an adequate solution. However, by focusing on particular behaviors we can make gen-eral statements which hint at attitudes—on the way in which class influenced the response of people to the circumstances in which they lived. Three of these behaviors are property ownership, school attendance, and fertility.

To nineteenth-century workingmen property ownership had a particular utility. The wages of manual workers usually declined as they aged. No provisions existed for retirement, and there were no pensions. Unless workingmen had been able to save something out of their low wages or unless they had children or relatives who could assist them, old age, past the time during which work was possible, could be a terrible experience, survived only through charity or in the poorhouse. In this situation the ownership of a home provided minimal security. It meant that a man and his wife would at least have a home of their own, a place to live free of the worry of rent. As some workmen pointed out, homeownership was not an unmixed advantage. Homes were not always a good investment; nor were they easy to sell. A depressed real estate market might tie a man to a job or a place when his economic interests dictated that he should move on. Indeed, em-ployers, so it was claimed, could exploit homeowners unable or unwilling to move.[30]

For those with more money, especially within the business class, homeownerhsip had a different meaning. Property was examined more often for its exchange than its use value. A mer-chant might consider whether or not he should put his capital into stock for his store, an investment such as a railroad, or into a home. Indeed, he would have had good reason to wonder, for a home was a risky investment in which many men lost money. Furthermore, for the affluent a home had a symbolic value; it was a measure of consumption, an indicator of rank. Thus, a man

---

30 The question of property-ownership is discussed in detail in "Property-Ownership: Use Value and Exchange Value," in Katz, Doucet, and Stern, *Social Organization*.

without the ready cash to buy a home that matched the position to which he aspired might well rent instead.

People at the margin—families of middling wealth—were in a particularly vulnerable position. Homeownership was difficult. It required saving a sizable downpayment and then paying-off a mortgage in a short period of time, usually five years at most. Thus, it required severe savings, sometimes underconsumption. For many at the economic margins this required a choice between acquiring a house and employing a servant.

What is particularly telling about class is the different way in which such a decision was made. Within the same middling economic rank, working-class men more often chose homeownership. Those in the business class more frequently chose a servant (Table 5).

Just as there were different class attitudes toward property, so were there differences in approach to education. In the 1850s, the facilities for the education of teenage children in Hamilton expanded dramatically with the opening of a new central school, and during the depression of the late 1850s the attendance at school of children from all social backgrounds increased markedly, for what little work had existed for teenagers in the commercial city had nearly disappeared. Children of more affluent parents stayed at school longer, but even the attendance of the poorest children within the working class increased. By 1871 the rapid introduction of industry had created new job opportunities.

Table 5   Proportion of Homeowners By Occupation Within 40–79th Economic Ranks: Hamilton, Ontario, 1871

	PERCENT	NUMBER
Lawyer	12.5	8
Physician	30.0	10
Merchant	19.1	47
Clerk	18.0	61
Carpenter	61.7	107
Tailor	36.8	38
Shoemaker	29.2	48
Laborer	43.0	114

SOURCE: See Table 2

Given the prospect of work, the school attendance of working-class teenagers dropped notably while—undoubtedly sensing a heightened connection between schooling and the retention of rank—business-class teenagers continued in school at their increased level (Table 6).[31]

Among parents of middling means, those in the working class probably saw the new industrial opportunities as a chance to start their children in work that would contribute to the collective well-being and advancement of the family. Most working-class children lived at home, where they gave most of their wages to their parents. By contrast, business-class families of the same economic rank were deferring the entry of their children into the workforce, sacrificing their own economic well-being to the future, individual mobility of their children.

The different class attitudes toward school attendance were reflected in approaches to family size and fertility. It is a commonplace that native white fertility began to fall during the nineteenth century, accelerating after about 1850. In Hamilton this trend was class related. Business-class men and women lowered their fertility within marriage between 1851 and 1871 as they found themselves caught between the desire for increasing levels

Table 6 Probability of School Attendance Among 13–16 Year-Old Males By Selected Occupations of Fathers: Hamilton, Ontario, 1851, 1861, 1871.

	PROBABILITY		
	1851	1861	1871
Professional			
Gentleman	a	a	73
High-Ranking Businessman	a	49	74
Middle-Level Business Employees	37	58	53
Workers in Apparel, Textile, Leather	29	51	42
Construction Workers	36	55	46
Laborers	36	68	31

SOURCE: See Table 1
a = insufficient cases

31 For a complete discussion of youth see Katz and Ian E. Davey, "Youth and Early Industrialization in a Canadian City," in John Demos and Sarane Spence Boocock (eds.), *Turning Points: Historical and Sociological Essays on the Family* (Chicago, 1978), S84–S87.

of consumption and the expense of education. More telling, it was the members of the class with the most modern occupations—the white-collar workers with specific job titles, such as accountant, salesman, or bookkeeper—in contrast to those who simply called themselves clerk, that lowered their fertility most notably. Indeed, figures for Buffalo that extend through 1915 show that it was this group that continually led the fertility decline (Table 7).

By contrast, the working class behaved differently. As jobs for teenagers became more available and the value of children increased, working-class fertility in Hamilton rose. In 1855 it was the capitalist class which had the highest marital fertility; by 1871 that situation had been reversed, not simply through a decline among the capitalist class but through an increase among the working class as well.[32]

Clearly, class was a powerful and independent influence upon behavior and upon the distribution of resources in nineteenth-century cities. However, the strength of a two-class model also can be its weakness. It can reduce the complexity of social structure by cutting through surface divisions and exposing the dynamic properties of a social formation, but, in the process, such a model can foster a false simplicity, obscuring very real differ-

Table 7 Percentage Change in Standardized Child-Woman Ratios, Major Groups, Hamilton, Ontario, 1851–1871

	PERCENT OF CHANGES	
Business Class		−4.3
Professional and Rentiers	+6.7	
Agents and Merchants	−8.6	
Business Employees	−11.7	
Masters and Manufacturers	−3.3	
Working Class		+6.0
Skilled Workers	+3.5	
Laborers	+7.9	

SOURCES: See Table 2

32 A detailed account of the fertility decline in Hamilton is included in Katz, Doucet, and Stern, *Social Organization*. On the fertility history in Buffalo see Stern, "The Demography of Capitalism," unpub. Ph.D. diss. (York University, 1979); Katz and Stern, "Fertility, Class, and Early Industrial Capitalism," *American Quarterly*, forthcoming.

ences between social structures, ignoring the effect of time and place, and by-passing the intricate task of unravelling the relations between the components of actual situations. The last task is best conceived as the analysis of stratification, which is distinct from the discussion of class. Within a two-class society it is by no means self-evident how the major components of stratification—wealth, occupation, ethnicity, age, and sex—will be related and how their relations will change under the impact of major social and economic events.

This article does not explore more than a few aspects of stratification. Nor does it mean to imply that class was the only influence at work in nineteenth-century cities. For social behavior was the result of many other factors which interacted with class in ways that remain to be understood. Rather, what the patterns portrayed here do show is that class was a central fact of life within nineteenth-century urban America. Class, not simply confused with stratification or occupational categories, but class defined as the social relationships derived from the way in which material life was reproduced, played a key role in shaping the most vital and intimate aspects of human experience.[33]

The demonstration that class had tangible implications, that the social morphology of nineteenth-century cities emanated from a series of basic relations which exerted an influence upon the rewards that people received, the way they earned their living, how they brought up their children, and, even, how they behaved in bed—these observations are not intended to foreclose research. Their point, rather, is to redirect it, to energize the analysis of social structure by showing the need for the serious consideration of class in North American historiography and by pointing to a way in which class can be made operational.

In order to make class operational historians must divide those people with artisanal titles into wage workers and employers. As early as the mid-nineteenth century, and probably earlier

---

33 On this point the observations of E. O. Wright and Perrone on their own study ("Marxist Class Categories," 50) are relevant here: "It must be recognized that class itself still explains only a relatively small proportion of the total variance in income . . . A full model explaining income variation would have to include many other variables. . . . The critical argument of this paper is not that class explains everything but, rather, that other variables must be examined in terms of their interactions with class position in order to unravel the nature of income determination."

if good data could be found, the two groups were distinct. North American cities contained a large group of skilled wage workers who did not grow up to be masters or manufacturers, and any analysis which obscures the distinction between worker and master will be inadequate. It is the existence of this distinction, heretofore largely neglected, that undercuts much of the recent historiography of social structure and social mobility in America. The failure to make the distinction, moreover, has given social structure an illusory middle, a very large group of people straddling the line between workers and owners, widely divergent in wealth and behavior, uneasily assimilated either to the groups above or below. But, break apart the artisan group and the pieces differ fundamentally, each being part of a different universe in a social world where their class basis no longer can be obscured or denied.

The task of systematically analyzing the variations within the two-class structure from place to place and over time, the unraveling of the interconnections between class and behavior, the penetration of the shifting consciousness of class among various groups—all of these tasks require an immense amount of historical research. That research, however, must not be aimless, atheoretical, or mindlessly empirical. For historians to advance beyond the vacant abstractions of sociologists they must pay attention, always, to context, to the variation in the objective expression of class, and to the mediation of the relation between class, behavior, and consciousness by a myriad of influences. At the same time they must adopt a posture of methodological eclecticism. Class does have an objective expression, an embodiment that can be located and described, or it means nothing. At the same time it is not a thing but a relation; it is seen in the activities of people, and refracted in the way that they view the world.

Thus, its analysis requires all of the tools that historians always have used, and more as well. Arguments about the appropriateness of quantification to class analysis, for instance, are pointless distractions from the task at hand. So are severely empirical rejections of social theory. The historical analysis of social structure has been hindered by the relatively uncritical adoption of the categories deployed in American sociology. Now it is being hampered by the reproduction within the profession of the methodological warfare within contemporary social science. The emancipation of history from the tyranny of conventional social science rests neither solely in a return to narrative or in "thick description" but in an irreverant eclecticism in which intelligent theory and the widest, most imaginative array of methods are brought to bear upon the central problems of human society, past and present.

Claudia Goldin

The Changing Economic Role of Women: A Quantitative Approach

In the early nineteenth century only a small fraction of women in the United States worked in the agricultural, industrial, and service components of the market sector. Within agriculture the wages of females relative to those of men were exceptionally low. But, wherever industry spread, relative wages for females increased, and their employment appeared linked to the diffusion of the factory system. The female labor force that expanded in the nineteenth century was primarily young and unmarried. It was not until the twentieth century that married women entered the market sector in any substantial way, first in the 1920s when young, and later, in the 1940s and 1950s, in their post-child-rearing years. Impressive gains in the participation of married women in the labor force were eventually achieved, with particular age groups affected during particular decades. This article explains the timing and the form of this expansion in the market role of married, white women in the United States.[1]

The focus is on those who are married because of their numerical importance among all women, and because changes in their economic role have had repercussions transcending the economic sphere. Single women are not, however, ignored. The labor force, education, and home experiences of young, single women have profoundly influenced their economic roles when married and have also affected the economic roles of their mothers. My methodology stresses a life-cycle approach to understanding change in the economic role of married women. Change

Claudia Goldin is Associate Professor of Economics at the University of Pennsylvania and Research Associate for the National Bureau of Economic Research.

Research for this article had been supported by N.S.F. Grant #SOC78-15037 and is part of the author's monograph, in progress, *Economic Change and American Women: An Economic History*.

0022-1953/83/040707-27 $02.50/0

1 Goldin and Kenneth Sokoloff, "Women, Children, and Industrialization in the Early Republic: Evidence from the Manufacturing Censuses, 1820 to 1850," National Bureau of Economic Research Working Paper, no. 795 (1981), forthcoming in *Journal of Economic History*.

during one part of the life cycle can affect employment in another part. Thus different cohorts at any point in time may respond differently to the same set of factors. The analysis is limited to the economic behavior of white women, because the labor force participation of black women has differed in significant ways from that of white women even in analyses accounting for income, education, and family size. Most studies of this phenomenon have concluded that white and black married women differ substantially in their labor supply functions.[2]

The use of labor force participation rates as an indicator of economic and social change has some limitations. It does not fully capture changes in occupations and in work conditions, nor does it fully reflect the alteration in economic roles as individuals move from the nonpaid to the paid sector. But these changes seem adequately proxied by variations in labor force participation rates. Indeed, Lewis, an eminent student of development, has commented that "the transfer of women's work from the household to commercial employment is one of the most notable features of economic development."[3]

---

2   See the discussion in Goldin, "Female Labor Force Participation: The Origin of Black and White Differences, 1870 and 1880," *Journal of Economic History*, XXXVII (1977), 87–108.

3   A more comprehensive measure of market work for married women including boardinghouse keepers, industrial homework, etc., is being constructed as part of Goldin, *Economic Change and American Women*. Labor force participation is used in this article as the primary indicator of the economic role of women in the market economy. Several empirical and theoretical issues arise, however, when using such a statistic. The distinction made here, an extension of that made in our national income accounts, is between work for pay, which is generally part of the market sector, and work at home or within the voluntary sector, which is not. This distinction, although generally useful, is not immune to problems, particularly regarding the type of work that women have generally pursued. How participation in the market economy is measured is another issue. The current definition of the labor force includes those seeking work but not currently employed, together with those at work. Prior to 1940, the definition used was whether or not the individual listed an occupation on the population census questionnaire. There has been concern that participation rates for married women have been understated in the past because of the reluctance of women to state an occupation, particularly when the work was performed in the home or done intermittently. These problems, however, have not significantly biased the data. The labor force participation rates of married women from census data in the early period seem consistent with those from, for example, studies of working-class families around 1900. The change in the definition also has not altered the meaning of the data. W. Arthur Lewis, "Economic Development with Unlimited Supplies of Labour," in A. N. Agarwala and S. P. Singh (eds.), *The Economics of Underdevelopment* (London, 1958), 404.

Whereas economists and sociologists have concentrated on the causes of the progressive entry of women into the labor market, the historical literature has focused on the social impact of such change. The most immediate impact has been on the family itself. Thus, notes Degler, "[w]ork for money, as opposed to work for family, generates different attitudes and relationships among family members," and, to Chafe, "the growing employment of married women after 1940 exerted a considerable influence on the distribution of tasks and authority within the family." Beyond the family lies change in social roles and in ideology. Although it is clear that economic change altered family life, the relationship between economic change and social norms has been less obvious. That the feminist movement did not spring from the rapid rise in female labor force participation in the 1950s has appeared paradoxical to some. Nor did the earlier feminist movement of the 1920s result in a radical altering of the market role of women.[4]

Although economic change need not have altered ideology, prevailing social norms may still have been a critical force in defining and containing the economic role of women. To many, the pervasive ideology inhibiting work for married women was the notion that such work was harmful to the family. Others stressed what Martineau noted was a particularly American sentiment, that a "husband's hair stands on end at the idea of [his wife's] working." But if the impediments to economic change for women were primarily ideological, then only a major break with the past, such as that effected by war, could have redefined economic roles. With some exception, there is general agreement with Chafe's view that World War II was that "watershed event." It "radically transformed the economic outlook of women" with an impact greater than even "the implementation of a well-developed ideology." Change, in this context, was catastrophic, not cumulative.[5]

4 Carl Degler, *At Odds: Women and the Family in America from the Revolution to the Present* (New York, 1980), 362; William H. Chafe, *The American Women: Her Changing Social, Economic, and Political Roles, 1920–1970* (New York, 1972), 222, 188.

5 E.g., Degler, *At Odds*, 362–394. Alice Kessler-Harris, "Women's Wage Work as Myth and History," *Labor History*, XIX (1978), 287–307, provides an insightful interpretation of the historical commentary about working women in light of such ideological considerations. Harriet Martineau, *Society in America* (New York, 1837), II, 227; Chafe, *American*

There has been virtual unanimity that little progress in the economic role of married women was achieved prior to World War II, with most adopting Oppenheimer's division of the twentieth century into two distinct periods. The earlier, pre-1940 period witnessed the evolution of work for single women. Beginning with the initial adoption of the factory system early in the nineteenth century, the labor force participation of single women expanded almost steadily until about 1940. This widening of an economic role for single women carried with it important implications for married women. With more daughters in the labor force there were fewer compelling reasons for their mothers to leave the household. But work for single women not only precluded that for married women, it may also have made future change more difficult. Tentler and others have argued that the manufacturing jobs given to single women were sufficiently arduous, dead-end, and sexually segregated that they reinforced the prevailing notion that the proper and preferred role for married women was in the home. Furthermore, Rotella's study of the emerging clerical sector reminds readers that this impressive transformation of women's jobs from 1870 to 1930 almost universally involved single, and not married women.[6]

Even for those who view World War II as initiating change in the economic role of married women, the continued increase in labor force participation rates has demanded further thought. Most of the explanations for change in the more recent period have come from economists. Historians have been understandably hesitant to analyze these recent, and thus brief, trends. Although

---

Woman, 195, 135. One exception to Chafe's view can be found in D'Ann Campbell, "Wives, Workers, and Womanhood: America During World War II," unpub. Ph.D. diss. (Univ. of North Carolina, 1979). Maurine Weiner Greenwald, *Women, War, and Work: The Impact of World War I on Women Workers in the United States* (Westport, Conn., 1980), emphasizes some of the less obvious changes in the female labor force resulting from that war.

6 Valerie Kincade Oppenheimer, *The Female Labor Force in the United States: Factors Governing Its Growth and Changing Composition* (Berkeley, 1970). See Winifred D. Wandersee, *Women's Work and Family Values, 1920–1940* (Cambridge, Mass., 1981), on changes from 1920 to 1940. Goldin and Sokoloff, "Women, Children, and Industrialization," and Goldin, "The Work and Wages of Single Women: 1870 to 1920," *Journal of Economic History*, XLI (1981), 81–89, discuss the evolution of work for single women. Leslie Woodcock Tentler, *Wage-Earning Women: Industrial Work and Family Life in The United States, 1900–1930* (New York, 1979); Elyce Rotella, *From Home to Office: U.S. Women at Work, 1870–1930* (Ann Arbor, 1980).

economists are not unanimous as to the precise line of causation, most have isolated a similar set of critical variables. But within the small group of noneconomists who have studied this topic, there is less consensus. Oppenheimer, a sociologist, emphasizes the demand side. The increased demand for labor in the post-1940s, combined with a relative short-fall of young, single women, led employers to seek a new pool of labor—older married women. Chafe, however, stresses family decision making, and thus labor supply factors. In his view, the post-war period gave rise to a new standard of living which made two primary earners per family a necessity. This reliance on changing consumption norms does not explain why such change occurred, nor, more important, why older and younger married women increased their roles in the labor force at different times.[7]

The framework employed in this article, in its emphasis on the life cycle of women, is a departure from that in the literature just summarized. Although change in the labor force participation rates of married women did accelerate after World War II, many of the preconditions for this expansion had been set decades before. The education, home roles, and occupations of single women, and the fertility behavior of married women, had lasting impacts on their later response to economic factors. The increased role of single women in the labor force prior to 1940, either in the manufacturing or in the clerical sectors, influenced the labor force patterns of these women at other points in their life cycles. New social norms of the 1920s may have influenced the decisions of many young women to delay leaving the labor force until their first pregnancy, rather than with marriage. Although this change may have affected only a small percentage of women, it may have provided that critical break on which future changes were founded. This point echoes and extends one made by Durand who, writing in 1948, was sensitive to the changes made from 1900 to 1945, and noted that "each successive generation of women seems to have retained the greater propensity to be in the labor force which it developed in early adulthood." Thus the historical evolution of market work for married women and the related changes in social roles and norms must be viewed by

7 Oppenheimer, *Female Labor Force*, 261; Chafe, *American Woman*, 174–195. On changing consumption norms see also Wandersee, *Women's Work and Family Values*.

considering women at every point in time to have had important past histories of their own.[8]

The incomplete nature of the data presently available cautions against forming rigid notions about the determinants of long-term change in the economic role of women. But despite the deficiencies of the data, the empirical results that follow are striking and persuasive. They indicate that long-term changes in the economic role of white married women have been the result of three sets of factors: cohort specific effects, primarily predetermined (education and fertility); point-in-time factors, under the assumption of exogenous wages (full-time earnings and unemployment rate); and a time trend, which probably proxies long-run changes in the structure of the economy, such as the growth of the service sector. Thus this almost century-long experience has had remarkable structural continuity, with political and social factors operating through variables such as education, income, and fertility rather than directly affecting this process.

DIMENSIONS OF CHANGE: THE DATA   Census marshals were first instructed to collect data on the occupations of women and children in 1860, and even though data on female employment were collected for the decades from 1860 to 1880, the printed census returns for these years yield only scant indication of how the national figure varies by age, race, nationality, and marital status. Trends in the labor force participation of women in the market economy can, at present, be calculated only for the period since 1890, although such data stratified by age, race, national origin, and marital status are not even conveniently available in the printed censuses for 1900 to 1930.[9]

8 John D. Durand *The Labor Force in the United States, 1890–1960* (New York, 1948), 124. On the role of past events in determining marriage, fertility, and labor force participation, see Sheila K. Bennett and Glen H. Elder, Jr., "Women's Work in the Family Economy: A Study of Depression Hardship in Women's Lives," *Journal of Family History,* IV (1979), 153–176.

9 For data on the 1820 to 1850 period see Goldin and Sokoloff, "Women, Children, and Industrialization," which uses manufacturing census information; Thomas Dublin, *Women at Work: The Transformation of Work and Community in Lowell Massachusetts, 1826–1860* (New York, 1979), which uses firm records and the population census for 1860. There are several studies which have sampled the 1870 and 1880 censuses, among them Goldin, "Female Labor Force Participation"; Tamara K. Hareven and Maris A. Vinovskis, "Patterns of Childbearing in Late Nineteenth-Century America: The Determinants of Marital Fertility in Five Massachusetts Towns in 1880," in Hareven and Vinovskis (eds.), *Family and Population in Nineteenth-Century America* (Princeton, 1978), 85–125.

Fig. 1   Labor Force Participation Rates of Cohorts of White, Married
Women, Born 1866 to 1955: Entire U.S.

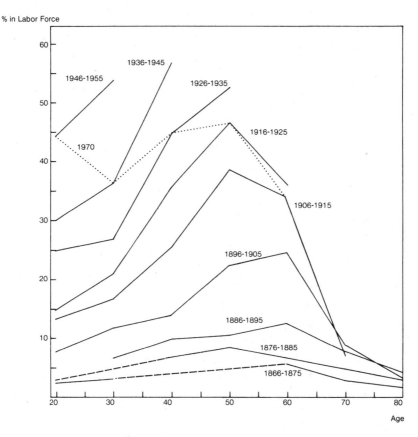

Dashed lines denote missing data. Data for 1890 to 1920 are for native-born women with
native-born parents. Dotted line is 1970 cross section.

SOURCE: Derived from population census data. Data appendix on request from author.

I have produced a matrix of cross-section and time-series
labor force participation rates by marital status, age, race, and
national origin for 1890 to the present which covers cohorts born
from 1816–1825 to 1946–1955. Figure 1 is part of this larger matrix
and summarizes the expansion of the labor force participation of
white married women born from 1866 to 1955. Each set of solid
(or dashed) lines represents the participation rate of a particular
birth cohort and traces its market role as it matured. Cross-section
data can also be read from this figure by connecting the relevant

points on the cohort lines; for example, the data for 1970 are given by the dotted lines.[10]

Several aspects of the data in Figure 1 should be recognized. The format used is termed an "experiential" one, in that the connected points represent participation rates for members of a birth cohort extending over its married life and reflect the actual experience of a cohort. There are, however, changes in the composition of each cohort as it ages that should be addressed. Individuals born in a particular year enter these data when they marry, and therefore as the cohort ages the size of this group changes. Furthermore, individuals who married late may have had different work histories than those who married early, and individuals who were widowed early and who exit from the data set may also differ. The geographical location of these cohorts also changed through time, as the population in the United States became more urbanized.

Despite these considerations the data in Figure 1 have a more or less transparent interpretation—for every cohort born since 1855 participation in the labor force has increased within marriage, at least until about age fifty-five. Despite the currently popular notion that married women universally experience interruptions in their work careers, the majority who have entered the labor force after their children began school had not experienced labor force work since they were single, if even at that time. The notion of interrupted work careers has arisen, in part, from the pattern of double-peaked labor force participation characteristic of cross-sectional data for women's work experiences in most contemporary developed nations. This pattern emerged in the United States in 1950 and is illustrated by the dotted line in Figure 1 giving participation rates for the cross section of married women in 1970. At that time the labor force participation rate for married women of fifteen to twenty-four years old was higher than for those twenty-five to thirty-four years old, and this rate rose again with those aged thirty-five to forty-four. Such a bimodal or double-peaked pattern has indicated to some an exiting of women

---

10 Goldin, *Economic Change and American Women*. Juanita M. Kreps and R. John Leaper, "Home Work, Market Work, and the Allocation of Time," in Kreps (ed.), *Women and the American Economy: A Look to the 1980s* (New York, 1976), construct cohort female labor force participation rates but do not derive them conditional on marital status.

from the labor force with the birth of their children and a later reentrance as their families matured.

But the actual labor force experience of these cohorts of women has universally consisted of increasing labor force participation rates until about age fifty-five. For reasons discussed later, each successive decade brought an expanded participation of married women in the market economy. Thus the cohort participation rates are substantially different from the cross-sectional ones. No generation of young women could have predicted solely from the experiences of their elders what their own work histories would have been. Indeed, in 1930 a cohort of twenty-year-old daughters born in 1910 would have been off by a factor of 3.6 in predicting their own participation rates in twenty-five years, had they simply extrapolated from the experiences of their forty-five-year-old mothers born in 1885. Had they, with more quantitative sophistication, partially utilized the model presented in the next section and recognized education and fertility differences between their and their mothers' cohorts, they would have been off by a factor of 2.1, considerably less. The remainder of the differences between these groups was accounted for by changes over time in the structure of the economy and thus economic opportunities for women and, among other factors, in increases in the earning capabilities of women.[11]

Interruptions in the work careers of women have been central to explanations for differences in the training and occupations of women relative to men. These cohort data do not eliminate entirely the notion of career interruption, but alter its significance and meaning. The large increases over time in labor force participation mean that many women must have entered the work force when older with very little, if any, work experience after marriage. Because a very high percentage of women worked at some time prior to marriage, many who worked when married were

---

11 The daughter's labor force participation rate was about 32% when she was 45 years old, whereas the mother's was only about 9%. The daughter, however, had 39% more years of schooling than her mother and, on average, 28% fewer children. Using the coefficients from Table 1 column (2) yields an expected labor force participation rate of 15.3% had the daughter extrapolated only on the basis of these two differences in the experience of her cohort and that of her mother. That is: dlog FLFP = (0.891) dlog SCH − (0.723) dlog CHILD = (0.891) log (11.5/8.3) − (0.723) log (2.3/3.2) = 0.53. Therefore, these two factors served to increase FLFP by 1.7 times, ($e^{0.53}$ = 1.7), or from 9% to 15.3%. (See Table 1 for variable name definitions.)

returning to occupations that they had when single. Because the clerical labor force, for example, consisted primarily of single women in the pre-1940 period does not mean that it was an entirely unimportant factor in shaping the labor force experiences of married women later in the century.[12]

In terms of time-series trends, participation rates increased for married white women in all age groups, except the very oldest, in every decade. Increases were slight, however, for most cohorts until the 1920s and then again in the 1940 and 1950 decades. Young, married women experienced somewhat larger increases than did older women during the 1920 to 1930 period. But from 1940 to 1960 participation rates for older women, say over thirty-five years, rose dramatically, and from 1960 to 1980 the rates for younger women, say those under thirty-five years, experienced similar increases.

These time-series trends can be seen more clearly with reference to Figure 2, which shows labor force changes over time for married women both twenty-five to thirty-four years old (younger) and forty-five to fifty-four years old (older). It is more evident from Figure 2 than it was from Figure 1 that the greatest expansion in the labor force participation of older women occurred in the World War II and post-war periods, when that for younger women increased far less. The younger women, however, have had relative expansions in their market work activity both in the earliest periods drawn and in the most recent ones. Such differences in labor market activity by age were explored by Easterlin whose explanation of them stressed a relationship between cycles in the economy and changes in birth rates.[13]

The cohort experiences and time series graphed in Figures 1 and 2 are for the entire United States, and thus, it might be claimed, reflect in large measure the long-run movement of the population out of agricultural and non-farm rural areas. But similarly constructed data for urban areas only (not shown) are virtually identical to the total data for the period after 1950 and differ

12 On the implications of career interruptions see Jacob Mincer and Solomon Polachek, "Family Investments in Human Capital: Earnings of Women," *Journal of Political Economy*, LXXXII (1974), S76-S108.
13 Richard Easterlin, *Birth and Fortune: The Impact of Numbers on Personal Welfare* (New York, 1980).

Fig. 2 Labor Force Participation Rates for Two Age Groups of White, Married Women, 1920 to 1980: Entire U.S.

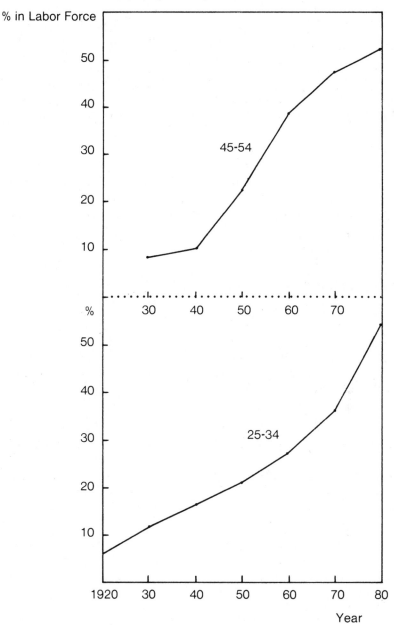

SOURCE: Fig. 1. Data appendix on request from author.

before 1950 only with respect to the greater increase in the labor force participation of young married women in urban areas from 1920 to 1930. This increase in young married women in the labor force of the 1920s suggests that they were either progressively exiting from the labor force after their first pregnancy or delaying their first birth. The urban data also indicate that within cities there were few substantial differences by nativity in average labor force participation rates of married women, a result which would have been difficult to demonstrate in the context of the national figures.

Each cohort has been influenced in its decision to participate in the labor force both by economic and social conditions at a particular date and by aspects of early socialization and training carried with it through time. Of the factors which may have differentiated one cohort's work history from another, three relate to their early experiences: schooling, work in the market economy, and work in the home.

The median years of schooling for female cohorts born from 1876 to 1952 and the percentage with four or more years of college are given in the left and right-hand graphs of Figure 3. The data on median years of schooling show a remarkable rise in the educational attainment of young American women beginning approximately with the cohorts born between 1900 and 1910. During a very brief period young women had increased their years of education by about one third, from about nine years to twelve years. This rapid rise in years of schooling was a product of the increase in high school education, with these individuals leaving school from 1915 to 1928. The cohort that achieved this educational transformation was precisely that which experienced substantial increases in its labor force participation both during its early years and even more so at the time, during the 1950s, that it was forty to fifty years old (see Fig. 1).[14]

Not only was the educational attainment of the cohort born from 1900 to 1910 a break with prior experiences, but it also achieved a high rate of labor force participation when single. The labor force participation rate of native-born white, single women

---

14 The increase in effective years of schooling would be even greater if days attended and expenditures per pupil were incorporated. Years of schooling for males did not rise as dramatically over the same period.

Fig. 3 Educational Attainment for Cohorts of White Women Born
1876–1952

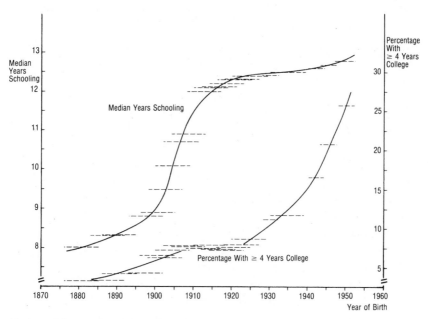

Horizontal lines indicate the width of the birth cohorts for which data on educational
attainment are given.

SOURCE: U.S. Bureau of the Census, *Current Population Reports,* Series P-20 for years 1940,
1947, 1962, 1966, 1968, 1970, 1972, 1974, 1977. Data appendix on request from author.

of fifteen to twenty-four years old was 30 percent in 1890, 33.5
percent in 1900, 45.1 percent in 1920, and about 40 percent from
1930 to 1960. Thus this cohort carried with it through time a
labor market experience and education that differed considerably
from those of prior generations of young women. It was also a
cohort that was employed to a large degree in the clerical sector
when it was single and when that sector employed young single
women almost exclusively.[15]

Cohorts of women born around the early twentieth century
were able to achieve both an increase in their educational attainment and an increase in their labor market experience when single,

15   On this point see Rotella, *From Home to Office*; Goldin, "The Historical Evolution of
Female Earnings Functions and Occupations," National Bureau of Economic Research
Working Paper, no. 529 (1980).

by spending considerably less time "at home," ostensibly helping their mothers. In 1880 over 50 percent of all unmarried urban daughters between sixteen and twenty-four years old (white with American-born parents) were full-time workers in their parents' households. By 1900 about 30 percent were, and by 1930 practically no post-adolescent single women were either not in school or not in the labor force. This shift away from home chores by teenaged girls and young women may have been an influential factor both in delaying the entrance of older married women into the labor market and in encouraging labor market work for these younger women when they married.[16]

After the initial schooling increase with the cohorts born from 1900 to 1910, median years of education increased only gradually, with the exception of the most recent cohorts. Changes in the educational attainment of the most recent cohorts can be seen more clearly on the right-hand portion of Figure 3, which graphs the percentage of women with four or more years of college. This indicator increased most rapidly with cohorts born after 1940, precisely those with substantially higher labor force participation in the most recent decades.

Yet another factor influencing the future labor force participation of these cohorts is fertility, although it might best be viewed as jointly determined with the work history. The well-known cycles in fertility which have marked the twentieth-century experience began with the trough produced by the cohorts born between 1905 and 1914. The peak of this cycle was achieved by the cohorts born from 1928 to 1932. Although it is still too early to know, another trough may have been produced by the cohorts born between 1948 and 1952. The relationships between education and fertility data are suggestive. Changes in schooling, by affecting early work experience and social norms, may have influenced fertility, although a complete model of fertility change

16 The 1880 data are for Philadelphia and are from Goldin, "Household and Market Production of Families in a Late Nineteenth-Century City," *Explorations in Economic History,* XVI (1979), 111–131. The 1900 data were computed from labor force and schooling data for Boston, Chicago, New York, Philadelphia, and St. Louis in *Population Census, 1900* (1902), Pt. 2 and the related volume *Women at Work* (1904); those for 1930 were computed from labor force and schooling data on the same cities in *Population Census, 1930* (1933), II, V. Data are in an appendix available upon request from the author.

must also incorporate an explanation for the "baby boom" of the post-World War II period.[17]

The data on the schooling, market work, and home work of post-adolescent daughters have suggested that experiences early in the life cycle of women may have greatly affected their market involvement when older. The data on educational attainment indicate that increases in median years of schooling were discontinuous and that certain cohorts experienced rapid increases in years of schooling. These same cohorts also had more years of labor market experience when young, but far less experience in household production than prior cohorts. Their early socialization may have provided a change in focus with that of past generations. The cohorts whose schooling and early labor force experiences rapidly approached contemporary levels were precisely those whose labor market participation rates, both in their early and in their later married years, substantially increased over previous levels. These cohorts also had smaller families than did those who were born before or, for some time, after. Recent changes in the percentage of women completing college may have affected the current labor force and fertility behavior of young married women.

The profiles of labor force participation for cohorts of white married women born from 1866 to 1955 show an unbroken upward trend to about age fifty-five. But there were distinct changes in participation rates during particular decades and for particular cohorts. The increases in labor force participation with age for each cohort appear to reflect two complementary sets of factors: those affecting point-in-time experiences, such as economic upturns or downturns, and those concerning characteristics that each cohort retained with it through its life cycle. The estimation in the next section addresses how much of the increase over time in labor force participation was due to increases in wages, employment opportunities, and changes in societal norms, and how much to changes in cohort specific factors.

---

17   For data sources see notes and sources for Table 1, CHILD variable. Deborah Dawson, Denise Meny, and Jeanne Clare Ridley, "Fertility Control in the United States Before the Contraceptive Revolution," *Family Planning Perspectives,* XII (1980), 76–86, examine the fertility experience of the cohort of females born from 1901 to 1910.

EXPLAINING CHANGE IN THE LABOR FORCE PARTICIPATION OF MARRIED WOMEN   Two distinct but complementary theories of change in the economic role of married women have been offered by economists. One, due to Easterlin, stresses the concept of relative income and the importance of fertility decisions; the other, associated primarily with Mincer, stresses the value of time and the importance of changes in female wages.[18]

As part of a more comprehensive theory of demographic, social, and economic change in the twentieth century, Easterlin has distinguished between changes in the labor force participation rates of younger and older women. The fertility rate is the prime determinant of changes in the economic behavior of both groups, but the mechanism of change is through alterations in the relative income of younger men, presumably the prospective husbands of the younger women. Relative income is a critical concept in this analysis, and Easterlin defined it as income in comparison to what one had anticipated earning, perhaps relative to the incomes of older cohorts. Thus, the children of the baby trough of the 1920s and 1930s married in the relatively prosperous post-World War II era. These young men were from a relatively small cohort and thus commanded relatively high incomes. They married young and had large families. The fertility rate rose, the labor force participation rate of younger women rose only slightly, but that of older women increased greatly. Older women were close substitutes for younger women, whereas older and younger men were presumably poor substitutes for each other. Younger women had small increases in their labor force participation rates for two reasons: they were raising larger families; and their husbands had relatively high incomes, generally a factor deterring female labor market participation.[19]

The recent baby slump and large labor force increases by all

---

18   Easterlin, *Birth and Fortune*; Mincer, "Labor Force Participation of Married Women: A Study of Labor Supply," in H .Gregg Lewis (ed.), *Aspects of Labor Economics* (Princeton, 1962), 63–105.
19   See also Easterlin, "What Will 1984 Be Like? Socioeconomic Implications of Recent Twists in Age Structure," *Demography*, XV (1978), 397–432; idem, *Population, Labor Force, and Long Swings in Economic Growth* (New York, 1968). Richard Freeman, "The Effect of Demographic Factors on Age-Earnings Profiles," *Journal of Human Resources*, XIV (1979), 289–318, has provided independent and substantiating evidence for the theory concerning both changes in relative incomes and the greater substitutability between older and younger women than between older and younger men.

age groups of married women have been viewed by Easterlin as rooted in the relatively lower incomes of the young cohorts in the 1970s. These lower incomes were produced by two coincident factors: large cohorts born in the post-World War II period have depressed the earnings of young men relative to old men; in addition, the economy was generally depressed in the early and mid-1970s. Young men, faced with relatively lower incomes (again, relative to what they might have expected) married later, and had smaller families. Easterlin's formulation has pointed to critical differences in the determinants of work for younger and older women, as well as the importance of perceived changes in standards of living. But his implicit model is a highly complex one and difficult to test over long periods of time.

Mincer's explanation of secular changes in labor force participation rates of married women is an application of neoclassical labor economics. He had set out to resolve a paradox which Long had noted earlier, that despite increases in real family incomes, which should have reduced market work for women, the labor force participation of married women rose steadily from 1890. Long had used cross-section estimates of economic concepts termed income and substitution coefficients to predict time-series changes in participation rates. But he found that the cross-section income effect was so strong that it offset changes from all other possible variables, particularly the substitution effect.[20]

The solution to Long's paradox was Mincer's recognition that the cross-section income effect might be a gross overstatement of the income effect in a time-series context. The cross-section income estimate was overstated for use in predicting time-series, because it reflected, in large measure, variations in income arising from transitory, not permanent factors. The time-series and cross-section results could, to some degree, be reconciled by correcting the income effect coefficient. The income and substi-

---

20 Mincer, "Labor Force Participation." Clarence Long, *The Labor Force Under Changing Income and Employment* (Princeton, 1962). The "income effect" refers here to the change (generally a decrease) in labor time with an increase in income. For example, in most cross sections married women with husbands whose earnings are high tend to work fewer hours or days per year during their lifetimes. The "substitution effect" refers to the change in labor time with a change in the wage rate, generally, positive. For example, in cross sections individuals with high actual or anticipated wages work more hours or days per year or more years within their lifetimes.

tution coefficients estimated by Mincer from a cross section of cities in 1950 were −0.53 and +1.52, respectively (where incomes and wages are in 1949 dollars $\times$ 10^{-2}), and the elasticities, measured about the mean, were −0.83 and +1.50, respectively. Because variations in incomes across cities presumably arise from permanent and not transitory factors, the estimated income effect would be applicable for predicting the trend in labor force changes over time. But when applied to the wage and earnings data for 1890 and 1980 that underlie the regressions presented in Table 1, the Mincer estimates severely overstate changes in labor force participation from 1930 to 1940 for both younger and older women, and severely understate the increases in the labor force participation of older women from 1940 to 1960. However, over the entire period from 1890 to 1980 Mincer's coefficients do account for 62 percent of the change for women twenty-five to thirty-four years old.

One might track the turning points with better precision by taking into account changes in unemployment and in fertility, particularly as the latter affected younger women. Although Mincer had found these variables to have no statistical significance, Cain's reworking of Mincer's data concluded the reverse. The more extensive cross-section estimates of Bowen and Finegan are consistent with those of Cain, yielding a negative impact for increases in unemployment, and thus account better for the 1930 and 1950 data. These estimates do not, however, account for a greater percentage of the change over the entire period, primarily because the effect of the female wage is smaller in the Bowen and Finegan study than it was in Mincer's. In addition, the impact of changes in the number of children is too small in the Bowen and Finegan study to increase the predictive power of their equation over the entire time period.[21]

In the years since Mincer's influential paper was written, there have been advances both in the estimation of coefficients and in the recognition of the complexity of change in the labor market participation of married women. This body of research has suggested a set of variables to include in a model of long-run economic change, and the discussion above of life-cycle effects has

21 Glen G. Cain, *Married Women in the Labor Force: An Economic Analysis* (Chicago, 1966), 22–24; William Bowen and T. Aldrich Finegan, *The Economics of Labor Force Participation* (Princeton, 1969).

suggested some extensions. But rather than applying cross-section coefficient estimates to time-series data, as Mincer had done, I have used a pooled time-series and cross-section model directly to confront the sources of long-run change.[22]

The variables of the preceding discussion can be divided into two groups, isolating the impacts of two sets of factors: (1) those influencing change over time for any particular cohort (point-in-time factors); and (2) those differentiating each cohort's experience from any other (cohort specific factors). Such a procedure enables a full analysis of the cohort and cross-sectional data given in Figure 1.

The first set of factors, which accounts for within cohort effects, includes the full-time earning capacity of women (FEARN), the income of other family members (MEARN) proxied by the actual income of all labor force participants or of males, and the unemployment rate (UN). Depending on the degree of precision used in stratifying the labor force data, factors such as the urbanization rate (URB) or merely a time trend (TIME) are needed to account for long-term structural change in the economy. Relative prices for market goods which had been primarily home produced and for labor-saving capital equipment are also important indicators, but are not readily available for the full period considered. The data in Figure 1 allow for, at most, nine equations of the general form of (1), one for each of the nine cohorts to explain (LFPR$_{i,t}$) the labor force participation rate of cohort i, at time t:

$$\text{LFPR}_{i,t} = f(\text{FEARN}_t, \text{MEARN}_t, \text{UN}_t, \text{TIME or URB}_t) \qquad (1)$$

where t=year, i=cohort, for all i.

The second set of factors, which accounts for cross cohort effects, includes schooling attainment (SCH) and fertility (CHILD).

22 An excellent introduction to the literature which extended Mincer's work on labor supply is James J. Heckman, Mark R. Killingsworth, and Thomas MaCurdy, "Empirical Evidence on Static Labour Supply Models: A Survey of Recent Developments," in Zmira Hornstein, Joseph Grice, and Alfred Webb (eds.), *The Economics of the Labour Market* (London, 1981), 73–124. I am aware of only one other time-series analysis of labor force participation rates for women: June A. O'Neill, "A Time-Series Analysis of Women's Labor Force Participation," *American Economic Review*, LXXI (1981), 76–80, which covers the 1948–1978 period and runs separate regressions by age and marital status. Although O'Neill's study does not include the same variables and its coefficients are not expressed as elasticities, the estimates presented below in Table 1 appear generally consistent with those of O'Neill.

Additional aspects of early socialization, work experience, and the time allocation of older children in the household cannot at present be incorporated. As summarized in equation (2) there are eight years of data, one for each of the census years from 1890 to 1980 (with the exception of 1910):[23]

$$\text{LFPR}_{i,t} = g(\text{SCH}_i, \text{CHILD}_i) \tag{2}$$

where i=cohort, for all t.

By pooling the cross-section and time-series data one can estimate a model of the form:

$$\text{LFPR}_{i,t} = h(\text{FEARN}_t, \text{MEARN}_t, \text{UN}_t, \text{TIME or URB}_t;$$
$$\text{SCH}_i, \text{CHILD}_i) \tag{3}$$

for all i,t.

The data underlying Figure 1 contain thirty-six observations on $\text{LFPR}_{i,t}$, beginning with fifteen to twenty-four year olds in 1890 from the birth cohort 1866–1875, ending with those twenty-five to thirty-four year olds in 1980 from the birth cohort 1945–1955, and omitting women over sixty-five years old. The data for the SCH_i variable are contained in Figure 3. Procedures for obtaining FEARN_t, MEARN_t, UN_t, URB_t, and CHILD_i are described in Table 1. All earnings are expressed in constant dollars, female earnings are for full-time employment, and male earnings adjust for unemployment. This asymmetry in measuring female and male earnings is deliberate and reflects the notion that women condition their labor force decisions on actual family income but determine hours or days worked by considering their full-time wage. Unemployment is included as a separate factor, a possibly discouraging element in labor force decisions.

Several variables are added to test hypotheses raised earlier and to account for differences among groups. A dummy variable for the oldest age group, women between fifty-five and sixty-four years, is included (OLD Dummy). An interaction between fertility and a dummy variable for women in their childbearing years (CHILD·YOUNG) is added to test whether increased fertility lowers a cohort's labor force participation rate only when it is young or whether family size has a more enduring impact. A

---

23 The 1910 data, because they included women in agricultural activities not included in other census years, have been omitted from the entire analysis.

dummy variable for 1950 (WAR Dummy) is included to test whether the increase in participation rates from 1940 to 1950 was due primarily to conventionally measured factors or whether the war had some residual impact.

The functional form used is double log (natural) and is given by:

$$\log \text{LFPR}_{i,t} = \beta_0 + \beta_1 \log \text{FEARN}_t + \beta_2 \log \text{MEARN}_t$$
$$+ \beta_3 \log \text{UN}_t + \beta_4[\log \text{URB}_t \text{ or } \text{TIME}]$$
$$+ \beta_5 \log \text{SCH}_i + \beta_6 \log \text{CHILD}_i$$
$$+ \sum_j \alpha_j D_j + \epsilon_{i,t} \qquad (4)$$

where all variables are defined above, the D_j are various dummies and interaction terms, and $\epsilon_{i,t}$ is the error term, assumed uncorrelated within cohorts and among years.[24] The results are given in Table 1, where the coefficients, with the exceptions of the dummy variables and the time trend, are elasticities, the magnitudes and signs of which are generally within the range of estimates from disaggregated studies. Although I discuss below the deficiencies of data and modeling, these estimates can, with caution, be employed to understand some of the sources of long-term change. The relative influences of cohort specific and point-in-time effects can be disentangled, and the role of special influences, such as World War II, can be assessed.

It can be seen in Table 1 that the impact of the female wage is strong, as suggested by cross-sectional studies such as Mincer's, with an elasticity of about 0.7 to 1. The role of a husband's or a family's income is insignificant, but unemployment generally has the predicted and somewhat significant discouraging impact. Because of the collinearity between female and male earnings over time, the equations were also estimated without the latter variable, as in columns (2) and (4). The cohort influences on schooling and fertility are both of the predicted sign, with elasticities around 0.9 for years schooling and −0.7 for average number of children.

The coefficients on the fertility and age interaction (log CHILD·YOUNG) and on fertility (log CHILD) alone indicate that labor force participation for a cohort remains significantly affected by its fertility experience beyond the period of childbearing and

---

24 A logit form for the equations in columns (2) and (4) of Table 1 yielded virtually the same elasticities, evaluated at the mean of the labor force participation rates.

Table 1 Explaining Variations in the Labor Force Participation of White Married Women, 1890 to 1980, for Age Groups 15–24 to 54–65

Dependent Variable = Log (Labor Force Participation Rate) for cohort i at time t. 't' statistics are given in parentheses below the coefficients. Independent variables are defined in the text and in the SOURCES. Number of Observations = 36 for all four regressions

	(1)	(2)	(3)	(4)
Constant	−9.112	−9.300	−11.070	−11.496
	(−3.53)	(−3.14)	(−6.52)	(−6.66)
Log FEARN	0.658	0.673	1.008	1.097
	(1.37)	(1.50)	(2.84)	(5.22)
Log MEARN	−0.015		0.040	
	(−0.07)		(0.17)	
Log UN	−0.078	−0.074	−0.003	−0.012
	(−1.32)	(−1.47)	(−0.05)	(−0.33)
Log SCH	0.892	0.891	0.957	0.945
	(3.48)	(3.48)	(3.80)	(3.74)
Log CHILD	−0.718	−0.723	−0.707	−0.711
	(−4.64)	(−4.75)	(−4.50)	(−4.57)
Log CHILD · YOUNG	−0.171	−0.173	−0.183	−0.182
	(−2.89)	(−2.95)	(−3.15)	(−3.18)
OLD Dummy	−0.312	−0.312	−0.305	−0.307
	(−5.46)	(−5.47)	(−5.33)	(−5.37)
TIME	0.014	0.014		
	(1.88)	(1.56)		
Log URB			0.794	0.688
			(1.73)	(1.44)
WAR Dummy		−0.001		−0.024
		(−0.14)		(−0.42)
R^2	0.990	0.990	0.989	0.989

NOTES AND SOURCES:

LFPR = labor force participation rate of white (native-born) married women for cohort i at time t, from Fig. 1.

FEARN = a weighted average of the annual full-time female wage in manufacturing and that in the clerical sector where weights are the share of female employment in each sector. Wages are from Rotella, *From Home to Office*; Paul F. Brissenden, *Earnings of Factory Workers, 1899–1927* (Washington, D.C., 1929); M. Ada Beney, *Wages, Hours, and Employment in the U.S. 1914–1936* (New York, 1936); U.S. Bureau of the Census, *Historical Statistics*, Series D838; U.S. Bureau of the Census, *Current Population Surveys*, Series P-60, 1945–1980. The wages are deflated to 1967 = 100 using the B.L.S. C.P.I., *Historical Statistics*, Series E135. For each year t, wages are an average of (t − 3) to (t − 1).

MEARN = male earnings adjusted for unemployment and are deflated to 1967 = 100. From Stanley Lebergott, *Manpower in Economic Growth: The American Record Since 1800* (New York, 1964), Series A-17, 524, non-farm wages for 1900–1960; Series A-19, non-farm

child-raising. The cohort does experience a greater impact from changes in fertility when it is young, but the effect is not contained in those years. Indeed, the elasticity with respect to number of children is reduced by only 20 percent for women above thirty-five years old.

Sources of long-term change in female labor force participation, derived from the regressions and the data underlying them, are given in Table 2. Point-in-time effects, which might also be thought of as demand-side factors, principally the rise in the earning ability of women, have exerted a powerful influence on participation rates, accounting for about one third of the total change from 1900 to 1980 or from 1920 to 1980. The impact of changes in education and fertility, termed cohort specific factors, have provided from 28 to 34 percent of the long-term movement. These cohort specific factors might also be thought of as supply-side factors. The time trend, which may be picking up either demand or supply factors, has accounted for about the remaining third.

I have shown elsewhere that, in the early twentieth century, earnings for women over their own life cycles in manufacturing jobs first rose sharply with age and then declined. Furthermore, such a decline persists even after adjusting for various factors, such as days worked per year, work experience, and marital status. But work in the clerical sector, at a somewhat later date,

---

wages for 1890–1900; *Current Population Surveys*, Series P-60, for urban white males, 1960–1980. For each year t, wages are an average of $(t-3)$ to $(t-1)$.

UN = national unemployment rate, five year average for $(t-6)$ to $(t-1)$, from *Historical Statistics*, Series D 85–86.

SCH = median years schooling for cohort i, from Fig. 3.

CHILD = average number of children born to white women in cohort i over its life cycle. Cohorts born 1865 to 1924 from *Historical Statistics* (Washington, D.C., 1976), Series B42–48, 53; cohorts born 1928 to 1952 from U.S. Bureau of the Census, *Current Population Reports*, Series P-20, No. 341, "Fertility of American Women" (1978).

CHILD · YOUNG = Child · dummy variable for women 15 to 34 years old.

OLD = dummy variable for women 55 to 64 years old.

TIME = number of years from 1890.

URB = percentage of U.S. population living in urban areas at time t, from *Historical Statistics*, Series A 57–72.

WAR Dummy = dummy variable for 1950.

Table 2 Explaining Long-Term Change in Female Labor Force
Participation Rates

TIME INTERVAL	1900–1980	1920–1980	
AGE GROUPS	25–34	25–34	35–44
Point-in-time factors	0.96	0.66	0.66
	(30%)	(29%)	(33%)
Cohort specific factors	1.00	0.77	0.56
	(31%)	(34%)	(28%)
Time trend	1.23	0.81	0.81
	(39%)	(36%)	(40%)

NOTES AND SOURCES:

The numbers in this table give the values of dlog FLFR predicted by the equation in
Table 1, column (2). The time intervals and age groups given were dictated by the
available data underlying Table 1, e.g. there are no data for 1910. The figures in
parentheses give the percentage of the predicted change in dlog FLFP explained by
the set of variables in each row. The definitions of each row are:

Point-in-time factors = 0.673 dlog FEARN − 0.074 dlog UN

Cohort specific factors =
0.891 dlog SCH − 0.723 dlog CHILD − 0.173 dlog CHILD · YOUNG

Time trend = 0.014 dTIME

Note that all three sets of factors fully exhaust the relevant variables in the regression
in Table 1, column (2).

did not exhibit such a pattern. Instead, its age-earnings or expe-
rience-earnings profile was flatter and did not peak within the
relevant range. It is possible, therefore, that an extensive participation of married women in the labor force had to await the
emergence of such an occupation, the earnings profile of which
did not decline at older ages. The time trend variable may be
picking up changes in the structure of the economy which increased the demand for occupations in the clerical sector. It may
also be picking up changes in social and individual norms and
ideals.[25]

The twentieth century has been punctuated by two wars and
one protracted economic depression, and change over this time
in the economic role of married women has frequently been
attributed directly to these events, apart from their indirect impact

25 Goldin, "Historical Evolution of Female Earnings Functions."

through such factors as economic variables. But the regressions in Table 1 indicate that change over the twentieth century has had a certain structural stability. The impact of World War II, for example, appears to have worked primarily through conventionally measured variables rather than as a separate factor, as can be seen by the insignificant coefficient on the variable (WAR Dummy).[26]

As encouraging and useful as this exercise may be in interpreting the past, it is not without problems regarding both the data and the underlying model. Several omitted variables have already been isolated. The income data are not age or race specific over the entire period for males or females, and although the fertility data are for white women, they are not specific to native-born women. The use of a time-trend or urbanization variable disguises the need for better indicators of economic structural change that have affected the demand for female workers. In terms of the model, the framework implies that female earnings are exogenous. Although this might be an acceptable assumption for the earliest periods, it becomes less viable as the percentage of females in the total labor force rises. The complexities raised by Easterlin concerning the endogeneity of fertility and the use of a relative income concept are further issues with which to contend.

Finally, nothing has been said about the constraints facing married women in the labor market. The occupations in which married women have been employed expanded greatly over the period analyzed. Whereas it was commonplace earlier in the century for women to be dismissed from their jobs upon marriage, particularly from teaching and clerical sector positions, this prohibition slowly disappeared. But its relaxation has been linked to certain economic factors, and thus its presence may not have been solely a function of social norms. One study of the local employment practices of a school board has found a marked increase in married women hired during the tight World War I labor market.

26 However Judith M. Fields, "A Comparison of Intercity Differences in the Labor Force Participation Rates of Married Women in 1970 with 1940, 1950 and 1960," *Journal of Human Resources,* XI (1976), 568–577, demonstrates that cross-sectional data yield vastly different labor-supply relationships over time. Although it is likely that the recent period demands more diligent modeling of factors relating to investment in human capital, differences among these decades may also be a function of greater geographical mobility in the later period.

In addition, unemployment in the 1930s led to a rationing of jobs among women by marital status. But there have been no quantitative studies of the precise impact of such practices, the ways in which they were relaxed, and how changes in the interval between marriage and first pregnancy, for example, affected them.[27]

The concentration in this article on economic role and, more specifically, on labor market participation, should not be interpreted to mean that society has measured the worth or position of individuals only in this manner. Nor do I mean to imply that men and women have had the same treatment or experience in the labor market. The focus on labor market participation stems from the notion that such a convenient measure conveys information. It may in some economies convey information about the harshness of life, but it may in others point to deeper social and economic change. Work for married women in the American past has frequently meant, as it has for men, economic necessity. But it has also implied, with more and more frequency, economic autonomy. The emergence of such independence and control has carried with it further implications, such as the formation of wider and less family-dependent social networks, a greater chance for marital dissolution, and the possibility of less constrained and structured sex roles. Across a wide variety of countries, the emergence of married women in the paid labor force has carried with it similar implications for social and economic change, and thus an explanation for changes in female labor force participation has been a topic of great importance.

In explaining the labor force behavior of married women, economists have stressed contemporaneous variables, primarily income, wage rates, family size, and unemployment. But precedents for economic change within the life cycles of individual cohorts, although harder to isolate, also merit inclusion. I have made a strong case for viewing individuals through time as having important past experiences. A pooled cross-section and time-series model was estimated across the years 1890 to 1980 to explain variations in female labor force participation, including at most

27 Robert Margo and Rotella, "Sex Differences in the Market for School Personnel: Houston, Texas, 1892–1923," unpub. ms. (1981).

five age groups in each year and using both cohort specific and point-in-time independent variables. The primary findings were that there apparently was structural stability in the process of change over the past century. Despite the importance of the female earnings variable and the time trend, the role of education and fertility in accounting for between cohort differences was significant, and these are only two of the variables that might capture aspects of a cohort's past.

Gale Stokes

Cognition and the
Function of Nationalism

It is perfectly well known that nationalism is a powerful and ubiquitous feature of modern European politics. The thing that is unclear is why this should be so.

Historians who have tried to explain nationalism have tended to follow the lead of Kohn and Hayes. As historians, both men believed that a historical description of the complex series of events that produced nationalism amounted to an explanation of it. At the same time both also realized that nationalism has a great psychological impact. "Nationalities are the product of the historical development of society," Kohn wrote, but "nationalism is first and foremost a state of mind," ... "a group-consciousness ... a psychological and a sociological fact." Nonetheless, Kohn believed that psychological or sociological explanations of nationalism were "insufficient" to explain it.[1] In this he was correct, because psychological and sociological theories must operate in a historical context. But Kohn's historicist understanding of explanation led him beyond this undeniable observation to the untenable belief that an understanding of psychological mechanisms at work in the individual were not necessary at all in the understanding of nationalism. And so his work, and the work of the many historians who have followed him, relies very little, if at all, on psychological theory.

Hayes also recognized that nationalism was a state of mind, or, as he might put it, a cultural phenomenon. "There must be something more than a philosophy, something more than a doctrine and an historical process, about modern nationalism," he wrote. "This something is obviously an emotion, an emotional loyalty to the idea or the fact of the national state, a loyalty so intensely emotional that it motivates all sorts of people. . . ." Hayes ascribed the strength of this intense loyalty to a man's deeply ingrained religious sense. Nationalism could bear evil fruit, Hayes believed, because this religious sense was a matter of faith rather than reason and therefore susceptible to perversion in a way

Gale Stokes is Assistant Professor of History at Rice University and the author of several articles on the nineteenth-century Balkans.

An earlier version of this paper, entitled "Communication, Cognition, and Nationalism," was presented at the fifth annual meeting of the American Association for the Advancement of Slavic Studies, in March, 1972.

1 Hans Kohn, *The Idea of Nationalism* (New York, 1944), 10, 13.

that a rational phenomenon would not be.[2] He concluded that the most plausible explanation of what he called nationalism's "vogue . . . in modern times" was "the underlying tendency . . . to regard the national state as the medium through which civilization is best assured and advanced," an argument notable more for its circularity than its explanatory power.[3]

Because of its balance, erudition, thoroughness, and moral force, Hayes' analysis of nationalism has approached the status of holy writ among historians. This has blurred the fact that underlying Hayes' explanation of nationalism's psychological potency lies the simple notion that nationalism appeals to the irrationality of the bulk of mankind, which he says is made up of "thoughtless persons."[4] But to dismiss nationalism's appeal as irrational, dependent on man's "religious sense," is different only on the surface from categorizing nationalism as a "state of mind" and then not investigating that state, as Kohn did. As Hayes himself probably would admit, classifying a phenomenon as irrational is an admission of ignorance.[5] In a similar way, historians a century ago "explained" that outbreaks of lower-class violence were expressions of the criminal irrationality of the mob. Only fairly recently has it been realized that such behavior was actually guided by norms which historians previously did not understand or were not willing to accept as legitimate.[6]

Most historians of nationalism have followed in the footsteps of Hayes and Kohn, admitting the importance of the psychological ingredient in nationalism, but writing historical narratives. Shafer points out that nationalism is, in his opinion, a sentiment, a belief held by a group of people that they constitute a nation. He then asks, quite properly, "How did groups of individuals . . . come to think they

2 Carlton J. H. Hayes, *Essays on Nationalism* (New York, 1928), 94; *idem, Nationalism: A Religion* (New York, 1960), 11; *Essays*, 95, 246.
3 Carlton J. H. Hayes, *The Historical Evolution of Modern Nationalism* (New York, 1931), 302.
4 Hayes, *Essays*, 3.
5 "What has given great vogue to nationalism in modern times? We really do not know" (Hayes, *Evolution*, 302). See also Jerzy F. Kercz, "Reflections on the Economics of Nationalism and Communism in Eastern Europe," *East European Quarterly*, V (1970), 234.
6 George Rudé, *The Crowd in History* (New York, 1964), 8. Social historians such as Rudé have begun to take seriously lower-class behavior that does not fit traditional concepts, e.g., E. J. Hobsbawm, *Primitive Rebels* (New York, 1965; Hobsbawm and Rudé, *Captain Swing* (London, 1969); E. P. Thompson, "The Moral Economy of the English Crowd in the 18th Century," *Past and Present*, L (1971), 76–136.

constituted a group?" His answer, despite mention of the socialization process and occasional use of psychoanalytic terms, is essentially a chronological review of the standard history of nationalism. This does not prevent Shafer from claiming in his final paragraph that "there is no [psychological] basis . . . for believing . . . that nationalism must be or will be permanent."[7] Without a more serious effort to establish the psychological basis of nationalism, the point cannot be proven.

More recent studies continue to repeat the methods, even almost the words, of the early masters. Sugar, in his introduction to the recent compilation of studies, *Nationalism in Eastern Europe*, relies heavily on Kohn and Hayes in establishing his theoretical underpinnings, and most of the rest of the authors present traditional narrative descriptions. Minogue, in his book, almost quotes Kohn when he says, "Psychological theories . . . do not amount to explanations of nationalism."[8] Without pursuing the point to exhaustion, it is noteworthy that one historian who has explicitly turned to a discussion of the psychology of nationalism, Snyder, has this to say: "Historians readily admit that nationalism, in its ideal sense, is a psychological fact, but they see it as a community of sentiment created only through the trials of historic circumstance."[9] As Snyder goes on to suggest, there is more to it than that.

It is understandable why many historians have not gone beyond Hayes and Kohn in investigating the mechanics of nationalism's psychic impact. In the first place, it is not a simple matter to understand human behavior. Worse yet, even if one should achieve a plausible theory, he must face the problem of how the individual's behavior becomes significant to the larger phenomenon which he is interested in, because psychic effects are experienced in individuals, not in abstract entities such as the nation. In order to begin constructing a hypothesis that might explain the power of nationalism, therefore, the investigator

7 Boyd Shafer, *Nationalism: Myth and Reality* (New York, 1955), 53, 237. It must be acknowledged, however, that Shafer is one of the few historians who has called for the use of Piaget in understanding nationalism. Besides *Nationalism*, 183, see his review of Leonard Doob, *Patriotism and Nationalism*, in *Journal of Modern History*, XXXVII (1965), 275.

8 Peter F. Sugar and Ivo J. Lederer (eds.), *Nationalism in Eastern Europe* (Seattle, 1969), esp. 8–11. See also R. V. Burks' review of this book in *American Historical Review*, LXXVI (1971), 795–796; Kenneth R. Minogue, *Nationalism* (London, 1967), 146.

9 Louis L. Snyder, *The Meaning of Nationalism* (New Brunswick, 1954), 109. However, in his more recent book, *The New Nationalism* (Ithaca, 1968), Snyder relies very little on psychological speculations.

must not only understand the psychology of individuals, but he must explain how the affected individuals make their impact felt on the larger social body.[10]

Contemplation of the first problem, individual psychology, brings most historians quickly to their knees, because it means turning to Freudian analysis, or at least it has almost universally meant that since Langer made Freud respectable in 1957. The handful of works in this tradition which have appeared in the past decade, and the rather larger number of calls to arms, show that a small but vigorous movement to apply psychoanalytic methods and insights to historical questions is under way.[11] So far, however, the efforts have had little effect. Most historians find ordinary examples of psychohistory entirely unconvincing. For example, Ketcham calls Binger's biography of Thomas Jefferson "an unhappy mixture of dubious psychology, inaccurate history, and recitation of well-known aspects of Jefferson's life," while David Donald describes the first four essays (of seven) in Wolman's collection as "almost totally without value" for the historian. Donald believes that the last three essays in the Wolman collection "serve as useful illustrations of how historians should not use psychoanalysis."[12] Rejecting poorly done psychohistory, historians without special training and interest find a complex interpretation such as the one offered by Fred Weinstein and Gerald M. Platt in *The Wish To Be Free* (Berkeley, 1969) utterly incomprehensible. Even a widely admired study (and the only one that seems to fall in this category is Erik

10   In fact, the problem is considerably more complex than that, since, among other difficulties, the relationship between the internal and external states of the individual is not clear to begin with. For a perceptive discussion of this and related matters, along with copious references, see Robert F. Berkhofer, Jr., *A Behavioral Approach to Historical Analysis* (New York, 1969).

11   William H. Langer, "The Next Assignment" (Presidential Address to the American Historical Association, December 1957), *American Historical Review*, LXIII (1958), 283–304. Frank E. Manuel reviews the field in "The Use and Abuse of Psychology in History," *Daedalus*, C (1971), 187–213. Much more penetrating and thought-provoking is Bruce (Mazlish, "What Is Psycho-History?" *Transactions of the Royal Historical Society*, XXI 1971), 79–99. A recent article that goes beyond the study of individuals to apply analytic insights to larger groups is Peter Loewenberg, "The Psychohistorical Origins of the Nazi Youth Cohort," *American Historical Review*, LXXVI (1971), 1457–1502.

12   Ralph Ketcham's review of Carl Binger, *Thomas Jefferson: A Well-Tempered Mind* (New York, 1970), appeared in *Journal of Southern History*, XXXVII (1971), 632. Donald's review of Benjamin B. Wolman (ed.), *The Psychoanalytic Interpretation of History* (New York, 1971), appeared in the same journal, XXXVIII (1972), 112. For a more thoroughgoing, and more cantankerous, critique of psychohistory, see Jacques Barzun, "History: The Muse and Her Doctors," *American Historical Review*, LXXVII (1972), 36–64.

Erikson's *Young Man Luther*) may be so overpowering and subtle that it seems a unique work of genius that most historians can scarcely hope to duplicate. As a result, although a small group of historians has turned to the Freudian tradition, most historians have rejected not only Freud, but the use of behavioral science in history altogether.[13]

This attitude of "Freud or nothing" has been unfortunate for at least two reasons. First, as Homans has demonstrated, it has obscured the fact that all historical explanations are constructed on the basis of some (usually unstated and unconscious) theory of human behavior. The statement, for example, that the industrial revolution was forwarded when English entrepreneurs saw an opportunity to make profits in textiles is so natural to us that we do not readily perceive the unstated view of behavior which underlies it, namely, that "men are likely to take actions that they perceive are, in the circumstances, likely to achieve rewarding results."[14] Obvious though this may seem, it is essentially a behaviorist rather than a psychoanalytic assumption about human behavior. Homans believes that assumptions such as this lie behind all historical propositions. He argues that it would be better for historians to investigate these implicit assumptions about behavior and in that way arrive at reasoned positions than to assume naively that their common-sense notions constitute an acceptable theory, something that they would never dream of doing when it comes to historical data and interpretations. The second unfortunate result of the fascination of historians with Freud is that it has kept them from noticing that behavioral scientists of all schools have largely abandoned Freudian concepts in their experimental and theoretical work because of the difficulty of formulating empirically testable propositions from them.[15] In

---

13 An exception is Berkhofer, *A Behavioral Approach*. See also W. H. Walsh's review of this book in *History and Theory*, X (1971), 241–246. Martin Duberman believes that even with the best of will, human motivation cannot be understood by use of historical methods. See Martin Dub.rman, *The Uncompleted Past* (New York, 1969), 42–59, 336–356.

14 George C. Homans, "The Sociological Relevance of Behaviorism," in Robert L. Burgess and Don Bushell, Jr. (eds.), *Behavioral Sociology* (New York, 1969), 10.

15 This view irks psychohistorians (e.g., Loewenberg, "The Nazi Youth Cohort," 1463), but is widely held. See Edward Zigler and Irvin L. Child, "Socialization," in Gardner Lindzey and Elliot Aronson (eds.), *The Handbook of Social Psychology* (Reading, Mass., 1969), III, 452; Calvin S. Hall and Gardner Lindzey, "The Relevance of Freudian Psychology and Related Viewpoints for the Social Sciences," *ibid.*, I, 284–285. For an effort to overcome this problem through the use of information theory see Emanuel Peterfreund, in collaboration with Jacob T. Schwartz, "Information, Systems, and Psychoanalysis. An Evolutionary Biological Approach to Psychoanalytic Theory,"

considering how children learn about what is at first a completely unknown and foreign world, for example, the Geneva school of child psychologists under the leadership of Jean Piaget has proposed powerful theories of child development based on empirical tests without recourse to Freudian analysis. The same is true in most other sub-specialties of psychology and social psychology.

The following argument tries to go beyond these widespread views of historians toward the behavioral sciences, but it is not a complete theory of the relationship of individual psychology to nationalism. That would require a comprehensive explication of human behavior. Instead, the hypothesis is that the development of interdependent economic systems has led to the creation of, in almost all members of society rather than in just a few, a cognitive state which is especially well suited to responding to the appeals of nationalism. Thus nationalism has become a powerful mobilizing and legitimizing ideology. However successful or unsuccessful the argument may be in throwing new light on the difficult question of why nationalism is strong, its basis in non-Freudian behavioral science may encourage others to seek out different paths from the ones now being trod by the psychohistorians and their critics.

The idea that lies behind the theories of child development worked out by Piaget is that children do not learn simply by accumulating data as they mature but rather that they develop knowledge by comparing schemata or models of reality which they have created in their brains to the actual world in which they must act.[16] When a child is born, he is not capable of conscious behavior because he has collected very little data to use for comparative purposes and has established few usable routines for manipulating these data. Very quickly, however, the infant constructs a hypothetical model of the world which he uses as his ex-

---

Psychological Issues, monograph 24/25 (1971). For a discussion of the potential value of developmental psychology to the historian see Kenneth Keniston, "Psychological Development and Historical Change," *Journal of Interdisciplinary History*, II (1971), 329–345.

16 Although Piaget does not rely on communication theory, a cybernetic model of brain operation would be consistent with his ideas. For an excellent discussion of communication theory in the social sciences see Karl Deutsch, *The Nerves of Government* (New York, 1963), esp. ch. 5. For an example of communication theory applied to mental processes see Michael A. Arbib and Roy M. Kahn, "A Development Model of Information Processing in the Child," *Perspectives in Biology and Medicine*, XII (1969), 397–416. A cybernetic model of brain operation is proposed in Earl Hunt, "What Kind of Computer Is Man?" *Cognitive Psychology*, II (1971), 57–98.

planation of reality, the standard on the basis of which he acts. At first this model is relatively simple, because the child's physical capacity is low and his world is uncomplicated. Quickly, however, the infant discovers that his simple model is inadequate to accommodate and explain the growing fund of experience data which he has been collecting and storing. When this happens the child becomes confused and begins groping for a more complete model which will take into account sufficient data to allow him to interpret his own acts successfully. Eventually, he creates such a new and more complex model and achieves a plateau of congruence between it and the real world. Soon, of course, this model in its turn will prove inaccurate and a new groping will occur. After passing through many such gropings and plateaus, the normal individual finally achieves the reasonably accurate model of reality used by normal adults.[17]

Piaget distinguishes three fundamental stages in this process.[18] During earliest childhood, from birth to eighteen months, the child rapidly organizes what was at first an undifferentiated environment to a level of coherence that permits him to act with a proficiency consistent with his physical growth. During this stage of sensory motor operation he learns, among other things, that objects have permanence. The first half of the second stage, from age two to seven (very approximately), is a period of elaboration of concrete operations. Even though the child learns a language in this stage and begins to use it to assist himself in dealing with the world, his thinking remains concrete in the sense that he does not distinguish between words and the objects which they represent. At about age seven, however, the child achieves his first abstract or formal thought structure. He learns at this point that words

17 Deutsch suggests four purposes the individual pursues through the process of reality testing here outlined: immediate satisfaction, self-preservation, preservation of the group, and preservation of process. These purposes require increasingly complex networks for solution and come within the capacities of the child only as his cognitive development proceeds to the adult level (*Nerves of Government*, 92–94). The question of whether it is necessary to impute purposes to understand behavior is heatedly debated among personologists.
18 The most authoritative and comprehensive summary of Piaget's work is John H. Flavell, *The Developmental Psychology of Jean Piaget* (Princeton, 1963). The best summary of Piaget's stages is Barbel Inhelder, "Some Aspects of Piaget's Genetic Approach to Cognition," in William Kessen and Clementina Kuhlman (eds.), *Thought in the Young Child* (New Haven, 1962), 19–28. Briefer studies include Hans Furth, *Piaget and Knowledge* (Englewood Cliffs, N. J., 1969); Herbert Ginsburg and Sylvia Opper, *Piaget's Theory of Intellectual Development* (Englewood Cliffs, N.J., 1969); David Elkind, *Children and Adolescents: Interpretive Essays on Jean Piaget* (New York, 1970).

are separable from objects, and from age seven to eleven he becomes increasingly capable of performing abstract cognitive operations. Finally, from age eleven to fifteen, the child becomes capable of formal thinking operations. During this last stage the final reorganization of his model of reality takes place and abstract, logical thought becomes fully possible.[19]

This bald statement of Piaget's stages of development does not hint at the subtlety and elegance, not to say massiveness, of Piaget's work, but it does suggest that the crucial step in a child's cognitive development is the change from concrete operations to formal or abstract operations. Until this transformation, the child makes no distinction between reality and the symbols used to describe reality. He does not understand the question "Why do you think the water changed color," only the question "Why did the water change color?" He cannot step outside of himself, so to speak, and see himself thinking about a category. Bruner calls this earlier stage realism, because the child cannot abstract his words from the things which they represent. He seems to think that the words inhere in the real objects around him and does not understand that they could also exist in his head separately from the objects themselves. When he does come to understand this fact at about age seven Bruner believes that the child is operational, that is, "able to apply the fundamental rules of category, hierarchy, function and so forth to the world *as well as* to his words."[20]

Investigators working with Bruner, notably Patricia Marks Greenfield, have found that the transition to operationalism is not a universal occurrence, but is a function of culture. Members of the Wolof tribe of Senegal never pass beyond the stage of realism if they remain in their natural group in the bush, nor do native Eskimos or even remote Mexican villagers.[21] Adults in such cultures continue to operate concretely, just as they did when they were children of five years of age, even though their language itself may be, and probably is, highly complex.

19 Flavell, *The Psychology of Piaget*, 86; Elkind, *Children and Adolescents*, 18–21; Inhelder, "Piaget's Approach," 19–28.
20 Jerome S. Bruner, "On Cognitive Growth: II," in Jerome S. Bruner et al., *Studies in Cognitive Growth* (New York, 1966), 46, italics mine.
21 Patricia Marks Greenfield, "On Culture and Conservation," in Bruner et al., *Studies in Cognitive Growth*, 225–256; Patricia M. Greenfield, Lee C. Reich, and Rose R. Olver, "On Culture and Equivalence: II," *ibid.*, 270–318; Patricia Marks Greenfield and Jerome S. Bruner, "Culture and Cognitive Growth," in David A. Goslin (ed.), *Handbook of Socialization Theory* (Chicago, 1969), 633–657; Jerome S. Bruner, *The Relevance of Education* (New York, 1971), 48. Cf. Keniston, "Psychological Development," 339–340.

Two major factors are involved in the failure of children in isolated societies to achieve operationalism. The first is that their learning process is essentially nonverbal.[22] The child in the isolated society learns the overwhelming majority of his skills and attitudes by participating, and very few or none of them by learning abstractions presented verbally. This direct instruction creates a correspondingly direct relationship in the mind of the individual between symbol and referent. As Goody and Watt have put it, "the meaning of each word is ratified in a succession of concrete situations,"[23] so that the individual has little need to establish the routines and models that would enable him to perform formal thinking operations. By contrast, in societies in which industrial development has occurred, it is impossible to pass on all of the skills an adult will need in the direct, palpable way in which the isolated community does. The universal solution to this difficult problem of teaching in modern societies has been the school. In school the child is removed from direct contact with the things which he is studying and therefore he must be taught through the use of abstractions.[24] If he is to function in his society, therefore, the school child must become operational, and, in fact, the transformation to operationalism in developed societies is well-nigh universal.

The achievement of operationalism is also related to whether the culture emphasizes community or individuality. In the community-stressing culture of the isolated society a child is not treated as a person who may grow to have functions separate from others.[25] In the case of the Wolof, Bruner, and Greenfield report, the child's "activity is not evaluated *per se* but in terms of its relation to group members." His efforts at "manipulation of the physical, inanimate world fail to be encouraged in isolation from social relations, and the personal desires and

22 Bruner, *The Relevance of Education*, 10–12.
23 Jack Goody and Ian Watt, "The Consequences of Literacy," *Comparative Studies in Society and History*, V (1963), 306.
24 "School forces . . . [the child] to rely on linguistic encoding as a way of communication, because by its remoteness from direct action it robs him of contextual and ostensive reference as a mode of carrying meaning" (Jerome S. Bruner, "An Overview," in Bruner et al., *Studies in Cognitive Growth*, 323). "It is always the schooling variable that makes qualitative differences in directions of growth," Bruner, *The Relevance of Education*, 47.
25 This view differs in emphasis from the traditional view that "the development of a sense of self must have occurred early in human evolution" and that "all human beings maintain such images of self" (Anthony F. C. Wallace, "Anthropological Contributions to the Theory of Personality," in Edward Norbeck et al., *The Study of Personality* [New York, 1968], p. 46).

intentions which would isolate him from the group are also discouraged." As the Wolof child grows older, "he becomes less and less an individual and more and more a member of a collectivity."[26] No reward is offered in the primitive society for becoming an autonomous person, and realism remains the common cognitive state.

In more complex societies, however, in which the manipulation of linguistic abstractions is important, the person who achieves operationalism can see himself as an individual separate from the community in an important sense. His ability to think does not depend on manipulating objects but on his capacity to manipulate words which are no longer attached to objects. This capacity is his own. The words exist in his head, and he can play with them there without regard to the community. The power of abstraction allows him to see himself as separate from others, to observe himself participating in nature rather than simply buffeted by it as is the realist. At the same time, the ability to abstract gives him a powerful tool for understanding his environment. The advantage which this ability gives him over the realist is analogous to the enormous explanatory capacity of modern science compared with Aristotelian science. Galileo discovered that an understanding of motion could be achieved by considering the behavior of an abstract and perfect sphere moving on an abstract and perfect incline much more certainly than by rolling real balls down real inclines.[27] This trick, as Butterfield calls it, of dealing with abstractions rather than with concrete objects eventually led science to the creation of extremely powerful explanations of reality. In a similar way, operationalism gives the individual a much more powerful tool for understanding and explaining phenomena than the realist can achieve. Thus, on the one hand the operational person's cognitive capacity allows him to see himself as an individual, and on the other hand his ability to abstract gives him a sense of his power of thought and explanation. In short, the operational person is able to conceive of himself as an autonomous, self-directed individual.

There have always been, in Western culture at least, a certain number of operational persons in society. At times, such as in Periclean Athens or in Renaissance Florence, operational persons must have constituted a significant portion of the population. For most of the history of Western Europe, however, the isolation of the majority of communities and the restricted access to education limited the achievement of

26 Bruner, *The Relevance of Education*, 31–32.
27 Herbert Butterfield, *The Origins of Modern Science* (New York, 1965), 17.

operationalism to a very small portion of the population, the stratum in which culture as we know it flourished. The vast majority of people had neither the cultural environment nor the schooling which would have led them beyond realism. An extreme was reached in Europe about the end of the first millennium. In the year A.D. 1000, for example, France as a whole was characterized by the isolation of its peasant communities. As Duby has described it, the "settled places are extremely scattered. Separating these little islands are wildernesses—wide, uncultivated expanses surrounding and isolating each group of hamlets, here and there immense areas of forests or bogs devoid of permanent habitation. This state of affairs reveals one of the essential traits of the civilization of that time: isolation."[28] It cannot be proven, but it seems highly likely that the cognitive structure of the villagers and peasants of France of the year 1000 was not dissimilar from that of isolated communities today; that is, they were overwhelmingly realists.

From the year 1000, French society developed rapidly and in many ways. Naturally, the more complex a society becomes, the more it must rely for its functioning on the linguistic interchange of data and thus the proportion of operational persons in it climbs. As time went on, it is likely that the vast majority of the intellectuals and the middle and upper classes achieved that capacity. But these groups still represented only a small portion of the total population. For the majority, isolation remained the essential characteristic of their experience and realism the characteristic cognitive level of their development. As Lefebvre has said, in the eighteenth century "the typical rural Frenchman is the peasant who farms for himself and, at best, for the nearest town." "One must wait until the eighteenth, even the nineteenth, century for the still-forming town to give life to the surrounding countryside" in France, says Mandrou.[29]

The complex family of changes that occurred first in England and then on the continent, however, altered this situation. The process, which was both a culmination of a long development and a sudden burst occasioned by the industrial revolution, has been characterized by Mannheim as "large numbers of people moving *away* from a life of local isolation, traditionalism and political apathy, and moving *into* a different or broader and deeper involvement in the vast complexities

28 George Duby and Robert Mandrou (trans. James Blakely Atkinson), *A History of French Civilization* (New York, 1964), 6. See also Charles T. Wood, *The Quest for Eternity: Medieval Manners and Morals* (Garden City, 1971), 36–49.
29 Quoted in Duby and Mandrou, *A History*, 207; *ibid.*, 228.

of modern life."[30] The greatly increased opportunities which this new life offered for interpersonal contacts, the premium which it placed on verbal communication, and the broadened organizational structures which it demanded, created a vast new pool of operational individuals out of the former realists and their children. In the space of only a few generations, the cognitive structure of the modernizing society changed. Formerly only a relatively few persons were operational. Suddenly almost everyone was. The modernizing process produced this change in part by destroying the isolated village that had given the realist his sense of community. But this very process created at the same time a vast number of persons who were capable of considering themselves self-directed. Political figures seeking to understand, control, and make use of these newly mobilized masses found in nationalism an ideology which appealed to the operational person because it seemed to offer him a satisfying community at the same time it claimed to offer him a chance to be truly self-directed. The new community, the nation, replaced the archaic, isolated community and thus restored his sense of security, while at the same time the nation-state provided a structure in which to exercise his new sense of autonomy. Other modern ideologies offered to fill one or the other of these needs, but none offered to fill both of them simultaneously. Therein lay nationalism's strength as a legitimizing and mobilizing concept.

The first of these two propositions, that nationalism offers individuals a sense of community, is widely accepted. The crucial question is why does the nation-state rather than some larger or smaller group provide the most satisfactory new community?[31] The answer lies in the unique importance of language, the basis of national consciousness. There has been a great deal of quibbling over this fact because some cases in Europe, notably Switzerland (but no longer Belgium), seem to weaken the directness of the linkage between nationalism and language. The most common proposal that seeks to explain the anomalies is that the national bond is cultural,[32] and in his justly renowned *Nationalism*

30 Karl Mannheim, *Man and Society in an Age of Reconstruction* (New York, 1940), as paraphrased by Karl Deutsch, "Social Mobilization and Political Development," *American Political Science Review*, LV (1961), 494. Cf. Cyril E. Black, *The Dynamics of Modernization* (New York, 1966), 81; Karl Deutsch, "The Growth of Nations: Some Recurrent Patterns of Political and Social Integration," *World Politics*, V (1953), 172, 182–183.
31 The following discussion owes much to Ernest Gellner, *Thought and Change* (Chicago, 1964), 147–178.
32 For a typically urbane and clear critique of this widespread view, see David Potter, *The South and the Sectional Conflict* (Baton Rouge, 1968), esp. 49–59.

and Social Communication (Boston, 1966), Deutsch seeks to improve on this idea by defining nationalism as complementarity of social communication. Successful and penetrating as these and other suggestions have been, the fact remains that the single most important national differentiating factor is language. When nationalists fear for the survival of their national identity, their first thought is to preserve the national tongue.[33] When nineteenth-century intellectuals discovered their people, the first active scholars were those who established the standard national language. Today, as Emerson points out, in the underdeveloped world "it is where ... a single language is lacking that the most dangerous situations are created once the nationalist urge has taken hold." Indeed, the connection between language and nationality seemed so self-evident to nineteenth-century nationalists that it was almost beyond the need for proof. "Those who speak the same language are joined to each other by a multitude of invisible bonds by nature herself," said Fichte, in 1806; and seventy years later Freeman concurred: "Mankind instinctively takes language as the badge of nationality."[34]

If we accept as plausible the hypothesis that increasing interdependence leads to the achievement of operationalism by large numbers of persons in complex societies, then the peculiar connection of community and language is not surprising.[35] Indeed, there is every reason to suspect that the sudden change in large numbers of people to an entirely new level of language use, the abstraction of word from thing, would create an intense interest in language as well as a predisposition in operational individuals to feel comfortable among people who manipulated abstractions in a readily understandable way. This is why the linguistic nation, not some larger group and not some smaller group, offered the most satisfying community to persons who were operational.

Besides easing the mobilized person's loneliness and insecurity by providing him with a renewed sense of community, nationalism

33 Scottish and Welsh are good examples. See Reginald Coupland, *Welsh and Scottish Nationalism: A Study* (London, 1954), 360–366, 395–396. According to Coupland, extreme Scottish nationalists hold that the very limited use of Gaelic "forbids the full fruition of the national renaissance" (396).

34 Rupert Emerson, *From Empire to Nation* (Cambridge, 1960), 138; Johann G. Fichte (ed. George A. Kelly) *Addresses to the German Nation* (New York, 1968), 190; Edward A. Freeman, "Race and Language," *Historical Essays* (London, 1879), 203, cited by Emerson, *From Empire to Nation*, 132.

35 Richard H. Pfaff points out that in the case of the Arabs, nationalism fulfilled precisely this search for community, which arose from what Lerner called the passing of the traditional society in the Arabic world ("The Function of Arab Nationalism," *Comparative Politics*, II [1970], 147–169).

paradoxically offered expression to his sense of autonomy as well. Nineteenth-century nationalists believed that the nation-state was the most desirable modern political unit because they believed it guaranteed the exercise of freedom.[36] Their argument had two sides to it, a right and a left, so to speak. All nationalists, whether conservative or liberal, believed that the creation or continuation of the nation–state as a sovereign body would insure the self-determination of the people as a whole and protect the nation's autonomy in world affairs.[37] Each person participated in the sovereignty of the nation of which he was an integral part. Its autonomy was a reflection of his autonomy, its strength an extension of his strength. Therefore, if the nation–state already existed, the goal of nationalists was to maintain its independence of action, its freedom. If the nation had not yet achieved legal status, then the task was unification into one independent state. Only when all members of the nation were organized as a recognized political unit could the sense of autonomy felt by the operational persons in that nation be satisfied in the political sphere.[38]

Some, but not all, nationalists went beyond this argument and sought to organize the nation's political and economic systems on the basis of the self-directing power of the individual. The organizing principle of these nineteenth-century liberals was that each individual is the "proprietor of his own person or capacities, owing nothing to society for them."[39] In politics, this notion led liberals to favor parliamentary governments in which those persons who had demonstrated their ability to direct their lives successfully, that is, the middle class, would

36 The assumptions of this statement are that nationalism is an attitude that exerts a dynamic rather than a directive influence and that the most important of the independent (source) variables which induce the attitude is nationalism's *message*: that one can find freedom in the nation-state. For a discussion of attitude theory, see William J. McGuire, "The Nature of Attitudes and Attitude Change," in Lindzey and Aronson, (eds.), *Handbook of Social Psychology*, III, 136–314, esp. 147–148 and 172–175.

37 Elie Kedourie bases much of his recent study of the intellectual origins of nationalism on just this idea, that nationalism is "largely a doctrine of national self-determination" (*Nationalism* [London, 1961], 31).

38 As Karl Deutsch puts it, nationalists wanted to achieve "governments that would in some sense be their own and that would give them a chance to . . . control their own fate" (*Nationalism and Its Alternatives* [New York, 1969], 50).

39 C. B. Macpherson, *The Political Theory of Possessive Individualism* (Oxford, 1964), 3. Cf. L. T. Hobhouse's classic definition of liberalism as "the belief that society can safely be founded on . . . [the] self-directing power of personality . . ." (*Liberalism* [Oxford, 1964], 66). The best description of mid-nineteenth-century liberalism now appears to be Theodore S. Hamerow, *The Social Foundations of German Unification, 1858–1871* (Princeton, 1969), 135–180.

have the controlling voice in the affairs of the nation. In economic theory, liberals believed that the prosperity of the nation was founded on the ability of each individual to seek his own legitimate self-interest. True, this idea did not always lead liberals to a narrowly nationalistic policy, as the French free trade movement of the 1850s demonstrates; but often liberals did make a connection between the right of the individual to be free and the duty of the nation to be autonomous. Thus, for example, liberal nationalists in Serbia in the 1860s demanded not only that the Prince of Serbia seek to unify all Serbs into one independent state, but that he make Serbia worthy of this great task by introducing freedom of the press, a responsible legislature, and other features of a liberal political system.[40] In the minds of these Serbian liberals, and of many liberals in the nineteenth century, self-direction of individuals went together with self-determination of the people as a whole.

In either case, whether nationalism was conservative or liberal, whether its protagonists concentrated on international freedom of action for the whole nation, or on individual freedom of action within the state, and whether or not they found a connection between these two elements, nationalism infused operational persons with the belief that they could be truly autonomous in the nation–state.

Nationalism's peculiar psychic strength, therefore, lies in its simultaneous offer to satisfy the operational person's sense of autonomy and his need for a natural community. Freedom and unity: These were the basic promises of nineteenth-century nationalism and the source of its impact on operational individuals. But how did these individuals have an effect on society? What is the mechanism by which individual propensity is translated into social action? An answer to this question would have to be complex indeed, but perhaps the key is nationalism's function as an ideology. The solution lies not so much in why this or that nationalist was influential, not on the psychological characteristics of one or another individual, but in how persons who sought and achieved power used nationalism.

Like other ideologies, nationalism performs two basic functions for political leaders. It legitimizes their authority and it mobilizes public support for them and their policies. Justifications are considered

---

40 The close connection between liberalism and nationalism is almost a truism among historians. See, e.g., Guido de Ruggiero, *The History of European Liberalism* (Boston, 1959), 407–413. For some perceptive remarks on the relationship of nationalism to liberalism see Potter, *The South*, 287–299; Dimitrije Djordjević, *Revolutions des Peuples Balkaniques* (Belgrade, 1965), 121.

legitimate when they are beyond the necessity of proof.[41] When a political figure can establish himself as the spokesman for a principle that is accepted without argument, he has in effect legitimized his right to hold and exercise power. Kings and nobility could do this, once it became necessary, by calling on the rights granted them by God, but by the nineteenth century this argument had lost its self-evident character. Nineteenth-century politicians found a new basis for legitimacy in their claim that they truly represented the nation. Appeals to similar sentiments, such as linguistic affinity, emotional attachment to one's native area, martial spirit, or hatred of an enemy, had been made in the past, but then the number of operational persons remained very small and the argument did not have widespread legitimizing impact.[42] With the industrial revolution, however, the number of operational persons actively introduced into the political process grew enormously and suddenly. The politician had to justify his pretensions to power to a public containing a high proportion of persons who were prepared to regard-the nation as a natural phenomenon. The politician may have been inaccurate in making the claim that he truly represented the nation. He may have represented only his own class or a small intelligentsia, or even just himself; but when the politically active public believed his claims, his right to exercise political power became legitimate.[43]

In those states of Europe where the nation–state emerged before or during the discovery of the nationalist argument, nationalism was put to use legitimizing the fact of power. Bismarckian Germany is a good example. As Berdahl has recently pointed out, it was not the ideas and ideology of German nationalists of the first half of the nineteenth century that "caused" German unification, but rather the political and

---

41 Max Weber, in the classic statement on the sources of legitimacy, says that it may be based on legal authority, traditional authority, or charismatic authority (*Theory of Social and Economic Organization* as reprinted by S. N. Eisenstadt [ed.], *On Charisma and Institution Building* [Chicago, 1968], 46). In each case the authority derives from the society's normative system and as such is beyond proof (cf. Charles F. Andrain, *Political Life and Social Change: An Introduction to Political Science* [Belmont, Cal., 1970], 141). On the function of ideology, see David E. Apter, *Some Conceptual Approaches to the Study of Modernization* (Englewood Cliffs, 1968), esp. 237–242.

42 E.g., Marin Pundeff, "National Consciousness in Medieval Bulgaria," *Südost-Forschungen*, XXVII (1968), 1–27.

43 As David Potter puts it, "the nature of the association which constitutes a people took on almost as mystical a quality as once pertained to the nature of the anointment which a crowned king received from God" (*The South*, 44). Cf. Gellner, *Thought and Change*, 150–151.

military acts of an aristocratic elite. "The Bismarckian state was . . . 'self-determined,' not by popular sovereignty or by the *Volk*, but by its leading statesmen," Berdahl says. "Culture did not 'form' the German state, it legitimized it." Berdahl maintains that for nationalists and politicians in Germany "nationalism was a functional concept" used primarily to justify a state already in being.[44] Bismarckian politicians encouraged the creation of the national myth because it legitimized what was in fact simply their consolidation of power by traditional means. Nationalism as an ideology justified their acts and gave them the right to continue in power. One reason, of many, why this argument was useful to them in the 1870s and later was that the modernization process had created a sufficient pool of operational persons who could respond to the dual appeal of the nationalist argument.

Legitimizing the right of certain groups to power, nationalism serves at the same time to mobilize mass support.[45] Hayes' cynical view of this well-known phenomenon is that "on the multitudes nationalism could be made to act as a sort of a laughing gas. . . ." More recently, Breton has suggested that nationality is a public consumption good, a form of capital that is not used up when it is consumed by different persons (like a park), and which can be "augmented through investment or reduced through depreciation and consumption."[46] Breton shows how middle-class elites appropriate the material benefit of modernization in part by satisfying the lower classes with nonmaterial (psychic) benefits in the form of this public consumption good (nationalism). In the underdeveloped successor states to the imperial empires, leaders use nationalistic appeals to mobilize support for difficult policies, to divert attention from unpleasant problems, or to keep themselves in power.[47]

---

44 Robert M. Berdahl, "New Thoughts on German Nationalism," *American Historical Review*, LXXVII (1972), 70–71. The argument I am making is similar to Berdahl's point that nationalism is a functional ideology which is a "force for the reintegration of society" (74), with two additions. Nationalism's strength lies not only in its integrative force, but also in its offer of autonomy to the operational person. Furthermore, its mobilizing function, although closely connected to its legitimizing function, serves a distinct purpose.

45 A provocative book on mobilization is J. P. Nettl, *Political Mobilization* (New York, 1967).

46 Hayes, *Essays*, 74; Albert Breton, "The Economics of Nationalism, "*Journal of Political Economy*, LXXII (1964), 377.

47 Leaders may see nationalism as a useful tool even when it hinders solution of the practical problems of independence or development (Rupert Emerson, "Nationalism and Political Development," *The Journal of Politics*, 22 [1960], 3–28).

Other ideological appeals have been used successfully for political mobilization, most notably socialism, but as recent experience in Eastern Europe has amply demonstrated, socialism's durability as a device for mass mobilization remains doubtful. It promises community, but community with persons of the same class, not of the same language.[48] The distant and culturally foreign composition of the international class makes it difficult to accept as a real community, in contrast to the linguistic group, the naturalness of which seems self-evident to the operational person. And of course socialism is not based on a principle of individual autonomy, but on man's social nature and responsibilities. Thus it can have little long-run staying power with nationalism in appealing to the operational person's sense of autonomy. Nationalism will continue effectively to mobilize political support for politicians as long as the operational person believes that a threat exists to the integrity of the nation which provides him his community and his field for exercising autonomy.

One hundred years ago, forecasts of the imminent demise of nationalism were not ususual, despite the belief of many that nationalism was the uniquely modern idea. In 1871 one Eastern European professor confidently predicted that "the era of nationalistic giddiness is on the verge of final decay. The current movements of this sort are its last dying convulsions."[49] That analysis, and all of the many announcements of nationalism's death that have appeared since, proved premature because the growth of highly interdependent economic systems created a large number of operational persons capable of a sense of autonomy at the same time it destroyed the isolated communities in which these persons had found satisfaction. The ability of nationalism to fill the need for community and autonomy that this process created made it a legitimizing and mobilizing ideology of unique force.

---

48 Yugoslav socialist theory is an exception. There Edvard Kardelj has suggested that the road to internationalism lies through (socialist) nationalism, and another leading theorist, Kiro Hadži-Vasilev, has suggested that national self-interest is the starting point of true internationalism (Michael B. Petrovich, unpub. paper presented at the Fifth Annual Convention of the American Association for the Advancement of Slavic Studies, 1972).

49 Quoted by Arpad Lebl, "Omladina i srpsko pitanje u peštanskom parlamentu 1867–1871" ["Youth and the Serbian Question in the Hungarian Parliament, 1867–1871"], in Nikola Petrović (ed.), Ujedinjena omladina srpska [The United Serbian Youth] (Novi Sad, 1968), 355.